GOETHE'S FAUST

PARTS I AND II

IN THE SIR THEODORE MARTIN TRANSLATION,
INTRODUCED, REVISED, AND ANNOTATED BY
W. H. BRUFORD

LONDON J. M. DENT & SONS LTD
NEW YORK E. P. DUTTON & CO INC

INTRODUCTION

'IF you search for the roots of *Faust* or of *King Lear*, you must dig to the depths from which Igdrasil grows, that tree on which all we mortal men hang like fluttering leaves.' In writing these words about *Faust*, Edward Dowden placed the work by implication on the same level as the greatest plays of Shakespeare, other nineteenth-century critics spoke of it as the *Divina Commedia* of the modern age, and it is still universally regarded as the greatest single work in German literature. Like all the supreme products of art, it seems to have something important to say to each successive generation because it draws, Dowden suggests, on depths of human experience which our knowledge of the life of its author does not suffice to explain. Yet no age with any historical sense can persuade itself, he reminds us, that it has at last been granted a final understanding of the masterpiece, for it remains an inexhaustible symbol, as Goethe thought all great poems should be. The one set of words evokes responses which will always vary from age to age and from reader to reader, according to the contents of the mind on which they impinge, for words are necessarily vague in poetry and many meanings can be read into them.

Certainly many different interpretations of *Faust* have been presented to German readers by the untiring 'Goethe-philologists' of the past century, and one thing on which they are all agreed is that in *Faust*, even an educated German reader finds certain difficulties which become more striking the more carefully he studies it, complexities due to the particular circumstances in which the play was composed. It was written, and portions of it were published, at intervals over a period extending from Goethe's twentieth to his eighty-second year. He wrote, moreover, in an age of confused beliefs, which looked to its poets for an answer to its questions about the meaning of life, to poets who, with far less support from any literary or cultural tradition than their English contemporaries, suffered just as much as they did from what Mr T. S. Eliot has called the 'split in sensibility,' the dissociation between intellect and emotion, resulting from the decay of Protestantism. It is surprising that a poet so dependent on inspiration was able to return to the same theme so frequently without losing interest, and to give as high a degree of unity as he did to the plot, the thought, and the recurrent symbolism of the drama. It was only possible, perhaps, because he expressed in each new section he wrote, as usual, his own deepest preoccupations at the time, and because he had given to his life, through his passion for self-culture, an unusual consistency of development, for one drawn in so many directions by multiple gifts and interests. He was quite conscious that despite all his efforts, there were loose ends in *Faust*. An abandoned explanatory poem about the drama contains the lines:

> This poem's like the life of any man:
> We knew well when it ended and began,
> But none can make a single whole of it.

However, a very considerable number have tried to do so, and published interpretations which it is difficult or impossible to reconcile with each other. Foreseeing their criticisms, Goethe put his manuscript away in a sealed packet to be published after his death, when he had completed the Second Part as well as he felt to be possible, saying to Eckermann: 'It will contain problems enough and certainly leaves some points obscure, yet it will satisfy a reader who knows how to take a look, a gesture, a gentle hint. He will even find more there than I could give.'

If the unity of *Faust* can be questioned, there is no doubt about its infinite variety. This romantic richness is just what anyone will expect to find who is acquainted with the manner of its composition and with the wide range of its author's experience of life, with the catholicity of his artistic, intellectual, and scientific interests, with the superb creativeness of his imagination down to old age and his capacity for self-renewal in repeated 'moultings.' In reading *Faust* we can hardly avoid asking ourselves how its various episodes are connected with Goethe's own life, so that even the briefest introduction must include something about the history of the play's composition. It is no doubt an artistic weakness of *Faust* that to this extent its unity lies outside, in Goethe's life, but it is only in this way that the retention of some scenes in the finished work can be explained at all.

Faust's opening monologue, the Earth Spirit scene and that with Wagner, the Student scene, Auerbach's Cellar, and almost the whole of the Gretchen tragedy were written down before Goethe went in 1775, at the age of twenty-six, to the court of Weimar, where he lived for the rest of his life. Owing to a lucky chance we know exactly what this earliest version of *Faust*, the so-called *Urfaust*, contained, although Goethe never published it in this form. It was copied out by a lady-in-waiting and rediscovered fifty years after Goethe's death. What Goethe made in his early twenties out of hints provided by an old chapbook and a puppet-play is much more an expression of himself and his age than a dramatization of the traditional legend of the wicked magician who, in the time of Luther, was said to have sold his soul to the devil for twenty-four years of earthly happiness, and to have been hauled off by the devil to hell, after warning his student admirers not to follow his example. Fresh from the university himself, Goethe could enter into the mind of a scholar whom the conventional studies of his time left unsatisfied, and could light-heartedly ridicule the four faculties in Mephistophelian vein. He could feel intensely how ignorant the wisest are of all the teaming life on earth and its mysteries, and yet conceive of the veil being lifted for a man of genius in a moment of insight, as if by magic. He could therefore invent the Earth Spirit scene, which is entirely his own, and imagine his young scholar-poet-mystic talking down to his plodding disciple Wagner as the 'geniuses' of the Storm and Stress period in Germany did to the short-sighted apostles of rational progress. Yet this same young poet, who felt himself the possessor of Promethean creative power, also had moments when his clear intellect mocked to scorn these dreams of human greatness and reminded him of the earth-bound animal in man. All the Voltairian irony, the free-thinking, disillusioned wit of Goethe, nourished by so many literary examples, especially from France, went into Mephistopheles, raised to a higher power of cynicism and sensuality by his imagination, just as his longing for a deeper understanding of life and for passionate emotional experience of all kinds was made absolute in Faust. The two characters are at bottom a pair of contrasted potentialities in Goethe, like his Clavigo and Carlos, his Tasso and Antonio.

The connection between the university scenes and the Gretchen tragedy is left unexplained in this original version. In 1826, when he was working on the Second Part, Goethe spoke of the Faust whom he had elaborated out of what he found in a crude popular tale as a man 'who feels himself impatient and ill at ease in the limitations of earthly existence, regarding even the possession of the highest wisdom, the enjoyment of the best that life can offer, as incapable of satisfying his aspirations in the least, so that he comes back from any experience he essays more unhappy than before.' This 'monster without aim or peace,' as he calls himself in the *Urfaust,* was bound in any modern version of *Faust* to seek the heights and to plunge into the depths of existence in a tragic love-affair, especially when portrayed by the author of *Werther,* 'ideally in love with emotion and with passion' (Barker Fairley). It is not surprising that what was intended as only one episode came to be expanded beyond all measure owing to the congeniality of the theme. No one, however, will quarrel with Goethe for that, for these scenes are counted among the most truly inspired in world literature, so seemingly simple and natural in every detail, yet so richly varied and so convincing in their painting of the heroine, as well as of the folk background and atmosphere, and so artlessly poetical in every line. They seem to have the inevitableness of Goethe's finest lyrical poems. The incomparable lyrical monologues of Gretchen are a central feature, and the structure of the whole Gretchen tragedy has been well compared with that of a folk-ballad, where the action leaps from one highlight in the story to the next, leaving what is unspoken to be filled in by the reader's imagination.   It is natural that these scenes should be thought of by many readers as the very heart of *Faust*, and that they should make up the greater part of Gounod's opera, with which the average Englishman is so much more familiar than with Goethe's drama.

In the Gretchen tragedy Faust himself is never for long the centre of interest, and in the first version there is little to remind us that he has sold his soul to the devil, for Mephistopheles is usually just a rakish companion experienced in seduction, and the tragedy makes the effect of a poeticized 'domestic drama' on one of the favourite themes for such plays in Goethe's youth, possibly evoked by the execution of a girl, also a Margaret, for child-murder in Frankfort in 1772.   He could draw on his own experience for the psychological relations between a man of senti-ment and a naïve girl of the people.   The catechization scene, however, reminds us of the deeper issues, even before the inevit-able tragic close.   Even in the first published version of the drama, *Faust, a Fragment* (1790), the 'great gap,' as the Goethe scholars call it, between the opening monologue and the scene where Mephistopheles directs a freshman's studies, is not filled. Goethe had left the play a fragment still, after attempting to finish it, like several other writings, for the first collected edition of his works.   In the hundred lines of dialogue between Faust and Mephistopheles which have been added before the student scene, Faust's longing for the fullest experience of life, even though he is convinced that nothing will satisfy him, is now made clear, and Mephistopheles is evidently already bound to him by some kind of contract.   The main additions are the 'Witches' Kitchen' scene, written in Rome, of all places, and reflecting the rejuvena-tion the poet had experienced there, by coming down to earth after the too protracted, Platonic wooing of Frau von Stein, and the scene 'Forest and Cavern,' inserted into the Gretchen tragedy between 'At the Well' and 'Zwinger,' with the effect of raising the character of Faust by giving expression to his qualms of con-science, while at the same time preparing the reader for the tragic issue, and incidentally reflecting once more the author in a new phase of his development, as a contemplative student of external nature.   The fragment closes with Margaret's full awakening to her moral guilt, at the burial service for her mother.

In the version of *Faust* published in 1808, the work which its author had despaired of finishing is rounded off up to the point reached in the *Urfaust*, the end of the Gretchen tragedy, and is presented as the First Part of a still incomplete tragedy.   The new writing had been done between 1797 and 1806, a quarter of a century after the *Urfaust*, by a poet whose attitude to his theme had insensibly changed in that time, partly because of his own natural development, partly through the influence of Schiller, the philosophical poet and dramatist with whom he exchanged thoughts so freely between 1794 and Schiller's death in 1805. It was only in response to Schiller's encouragement that he took up *Faust* again at all, and Schiller's first suggestion was that Goethe should make the symbolic meaning clearer which Schiller himself saw in the *Fragment*. It was now that Goethe elaborated the compact with Mephistopheles on completely new lines, leaving open the possibility of saving Faust at the end, and that he composed, in accordance with this interpretation of the compact, the 'Prologue in Heaven,' thus giving the whole action of the drama a supernatural framework. The Gretchen tragedy still had a very different character from that of the scenes in Faust's study, but 'Before the town gate,' with its panoramic view of the life of the common people, makes an admirable transition from the one world to the other. In addition to the many scenes which had been there from the beginning, where Christian beliefs and ritual are so important an element that they suggest to us a civilization still rooted in religion, we have now in the 'Walpurgis Night' further hints of popular superstitions and mythology which amplify the 'Witches' Kitchen' and link up, as we shall see, with the 'Classical Walpurgis Night' in the Second Part.

The beginning of the Third Act of the Second Part, introducing Helena in scenes closely modelled on Greek tragedy, was also written at this time, just after Goethe had produced his German epic in hexameters, *Hermann und Dorothea*, at the height of the classicistic phase of his and Schiller's development. It was a central feature of the old legend that at the Emperor's court Faust fell in love with Helena, whom he had called up by magic to please his royal master, and the episode became now a symbol of European and more especially German Hellenism, a last flowering of the ideas of the Renaissance, seen by Goethe naturally in its intimate connection with the beginnings of Romanticism. It is beyond the scope of a brief introduction to trace in full the evolution of the Second Part of *Faust*, the remainder of which was written between 1825 and 1831, not, like the *Urfaust*, in bursts of inspiration, but methodically, following a scheme which was already complete in essentials in 1800. In innumerable ways this part reflects the older Goethe and his broodings over man and society and nature. The scenes at court, for example, in the first and the fourth acts, read into the old story an interpretation of some basic problems of government, clearly suggested, in spite of the ostensibly medieval setting, as much by Goethe's personal knowledge of the ruling class as by his reading of history. Here Faust himself, apart from his calling up of Paris and Helena, is a secondary figure, and as far as the central action is concerned, we can best regard these acts as bridges, Act I to the union of Faust and Helena in

Act III, and Act IV to his experiments in government on his own account in Act V, when he has been granted a stretch of seashore as a fief from the Emperor, in return for his services, or rather those of Mephistopheles, in the civil war.

Apart from the introductory scene 'A beautiful landscape' at the beginning of the Second Part, linking it up with the First Part by showing Faust, helped by the healing forces of time and natural beauty, as he lives down, too easily for the taste of some readers, the sense of guilt evoked in him by the fate of Gretchen, Acts III and V are the only ones where Faust himself still occupies the centre of the stage, and even here he is less an individual man than a representative of modern European civilization, as it appears to Goethe's critical eye.   If the growth of this civilization is taken as the real theme of the Second Part, the acts in which Faust's own action is not a central feature can nevertheless be seen to form an integral part of the whole, though they are not concerned with what most deeply interested Goethe, as a typical German of his time.   They deal with the means and not the ends of true culture as then conceived.   Reading them we are reminded of Friedrich Schlegel's aphorism about not squandering faith and love on the world of politics, but rather offering up one's inmost self on the altar of personal culture.   The things of the mind alone really mattered, so the central act is devoted to Faust's union with Helena, symbolizing the passionate admiration of the modern, 'romantic' man of cultivation for ancient Greece and all its works, that supreme revelation of beauty and harmonious living.   But no man can fully recapture the reality of life as lived by the ancients.   It can only live on in art, the robe and veil left behind by Helena.

Now in Schiller's theories concerning aesthetic education, the love of beauty is said to lead on to action.   'To lead the aesthetically educated man to moral insight and to greatness of soul, all that is necessary is to provide situations which clearly call for the exercise of these qualities'—a situation such as that in which Faust finds himself at the beginning of Act IV, when from a high mountain he notices how much energy goes to waste in the movement of the tides.   The shaping of the real world, not a world of symbols, in accordance with his inner vision, is what now attracts him, and we find him in Act V, having won his fief, establishing a colony on land reclaimed from the sea and initiating great trading enterprises, still with the help of Mephistopheles.   Finally as an old man (a hundred years old, Goethe said to Eckermann) he dies, at a moment when, having forsworn magic, he is looking forward to contentment at last in a community no longer dominated by him, but actively free, through co-operation in tasks necessary for the common good.

As a scholar, a lover, a devotee of ideal beauty, and a builder of economic and political power in the world of men, Faust has shown himself throughout great in conception and aspiration, but self-centred and wilful, so that from the ethical point of view, his successive activities have resulted in as much evil as good. Is this to be taken as a glorification of a 'dynamic' philosophy, a Nietzschean 'will to power'? That was a common interpretation in the expansive era of German history, when 'Faustian' was a term of the highest praise. Or is it rather, as scholars like Burdach and Böhm would have it, 'the tragic story of an erring life,' ending at last in a certain measure of self-knowledge and repentance? We should certainly not forget the other works of Goethe's old age, where there is no praise of self-assertion at all costs, works like *Wilhelm Meister's Travels*, the *Divan of East and West*, or the poems in the section *God and the World*. At all events, Faust's soul is not captured by the minions of Mephistopheles, in that final scene on earth, where Goethe's sympathy with his hero is still, as so often, mingled with irony. In the last scene of all, a pendant to the 'Prologue in Heaven,' Goethe shows us, using catholic symbolism partly derived from paintings, 'the immortal in Faust,' thought of as the essence of his character, his Aristotelian 'entelechy,' not indeed already in Heaven, but in a kind of purgatory on the way to it, and still pursuing a higher form of existence, aided from within by the love of the ideal, which is still conceived by him, as by Goethe himself, in the feminine, and from without by the grace of God which passes all understanding.

The higher, universal insights of religion have always had to find a *modus vivendi* with surviving remnants of nature-demonism and the worship of local divinities, so the supernatural background of the Second Part, as well as of the First, includes a Walpurgis Night, a discussion of which must be left mainly to the notes. Goethe's presentation in this 'Classical Walpurgis Night' of the mythological antecedents of the fully developed Greek view of religion and art does not now frighten the German reader quite so much as it formerly did, so successfully has Goethe's intention been expounded by modern interpreters, so that Act II is no longer a series of learned riddles for them, but a poetic achievement of the first order. One element in it is the search of Homunculus for a body. The bottle-imp, who has resulted from the attempt of Wagner, Faust's old Famulus, to produce life by artificial means—an attempt that is only successful owing to timely help by Mephistopheles—is disembodied spirit, like Faust's 'entelechy' in the last scene, but it is a useful corrective to the construction sometimes put upon that scene to realize what Goethe seems to be saying through Homunculus, namely that here, on earth, the first need of such a spirit, if it could be produced, would be precisely the body, which so often appears to Faust to be the chief enemy of the spirit. In this way one part of this vast poem is constantly, as we read and re-read it, throwing light on another, and though close scrutiny reveals inconsistencies too, they are trifling in comparison with our growing understanding of the 'contrasted and, as it were, mutually reflected images' of which Goethe himself felt the work to consist, complex symbols expressing a total vision of life.

A NOTE ON THE TRANSLATOR

Sir Theodore Martin (1816–1910), the son of a solicitor in Edinburgh, began to write verses there as a student and found time in the course of a busy career as a parliamentary solicitor in London for an astonishing amount of literary work, including articles on the theatre (his wife was the actress Helen Faucit), biographies (especially the five-volume life of the Prince Consort), and translations from German, Italian, Latin, and Danish. He wrote his last article for 'Blackwood' at the age of ninety.

Martin's translations are marked by great versatility, fluency, and metrical skill. In the present revised edition of his *Faust* (of which Part I was first published in 1865, 9th ed. 1910, and Part II in 1886), the editor has corrected some few misunderstandings of the text, slightly modernized some lines and converted the metre of a scene in Act IV of the Second Part to that of the original, alexandrines, for reasons indicated in the notes. Apart from this scene, the very varied metres of the original were closely imitated by Martin.

1954   W. H. BRUFORD

BIBLIOGRAPHY

THE introduction and notes in this edition are intended to give the minimum of help required by the general reader. Most of the literature about Goethe and *Faust* is of course in German. There is a good select bibliography in the excellent recent edition of *Faust* by Erich Trunz, Hamburg, 1949.

SELECT BIBLIOGRAPHY OF WORKS AVAILABLE IN ENGLISH

Lives of Goethe and general studies:

Carlyle, *Critical Essays*, vols. i and ii.
G. H. Lewes, *Life of Goethe* (1855). Republished in Everyman's Library, No. 269.
Eckermann, *Conversations with Goethe*, translated by J. Oxenford (1850). Republished in Everyman's Library, No. 851.
E. Dowden, *New Studies in Literature*, London, 1895.
J. G. Robertson, *The Life and Works of Goethe*, London, 1932.
Barker Fairley, *Goethe as revealed in his Poetry*, London, 1932; *A Study of Goethe*, Oxford, 1947.
Essays on Goethe, edited by W. Rose, London, 1949.

Faust:

Annotated editions: of the German text, by Calvin Thomas, Part I, 3rd ed., 1912, Part II, 1897; of *Urfaust* and *Faust, ein Fragment*, by L. A. Willoughby, Oxford, 1943; of Bayard Taylor's translation, introduction by Marshall Montgomery, notes by Douglas Yates, Oxford (World's Classics), 1932.
W. H. Van der Smissen, *Goethe's 'Faust' done into English Verse*, Toronto, 1926 (including the *Urfaust*).

Commentaries:

G. Santayana, *Three Philosophical Poets*, Harvard, 1910.
F. Melian Stawell and G. Lowes Dickinson, *Goethe and 'Faust,'* London, 1928.
Marshall Montgomery, *Studies in the Age of Goethe*, Oxford, 1931.
Barker Fairley, *Goethe's 'Faust,' Six Essays*, Oxford, 1953.

The Faust Legend, and special points:

Doctor John Faustus, edited by W. Rose, London, 1925.
E. M. Butler, *The Myth of the Magus*, Cambridge, 1948; *Ritual Magic*, Cambridge, 1949; *The Fortunes of Faust*, Cambridge, 1952.
H. Trevelyan, *Goethe and the Greeks*, Cambridge, 1942 (for the Helena act).
R. D. Gray, *Goethe the Alchemist*, Cambridge, 1952.
A. R. Hohlfeld, *Fifty Years with Goethe*, Madison, 1953.
Publications of the English Goethe Society, 11 volumes, London, 1880–1910; *New Series*, 1924–.

CONTENTS

		PAGE
Introduction	. . . .	v
Bibliography	. . . .	xiii
DEDICATION	. . . .	xix
PRELUDE AT THE THEATRE	. . . . . .	1
PROLOGUE IN HEAVEN	. . . . . .	9

THE FIRST PART

NIGHT
A high-vaulted, narrow Gothic chamber—FAUST in restless mood seated at his desk 13

BEFORE THE TOWN GATE
Promenaders of all kinds pass out 27

FAUST'S STUDY
FAUST (entering with the poodle) 39

FAUST'S STUDY
The compact between FAUST and MEPHISTOPHELES, and MEPHISTOPHELES' interview with the student 51

AUERBACH'S CELLAR IN LEIPZIG 69

WITCHES' KITCHEN 83

STREET
FAUST, MARGARET (passing along) 94

EVENING
A tidily appointed little room. MARGARET (braiding and binding up her hair) 97

PUBLIC PROMENADE 101

THE NEIGHBOUR'S HOUSE 104

STREET 111

GARDEN
MARGARET on FAUST's arm. MARTHA with MEPHISTOPHELES walking up and down 114

		PAGE
A SUMMERHOUSE		120
FOREST AND CAVERN		122
MARGARET'S ROOM MARGARET (at her spinning-wheel alone) . . .		127
MARTHA'S GARDEN		128
AT THE WELL		133
ZWINGER In the niche of the wall a devotional image of the *Mater Dolorosa*, and in front of it pots of flowers . . .		135
NIGHT Street in front of MARGARET'S door		136
CATHEDRAL		142
WALPURGIS NIGHT		144
WALPURGIS NIGHT'S DREAM		158
A GLOOMY DAY. OPEN COUNTRY		164
NIGHT. OPEN COUNTRY FAUST, MEPHISTOPHELES, sweeping along on black horses		166
A DUNGEON		167

THE SECOND PART

ACT I

A BEAUTIFUL LANDSCAPE		175
IMPERIAL PALACE. THRONE ROOM . . .		178
SPACIOUS HALL		188
PLEASURE-GARDEN. MORNING SUN . . .		214
A DARK GALLERY		221
A HALL BRILLIANTLY ILLUMINATED . . .		226
BARONIAL HALL DIMLY ILLUMINATED . . .		229

ACT II

A HIGH-VAULTED, NARROW GOTHIC CHAMBER, FORMERLY FAUST'S; UNALTERED		237

PAGE

LABORATORY 245

CLASSICAL WALPURGIS NIGHT
  Pharsalian Fields—Darkness 251
  On the Upper Peneios 255
  On the Lower Peneios 261
  On the Upper Peneios as before 269
  Rocky Bays of the Aegean Sea 285

ACT III

IN FRONT OF THE PALACE OF MENELAUS AT SPARTA . . 301

INNER COURT OF THE CASTLE 322

ACT IV

A HIGH MOUNTAINOUS REGION 351

ON THE SPUR OF THE MOUNTAIN 361

THE RIVAL EMPEROR'S TENT 374

ACT V

OPEN COUNTRY 383

IN THE LITTLE GARDEN 385

PALACE 386

DEEP NIGHT 391

MIDNIGHT 394

GREAT FORE-COURT OF THE PALACE 398

BURIAL 401

MOUNTAIN DEFILES, FOREST, ROCK, WILDERNESS . . 408

DEDICATION [1]

Ye come, dim forms, as in youth's early day
    Ye bless'd these eyes, which now so lonely grieve!
Still, still, to hold you fast shall I essay,
    Still let my heart to that delusion cleave?
Ye throng me round! Well! lord it how ye may,
    As from the mists ye rise, that round me weave!
Ye waft a magic air, that shakes my breast
With youth's tumultuous, yet divine unrest.

Visions ye bring with you of happy days,
    And many a dear, dear shade ascends to view;
Like some faint haunting chime of ancient lays,
    Come love, first love, and friendship back with you;
The heart runs back o'er life's bewilder'd maze,
    And pangs long laid to sleep awake anew,
And name the loved ones lost—before their day
Swept, whilst life yet was beautiful, away.

Alas, alas! These strains they cannot hear,
    The souls to whom my earliest lays I sang;
Gone are they all, that band of friends so dear,
    The echoes hush'd, that once responsive rang;
My numbers fall upon the stranger's ear,
    Whose very praise is to my heart a pang,
And all who in my lays took pride of yore,
Are lost in other lands, or else no more.

And yearnings fill my soul, unwonted long,
    To yonder still, sad, spirit-world to go;
Now, like Aeolian harp, my faltering song
    Rises and falls in fitful cadence low;
A shudder thrills me, as old memories throng,
    The strong heart melts, tears fast on tear-drops flow;
What I possess seems far, far-off to be,
And what hath pass'd away becomes reality.

[1] The poet's dedication of the work he is taking up again in 1797 to the
friends of his youth reminds us that its composition has extended over many
years and that his own attitude towards it has changed with time.

PRELUDE AT THE THEATRE [1]

MANAGER, POET OF THE THEATRE, MERRYMAN

MANAGER

OLD friends and true, my proved allies
In times of trouble and of need,
Say, how you think our enterprise
Will here on German soil succeed.
My aim and chief delight would be
To please the crowd, especially
As 'Live and let live' is their creed.
Our booth is up, both wind and water tight,
And all are looking forward to a treat:
Even now they sit, with eyebrows raised, and quite
For marvels primed to lift them off their feet.
Well know I how to hit the public taste,
Yet ne'er felt so perplex'd as now I feel;
'Tis true, they're not accustomed to the best,
But then the rogues have read an awful deal.
How to contrive, then, something fresh and new,
To set them thinking, yet amuse them too?
For, sooth, it glads my heart the crowd to view,
When, setting towards our booth with streamlike rush,
They pour along, wave coursing wave, and through
The narrow doorway elbow, squeeze, and crush:
When in broad day, by three, or even before,
They make a dash at the pay-taker's wicket,
Like starving men, that storm a baker's door
For bread, their ribs imperilling for a ticket.
This miracle on men so various may
The poet only work.   Work thou it, friend, to-day!

[1] This prelude is not strictly part of the play, but it prepares us for its novel
character, much as a similar dramatic prelude does which Goethe had
admired in Kalidasa's *Çakuntala*.   Besides writing for the theatre, Goethe
had frequently acted in amateur performances, and he had now been
managing the Weimar Court Theatre for several years.   The justifiably
differing points of view of manager, dramatist, and actor (represented here
by the clown of the travelling company) have probably never been more
effectively contrasted.   The company is thought of as such companies were
until the last twenty or thirty years of the eighteenth century, when permanent
theatres became numerous, but the public is drawn much as it still was at the
time of writing.   The prelude should not mislead us into thinking that *Faust I*
was written with a view to performance.   It was not performed even in
Weimar until 1829, when Goethe had long ceased to control the theatre.

POET

Oh, tell me not of yonder motley crew,
Which scares our spirit with its aspect coarse,
Yon surging throng, oh, veil it from my view,
Which in its eddies drags us down perforce!
No, lead me to some heaven-calm nook, where true
Delight hath for the bard alone its source,
Where love and friendship wake, refine, expand
Our heart's best blessings with celestial hand.

What there has touch'd the spirit's inward ear,
And on the lips a trembling echo found,
Uncertain now, now full, perchance, and clear,
Is in the wild world's dizzying tumult drown'd.
Oft only after throes of year on year
With perfect form our spirit's dream is crown'd;
The showy lives its little hour; the true
To aftertimes bears rapture ever new.

MERRYMAN

Truce to this prate of aftertimes!   Were I
Of aftertimes to babble thus, why, who
With fun would these our present times supply,
Yet fun they will have, and with reason too?
A jovial presence, readiness, address,
Go far, believe me, to command success.
He that can put what he has got to say
Into the compass of a pleasant piece,
And send his points home well, he, come what may,
Will ne'er be sour'd by popular caprice.
He wants a large wide public for his sphere;
There burns his genius with a tenfold ardour,
For there he knows he's sure to catch their ear,
To move them deeper, and to hit them harder.
Coragio, then—to work!   And let them see
The very type of what a piece should be.
Fancy with all her ministering train—
Thought, Reason, Feeling, Passion, Melancholy—
Make these to speak, each in her proper strain,
And, last not least, forget not, mark me, Folly!

MANAGER

But put, be sure, whatever else you may,
Enough of incident into your play,
Plenty to look at, that's what people like,
'Tis what they come for; dazzle, then, their eyes

With bustle, plot, spectacle—things that strike
The multitude with open-mouth'd surprise,
'Superb! sublime!' they cry, 'what breadth! what power!'
And you become the lion of the hour.
Only by mass can you subdue the masses,
A sop for every taste, for every bent;
He that brings much brings something for all classes,
And everybody quits the house content.
If you're to give a piece, in pieces give it!
With a ragout like that succeed you must.
To serve it up so is quite easy—just
As easy anyhow as to invent it.
In one organic whole though you present it,
Harmonious and compact, it little matters;
The public's sure to tear it into tatters,
Blur every tint, and every joint unrivet.

POET

You do not feel, how all unworthy is
Such vulgar handicraftsman's work as this;
How little consonant with every aim,
That spurs the genuine artist on to fame.
Mere paltry patchwork of a bungling fool,
Which you, I see, have justified by rule.

MANAGER

Rail on! I care not how you thrust.
Whoe'er would work to purpose must
Choose tools that best his purpose fit.
Think what soft wood you have to split,
And only look for whom you write.
One comes to seek a brief respite
From *ennui*, if he can, and vapours;
Another stupid from a heavy meal,
And, what is worse than all a deal,
Scores fresh from reading magazines and papers.
They rush to us as to a masquerade,
Quite in the cue for dissipation,
And the mere prospect of a new sensation
Wings all their footsteps, man and maid.
The ladies, in their best arrayed,
Think only how to catch the eye,
And with our own performers vie,
Themselves performers though unpaid.
Your poet-dreams, your soarings high,
What sort of house will these things draw?

Regard your patrons closely.   Why,
They're one half cold, the other raw.
One's longing for the play to end,
That he may have his game of cards in quiet,
Another's eager to be off to spend
The night upon a wench's lap in riot.
Why then, ye simpletons, for such a pack
Put the sweet, gracious Muses on the rack?
I tell you, only give enough to hear and see,
No matter what the quality may be!
Then you can never miss your mark.   Contrive
To keep folk's curiosity alive,
Their senses stun, and mystify their brains;
To satisfy them's more than man can do.
How!   What's amiss?   Are these poetic pains,
Or stomach-qualms that have got hold of you?

POET

Begone, and seek elsewhere some other man,
Lackey in soul, to work on such a plan!
What! shall the poet fool at thy behest
The right away, 'twere sin if he forsook,
His human-heartedness, the noblest, best
Endowment which from Nature's hands he took?
What is it stirs all hearts and can compel
Each natural element to work his spell?
Oh, is it not the harmony that rings
From his full soul with unconstrainèd art,
And, circling round creation's orbit, brings
The whole world back in music to his heart?
When Nature winds her endless threads along
The spindles, heedless how they cross or tangle,
When all created things, a jarring throng,
In chaos intermingling, clash and jangle,
Who parts them, till each living fibre takes
Its order'd place, and moves in rhythmic time,
Who in the general consecration makes
Each unit swell the symphony sublime?
Who links our passions with the tempest's glooms,
Our solemn thoughts with twilight's roseate red,
Who scatters all the springtide's loveliest blooms
Along the path the loved one deigns to tread?
Who of some chance green leaves doth chaplets twine
Of glory for desert in every field,
Assures Olympus, gives the stamp divine?
Man's power immortal in the bard reveal'd!

MERRYMAN

To work, then, with these powers so rare,
And ply your task of bard and singer,
As people push a love-affair;
They meet by accident, are smitten, linger,
And get themselves somehow into a tangle;
All's love and bliss, then comes a tiff, a wrangle,
In heaven one hour, the next, despair, distraction,
And, presto, lo! a whole romance in action!
After this fashion let us, too,
Construct our piece; but see that you
Go straight at all the stir and strife,
That agitate our human life;
All have it, but not many know it.
Get hold of it, where'er you will,
In all its motley mixture show it,
And it is interesting still.
A medley give of personages wheeling
'Neath impulses half seen, half hid from view,
With much that's false to nature and to feeling
Mix here and there a spice of something true:
So you a famous beverage compound,
To rouse and edify the house all round.
Then to your play throngs youth's prime flower, intent
To see its future there made clear and plain,
Then tender souls from it seek nourishment,
To feed withal their melancholy vein.
Call up now this, now that, love, hate, mirth, rage, despair,
And all will then behold what in their heart they bear.
They still are of that happy age, when they
Are equally prepared to laugh or weep;
They still can find a pleasure in display,
Still reverence bold imagination's sweep.
He that is past his growth, hard, formal, set,
There's no contenting him, howe'er you sing:
The young, with all their growth before them yet,
Will thank you heartily for all you bring.

POET

Then give, give me too back the days,
When I myself, like them, was growing,
When forth gush'd thronging lays on lays,
As from a fountain ever flowing;
When to my wondering eyes the world
As in a veil of mist was set,
And every bud gave promise yet
Of marvels in its leaves upcurl'd;

When swiftly sped the happy hours,
As roaming like a summer gale,
I pluck'd at will the thousand flowers,
That richly studded every vale.
Nought had I then, yet had in sooth
Such wealth as nothing could enhance,
The indomitable thirst for truth,
The blest delusions of romance.
Give each bold impulse back to me,
The deep wild joy, that thrill'd like pain,
The might of hate, love's ecstasy,
Give me my youth again!

MERRYMAN

Of youth, good friend, you would have need, no doubt,
If foes on battle-plain were round you pressing,
If some fond wench had flung her arms about
Your neck, and plied you hard with her caressing;
If from a far-off goal, nigh out of sight,
The wreath for him that wins the prize were blinking,
If, after dancing madly half the night,
You settled down to spend the rest in drinking.
But on the lyre's familiar strings to lay
Your grasp with masterful, yet sweet control,
And there meandering gracefully to stray
On to your shining self-appointed goal,
This the vocation is of you old fellows,
Nor do we therefore prize you less, my friend.
Age does not make men childish, as folks tell us
It only finds them children to the end.

MANAGER

Enough of talk! At all events,
I fain would see you up and doing:
While you are turning compliments,
Something to purpose might be brewing.
Why speak of waiting for the mood?
Wait, and 'twill never come at all!
You set up for a poet—good!
Then hold your poetry at call.
You know the article we want,
A drink strong, sharp, and stimulant,
So get to work, and brew away!
Full well we wot, and to our sorrow,
That what's not set about to-day
Is never finish'd on the morrow.
No man of sense will waste in such

Delays one day, one single hour,
No, he will by the forelock clutch
Whatever lies within his power,
Stick fast to it, and neither shirk,
Nor from his enterprise be thrust,
But, having once begun to work,
Go working on because he must.
On German stages one expects,
You know, vagaries wild and daring,
So of mechanical effects,
And gorgeous scenery be not sparing!
Turn on heaven's greater light and less,
Be lavish of the stars withal,
Fire, forest, sea, crag, waterfall,
Birds, beasts into your service press,
So in this narrow booth the wide
Broad circle of creation stride,
And, with such speed as best will tell,
From heaven post through the world to hell!

PROLOGUE IN HEAVEN [1]

THE LORD, THE HEAVENLY HOSTS, *Afterwards*
MEPHISTOPHELES

The THREE ARCHANGELS *come forward*

RAPHAEL

THE sun in chorus, as of old,
   With brother spheres is sounding still,
And on with crash of thunder roll'd,
   Doth its appointed course fulfil.
The angels as they gaze grow strong,
   Though fathom it they never may;
These works sublime, untouch'd by wrong,
   Are bright as on the primal day.

GABRIEL

And swift, beyond conceiving swift,
   The earth is wheeling onward; mark!
From dark to light its surface shift,
   From brightest light to deepest dark!
And, see, in foam broad billows leap,
   And lash the rocks with giant force,
And rock and billow onward sweep
   With sun and stars in endless course.

MICHAEL

And battling storms are raging high
   From shore to sea, from sea to shore,
And radiate currents, as they fly,
   That quicken earth through every pore.

[1] The Prologue, written about 1800 (see the introduction), was clearly suggested by the Book of Job (particularly Chap. I, vv. 6–12), but to introduce a play which will justify the works of man, within the cosmic order celebrated by the Archangels. The mocking spirit Mephistopheles, though opposed to every kind of idealism, is not rejected by the Lord, but has his role in the total order. For this 'Pelagian' view of evil and the implied rejection of the notion of original sin, we may compare such sayings of Goethe as: 'What we call evil is only the reverse of good, which belongs as necessarily to its existence and to the whole as the torrid zone must burn and Lapland freeze in order that there may be a temperate region' (1771), or: 'Nature is an organ on which the Lord plays, while the devil blows the bellows' (1815).

There blasting lightnings scatter fear,
   And thunders peal; but here they lay
Their terrors down, and, Lord, revere
   The gentle going of Thy day.

THE THREE

The angels, as they gaze, grow strong,
   Yet fathom Thee they never may;
And all Thy works, untouch'd by wrong,
   Are bright as on the primal day.

MEPHISTOPHELES

Since Thou, O Lord, amongst us com'st once more,
To ask how things are getting forward here;
And since Thou'st commonly been kind before,
I at Thy levee with the rest appear.
I can't talk grandly, not though these fine folks
Should all upon my homeliness cry scorn;
My pathos surely would Thy mirth provoke
If Thou hadst not all merriment forsworn.
Of sun and worlds I nothing have to say,
I only see how mortals fume and fret.
The world's small god retains his old stamp yet,
And is as queer as on the primal day.
He had been better off, hadst Thou not some
Faint gleam of heavenly light into him put;
Reason he calls it, and doth yet become
More brutish through it than the veriest brute.
He seems to me, if I my thought may state,
One of those grasshoppers, with legs ell-long,
That flies and leaps, and flies again, and straight
Down in the grass is piping its old song!
If to the grass he kept, his grief were less,
But he will thrust his nose in every dirty mess!

THE LORD

Hast thou, then, nothing else to say but this?
Comest thou ever only to complain?
Art thou with nothing upon earth content?

MEPHISTOPHELES

No, Lord! I find things there, as ever, much amiss.
Men and their troubles cause me genuine pain;
Not even I would the poor souls torment.

THE LORD

Dost thou know Faust?

MEPHISTOPHELES

What! Doctor Faust?

THE LORD

My servant.

MEPHISTOPHELES

Thy servant? Well, his service may be fervent,
But it is surely of the strangest kind;
Not upon earth, the fool! is he
Content his food or drink to find;
Craving for what can never be,
Yet sure to his own madness blind,
He would be soaring far and free,
In hopes to clutch Immensity.
From heaven he asks its fairest star,
From earth its every chief delight,   *& will to power*
Yet all that's near, and all that's far,
Although they lay within his might,
Would never yield the look'd-for zest,
Nor still the tumult of his breast.

THE LORD

Though now he serve me stumblingly, the hour
Is nigh, when I shall lead him into light.
When the tree buds, the gardener knows that flower
And fruit will make the coming seasons bright.

MEPHISTOPHELES

What will you wager? If you only let
Me lead him without hindrance my own way,
I'll answer for it, you shall lose him yet!

THE LORD

So long as on the earth he lives, you may
Your snares for him and fascinations set—
Man, while his struggle lasts, is prone to stray.

MEPHISTOPHELES

For this you have my thanks; for I protest,
That with dead men I never cared to deal;
Plump, rosy cheeks are what I like the best.
When corpses call, I'm out; for, sooth, I feel,
Like cats with mice, 'tis life that gives the zest.

THE LORD

Enough, 'tis granted!   From the source, where he
His being had, this spirit turn aside,
And lead him, if thou'rt able, down with thee
Along thy way, that pleasant is and wide;
And stand abash'd, when thou art forced to own,
A good man, in the darkness and dismay
Of powers that fail, and purposes o'erthrown,
May still be conscious of the proper way.

MEPHISTOPHELES

Good!   But at rest the point will soon be set;
I'm not at all alarm'd about my bet.
If I should win and crow too loudly, you
Will not amiss my little triumph take?
Dust shall he eat, ay, and with relish, too,
Like that old cousin of mine, the famous snake.

THE LORD

In this, as in the other, thou art free;
I ne'er have look'd with hate on such as thee.
Among the spirits that deny,
The scoffer doth offend me least of all.
On men's activity who may rely?
Into indulgent ease 'tis apt to fall.
Whatever his beginnings, soon he grows
To have a taste for undisturb'd repose;
And therefore am I always glad to yoke
In fellowship with him a comrade, who
Is ever ready to incite, provoke,
And must, as devil, be busy, such as you.

But, ye true sons of heaven, rejoice to share
The wealth exuberant of all that's fair,
Which lives, and has its being everywhere!
And the creative essence which surrounds,
And lives in all, and worketh evermore,
Encompass you within love's gracious bounds;
And all the world of things, which flit before
The gaze in seeming fitful and obscure,
Do ye in lasting thoughts embody and secure!
              [*Heaven closes; the* ARCHANGELS *disperse.*

MEPHISTOPHELES (*alone*)

The Old One now and then I like to see,
And not to break with him take special heed.
'Tis very good of such a great grandee
To be so civil to me—'tis indeed.

FAUST: A TRAGEDY

THE FIRST PART

NIGHT [1]

A high-vaulted, narrow Gothic chamber—FAUST *in restless mood seated at his desk*

FAUST

ALL that philosophy can teach,
The lore of jurist and of leech,
I've master'd, ah! and sweated through
Theology's dead deserts, too,
Yet here, poor fool! for all my lore,
I stand no wiser than before.
They call me magister, save the mark!
Doctor, forsooth! and these ten years I
Have been leading my pupils a dance in the dark,
Up hill, down dale, through wet and through dry—
And yet that nothing can ever be
By mortals known, too well I see!
This is burning the heart clean out of me.
More brains have I than all the tribe
Of doctor, magister, priest, and scribe.
From doubts and scruples my soul is free;
Nor hell nor devil has terrors for me:
But just for this I am dispossess'd
Of all that gives pleasure to life and zest.
I can't even juggle myself to own,
There is any one thing to be truly known,
Or aught to be taught in science or arts,
To better mankind and to turn their hearts.
Besides, I have neither land nor pence,
Nor worldly honour nor influence,
A dog in my case would scorn to live;
So to magic I've vow'd myself to give,

---

[1] The opening monologue on the vanity of learning and the charm of magic had been traditional in Faust plays since Marlowe's *Doctor Faustus*, the first of them. Though Goethe did not read the play till late in life, it had been taken over to Germany by the English Players before 1600, and it formed the basis of German popular plays which Goethe had known in the degenerate form of a puppet-play since his childhood.

And see if through spirit's might and tongue
The heart from some mysteries cannot be wrung;
If I cannot escape from the bitter woe
Of babbling of things that I do not know,
And get to the root of those secret powers,
Which hold together this world of ours,
The sources and centres of force explore,
And chaffer and dabble in words no more.

Oh, broad bright moon, if this might be
The last of the nights of agony,
The countless midnights of toil and ache,
I've pass'd at this dreary desk awake!
Then, sad-eyed friend, thy wistful looks
Found me imprison'd 'mongst paper and books;
But oh! might I wander in thy dear light
O'er the trackless slopes of some mountain height,
Round mountain caverns with spirits sail,
Or float o'er the meads in thy hazes pale;
And freed from the fumes of a fruitless lore,
Bathe in thy dews and be whole once more! [1]

Ah me! am I penn'd in this dungeon still?
Accursèd doghole, clammy and chill!
Where heaven's own blessèd light must pass,
Shorn of its brightness, through painted glass,
Narrow'd and cumber'd by piles of books,
Gnaw'd at by worms and grimed with dust,
Which, with its smoke-stain'd paper, looks
Swathed to the roof in a dingy rust;
Stuck round with phials, and chests untold,
With instruments litter'd, and lumber'd with old
Crazy, ancestral, household ware—
This is your world!   A world most rare!

And yet you ask, why it is your soul
Is numb'd within your breast, and why
A dead, dull anguish makes your whole
Life's pulses falter, and ebb, and die?
How should it be but so?   Instead
Of the living nature, whereinto
God has created man, things dead
And drear alone encompass you—
Smoke, litter, dust, the skeletons
Of birds and beasts, and dead men's bones!

[1] 'Oh, broad bright moon. . . .'   The attitude to nature here is decidedly
Ossianesque.   There are close parallels to this passage in the one translated
from Ossian in Goethe's *Werther* (letter of 12th October).

Up, up!   Away to the champaign free!
And this mysterious volume, writ
By Nostradamus' self,[1] is it
Not guide and counsel enough for thee?
There wilt thou learn, by what control
The stars within their orbits roll;
And if thou 'lt let boon Nature be
The guide and monitress to thee,
Thy soul shall swell with tenfold force,
As spirit with spirit holds discourse.
Dull poring, think not that can here
Expound these holy signs to thee!
Ye spirits, ye are hovering near,
If ye can hear me, answer me!

[*Throws open the book, and discovers the sign of the
    Macrocosm.*[2]

Ha! as I look, what rapture gushes
Through every pulse and nerve!   Amain
A thrill of life—young, glorious—flushes
With sudden glow each nerve and vein!
Was it a god who traced these signs,
Which thus my inward tumult still,
The poor heart with such transport fill,
And show reveal'd in clearest lines
The powers of Nature to my sight?
Am I a god?   All grows so bright.
In these pure outlines I behold
Nature at work before my soul unroll'd.
Now can I read the sage's saw aright:
'Not barr'd to man the world of spirits is;
Thy sense is shut, thy heart is dead.
Up, student, lave—nor dread the bliss—
Thy earthly breast in the morning-red!'

                              [*Gazes intently at the sign.*

How all things in one whole do blend,
One in the other working, living!
What powers celestial, lo! ascend, descend,
Each unto each the golden pitchers giving!
And, wafting blessings from their wings,
From heaven through farthest earth career,

[1] Michel de Notre Dame (1503–66), a contemporary of the historical
Faust, did not really write this kind of thing, but his name suggests the time
and the atmosphere required.   The ideas resemble those of Swedenborg.
[2] The 'Sign' is a geometrical symbol representing the universe as a system
of harmoniously combined forces.   A mere glance at it suggests to Faust
rapturous thoughts of the possibility of understanding all things in heaven
and earth.   The lines in inverted commas are not an actual quotation, but
they express ideas similar again to those of Swedenborg, and also of Herder.

While through the universal sphere
One universal concord rings!

Oh, what a show!   But woe is me!
'Tis but a show.   Where, where shall I,
Infinite nature, grasp at thee,
Say, where is that I shall hold thee by?
Ye breasts, where are ye?   You, ye springs
Of all that lives, whereon depend
Both earth and heaven, as to a friend
To you the blighted bosom clings—
Ye well forth bounteous nourishment divine,
Yet I for you am doom'd so bootlessly to pine! [1]
   [*Turns the leaves of the book angrily, and sees the sign
      of the Earth Spirit.*
How differently I feel before this sign!
Earth Spirit, thou to me art nearer;
My faculties grow loftier, clearer,
Even now I glow as with new wine.
Courage I feel into the world to roam,
To bid earth's joys and sorrows hail,
'Mid storm and struggle to make my home,
And in the crash of shipwreck not to quail.
Clouds gather o'er my head;
The moon conceals her light,
The lamp's gone out.   The air
Grows thick and close!   Red flashes play
Around me.   From the vaulted roof
A shuddering horror creeps,
And binds me in its grasp!
Spirit invoked, I feel
Thou'rt hovering near, thou art, thou art!

---

[1] "*'Tis but a show. . . .*'   A mere symbol does not satisfy Faust for long.
He requires, in addition to intellectual understanding, direct acquaintance
with reality through his senses, or in an imaginative vision like a poet's,
fed by the senses.   (Cf. the 'two souls' passage in 'Before the Town Gate.')
The Earth Spirit's symbol suggests unlimited physical experience of life.
The alchemists and early natural philosophers imagined a spirit in every
star, and a similar one in the earth, controlling nature in all its aspects (in
Paracelsus 'archeus terrae,' in Giordano Bruno 'anima terrae').   Goethe
extends this notion to that of an 'Earth Spirit' (his own word), defined by him
as a 'Genius of the world and of deeds,' a collective soul of all organic life,
including humanity.   What the nineteenth century called 'vitalism' was
often associated with feelings of heightened vigour similar to those of Faust
here.   (Cf. the *Nature Fragment* of 1781, inspired if not written by Goethe.)
A drawing of Goethe's suggests that at any rate in later life (*c.* 1810) he
thought of the Earth Spirit as striking terror into Faust not by the over-
whelming power or incomprehensibility of its appearance, but by its majesty.
He depicts it like the head of a Jupiter, beardless and radiating light from
wide-open eyes.

Unveil thyself!
Ha!   What a tugging at my heart!
Stirr'd through their depths, my senses reel
With passions new and strange!   I feel
My heart is thine, thine wholly!   Hear!
Thou must! ay, though it cost my life, thou must appear!
> [*Seizes the book, and utters the sign of the Spirit mysteri-
> ously.   A flickering reddish light is seen, in which
> the Spirit appears.*

SPIRIT

Who calls?

FAUST (*turning away*)
Dread vision! mystery!

SPIRIT

By potent art thou'st dragg'd me here;
Thou'st long been sucking at my sphere
And now—

FAUST

I cannot look on thee!

SPIRIT

To view me were thy prayer and choice,
To see my face, to hear my voice.
Well! by thy potent prayer won o'er,
I come.   And thou, that wouldst be more
Than mortal, having thy behest,
Art with a craven fear possess'd!
Where is thy pride of soul—the breast,
Which in itself a world created,
Sustain'd and foster'd—which dilated
With throes of rapture, in the hope
As peer with spirits such as me to cope?
Where art thou, Faust, whose summons rang so wide,
Who storm'd my haunts, and would not be denied?
Is this thing thou?   This, my mere breath doth make
Through every nerve and fibre quake?
A crawling, cowering, timorous worm?

FAUST

Thou film of flame, art thou a thing to fear?
I am, I am that Faust!   I am thy peer!

SPIRIT

In Life's wild currents, in Action's storm,
Hither and thither, and up and down
I flit and I wave
In eddying motion!
Birth and the grave,
An infinite ocean,
A web ever growing,
A life ever glowing,
Thus at Time's whizzing loom I ply,
And weave the vesture of God, that thou
　　　know'st him by!

FAUST

Thou busy Spirit, who dost sweep
From sphere to sphere, from deep to deep,
Ranging the world from end to end,
How near akin I feel to thee!

SPIRIT

Thou'rt like the Spirit, thou dost comprehend,
But not like me!　　　　　　　　　　[*Vanishes.*

FAUST

But not like thee!
Whom, then?　What!　I,
The image of the Deity!
Yet not to be compared to thee?　　　[*A knock.*

O death!　My Famulus!　At time like this
To drag me from the top of bliss!
That such a soulless driveller should
Disturb this vision's full beatitude!

Enter WAGNER,[1] *in his dressing-gown and night-cap, with a lamp
　　in his hand.* FAUST *turns away impatiently*

WAGNER

I heard you, did I not, declaim?
From one, no doubt, of the old Greek plays?
And so to take a hint I came;
The art is much in favour now-a-days.
I've often heard it said, at least,
An actor might instruct a priest.

[1] Wagner, Faust's plodding assistant, believes, as the Enlightenment
generally did, in the possibility of man's steady progress through reason,
and Faust speaks like a poet of the German 'Storm and Stress' movement,
who writes from the heart.

FAUST

Yes, if the priest an actor be,
As sometimes happens, certainly.

WAGNER

Ah, when one's in his study pent, you see,
And sees the world but on a rare occasion,
And then far off, on some chance holiday,
And through a telescope, as one may say,
How can one ever hope to sway
Or govern it by eloquent persuasion?

FAUST

That is a power, which is not to be taught.
It must be felt, must gush forth from within,
And, rising to the lips in words unsought,
The hearts of all too deep emotion win.
Sit on for ever!   Till you ache,
Your patchwork and mosaics make;
With scraps at others' banquets found
A ragout of your own compound,
And, blowing at your ash-heap, fan
What miserable flame you can;
Children and apes may praise your art—
A dainty triumph, you must own—
But you will never make heart throb with heart,
Unless your own heart first has struck the tone.

WAGNER

Delivery makes the orator's success.
In that I'm far behind, I must confess.

FAUST

Scorn such success!   Play thou an honest game!
Be no mere empty tinkling fool!
True sense and reason reach their aim
With little help from art or rule.
Be earnest!   Then what need to seek
The words that best your meaning speak?
Oh, your orations, garnish'd, trimm'd, refined,
Shreds of old thought tricked out to look like new,
Are unrefreshing as the drizzling wind,
That the sere leaves in autumn whistles through.

WAGNER

Alas, sir, art is long!
And mortal life is brief;
And often, as I work, a pain
Sits leadlike on my heart and brain,
And struggles for relief.
How hard it is to reach the fountains, where
The streams of life and vital knowledge lave!
And ere a man is even half way there,
He's shoulder'd off, poor devil, to his grave.

FAUST

Is parchment, then, the sacred fount, can give
The stream that shall allay thy thirst for ever?
Man never quaff'd a draught restorative,
That from his own soul well'd not—never, never!

WAGNER

Excuse me, surely 'tis a joy sublime,
To realize the spirit of a time,
To see how sages long ago have thought,
And the high pass to which things now-a-days are brought.

FAUST

High pass!   Oh yes!   As the welkin high!
My friend, to us they are, these times gone by,
A book with seven seals, and what you call
The spirit of the times, I've long suspected,
Is but the spirit of the men—that's all—
In which the times they prate of are reflected.
And that's a sight, God wot, so poor, so mean,
We run away from it as soon as seen;
Mere scraps of odds and ends, old crazy lumber,
In dust-bins only fit to rot and slumber;
At best a play on stilts, all strut and glare,
Gewgaws and glitter, fustian and pretence,
With maxims strewn of sage pragmatic air,
That, mouth'd by puppets, pass with fools for sense.

WAGNER

Ay, but the world!   The heart and soul of man,
Something of these may, sure, be learned by all.

FAUST

As men call learning, yes, no doubt, it can!
But who the child by its right name will call?

The few, who something of that knowledge learn'd,
And were not wise enough a guard to keep
On their full hearts, but to the people show'd
The reaches of their soaring thoughts, the deep
Emotions that within them glow'd,
Men at all times have crucified and burn'd.
I prithee, friend, 'tis far into the night,
And for the present we must say adieu!

WAGNER

I'd gladly watch till dawn, for the delight
Of such most edifying talk with you.
To-morrow, being Easter-day,
Good sir, if I so far might task you,
Some things there are I'd like to say,
Some questions I should like to ask you;
My zeal has in my studies not been small;
Much, it is true, I know, but I would fain know all.

[*Exit.*

FAUST

Strange, that all hope has not long since been blighted
In one content on such mere chaff to feed,
Who digs for treasure with a miser's greed,
And if he finds a muck-worm is delighted!
Dare such a thing as this to babble now,[1]
When all around with spirit-life is teeming?
Yet ah, I thank thee, though the sorriest thou
Of all that tread the earth in mortal seeming.
Thou rescuedst me from the despair, that fast
Was wildering my brain with mad surmise.
Ah, yonder vision was so giant-vast,
I shrunk before it to a pigmy's size.

I, God's own image, I who deem'd I stood
With truth eternal full within my gaze,
And of this earthly husk divested, view'd
In deep contentment heaven's effulgent blaze;
I, more than cherub, whose free powers, methought,
Did all the veins of nature permeate,
I who—so potently my fancy wrought—
Conceived that, like a god, I could create,

---

[1] '*Dare such a thing. . . .*' What follows, down to p. 58, 'All forms of woe,'
was written a quarter of a century later than the earlier part of the scene.
The style is noticeably more contemplative, less terse and vigorous.

And in creating taste a bliss supreme,
How must I expiate my frenzied dream?
One word, that smote like thunder on my brain,
Swept me away to nothingness again.
I dared not deem myself for thee a peer;
Though to evoke thee I the power possess'd,
Yet was I impotent to keep thee here.
Oh, in the rapture of that moment blest
I felt myself so little, yet so great!
But thou didst thrust me back with cruel scorn
Upon the sad uncertainties forlorn
Of man's mere mortal state.
Where is a teacher to be found?
What shall I shun?   What shall I dare?
Shall I succumb to, or control
The impulses that rise within my soul?
Alas! our way of life is cramp'd and bound
By what we do no less than what we're doomed to bear!

Around our spirit's dreams, our noblest, best,
Some base alloy for ever clings and grows;
Once of the good things of this world possess'd,
We call a better wealth but lying shows.
The glorious feelings, those that most we prized,
That made indeed our very life of life,
In the world's turmoil and ignoble strife
Are sear'd and paralysed.

If fancy, for a season flush'd with hope,
Through boundless ether soars with wing uncheck'd,
A little space for her is ample scope,
When in Time's quicksands joy on joy lies wreck'd.
Anon care creeps into our nether heart,
And there of secret sorrows breeds great store;
Uneasily she sits, and mopes apart,
Marring our joy and peace; and evermore
Fresh masks she dons, to work us bitter dole;
Turn where we will, she haunts our life,
As house and land, as child and wife,
As fire and flood, as knife and poison'd bowl.[1]
I am not like the gods, too well I feel!
No!   Like the worm that writhes in dust am I,
Which, as it feeds on dust, the passer by
Stamps into nothingness beneath his heel.

[1] '*If fancy, for a season. . . .*'   The theme of care is not met with again until Faust renounces magic in the fifth act of Part II, for with the help of Mephistopheles he has been able to indulge every wish and banish care.

For what but dust, mere dust, is all
Which, piled in endless shelf and press,
From floor to roof, contracts this lofty wall?
The trash, all frippery and emptiness,
Which here in this moth-swarming hole
Cramps, cabins, and confines my soul?
How shall I e'er discover here
The light and lore, for which I yearn?
Is all my poring year by year
On books by thousands, but to learn,
That mortals have been wretched everywhere,
And only one been happy here and there?
What, hollow skull, what means that grin of thine?
But that thy brain was once, like mine, distraught,
Did after truth with rapturous passion pine,
And, while the radiance of the day it sought,
Grew at each step less certain of its way,
And in the twilight went disastrously astray?
Ye instruments, at me ye surely mock
With cog and wheel and coil and cylinder!
I at the door of knowledge stood, ye were
The key which should that door for me unlock;
Your wards, I ween, have many a cunning maze,
But yet the bolts ye cannot, cannot raise.
Inscrutable in noon-day's blaze,
Nature lets no one tear the veil away,
And what herself she does not choose
Unask'd before your soul to lay,
You shall not wrest from her by levers or by screws.
Old lumber, that hast ne'er been used by me,
The reason, and the only, thou art here,
Is that my father work'd of yore with thee!
And thou, old roll, hast rotted here and moulder'd,
Smear'd with the fumes of smoke year after year,
Since first upon this desk the dull lamp smoulder'd.
Oh, better far, had I with hand profuse
Squander'd the little I can call my own,
Than with that little here to sweat and groan!
Would you possess, enjoy and turn to use
What from your sires you have inherited.
What a man owns, but knows not to employ,
A burden is, that weighs on him like lead;
Nought can avail him, nought can he enjoy,
Save what is by the passing moment bred.

Why is my gaze on yonder corner glued?
Yon flask, is it a magnet to my sight?

Why, why is all at once as lovely, bright,
As sudden moonshine in a midnight wood? [1]

All hail, thou priceless phial, which I here
Take from thy shelf with reverential hand!
In thee man's skill and wisdom I revere.
Thou quintessence of all the juices bland,
That drowse the brain with slumber—abstract thou
Of all most subtle deadly agencies,
Bestow thy grace upon thy master now!
I see thee, and my anguish finds a balm,
I touch thee, and the turmoil turns to calm;
My soul's flood-tide is ebbing by degrees.
A viewless finger beckons me to fleet
To shoreless seas, where never tempest roars,
The glassy flood is shining at my feet,
Another day invites to other shores.

A car of fire, by airy pinions driven,
Flits o'er me: and I stand prepared to flee,
By tracks untrodden, through the wastes of heaven,
Up to new spheres of pure activity.
This life sublime, this godlike rapturous thrill,
Can these by thee, a worm but now, be won?
Yes, so thou turn with a resolvèd will
Thy back on earth, and on its kindly sun!
The gates, most men would slink like cravens by,
Dare thou to burst asunder! Lo, the hour
Is here at hand by deeds to testify,
Man's worth can front the gods in all their power;
To gaze unblenching on that murky pit,
Where fancy weaves herself an endless doom,
To storm that pass, whose narrow gorge is lit
By blasting hell-fires flickering through the gloom;
Serene, although the risk before thee lay,
Into blank nothingness to melt away!

Then come thou down, pure goblet crystalline,
Out from that time-stain'd covering of thine,
Where I unmark'd for years have let thee rest.
Thou sparkled'st, when my grandsire's feasts were crown'd,
Lit'st up the smiles of many a sad-brow'd guest,
As each man t   his neighbour pass'd thee round.

[1] '*Why is my gaze. . . .*' At this moment of deepest depression, Faust
(like Werther again) sees his only consolation in life in the 'freedom' he
possesses to throw it away. For the situation compare that of the atheist
Kirilov in Dostoevsky's *The Possessed*, when he declares: 'I shall kill myself to prove my independence and my terrible new freedom.'

Thy figures, marvels of the artist's craft,
The drinker's task, to tell their tale in rhyme,
And drain thy huge circumference at a draught,
Bring many a night back of my youthful prime.
I shall not pass thee now to comrade boon,
Nor torture my invention to explain
The quaint devices of thy graver's brain.
Here is a juice intoxicates full soon;
Its current brown brims up thy ample bowl.
Now be this draught, the last I shall prepare,
In festive greeting quaff'd, with all my soul,
Unto the morn, that soon shall dawn on me elsewhere!

> [*Raises the goblet to his lips. Pealing of bells, and choral song.*

CHORUS OF ANGELS [1]

Christ is ascended!
Hail the glad token,
True was it spoken,
Sin's fetters are broken,
Man's bondage is ended!

FAUST

What deepening hum is this, what silver chime
Drags from my lips perforce the cup away?
Ye booming bells, do you proclaim the time
Is here once more of Easter's festal day?
And you, ye pealing choirs, do you the songs
Of consolation and glad tidings chant,
Hymn'd round the sepulchre by angel throngs,
Pledge of a new and nobler covenant?

CHORUS OF WOMEN

With myrrh and with aloes
We balm'd and we bathed Him,
Loyally, lovingly,
Tenderly swathed Him;
With cerecloth and band
For the grave we array'd Him;
But oh, He is gone
From the place where we laid Him!

CHORUS OF ANGELS

Christ is ascended!
The love that possess'd Him,

[1] Early on the morning of Easter Sunday a liturgical play is being performed in a neighbouring church. The 'Angels,' 'Women,' etc., are different groups of those taking part in it.

The pangs that oppress'd Him,
To prove and to test Him,
In triumph have ended!

FAUST

Celestial strains, soft yet subduing, why,
Why seek ye me, a crawler in the dust?
Ring out for men more pliant-soul'd than I!
The message though I hear, I lack the faith robust.
Faith's darling child is miracle.   I must,
I dare not strive to mount to yonder spheres,
Whence peal these tidings of great joy to men;
Yet does the strain, familiar to mine ears
From childhood, call me back even now to life again.
Ah, then I felt the kiss of heavenly love
On me in Sabbath's holy calm descending,
The bells rang mystic meanings from above,
A prayer was ecstasy that seem'd unending;
A longing sweet, that would not be controll'd,
Drove me through field and wood; and from my eyes
Whilst tears, whose source I could not fathom, roll'd,
I felt a great glad world for me arise.
This anthem heralded youth's merriest time,
The gambols of blithe Spring: now memories sweet,
Fraught with the feelings of my childhood's prime,
From the last step decisive stay my feet.
Oh, peal, sweet heavenly anthems, peal as then!
Tears flood mine eyes, earth has her child again.[1]

CHORUS OF DISCIPLES

He that was buried
Oh high has ascended;
There lives in glory,
Sublimely attended.
In heaven whilst He reigneth,
For us Who was slain here,
On earth we, His chosen,
To suffer remain here—
To suffer and languish
Midst pain and annoy;
Lord, in our anguish,
We envy Thy joy.

[1] '*Celestial strains. . . .*'   The associations of Easter, of which Faust is
reminded by the Easter music, with his own youthful faith and with the
hope that springtime brings, arouse the love of life still lingering in him, in
spite of all he has said.
    The liturgical choruses, in metres imitated from medieval Latin hymns,
sound like translations, but they are original.

CHORUS OF ANGELS

From the lap of corruption,
Lo! Christ has ascended!
Rejoice, for the fetters
That bound you are rended!
Praise Him unceasingly,
Love one another,
Break bread together, like
Sister and brother!
Preach the glad tidings
To all who will hear you,
So will the Master be
Evermore near you!

BEFORE THE TOWN GATE [1]

Promenaders of all kinds pass out

A PARTY OF APPRENTICES

But why are you turning up the hill?

ANOTHER PARTY

We for the Jägerhaus are bound.

FIRST PARTY

We think of strolling towards the mill.

AN APPRENTICE

Best by the Wasserhof go round.

SECOND APPRENTICE

The road there is none of the prettiest.

---

[1] The life to which Faust has been given back is seen here at its most natural, among the common people.   Although Faust, unlike Wagner, the pure intellectual, delights in the warm contact with the life of earth, he is more conscious of his loneliness than ever among the crowd, like A. H. Clough's *Dipsychus* among the Venetian crowd, in the dialogue clearly inspired by this scene.   The schematic way in which Goethe introduces the various age groups and classes is characteristic of his style in middle life. Very different are the Shakespearian crowd scenes in his *Egmont*.

THE OTHERS

And where are you for?

THIRD APPRENTICE

                    I go with the rest.

FOURTH APPRENTICE

Come up to the Burgdorf!   That's the place,
Where one is sure to find the best of cheer,
The prettiest wenches, and the strongest beer,
And a good jolly row in any case.

FIFTH APPRENTICE

You pestilent scapegrace,
A third time do you want to be well whack'd?
I don't half fancy going there; in fact,
I have a perfect horror of the place.

SERVANT GIRL

I will go back to town, I will, that's flat!

SECOND SERVANT GIRL

We're sure to find him at the poplars yonder.

FIRST SERVANT GIRL

And much the better I shall be for that!
By whose side will he walk, I wonder?
Why, yours!   And dance with you, and you alone!
So, while you have your frolic, I may moan.

SECOND SERVANT GIRL

He's sure to have a friend!   Ah, come now, do!
He said that Curlylocks was coming, too.

STUDENT

Lord! how these strapping girls step out!
Come, brother, come, let's join them for a bout.
A beer that stuns, a pipe that bites,
And a wench in her braws are my delights.

CITIZEN'S DAUGHTER

These fine young fellows, look where they go!
'Tis a downright shame; when they might know
The best of company, if they please,
To be running after drabs like these.

SECOND STUDENT (*to the first*)

Not quite so fast! Behind us, yonder, see,
A brace of wenches rigg'd out smart and neat!
One lives almost next door to me,
And on the girl I'm very sweet.
For all their looking so demure,
They'll take us with them presently, I'm sure.

FIRST STUDENT

No, no! all prudes are bores.   Quick, come away,
Or we shall let the game slip.   'Tis confess'd,
The hand, that twirls the mop on Saturday,
Fondles on Sunday with peculiar zest.

CITIZEN

What, our new burgomaster?   Nay,
He is a man I cannot bear.
He grows more overbearing every day,
Since he was call'd into the chair.
And what, pray, does he for the town?
Are things not daily growing worse?
Are we not more and more kept down,
And pull'd at more and more in purse?

BEGGAR (*sings*)

Kind sirs, and ladies fair and sweet,
    With rosy cheeks and handsome dresses,
Look down upon me, I entreat,
    Observe, and lighten my distresses.
In pity listen to my voice!
    Free hands make merry hearts and gay;
So make this day, when all rejoice,
    To me a very harvest day.

SECOND CITIZEN

There's nothing more my heart on Sundays cheers,
Or holidays, than a gossip about war
And warlike rumours, when the peoples far
Away in Turkey all are by the ears.
We by the window stand, toss off our glass,
And down the river watch the painted vessels gliding;
Then home at evening merrily we pass,
And bless the comforts of a peace abiding.

THIRD CITIZEN

Ay, neighbour, nor care I what lengths they go.
Why, they may cleave each other's pates, they may,
And turn the whole world topsy-turvy, so
They leave things here at home to jog on the old way.

OLD WOMAN (*to the Citizen's daughters*)

Well, well! How smart! The pretty dears! Who'd not
Be fairly smitten, now, that met you?
You needn't be so haughty, though, for what
You both desire I know the way to get you.

CITIZEN'S DAUGHTER

Come, Agatha! I do not want to greet
A witch like this upon the public street;
But on Saint Andrew's Eve she let me see
In flesh and blood my lover that's to be.

THE OTHER

Mine, too, she show'd me in the glass,
A soldier, one of a dare-devil set;
Here, there, all wheres I seek him, but alas!
I have not come across him yet.

SOLDIERS (*sing*)

Towns, with loud defiance sent
Down from tower and battlement;
Maidens, rosy as the morn,
Flashing round them looks of scorn,
These alike for us have charms,
Sound alike the cry, 'To arms!'
When such glorious prizes call us,
Death nor danger can appal us.

When we hear the trumpets blow,
On to death or bliss we go!
What is like the soldier's trade?
What can match such escalade?
Forted towns, and maidens tender
Must alike to us surrender.
When such glorious prizes call us,
Death nor danger can appal us.

CHORUS

Maids or widows may be sighing,
On we march with colours flying!

FAUST

Freed from the ice are river and rill
By the quickening glance of the gracious Spring;
Green with promise are dale and hill.
Old winter, palsied and shivering,
Back has crept to his mountains bleak,
And sends from them, as he flies appall'd,
Showers of impotent hail, to streak
The fields that are green as emerald.
But the sun in his might disdains to bear
One trace of the snow, and everywhere
The stirrings and strivings of growth are rife,
And all things don the bright hues of life.
Flowers are scant, but the landscape is gay
With multitudes dress'd for a holiday.
Turn round, and from this height look down
Over the vineyards upon the town.
The motley rabble is making its way
Out from the murky wide-mouth'd gate.
Blithely they bask in the sun to-day;
The Saviour's Rising they celebrate,
For they have risen themselves, I ween,
From the close, damp rooms of their hovels mean,
From the bonds of business, and labour, and care,
From the gables and roofs that oppress them there,
From the stifling closeness of street and lane,
From the churches' awe-inspiring night,
They all have emerged into the light.
But, see, how they are spreading amain
Across the gardens and fields, and how
The river, as far as the eye can note,
Is all alive with shallop and boat!
And look! the last departing now,
Laden so deeply it scarce can float.
Far up on the hills as the pathways run,
Gay dresses are glistening in the sun.
Hark now the din of the village!   Here
Is the people's true heaven.   With hearty glee
Little and great, how they shout and cheer!
Here I am man, nor such need fear to be.

WAGNER

To walk about with you, sir doctor, so
Is honour, yea, and profit.   Still, were I alone,
I would not here be loitering thus, I own,
Seeing of all that's coarse I am the foe.

Your fiddling, shouting, skittle-playing, all
Are noises which I loathe and quite resent.
These creatures rave, as if the devil drove, and call
Their riot song, forsooth, and merriment.

PEASANTS (*under the linden tree*)
Dance and Song

The shepherd for the dance was dress'd;
All trick'd out in his Sunday best,
 With ribbons gay and sightly.
Throng'd round the linden lass and lad,
And all were dancing there like mad,
  Huzza! huzza!
  Hip! hip! huzza!
 The fiddle bow went sprightly.

Into the thick of them he paced,
And clipp'd a damsel round the waist,
 His arms about her bending;
The buxom wench turn'd round and said,
'You stupid oaf, where were you bred?'
  Huzza! huzza!
  Hip! hip! huzza!
 'Your manners, sir, want mending!'

But faster grew the fun, and right
And left they wheel'd; it was a sight
 To see the kirtles flying!
And they grew red, and they grew warm,
And then they rested, arm in arm,
  Huzza! huzza!
  Hip! hip! huzza!
 Such panting, and such sighing!

'Hold off your saucy hands!   You men
Are all deceit and falsehood, when
 You find a girl undoubting.'
But he coax'd her, and she stepp'd aside,
While from the linden echoed wide,
  Huzza! huzza!
  Hip! hip! huzza!
 The fiddling and the shouting.

OLD PEASANT

Sir Doctor, this is kind of you,
To think no scorn of us to-day;
And you such a grand scholar too,
To mix with simple folks this way!

Here, take this jug, 'tis handsome ware,
Nor is the liquor of the worst,
I pledge you in it, with the prayer,
It may not only quench your thirst,
But that each drop within it may
Add to your life another day!

FAUST

Right gladly I obey your call,
And drink with thanks good health to all!
                    [*The people gather round him in a circle.*

OLD PEASANT

Indeed this is most kindly done,
To mingle in our mirth to-day,
Ah, sir, you stood our friend in times,
When we were anything but gay.
There's many a hale man standing here,
Your father rescued from the clutch
Of raging fever, when he stay'd
The plague that wasted us so much.
Though but a lad, from house to house
You sought the sick and dying too:
They bore out many stark and stiff,
But nothing ever ail'd with you.
Your trials many were and sore,
You bore them with a spirit brave,
And the great Saviour of us all
Saved him that lent a hand to save

ALL

Health to the trusty friend, and may
He live to help us many a day!

FAUST

To Him above be homage paid,
Who only counsel can, or aid!
                    [*Walks on with* WAGNER.

WAGNER

What must you feel, to think, illustrious man,
This crowd reveres you with a love so deep?
Oh happy, who from his endowments can
So fair a harvest of advantage reap!
The father points you to his son,
The people whisper, crowd, and run,

The fiddle stops, and lad and lass
Break up the dance midway to stare;
They stand in rows for you to pass,
Their caps fly up into the air;
Upon their knees they dropp'd almost,
As though it were the passing of the Host.

FAUST

Some few steps farther, up to yonder stone!
Here will we rest, and taste the evening air,
Ofttimes I sat here, wrapt in thought, alone,
And rack'd myself with fasting and with prayer.
Brimm'd full with hope, in faith unwavering,
By tears and sighs and beatings of the breast
From the great Lord of Heaven I sought to wring
Cessation of that devastating pest.
Like mockery now rings yonder crowd's applause;
Oh, could you look into my soul, and read,
How little worthy son or father was
Of such repute as they to us decreed.
My father was a good man, queer, maybe,
Who, by strange notions of his own deluded,
In all good faith, and quite unwearyingly,
On Nature and her sacred circles brooded;
Who shut himself with his adepts away
In a laboratory, black, grim, and mystic,
And fused and fused by rule and recipe
Things that by nature are antagonistic.
The Lion Red, bold wooer, bolder mate,
In tepid bath was to the Lily married,[1]
And then were both by open fire-flame straight
From one bride-chamber to another harried.
Thus in due time the Youthful Queen inside
The glass retort in motley colours hover'd:
This was the medicine; the patients died,
And no one thought of asking who recover'd.
So 'mongst these hills and vales our hell-broths wrought
More havoc, brought more victims to the grave

---

[1] '*The Lion Red. . . .*' 'Red Lion' and '(White) Lily' are one pair among
the many allegorical names given by the alchemists (influenced by the
'emblematic' tradition of the sixteenth century and later) to the opposing
principles, active and passive, which they united, in the form of chemical
substances, in the hope of producing the philosophers' stone, one name for
which was the 'Young Queen.' Here it appears as an iridescent deposit
on the retort. The true stone, it was believed, would not only be a substance capable of transmuting base metals into gold, but also a panacea,
curing all diseases. (Cf. R. D. Gray, *Goethe the Alchemist*, Cambridge,
1952, Chap. I.)

By many than the pestilence had brought.
To thousands I myself the poison gave:
They pined and perish'd; I live on to hear
Their reckless murderers' praises far and near.

WAGNER

But why let this distress you—why?
Can any honest man do more,
Than conscientiously to ply
His craft as by its masters plied before?
If you, as youth, revere your father, you
Of course accept from him what he can teach;
If you, as man, see farther, wider too,
Your son in turn a higher mark may reach.

FAUST

Oh happy he, who still can hope
Out of this sea of error to arise!
We long to use what lies beyond our scope,
Yet cannot use even what within it lies.
But let us not by saddening thoughts like these
The blessing of this happy hour o'errun.
See, how they gleam, the green-girt cottages,
Fired by the radiance of the evening-sun!
It slopes, it sets; day wanes.   On with a bound
It speeds to wake new worlds to life amain;
O God, for wings to lift me from the ground,
Onward, still onward after it to strain!
Beneath me I should see, as on I press'd,
The hush'd world ever bathed in evening's beams,
Each mountain top on fire, each vale at rest,
The silver brook flow into golden streams.
Nor peak nor mountain chasm should then defeat
My onward course, so godlike and so free;
Lo, with its bays all winking in the heat,
Bursts on my wonder-smitten eyes the sea!
But now the god appears about to sink!
Fresh impulse stirs me, not to be confined.
I hurry on, his deathless light to drink,
The day before me, and the night behind,
The heavens above me, and the waves below.
A lovely dream!   Meanwhile, the sun his face
Has hid.   Ah, with the spirit's wings will no
Corporeal wings so readily keep pace.
Yet is the yearning with us all inborn,
Upwards and onwards to be struggling still,
When over us we hear the lark at morn
Lost in the sky her quivering carol trill;

When o'er the mountains' pine-clad summits drear
The eagle wheels afar on outstretch'd wing,
When over flat and over mere
The crane is homewards labouring.[1]

WAGNER

I too have often had my whims and moods,
But never was by such an impulse stirr'd.
A man soon looks his fill at fields and woods;
The wings I ne'er shall envy of a bird.
How differently the spirit's pure delights
Waft us from book to book, from page to page!
They give a beauty to the winter's nights,
A cheerful glow that can its chill assuage.
And some fine manuscript when you unroll,
Ah, then all heaven descends into your soul!

FAUST

One only aspiration thou hast known,
Oh, never seek to know the other, never!
Two souls, alas! within my bosom throne;
One from the other wildly longs to sever.
One, with a passionate love that never tires,
Cleaves as with cramps of steel to things of earth,
The other upwards through earth's mists aspires
To kindred regions of a loftier worth.
Oh, in the air if spirits be,
That float 'twixt earth and heaven, and lord it there,
Then from your golden haze descend, and me
Far hence to fields of new existence bear!
Yes, if a magic mantle were but mine,
To stranger lands to waft me at my call,
I'd prize it more than robes of costliest shine,
I would not change it for a monarch's pall.

WAGNER

The too familiar throng invoke not, who,
In trailing vapours spread upon the wind,
Come trooping from all quarters, where they brew
Unnumber'd plagues and perils for mankind.
The sharp-fang'd spirits of the North, lo, they,
Come rushing down on you with arrowy tongues,
Those of the East they parch you dry as hay,
And suck a slow nutrition from your lungs.

[1] '*Oh, happy he. . . .*' This eloquent expression of romantic longing for a
'new life,' expressed through the symbol of flight, admirably prepares us
for Faust's escape into magic through Mephistopheles, who fittingly makes
his appearance very soon.

If from the desert sands the South sends out
Those that heap fire on fire around your brain,
The West brings those that first refresh, no doubt,
But end with drowning you, and field, and plain.
They watch our every word, on mischief bent,
Obey each wish, yet turn them all awry,
They look as if from heaven expressly sent,
And lisp like very angels when they lie.
But let us go! the earth is wrapt in grey;
The air grows chill, the mists are falling.
'Tis evening makes us prize our homes.   But, hey,
Why stare you thus, as at some sight appalling?
What in the dusk there fills you with such trouble?

FAUST

See'st thou yon black dog coursing through the stubble?

WAGNER

I saw him long ago, but heeded not the least.

FAUST

Observe him well!   For what tak'st thou the beast?

WAGNER

Why, for a poodle, trying to hark back
In doglike wise upon his master's track.

FAUST

See how he doth in spiral circles make
A circuit round us, wheeling nigh and nigher!
And after him—it can be no mistake—
There follows, as he runs, a trail of fire.

WAGNER

Nought but a coal-black poodle can I see;
It must some optical illusion be.

FAUST

To me it seems, that round our feet he draws
Fine magic toils to snare us, fast and faster.

WAGNER

Round us he runs perplex'd and shy, because
He sees two strangers here, and not his master.

FAUST

The circle narrows.   He touches us almost.

WAGNER

'Tis a mere dog, you see, and not a ghost.
He growls, hangs back, lies down, begins to whine,
Waggles his tail—all practices canine.

FAUST

Here, go along with us!   Come hither, come!

WAGNER

A merry beast it is, and frolicsome.
Stand still, and he sits up and begs,
Speak to him, and he jumps upon your legs;
Lose anything, he'll find it for you quick,
And leap into the water for your stick.

FAUST

Thou 'rt right!   I find not of a spirit here
One single trace: 'tis training all, that's clear.

WAGNER

The dog, if well brought up, may be
Even for the sage good company:
Your favour, possibly your thanks,
He certainly deserves to earn;
The students, sir, have taught him all these pranks,
Which he has shown much aptitude to learn.
                    [*They pass in at the gate of the town.*

FAUST'S STUDY [1]

FAUST (*entering with the poodle*)

MEADOW I've left, and dale and hill,
In night's deep gloom array'd, that wakes
Within us with a solemn thrill
The mood which most of heaven partakes:
Each wild desire is lull'd to rest,
That rent the heart, or rack'd the brow;
The love of man now fires the breast,
The love of God is kindling now.
Peace, dog, be quiet! Your restlessness wearies!
Why sniff you so at the threshold there?
Down, sir, behind the stove! See, here is
The best of my cushions to make you a lair.
We did not object to your coursing and leaping,
It served to amuse us up there on the hill,
But if you are to remain in my keeping,
You must learn, like a well-manner'd guest, to be still.

Ah, when within our narrow room
The friendly lamp again is lit,
Then from our spirit flies the gloom,
That dull'd and overshadow'd it.
Reason begins once more to speak,
And hope again to plume her wings;
After life's streams we pant, yea, seek
The very fountain whence it springs.

Cease, dog, to growl! The brutish sound
Jars with the hallow'd tones that all
My soul at this sweet hour enthral!
We think it not strange, when men around

---

[1] Faust's 'second soul' reveals itself, for the last time until the scene 'Forest and Cavern.' But the biblical translation is as subjective as any of his lyrical outbursts, for what he puts down for 'word' is not what the Greek means, but what Faust can accept as true. The poodle shows signs of uneasiness whenever God is even indirectly referred to, and when it begins to change its shape, Faust uses upon it first an incantation from the medieval book of magic, *Clavicula Salomonis*, which purported to go back to King Solomon, was known in many languages from the sixteenth to the eighteenth century and indeed is said to be still circulating to-day. (Cf. E. M. Butler, *The Myth of the Magus*, Cambridge, 1948, p. 37). The particular formula used here is one directed against the spirits of the four elements of the Aristotelian physics. When this fails, Faust employs a crucifix.

Deride the things they comprehend not,
And all that is fairest and best contemn,
For how should such things their vile natures offend not?
Would the hound be snarling at these, like them?

But ah! I feel, strive as I may, that peace
Will well forth from my bosom never more.
Yet, wherefore should its stream so quickly cease,
And we lie parch'd and panting as before?
So oft have I been doom'd thus low to fall.
Yet for this want we may have compensation;
We learn to prize the supernatural,
And cry with yearning hearts for Revelation,
Which nowhere burns more worthily and clear,
Than all through the New Testament.   So here
I turn me to the primal text, elate
With a wild longing, line for line,
The great original divine
Into my own dear German to translate.
                    [*Opens the volume, and prepares to write.*
'In the Beginning was the Word!'   'Tis writ.
Here on the threshold I must pause, perforce;
And who will help me onwards in my course?
No, by no possibility is 't fit,
I should the naked Word so highly rate.
Some other way must I the words translate,
If by the spirit rightly I be taught.
'In the Beginning was the Sense!'   'Tis writ.
The first line ponder well.   Is it
The Sense, which is of each created thing
The primal cause, and regulating spring?
It should stand thus: 'In the Beginning was
The Power!'   Yet even as I write, I pause.
A something warns me, this will not content me.
Lo! help is from the Spirit sent me!
I see my way; with lightning speed
The meaning flashes on my sight,
And with assured conviction thus I write:
'In the Beginning was the Deed!'

        My chamber if you wish to share,
        This howling, poodle, straight forbear,
        This barking, and this riot!
        To brook a comrade so unquiet
        Is more than I am able.
        Here both of us cannot remain,
        And, though it goes against my grain,
        To be inhospitable,

There is the door, and you are free
To go!   But what is this I see?
How can such transformation be?
Is it a real thing, or throws
Some glamour over me its spells?
How long and broad my poodle grows!
It rises, it dilates and swells.
This is no dog: what can it be,
This fiend I have brought home with me?
Now with his fiery eyes, and rows
On rows of horrid teeth, he shows
Like any hippopotamus!
Ha!   Now I know you!   Is it thus?
For such half-hell-begotten brood
The seal of Solomon is good.

SPIRITS (*in the passage outside*)

One we know well
Is caught fast within there.
Mind what you're doing,
No one go in there!
An old lynx of hell,
Like a fox in a gin, there
Is quaking and stewing.
Have a care!   Have a care!
Unseen, through the air,
Flit ye and hover,
To and fro, round about,
Now under, now over,
And he will get out!
Aid him all, if aid ye may!
He has done us ere to-day
Pleasures manifold and rare!
Help him, then, in his despair!

FAUST

To grapple with the monster I
The Spell of the Four at first will try.

Salamander, he shall glow,
Into streams Undine flow,
Vanish Sylph, and, Kobold, double
Shall his turmoil be and trouble!

If a man know not the lore
Of the Elemental Four,
The power of each and property,
Of the world of spirits he
Never will the master be.

Hence as ye came in flash and flame,
        Salamander!
Flow out and be seen a rushing stream,
        Undine!
Blaze on the air a meteor fair,
        Sylph!
Us with timely help befriend,
        Incubus!   Incubus!
Come forth, come forth, and make an end!

No one of the Four is lodged in the beast.
'Tis plain I have not touch'd the case.
Quite still he lies, and grins in my face,
His withers I have not wrung in the least.
Now shall ye hear me, whatever ye are,
Conjure with a spell more potent by far.
Com'st thou here, from hell's confine
A fugitive, behold this sign,
Holy emblem, 'neath whose power
All the fiends of darkness cower!

Its bristles rise!   Behold it now to monstrous size dilate!

Thou thing accursed and reprobate!
Canst thou read the holy token,
Him that never was create,
Him that never may be spoken,
All from sky to sky pervading,
Vilely done to death degrading?

Spellbound behind the stove it stands,
And like an elephant expands!
It fills the alcove up complete:
Into a mist 'twill melt away.
Ascend not to the ceiling!   Lay
Thyself down at the master's feet.
Thou see'st, I threaten not in vain.
I'll scorch thee up with holy fire!
For that dread light best not remain,
Which burns with threefold glow!   Retire,
Nor wait till I, thou spawn of hell,
Let loose on thee my mightiest spell!

MEPHISTOPHELES (*comes forward, as the mist subsides, in the
        dress of a travelling scholar, from behind the stove*)

What is the use of all this mighty stir?
Can I in anything oblige you, sir?

FAUST

So this, then, was the kernel of the brute!
A travelling scholar?   Here's a pleasant jest!

MEPHISTOPHELES

Your learned worship humbly I salute.
You gave me a fine sweating, I protest.

FAUST

What is thy name?

MEPHISTOPHELES

                    Methinks the question's mean,
For one who holds the Word so very cheap,
Who, scorning all mere semblances, has been
Brooding on things in their quintessence deep!

FAUST

Of gentlemen like you one may
The nature mostly from the names surmise,
Where what ye are they all too plainly say,
When they 'Destroyer' style you, 'Flygod, Prince of lies!'
Speak, then!   Who art thou?

MEPHISTOPHELES

                    Part of the power, that still
Produces Good, while still devising Ill.[1]

[1] '*Part of the power. . . .*'   Mephistopheles's description of himself is an
'enigma' which may be read in various ways.   He would be speaking out
of character if he meant what is suggested in the Prologue in Heaven, that
evil is a spur to good.   He regards himself rather, nihilist as he is, as 'the
surgeon to the disease of life' (Santayana).   The light myth by means of
which Mephistopheles explains himself is a parallel to the passage in *Poetry
and Truth*, Book 8, where Goethe describes how, round about 1770, he
pictured to himself the creation of the world, following in the main the
Neoplatonists and alchemists, but Mephistopheles omits any mention of
God, the source of all in this other version.   In both, however, the world has
been the scene since its origin of a struggle between two opposing principles,
light and darkness.   With light is associated the thought of mind, the power
to soar and to approach perfection, with darkness that of matter and
immobility.   These symbols recur over and over again in *Faust* and in
other works of Goethe, even in the scientific writings.   On 'recurring
themes' see Barker Fairley, *Goethe's 'Faust,'* Oxford, 1953, Chap. V.

FAUST

A rare enigma!   Say what it implies.

MEPHISTOPHELES

The spirit I, that evermore denies.
And rightly am I thus employ'd,
For surely nought was e'er begot,
But it deserved to be destroy'd;
So were it better, things should not
Be into being brought at all.
Thus all these matters, which you call
Sin, Mischief—Evil in a word,
Are my congenial element.

FAUST

I heard
You call yourself a part, yet see
You stand there whole as whole can be.

MEPHISTOPHELES

Truth, truth, I vow, all truth and modesty!
Though man, that Microcosm of Folly, seem
A perfect whole to his own self-esteem,
Myself I, being less pretentious, call
Part of the part, which at the first was all;
Part of the darkness, from whose womb sprang light,
Proud light, which now doth with its dam contest
Her ancient rank, the space she fill'd of right;
And yet it can't succeed, for, strive its best,
It cleaves to bodies, fetter'd to them fast:
It streams from bodies, makes them fair and bright;
A body intercepts its passage, so
I hope, when bodies come to grief at last,
It will with them to sheer perdition go.

FAUST

Your high vocation now I understand.
You find you can't annihilate wholesale,
So on a smaller scale you try your hand.

MEPHISTOPHELES

And let me own, to very small avail.
That which is nothing's opposite,
This something, this great lumbering world, although
I've launch'd at it, with all my might,
Storm, deluge, earthquake, levin-brand,
I can't effect its overthrow;
It hangs together still, good sea and land.
And then these misbegots accurst,
This spawn of brutes and men, alas!
Defy me, let me try my worst.
How many have I sent to grass,
Yet young fresh blood, do what I will,
Keeps ever circulating still.
In water, in the earth, in air,
In wet, dry, warm, cold, everywhere
Germs without number are unfurl'd.
And but for fire and fire alone,
There would be nothing in the world,
That I could truly call my own.

FAUST

So, that cold devil's fist of thine
Thou dost not scruple to oppose
To the unsleeping power benign,
Beneath whose breath all lives and grows;
It laughs to scorn your threats malign.
Strange son of chaos, hadst thou not
Best start upon another tack?

MEPHISTOPHELES

It certainly is worth a thought!
More about this when I come back,
But for the present have I leave,
Your leave to take myself away?

FAUST

Why you should ask, I can't conceive.
We're strangers from this hour no more;
So visit me in future, pray,
Just when and how the fancy strikes you.
Here is the window, here the door,
And there a chimney, if it likes you.

MEPHISTOPHELES

I'd very quickly make my exit,
But that a trifling hindrance checks it;
The wizard's foot—alas! 'tis true—
Upon your threshold—

FAUST

Ha, 'tis well!
The Pentagram perplexes you.
But answer me, thou son of hell,
If that can thrust you backward, how
Contrived you to get in but now?
How came a spirit so astute
To tumble into such a snare?

MEPHISTOPHELES

You'll find, if you look closely to 't,
It is not drawn with proper care.
The outer angle's incomplete.
You may discover at a glance,
The lines converge, but do not meet.

FAUST

That was indeed a lucky chance!
So you should be my prisoner, then?
Most rare good fortune, truly!

MEPHISTOPHELES

When
The poodle bounded in, he took
No heed of what he was about.
Now things wear quite another look;
The devil's in, and can't get out.

FAUST

Why through the window not withdraw?

MEPHISTOPHELES

Of fiends and goblins 'tis a law,
Get in howe'er they please, but so
As they came in they out must go.
Free in the first choice, in the last
We're very slaves!

FAUST

So even hell
Has got its legal code.   'Tis well.
Then with you gentlemen a fast
And binding contract [1] may be made?

MEPHISTOPHELES

Ay, and implicitly obey'd.
Whate'er is promised you by us
You to the letter shall enjoy,
Without abatement or alloy.
A theme too grave this to discuss
So hurriedly; when next we meet,
We'll talk it fully out; but now
I beg, nay earnestly entreat,
This once you'll let me make my bow.

FAUST

One moment, by your leave!   I burn
For such rare news as yours must be.

MEPHISTOPHELES

Let me go now, I'll soon return,
And then ask what you like of me.

FAUST

Of choice, and not by my device,
You ran yourself into this plight.
Once catch the devil, hold him tight!
He'll scarcely let you catch him twice.

MEPHISTOPHELES

Well, if you wish it, here I stay,
On one condition, that the while
I with my sleights familiar may
Your moments worthily beguile.

[1] This is the point of the preceding hocus-pocus about the pentagram.
Goethe leads up to the compact scene gradually, so Mephistopheles is
enabled to escape by the 'spirits in the passage,' already known from their
previous appearance to be friendly to him.   They induce a vision of purely
sensual delights appealing to that soul in Faust which 'cleaves to the things
of earth' and is eager for the wider experience of them which Mephistopheles
later provides.

FAUST

Agreed! you have my leave—but mind
Your sleights are of the pleasing kind!

MEPHISTOPHELES

Within this hour, my friend, be sure,
You for your senses shall procure
More than you heretofore have found
Within the year's unvaried round.
The songs my dainty spirits sing,
The lovely visions which they bring,
Are no mere empty glamour, no!
Your very smell entranced shall be,
Your palate lapp'd in ecstasy,
Your every nerve with rapture glow.
No preparation here we need.
We're in our places, so proceed!

SPIRITS

Disappear, disappear,
Ye dark arches drear!
Let the blue sky of heaven
Look down on us here,
The beautiful blue sky
With friendliest cheer!
Hence, clouds, begone,
That gloomily darkle!
Lo now, anon,
Little stars sparkle,
Mellower suns
Shine in on us here.
Heaven's sons, bright
In the spirit's arraying,
In hovering flight
Are bending and swaying.
Souls with a passionate
Upward aspiring,
View them, pursue them,
Soaring untiring!
And ribbons gay
Are flashing and gleaming
Where lovers stray,
Musing and dreaming,

Stray on by grove
And meadow, requiting
Love with return of love,
Life for life plighting!
Bower on bower shining!
Tendrils entwining!
Grapes in huge clusters
Piled o'er and o'er,
Under the winepress
Spurting their gore.
Seething and foaming,
Wines gush into rills,
O'er the enamell'd stones
Rush from the hills,
Broaden to lakes, that
Reflect from their sheen
Mountains and brakes, that
Are mantled in green.
And birds of all feather,
Pure rapture inhaling,
Sunwards are sailing,
Sailing together,
On to the isles,
That lie smiling and dreaming,
Where the bright billows
Are rippling and gleaming;
Where we see jocund bands
Dance on before us,
Over the meadow lands
Shouting in chorus,
All in the free air
Every way rambling;
Some up the mountains
Climbing and scrambling;
Some o'er the lakes and seas
Floating and swimming,
Others upon the breeze
Flying and skimming;
All to the sources
Of life pressing onward,
Flush'd by the forces,
That carry them sunward;
On to the measureless
Spaces above them,
On where the stars bless
The spirits that love them.

MEPHISTOPHELES

He sleeps! Well done, ye little airy sprites!
You've fairly lullabied his wits to sleep:
I'm in your debt for these melodious sleights.
Thou'rt not the man, at least, not yet, to keep
The devil in thy clutch. Around him play
With soothing visions from the realms of dream;
Across his brain let wild illusions stray,
And fool his fancy with their meteor gleam!
Ha! tooth of rat, methinks, would serve me well,
To break me up this threshold's spell.
No need of lengthen'd conjuration. Hark!
There rustles one, my voice will quickly mark!

     The master of the rats and mice,
     Of flies, and frogs, and bugs, and lice,
     Commands you straightway to appear,
     And nibble at this threshold here,
     Where now he smears it o'er with oil.
     Ha! Here you are! Now, to your toil!
     The point that kept me back lies there
     Just in the front beside the stair.
     One nibble more, your task's complete!
     Now, Faustus, now dream on till next we meet.

                                     [*Exit.*

FAUST (*awaking*)

Am I again befool'd? Vanish they so,
The throng of spirits that my fancy shaped?
Was then the fiend a dream, a lying show,
And that a poodle, which but now escaped?

FAUST'S STUDY

Faust, Mephistopheles

FAUST

A KNOCK? Come in! Again my quiet broken?

MEPHISTOPHELES

'Tis I.

FAUST

Come in!

MEPHISTOPHELES

Thrice must the words be spoken.

FAUST

Come in, then!

MEPHISTOPHELES (*entering*)

So! That job's discuss'd.
We shall be firmer friends, I trust;
For, to dispel your fancies grim,
Behold me here, a springald trim,
In jerkin red, and laced with gold,
A cape of stiffest silk, a bold
Cock-feather in my cap; and see!
A long sharp rapier to boot!
Now, prithee, be advised by me,
And get just such another suit;
So, casting every trammel loose,
You'll learn what life is, and its use.

FAUST

In every dress I'm sure to feel the dire
Constraints of earthly life severely:
I am too old to trifle merely,
Too young to be without desire.
What from the world have I to gain?
'Thou shalt refrain! Thou shalt refrain!'
This is the everlasting song,
That's humm'd and droned in every ear,
Which every hour, our whole life long,
Is croak'd to us in cadence drear.

I wake each morning in despair,
And bitter tears could weep, to see the sun
Dawn on the day, that in its round will ne'er
Accomplish one poor wish of mine, not one—
Yea, that with froward captiousness impairs
Each joy, of which I've dreamt, of half its zest,
And with life's thousand mean and paltry cares
Clogs the creations of my busy breast.
And when at evening's weary close
I lay me down in anguish on my bed,
There, even there, for me is no repose,
Scared as I am by visions wild and dread.
The god, who in my breast abides,
Through all its depths can stir my soul,
My every faculty he sways and guides,
But all outside me lies beyond control.
And thus by life, as by a load, oppress'd,
I long for death, existence I detest.

MEPHISTOPHELES

And yet death never is a wholly welcome guest!

FAUST

Oh, happy he, around whose brows he winds
In victory's glorious hour the blood-stain'd bays,
Whom on the bosom of his girl he finds,
Warm from the dance's wild and maddening maze!
Oh had it been, 'neath that high spirit's might,
My fate, while tranced in bliss, in death to sink!

MEPHISTOPHELES

Yet was there one, who on a certain night
A certain dark-brown mixture fear'd to drink.

FAUST

Eaves-dropping, then, is your delight, I see!

MEPHISTOPHELES

Omniscient I am not, yet much is known to me.

FAUST

If, when my brain was rack'd and reeling,
A sweet and old familiar chime
Beguiled my all of childish feeling
With memories of a happier time;

Now do I curse whate'er doth pen
With wizard coil these souls of ours,
And chains them to this dreary den
With cozening and deceitful powers.
And first be curst the proud conceit,
Which girds our minds as with a fence,
Curst be the semblances that cheat,
And play and palter with our sense!
Curst be the false and flattering dream
Of fame—a name beyond the grave,
Curst all that ours we fondly deem,
As wife and child, as plough and slave!
Be Mammon curst, when he with pelf
Inspires to deeds that win renown,
When he, to sot and pamper self,
Makes silken smooth our couch of down!
Curse on the vine-grape's juicy balm,
Curse on love's soul-entrancing thrall,
A curse on hope, on faith, on calm,
And on endurance more than all!

CHORUS OF INVISIBLE SPIRITS

Woe, woe!
Thou hast laid it low,
The beautiful world,
With merciless blow.
It totters, it crumbles, it tumbles abroad,
Shatter'd and crush'd by a demigod.
We trail
The ruins to chaos away,
And wail
The beauty that's lost, well-a-day!
Mighty one thou
Of the sons of clay,
Haughty one, now
Build it once more,
Within thine own breast build it!   Here
A new career
Of life commence
With undimm'd sense,
And songs, unheard before,
Shall chime upon thine ear!

MEPHISTOPHELES

These my tiny spirits be.
Hark, with what sagacity
They advise thee to pursue
Action, pleasure ever new!

Out into the world so fair
They would lure and lead thee hence,
From this lonely chamber, where
Stagnate life and soul and sense.

No longer trifle with the wretchedness,
That, like a vulture, gnaws your life away!
The worst society will teach you this,
You are a man 'mongst men, and feel as they
Yet 'tis not meant, I pray you, see,
To thrust you 'mong the rabble rout—
I'm none of your great folks, no doubt,
But if, in fellowship with me,
To range through life you are content,
I will most cheerfully consent
To be your own upon the spot,
Your close companion, and if what
I offer pleases, you shall have
Me as your servant, yea, your slave!

FAUST

And in return what must I do for you?

MEPHISTOPHELES

Oh, time enough to talk of that!

FAUST

Nay, nay!
The devil's selfish—is and was alway—
And is not like for mere God's sake to do
A liberal turn to any child of clay.
Out with the terms and plainly!   Such as thou
Are dangerous servants in a house, I trow.

MEPHISTOPHELES

I bind myself to serve you here—to do
Your bidding freely and untiringly,
And when we come together yonder, you
Are then to do the same for me.

FAUST

I prize that yonder at a rush!
This world do thou but once to atoms crush,
Then may another, if it can, arise!
From earth my every pleasure flows,

Yon Sun looks down upon my woes,
Let me but part myself from those,
Then come what may, in any guise!
To idle prate I'll close mine ears,
If we hereafter hate or love,
Or if there be in yonder spheres,
As here, an Under and Above!

MEPHISTOPHELES

You're in the mood to venture!   Bind
Yourself, and pleasure in my sleights you'll find,
While this life lasts.   I'll give you more,
Than eye of man hath ever seen before.

FAUST

What wilt thou give, thou sorry devil?   When
Were the aspiring souls of men
Fathom'd by such a thing as thee?
Oh, thou hast food that satisfieth never,
Gold, ruddy gold thou hast, that restlessly
Slips, like quicksilver, through the hand for ever;
A game, where we must losers be;
A girl, that, on my very breast,
My neighbour woos with smile and wink;
Fame's rapturous flash of godlike zest,
Yet fated, meteor-like, to sink.
Show me the fruit, that ere 'tis pluck'd, doth rot,
And trees that every day grow green anew! [1]

MEPHISTOPHELES

Such task as this affrights me not.
Such treasures have I at command for you.
But, my good friend, the time draws nigh,
When we may banquet on the best in peace!

---

[1] '*What wilt thou give. . . .*'   This speech, like the preceding curse, is an
expression of despair, a highly self-conscious despair in which Faust strikes
a superior attitude.   He does not want to be satisfied, but to be proved
right in his claim that nothing will ever satisfy him, so he asks for pleasures
which bring an immediate revulsion.   The compact which follows is, as
Korff puts it, 'a mask for Faust's will to live.'   The compact of the legend,
guaranteeing to Faust twenty-four years of power and pleasure in return
for his immortal soul, is turned into a wager expressing Faust's romantic
idealism, half a divine discontent and half the expression of imperious
self-will.

FAUST

If e'er at peace on sluggard's couch I lie,
Then may my life upon the instant cease!
Cheat thou me ever by thy glozing wile,
So that I cease to scorn myself, or e'er
My senses with a perfect joy beguile,
Then be that day my last! I offer fair,
How say'st thou?

MEPHISTOPHELES

Done!

FAUST

                                    My hand upon it! There!
If to the passing moment e'er I say,
'Oh, linger yet! thou art so fair!'
Then cast me into chains you may,
Then will I die without a care!
Then may the death-bell sound its call,
Then art thou from thy service free,
The clock may stand, the index fall,
And time and tide may cease for me!

MEPHISTOPHELES

Think well; we shan't forget the terms you name.

FAUST

Your perfect right I must allow.
Not rashly to the pact I came.
I am a slave as I am now;
Yours or another's, 'tis to me the same!

MEPHISTOPHELES

Then at the Doctor's feast this very day
Will I my post, as your attendant, take.
Just one thing more! To guard against mistake,
Oblige me with a line or two, I pray.

FAUST

Pedant, must thou have writing too?
Man, or man's word, hast thou, then, never known?
Is not my word of mouth enough for you,
To pledge my days for all eternity?

Does not the universe go raving on,
In all its ever-eddying currents, free
To pass from change to change, and I alone,
Shall a mere promise curb or fetter me?
Yet doth man's heart so hug the dear deceit,
Who would its hold without a pang undo?
Blest he, whose soul is with pure truth replete,
No sacrifice shall ever make him rue.
But, oh, your stamp'd and scribbled parchment sheet
A spectre is, which all men shrink to view.
The word dies ere it quits the pen,
And wax and sheepskin lord it then.
What would you have, spirit of ill!
Brass, marble, parchment, paper?—Say,
Am I to write with pen, or style, or graver?
I care not—choose whiche'er you will.

MEPHISTOPHELES

Why throw your eloquence away,
Or give it such a very pungent savour?
Pshaw!   Any scrap will do—'tis quite the same—
With the least drop of blood just sign your name.

FAUST

If that will make you happy, why, a claim
So very whimsical I'll freely favour.

MEPHISTOPHELES

Blood is a juice of quite peculiar kind.

FAUST

Only fear not the compact I'll evade!
My life's whole struggle, heart and mind,
Chimes with the promise I have made.
Too high I've soar'd—too proudly dreamt,
I'm only peer for such as thee;
The Might Spirit spurns me with contempt,
And Nature veils her face from me.
Thought's chain is snapt—for many a day
I've loathed all knowledge every way.
So quench we now our passions' fires
In sense and sensual delights,
Unveil all hidden magic sleights
To minister to our desires!

Let us plunge in the torrent of time, and range
Through the weltering chaos of chance and change,
Then pleasure and pain, disaster and gain,
May course one another adown my brain.
Excitement, and only excitement, can
Appease the unsatisfied spirit of man.

MEPHISTOPHELES

To you is set nor goal nor stint.
If you'd sip the sweetest of everything,
And hawk at pleasure upon the wing,
Much joy, I'm sure, I wish you in 't.
Only fall to, and don't be coy.

FAUST

Again I say, my thoughts are not of joy.
I devote myself to the whirl and roar,
To the bliss that throbs till it turns to pain,
To the hate that we dote on and fondle o'er,
The defeat that inspirits both nerves and brain.
Of its passion for knowledge cured, my soul
Henceforth shall expand to all forms of woe,
And all that is all human nature's dole
In my heart of hearts I shall feel and know;
With highest, lowest, in spirit I shall cope,
Pile on my breast their joys, their griefs, their cares,
So all men's souls shall come within my scope,
And mine at last go down a wreck like theirs.

MEPHISTOPHELES

Oh, trust to me, who have through many a year
On this tough morsel chew'd the cud,
That from the cradle to the bier
No man of mortal flesh and blood
Hath e'er digested the old leaven.
Trust one of us, this whole so vast
Is only for the God of Heaven!
In radiance endless He is glass'd,
Us hath He into darkness cast,
And you, you mortals, only may
See day succeed to night, and night to day.

FAUST

Nay, but I will.

MEPHISTOPHELES

                    That's well enough to say;
Only I don't quite see my way.
Art's long, time short.   You'd best permit
Yourself to be advised a bit.
Club with a poet: soaring free,
Let him the realm of fancy sweep,
And every noble quality
Upon your honour'd forehead heap;
The lion's magnanimity,
The fleetness of the hind,
The fiery blood of Italy,
The Northern's constant mind.
Let him for you the art divine,
High aims with cunning to combine,
And, with young blood at fever full,
To love on system and by rule.
I should myself be glad to find
A Sir Microcosmus of such a kind.

FAUST

What am I, then, if never by no art
The crown of mortal nature may be gain'd,
For which our every energy is strain'd?

MEPHISTOPHELES

Thou art, when all's done, what thou art.
A periwig with countless ringlets buy,
Array thy feet in socks a cubit high,
Still shalt thou be no more than what thou art.

FAUST

'Tis true, I feel!   In vain have I amass'd
Within me all the treasures of man's mind,
And when I pause, and sit me down at last,
No new power welling inwardly I find;
A hairbreadth is not added to my height,
I am no nearer to the Infinite.

MEPHISTOPHELES

Good sir, you view these matters just
As any common mortal would;
But take a higher strain we must,
Not let life's joys our grasp elude.

Why, what the deuce!   Sure, foot and hand
And head and heart are yours!   And what
I can enjoy, control, command,
Is it the less my own for that?
If I for horses six can pay,
Their powers are added to my store;
A proper man I dash away,
As though I had legs twenty-four.
Up then, no more a dreamer be,
But forth into the world with me!
I tell you what; your speculating wretch
Is like a beast upon a barren waste,
Round, ever round, by an ill spirit chased,
Whilst all beyond fair verdant pastures stretch.

FAUST

But how begin?

MEPHISTOPHELES

We start at once.
Ugh! what a place of torture dire!
Call you this life—yourself to tire,
And some few youngsters, each a dunce?
Leave that to neighbour Paunch to do.
Why plague yourself with threshing straw?
What's best of all that's known to you,
You dare not tell these striplings raw.
I hear one now upon the stair.

FAUST

I cannot see him.

MEPHISTOPHELES

Long and late,
Poor boy, he's waited.   In despair
We must not send him from the gate.
Give me your cap and gown: the mask,
You'll see, will fit me to a hair.   [Changes his dress.
Now leave all to my wit.   I ask
But fifteen minutes.   Go now!   There!
And for our pleasant trip prepare.   [Exit FAUST.

MEPHISTOPHELES (*putting on* FAUST's *gown*)

Only scorn reason, knowledge, all that can
Give strength, or might, or dignity to man,
And let thyself be only more and more
Besotted by the spirit of lies
With faith in necromantic lore,
Its shams, delusions, sorceries,
And thou art mine beyond recall!—
Fate to this man a soul has given,
That brooks not to be held in thrall,
But onward evermore is driven,
And, on its own mad fancies bent,
In earth's delights finds no content.
Him will I drag through wilds of excess,
Through shallows of life that are meaningless.
Oh, he shall sprawl, be stunn'd, stick fast,
Dainties and drink shall dance before
His fever'd lips; nor shall he taste
The peace he'll pray for evermore.
Even if no contract with me bore his name,
He'd go to the devil all the same.[1]

Enter a STUDENT

STUDENT

To town quite recently I came,
And make it, sir, my earliest care
To see and talk with one, whose name
Is named with reverence everywhere.

MEPHISTOPHELES

You're too polite!   A man you see,
Like scores of other men, in me.
Elsewhere have you not found your way?

---

[1] '*Only scorn reason. . . .*' Mephistopheles appears to speak out of character, for he has just accepted a wager, to win which he must satisfy Faust.   The passage appeared first, however, in the *Faust, a Fragment* of 1790, before the compact scene had been worked out, and Goethe has let it stand, possibly, as Santayana suggests, because it gives the real import of the play, the devil being only a convenient symbol.   The moral experiences of Faust are simply those of any romantic, who will not learn from experience.   In its new context the speech may, however, be taken as meaning that Mephistopheles is too intelligent to think that he can ever satisfy Faust.   He hopes nevertheless to tire him out.

STUDENT

Take me in hand, oh do, sir, pray!
I've every wish, nay have, in truth,
A very passion to be taught,
Some money, too, and health and youth;
My mother scarcely could be brought
To part with me; but come I would,
To learn whate'er 'tis best I should.

MEPHISTOPHELES

If such be really the case,
You've come to just the proper place.

STUDENT

Yet I, the honest truth to say,
Already wish myself away!
These walls and lecture rooms I find
By no means of a pleasant kind.
All is so close, so cramp'd, so mean,
No trees, nor anything that's green—
Mew'd up in them, my spirits sink;
I neither hear, nor see, nor think.

MEPHISTOPHELES

Habit alone cures that.   Just so
The child at first will not, you know,
Take kindly to its mother's breast,
But soon it suckles there with zest.
Even thus at wisdom's breast will you
Each day find pleasure ever new.

STUDENT

Upon her neck I'll hang with joy; the way
To clamber there, do you, sir, only say.

MEPHISTOPHELES

Ere you go further, say, on which
Of all the faculties your fancies pitch.

STUDENT

Sir, my ambition is to be
A scholar widely read and sound,
All things on earth, in heaven, or sea,
To grasp with comprehensive view,
In short, to master all the round
Of science and of nature too.

MEPHISTOPHELES

You're on the right track; only don't
Get scatter-brain'd in the pursuit.

STUDENT

Oh, never fear, sir—that I won't.
Body and soul I'll buckle to't.
Yet should I like upon occasion
Some freedom, some small relaxation,
When skies are bright, and fields are gay,
Upon a summer's holiday.

MEPHISTOPHELES

Use well your time—so fast it flies;
Yet Method teaches, in what wise
Of time itself you may make prize.
And, first and foremost to that end,
I counsel you, my dear young friend,
A course of Logic to attend.
Your mind will then be so well braced,
In Spanish boots so tightly laced,
That henceforth, by discretion taught,
'Twill creep along the path of thought,
And not, with all the winds that blow,
Go Will-o'-Wisping to and fro.
Then many a good day will be spent
In teaching, that the things you used
To knock off at a stroke, with just
As little thought or pains, as went
To eating or to drinking, must
Be by First!   Second!   Third! produced.
The web of thought, we may assume,
Is like some triumph of the loom,
Where one small simple treddle starts
A thousand threads to motion—where
The flying shuttle shoots and darts,
Now over here, now under there.
We look, but see not how, so fast
Thread blends with thread, and twines, and mixes,
When lo! one single stroke at last
The thousand combinations fixes;
In steps me then Philosophy, and shows,
How everything must happen as it does.
The First was so, the Second so,
Ergo the Third and Fourth ensued;
But given no First nor Second, no
Third, yea, nor Fourth had been or could.

Scholars in matters of this kind
Are everywhere profound believers,
Yet none of them, that I can find,
Have signalized themselves as weavers.
He that would study and portray
A living creature, thinks it fit
To start with finding out the way
To drive the spirit out of it.
This done, he holds within his hand
The pieces to be named and stated,
But, ah! the spirit-tie, that spann'd
And knit them, has evaporated.
This process chemic science pleases
To call Naturae Encheiresis,
And, in the very doing so, it
Makes of itself a mock, and does not know it.

STUDENT

I don't entirely comprehend.

MEPHISTOPHELES

In that respect you'll quickly mend,
When once you learn, with true insight
To classify all things aright.

STUDENT

I'm as perplex'd with what you've said,
As if I'd a mill-wheel in my head.

MEPHISTOPHELES

Before all other studies you
Must Metaphysics next pursue.
There see, that you profoundly scan
What ne'er was meant for brain of man;
Be thought or no thought in your head,
Fine phrases there will do instead:
And mind, that this half year in all
You do you're most methodical.
Five hours of lecture daily; so
Be in your seat right to the minute!
Prepare the subject, ere you go,
Be thoroughly well read up in it.
Thus see, that the professor's stating
No more than all the textbooks show;
Yet still write down each word, as though
He were the Holy Ghost dictating.

STUDENT

No need to say that to me twice.
I see 'tis excellent advice;
For we take home, and study, quite
At ease, what's down in black and white.

MEPHISTOPHELES

But choose some Faculty.

STUDENT

　　　　　　　At the mere name
Of Jurisprudence I rebel.

MEPHISTOPHELES

In that, I own, you're not so much to blame,
For what that science is, I know full well.
Laws are transmitted, as one sees,
Just like inherited disease.
They're handed down from race to race,
And noiseless glide from place to place.
Reason they turn to nonsense; worse,
They make beneficence a curse!
Ah me! That you're a grandson you,
As long as you're alive, shall rue.
The natural law that's born within us,
That law, alas! is no man's business.

STUDENT

My loathing is now stronger far.
How fortunate your pupils are!
I almost think, Theology
Would be the study best for me.

MEPHISTOPHELES

I should not wish, friend, to mislead you;
Yet in that branch of lore, indeed, you
Will find it hard to keep away
From paths, that carry far astray.
In it so much hid poison lies,
Which you may fail to recognize,
Nay, will most probably confound
With the true medicine around.
But here again one rule is clear;
To one, and but one guide, give ear,

Take all his words as gospel in,
And swear by them through thick and thin.
As a broad principle, hold on
By words, words, words!   So you, anon,
Through their unfailing doors the fane
Of perfect certainty will gain.

STUDENT

But surely, sir, a meaning should
In words be always understood?

MEPHISTOPHELES

No doubt, no doubt!   Yet 'twere absurd,
Upon that point to feel too much concern;
Since just where meaning fails, a word
Comes patly in to serve your turn.
Words, my young friend—why, nothing suits
So well as matter for disputes;
With words your systems you can weave in,
Words are such fine things to believe in,
And from a word no jot or tittle
Can be abstracted, much or little.

STUDENT

I fear my numerous questions tease you;
Yet once more I must trouble you.
On Medicine I would fain, so please you,
Receive a pregnant word or two?
Three years, they slip away so fast,
And, Heavens! the field is quite too vast.
Still with a hint a man may hope
His way with more success to grope.

MEPHISTOPHELES (*aside*)

This prosing bores me.   I must play
The devil now in my own way.   [*Aloud.*]
Well, any simpleton may seize
The soul of Medicine with ease—
You simply study through and through
The world of man and nature too,
To end with leaving things to God,
To make or mar them.   'Tis in vain,
That you go mooning all abroad,
Picking up science grain by grain:

Each man learns only what he can.
But he that has the gift and power,
To profit by the passing hour,
He is your proper man!
You're not ill-built—will, I conceive,
Shew mettle on occasion due—
If you but in yourself believe,
Others will then believe in you.
Especially be sure to find
The way to manage the womenkind.
Their everlasting Ohs! and Ahs!
Of this be sure,
Whate'er their fashion or their cause,
All from one point admit of cure.
With air respectful and demure
Approach as they advance, and, mum!
You have them all beneath your thumb.
But a degree must first instil
Conviction in them, that your skill
Surpasses other people's; then
At once they make you free of all
Those tête-à-tête endearments small,
Years scarce secure for other men:
The little pulse adroitly squeeze,
With looks on fire with passion seize,
And boldly clasp the tapering waist,
To see if it be tightly laced.

STUDENT

Oh, that is much more in my way!
One sees at least the where and how.

MEPHISTOPHELES

Dear friend, all theory is grey,
And green life's golden tree.

STUDENT

            I vow,
I'm like one in a dream.   Might I
Intrude on you some other time, to hear
Your wisdom make the grounds of all this clear?

MEPHISTOPHELES

So far as I can serve you, I will try.

STUDENT

I cannot tear myself away,
Let me before you, sir, my album lay;
Some small memorial of your favour, pray?

MEPHISTOPHELES

With all my heart.   [*Writes and returns the book.*

STUDENT (*reads*)

Eritis sicut Deus, scientes bonum et malum.
                              [*Closes it reverentially and retires.*

MEPHISTOPHELES

Take for your law the ancient saw, and that cousin of
    mine, the snake,
And, with that likeness of yours to God, your heart is
    like to break.

FAUST (*entering*)

And now where shall we go?

MEPHISTOPHELES

                              You've but to name
What place you choose—to me 'tis quite the same.
Suppose we see the small folk first,
And then upon the great ones burst.
With what delight, what profit, too,
You'll revel the pleasant circuit through!

FAUST

But with my long beard can I face
Society?   I want the grace,
The easy, smooth, and polish'd air,
That of a man's expected there.
Nor could I learn it, if I would.
Adapt myself I never could
To what the world demands of all.
And in a crowd I feel so small,
'Tis certain I shall always be
Embarrass'd when in company.

MEPHISTOPHELES

All that will come in time.   Be self-possess'd!
In that one word is life's whole art express'd.

FAUST

But how are we to travel?   Where
Are horses, servants, carriage, pray?

MEPHISTOPHELES

This cloak out so we've but to lay,
And 'twill transport us through the air.
In this bold trip, no need to cumber
Yourself with luggage and such lumber.
A little gas, which I've at hand,
Will waft us straight o'er sea and land,
And, as we travel lightly, too,
On at a rattling pace we'll spin.
I wish you joy, friend, of the new
Career of life you now begin.

AUERBACH'S CELLAR IN LEIPZIG

A Drinking Party of Boon Companions

FROSCH

WILL nobody drink?   Is there never a joke
Among you, or bit of fun to poke?
At other times you can blaze away;
But, egad, you're all like damp straw to-day.

BRANDER

Your fault!   You do nothing to make us jolly,
No beastliness, no stupid folly.

FROSCH (*flings a glass of wine at his head*)
There's both for you!

BRANDER

Brute!   Beast!

FROSCH

You sought it,
My lad of wax, and now you've caught it!

SIEBEL

Any fellow that quarrels, kick him out!
Come, clear your throats, boys, swill and shout
Hip, hip, huzza!

ALTMAYER

I'm lost!   Oh dear!
Some cotton!   This rowdie splits my ear!

SIEBEL

Until the vaults with the echo reel,
The strength of the bass you never feel.

FROSCH

Right!   Those that don't like it needn't stay!
     Ah, tara, lara, da!

ALTMAYER

     Ah, tara, lara, da!

FROSCH

Our throats are tuned up, so fire away!

(*Sings*)

The dear old Roman Empire, how
Does it manage to hang together?

BRANDER

A filthy song!   A political song!   Fie, fie!
A most offensive song, say I.
Thank God each morning it's not your fate
To keep the Roman Empire straight.
I hold it a thing to be grateful for,
That I'm neither Kaiser nor Chancellor.
Still, we should have a chief, and may, I hope.
We will, we shall, we must elect a Pope!
I need not tell you, for you're all aware,
What qualities weigh heaviest there,
And lift a man into the chair.

FROSCH (*sings*)

Fly away, fly away, Lady Nightingale,
Over the mountain, and over the dale!
Fly to my sweetheart out over the sea,
And greet her a thousand times from me.

SIEBEL

No greetings, ho, to sweetings!   'Tis exceedingly improper!

FROSCH

I will greet her, kiss her, treat her!   You shan't put on me
   a stopper.

(*Sings*)

Undo the bolts at dead of night,
And let the lad that loves you in,
But in the grey of the morning light
Bar him without, and yourself within!

SIEBEL

Sing on!   Our ears with her perfections din!
My time will come to laugh, when you look blue.
She led me a fool's dance, and so she will lead you.
I'd give her for a lover a hobgoblin,
To toy with her on cross-roads in the dark;
An old buck-goat, back from the Blocksberg hobbling,
Might tickle her up in passing for a lark!
The blood and bone of any stout young blade
Are much too good for such an arrant jade.
No, no, the only greeting I will hear of
Is smashing all the gipsy's windows clear off.

BRANDER (*striking the table*)

Silence!   Silence!   To me give ear!
You'll all admit that I know what's what.
We have some love-sick spoonies here,
And I must treat them to something pat,
And like to enliven their doleful cheer.
Of the very last fashion is my strain.
Full chorus, mind, for the refrain!

(*Sings*)

Once in a cellar there lived a rat,
   His paunch it grew a thumper,
For he lived on nothing but butter and fat,
   Not Luther's self was plumper.
The cook laid poison for him one day,
And he fell into a terrible way,
   As if love's tortures twinged him!

CHORUS

As if love's tortures twinged him!

And he ran out, and round about,
    And he could not think what ail'd him,
And he scratch'd, and claw'd, and nibbled, and gnaw'd,
    But his fury nought avail'd him;
He felt the pains shoot from head to foot,
'Twas soon all up with him, poor brute,
    As if love's tortures twinged him!

CHORUS

As if love's tortures twinged him!

In pain, in dismay, in broad noon-day,
    He dash'd into the kitchen,
Fell down on the hearth, and there he lay,
    Convulsed with a woeful twitching;
But the cook she laugh'd when his pain she spy'd,
'Ha! Ha! He's at his last gasp!' she cried,
    As if love's tortures twinged him!

CHORUS

As if love's tortures twinged him!

SIEBEL

How easy it is to tickle flats!
To lay down poison for poor rats
Is wit of such a spicy flavour!

BRANDER

No doubt they stand high in your favour.

ALTMAYER

Fatguts is down in his luck—'tis that
Makes him soft-hearted and dejected;
Poor devil, he sees in the bloated rat
The image of himself reflected.

Enter FAUST *and* MEPHISTOPHELES

MEPHISTOPHELES

Before all things I must bring you to
A circle of jolly dogs, that you

May see how lightly life can sit.
Every day is a feast with such
Hard-drinking fellows as these.   With much
Self-satisfaction and little wit,
Day after day, they may all be found,
Spinning along the same narrow round,
Like a young kitten pursuing its tail.
So long as their heads don't ache or ail,
And with mine host they can score their way,
No care, or misgiving at all have they.

BRANDER

Strangers, and just arrived, that's clear,
Their cut and deportment are so queer!
Not been an hour in town, I'll swear.

FROSCH

For once you're right, old fellow, there.
Leipzig for ever!   'Tis Paris in small!
It gives us a style, sir, a style to us all.

SIEBEL

For what do you these strangers take?

FROSCH

Just leave them to me.   In a brace of shakes
Out of these fellows I'll worm the truth,
As easy as draw you a young child's tooth.
Noblemen I should say they were,
They've such a haughty dissatisfied air.

BRANDER

Mountebanks!   That's about their level!

ALTMAYER

Perhaps!

FROSCH

I'll trot them.   Pray you, note!

MEPHISTOPHELES (to FAUST)

These scum would never surmise the devil,
Although he had them by the throat!

FAUST

Your servant, sirs!

SIEBEL

The same to you!
[*Aside, looking askance at* MEPHISTOPHELES.
Limps on one foot?   So queerly, too!

MEPHISTOPHELES

Beside you have we leave our chairs to set?
Instead of good drink, then, which here we cannot get,
We shall have your good company for cheer.

ALTMAYER

You're mighty hard to please, it would appear!

FROSCH

Just fresh from Rippach, ain't you?   I dare say
You supp'd, now, with Squire Hans, upon the way?

MEPHISTOPHELES

To-day we gallop'd past his door;
But had much talk with him, the time before,
About his cousins here; and he presents
To each of you through us his special compliments.
[*Bowing towards* FROSCH.

ALTMAYER (*aside*)

That's home!   A knowing dog!

SIEBEL

A biting wit!

FROSCH

I'll serve him out, you'll see.   Just wait a bit!

MEPHISTOPHELES

Did we not hear—I can't be wrong—
Well-practised voices chanting chorus?
No doubt, the vaulted ceiling o'er us
Must echo rarely to a song.

FROSCH

You are a connoisseur of some pretence?

MEPHISTOPHELES

Oh no!   My powers are weak, my love immense.

ALTMAYER

Tip us a stave!

MEPHISTOPHELES

A score, if you incline.

SIEBEL

Brand new, then, let it be, some jolly strain!

MEPHISTOPHELES

We have quite recently return'd from Spain,
That beauteous land of song and wine.

(*Sings*)

A king there was, be 't noted,
    Who had a lusty flea.

FROSCH

Mark him, a flea!   You take the jest?
Now, by my faith, a royal guest!

MEPHISTOPHELES (*sings*)

A king there was, be 't noted,
    Who had a lusty flea,
And on this flea he doated,
    And loved him tenderly.
A message to the tailor goes,
    Swift came the man of stitches;
'Ho, measure the youngster here for clothes,
    And measure him for breeches!'

BRANDER

Mind you impress on Snip to take
Especial care about the fit,
And, as he loves his head, to make
The breeches without wrinkles sit.

MEPHISTOPHELES (*resumes his song*)

In silk and satin of the best
  Soon was the flea array'd there,
Ribbons had he upon his breast,
  Likewise a star display'd there;
Prime minister anon he grew,
  With star of huge dimensions,
And his kindred, male and female too,
  Got titles, rank, and pensions.

And lords and ladies, high and fair,
  Were grievously tormented;
Sore bitten the queen and her maidens were,
  But they did not dare resent it.
They even were afraid to scratch,
  Howe'er our friends might rack them,
But we without a scruple catch,
  And when we catch, we crack them.

CHORUS

But we without a scruple catch,
  And when we catch, we crack them.

FROSCH

Bravo!   First rate!

SIEBEL

            So perish all
The race of fleas, both great and small.

BRANDER

Catch me them daintily on the hip
Between the nail and the finger-tip!

ALTMAYER

Huzzah for freedom!   Huzzah for wine!

MEPHISTOPHELES

To pledge a bumper glass to freedom, I'd be glad,
Were not this wine of yours so execrably bad.

SIEBEL

Let's hear no more of that, Sir Superfine!

MEPHISTOPHELES

But that our host were apt to be offended,
I'd give these worthy fellows here
From our own cellar something splendid!

SIEBEL

I'll make that square, so never fear.

FROSCH

Make good your words, and you're a trump.   The sample,
I charge you, though, to make it ample.
For, if I have to judge of tipple, I
Must have a good mouthful to judge it by.

ALTMAYER (aside)

Soho!   They're from the Rhine, I see.

MEPHISTOPHELES

A gimlet here?

BRANDER

For what, now, can that be?
You can't have got the hogsheads at the door?

ALTMAYER

The landlord's tool-chest's yonder on the floor.

MEPHISTOPHELES (taking the gimlet, to FROSCH)

Now say, for which you have a mind?

FROSCH

What!   Have you them of every kind?

MEPHISTOPHELES

Name each his choice, strong, sparkling, old, or heady?

ALTMAYER (to FROSCH)

Aha, your lips are watering already.

FROSCH

Let it be Rhenish, if I may command.
For best of cheer I'll back old Fatherland.

D 335

MEPHISTOPHELES (*boring a hole in the edge of the
table where* FROSCH *is sitting*)

A little wax to stop the hole!   Quick, quick!

ALTMAYER (*to* FROSCH)

Pshaw, this is palpably a juggler's trick!

MEPHISTOPHELES (*to* BRANDER)

And you?

BRANDER

Champagne, champagne for me!
Creaming and sparkling cheerily.
[MEPHISTOPHELES *bores; meanwhile one of the party
has made stoppers of wax, and stopped the holes.*

BRANDER

One cannot at all times dispense
With foreign things, and foreign sense,
For what is good, and what we prize,
So far away so often lies.
No real German, 'tis most sure,
Could e'er a son of France endure;
Yet will he readily incline
To do full justice to his wine.

SIEBEL (*as* MEPHISTOPHELES *approaches him*)

The sour, I own, I can't away with.
Pure sweet, I'd like a glass of that.

MEPHISTOPHELES (*bores*)

You shall, sir, have Tokay to play with.

ALTMAYER

No, no, sir, no!   I tell you what,
You're making game, you are, of us.

MEPHISTOPHELES

That were somewhat too venturous
With men of mark like you.   You doubt it?
Quick!   Tell me without more ado,
What wine I am to serve for you?

ALTMAYER

Any!   So that you don't stand haggling long about it!

After all the holes have been bored, and stoppers put into them, MEPHISTOPHELES (*with strange gestures*)

> Wine-grapes of the vine are born,
> Front of he-goat sprouts with horn,
> Wine is juice, and vine-stocks wood,
> Wooden board yields wine as good!
> Here is truth for him that sees
> Into nature's mysteries;
> Miracles when you receive,
> You have only to believe!

Now draw your stoppers, and fall to!

ALL (*as they draw the stoppers, and the wine each has selected runs into his glass*)

Oh, fountain, beautiful to view!

MEPHISTOPHELES

Be very careful!   Drink your fill,
But see, that not a drop you spill!

[*They drink repeatedly.*

ALL (*sing*)

> As savagely jolly are we,
> As any five hundred porkers!

MEPHISTOPHELES

These sots from all restraint are freed,
And so are blest, and blest indeed.

FAUST

I'm sick of this, and would be gone.

MEPHISTOPHELES

Only a little moment stay;
You'll see a glorious display
Of what mere beasts they are, anon.

SIEBEL (*drinks carelessly; wine is spilt on the
ground and turns into flame*)

Help! Hell's broke loose! We all are shent!

MEPHISTOPHELES (*adjuring the flame*)

Be quiet, kindly element!   [*To the topers.*
This time 'twas nothing but a tiny spark
Of purgatorial fire, not worth remark!

SIEBEL

Just wait, and your cock's comb I'll mar.
You do not know, it strikes me, who we are.

FROSCH

His tricks a second time just let him try.

ALTMAYER

Let's send him to the right-about, say I.

SIEBEL

Confound you, coming to provoke us
With playing off your hocus-pocus!

MEPHISTOPHELES

Silence, old vat!

SIEBEL

You broomstick, you!
And so you'd fain be saucy, too?

BRANDER

Wait, and I'll thrash you black and blue.

ALTMAYER (*draws a stopper from the table; fire
shoots out towards him*)

I burn! I'm all on fire!

SIEBEL

The wizard!
Down with him! Stick him through the gizzard!
[*They draw their knives, and make a rush at* MEPHISTOPHELES.

MEPHISTOPHELES (*with solemn gesticulations*)

> Voices, that delude the ear,
> Forms, that mock the eye, appear!
> Let the distant seem the near,
> Be ye there and be ye here!
> > [*They stand amazed and stare at each other.*

ALTMAYER

Where am I?   What a lovely land!

FROSCH

Vineyards!   How strange!

SIEBEL

> And grapes that court the hand!

BRANDER

Here, under these green leaves by me,
See, what a stem!   What branches, see!
> [*Seizes* SIEBEL *by the nose.   The rest do the same with
> each other, and brandish their knives.*

MEPHISTOPHELES (*as before*)

> Phantoms of delusion, rise,
> Lift the bandage from their eyes!
> And take note, ye swinish soaks,
> In what wise the devil jokes!
> > [*He disappears with* FAUST. *The topers recoil from
> > one another.*

SIEBEL

What's this?

ALTMAYER

> How's this?

FROSCH

> Was that thy nose?

BRANDER (*to* SIEBEL)

On thine, too, see, my fingers close!

ALTMAYER

It sent a shock through all my limbs!
A chair!   I'm falling!   My head swims!

FROSCH

What ails you all?

SIEBEL

                    Where is he?   Where?
If I can catch the knave, he dies, I swear.

ALTMAYER

Out of the cellar-door, astride
A huge wine-tun, I saw him ride.
I feel like lead about the feet.
                              [*Turning towards the table.*
My!   Should the wine be running yet!

SIEBEL

'Twas all a sham, a trick, a cheat!

FROSCH

Yet, that it was wine, I would bet.

BRANDER

But how about the grapes?

ALTMAYER

                    Well, after that,
Doubt miracles who may, I won't, that's flat.

WITCHES' KITCHEN

*A large cauldron suspended above the fire upon a low hearth.
Through the fumes that ascend from it various figures are
visible. A female ape sits beside the cauldron skimming
it, and watching that it does not boil over. The male ape
with the young ones sits near her, and warms himself. Walls
and ceiling are decorated with witches' furniture of the most
fantastic kind.*

FAUST, MEPHISTOPHELES

FAUST

I LOATHE this wizard trash; yet you repeat,
That in this chaos of insane conceit
I shall my wasted strength repair?
Take counsel of an aged hag? Oh, shame!
Can the foul mess, that simmers there,
Strike thirty winters from my frame?
If you know nothing better, woe is me!
Already hope has left me. Is there not
Some natural balsam or elixir, wrought
By spirit high for such extremity?

MEPHISTOPHELES

Now with your old sagacity you speak!
There is a natural means to make you young; but you
In quite a different book for that must seek,
And in a chapter of the strangest, too!

FAUST

Speak! Let me know it on the spot!

MEPHISTOPHELES

Good! 'Tis a remedy that's to be got
Sans sorcery, gold, or medicine.
Straight to the fields away! Begin
To hack and delve with might and main,
Yourself and your desires confine
Within the very narrowest line,
On simple food yourself sustain,
With beasts live as a beast, and think it not a bore
Yourself to dung the field you are to reap.
This, trust me, is the best of ways to keep
The fire of youth within you to fourscore.

FAUST

I am not used to toil, and 'tis too late to force
Myself to wield the spade.   A life so bare,
So cramp'd, would drive me to despair.

MEPHISTOPHELES

Then is the witch our sole resource.

FAUST

But why this beldame?   Cannot you
Without her aid the potion brew?

MEPHISTOPHELES

That were fine waste of time.   Go to!
Rather would I a thousand bridges build,
Within the time 'twould take to brew it.
No matter how you may be skill'd,
You must give tireless patience to it.
A quiet spirit works at it for years;
Time, only time, the fermentation clears,
And concentrates its subtle force.
All the ingredients of the stew
Are wondrous in their kind, and source.
The devil taught the witch, 'tis true,
But, make it, that he cannot do.   [*Turning to the Apes.*
A handsome brood as ever was!
This is the lad, and this the lass.   [*To the Apes.*
The dame is not at home, it seems?

THE APES

She takes her 'rouse
Outside the house,
Up by the chimney among the beams.

MEPHISTOPHELES

And how long is she apt to stay,
When she is out for such a cause?

THE APES

We just have time to warm our paws,
And nothing more, while she's away.

MEPHISTOPHELES (*to* FAUST)

How like you them, the dainty brutes?

FAUST

Such loathsome creatures have I never seen.

MEPHISTOPHELES

Nay, nay!   A chat like this, I ween,
Is just the thing that best my fancy suits! [*To the Apes.*
Tell me, ye whelps accurst, what you
Are stirring there at such a rate?

THE APES

Coarse beggar's broth we boil and stew.

MEPHISTOPHELES

Your custom for it will be great.

THE HE-APE (*approaching and fawning upon*
MEPHISTOPHELES)

Tarry not, but in a trice,
Shake the box, and fling the dice!
I am poor, so let me win;
Poverty is such a sin;
But, if money once I had,
Who would say, that I was mad?

MEPHISTOPHELES

How happy, now, it would the monkey make,
If in the lottery he might only stake!
[*The young Apes, who have meanwhile been playing with
a large globe, roll it forwards.*

THE HE-APE

This is the world,
Evermore twirl'd
Round about, round about,
Destined to bound about!
Mounting and sinking,
Like crystal clinking;
Smashing like winking
Certain to follow!
All within hollow.

* D 335

> Here 'tis all o'er bright,
> Here even more bright!
> Living am I.
> Dear sire, get away!
> Back, be afraid of that,
> For thou must die!
> 'Tis fashion'd of clay,
> Potsherds are made of that!

MEPHISTOPHELES

For what is the sieve here?

THE HE-APE (*takes it down*)

> Came you to thieve here,
> Straight 'twould show me why you came.
> [*Runs to the She-Ape, and makes her look through it.*
> Through the sieve look, look!   Dost thou
> Recognize the thief, and now
> Art afraid to name his name?

MEPHISTOPHELES (*approaches the fire*)

And this pot?

THE APES (*male and female*)

> The crack-brain'd sot,
> He knows not the pot,
> He knows not the kettle!

MEPHISTOPHELES

Unmannerly brute!

THE HE-APE

> Look ye now, put
> This whisk in your hand, and sit down on the settle.
> [*Forces* MEPHISTOPHELES *to sit down.*

FAUST (*who has, meanwhile, been standing before a mirror,
now advancing towards, and now retiring, from it*)

> What form divine is this that seems to live
> Within the magic glass before mine eyes!
> Oh love, to me thy swiftest pinion give,
> And waft me to the region where she lies!
> Oh, if I stir beyond this spot, and dare
> Advance to scan it with a nearer gaze,
> The vision fades and dies as in a haze.

A woman's form beyond expression fair!
Can woman be so fair? Or must I deem,
In this recumbent form I see reveal'd
The quintessence of all that heaven can yield?
On earth can aught be found of beauty so supreme?

MEPHISTOPHELES

Why, when a God works hard for six whole days,
And when his task is over, says, 'Bravo!'
That he should turn out something to amaze,
Is nothing more than natural, you know.
Gaze on your fill! As choice a treasure
My power for you can soon provide;
And happy he beyond all measure,
Who has the luck to bear home such a bride!

> FAUST *continues to gaze into the mirror.* MEPHISTO-
> PHELES, *lounging on the settle and playing with the*
> *whisk, continues:*

Here like the king upon my throne I sit,
My sceptre here!   My crown, though, where is it?

THE APES (*who up to this time have been indulging in all sorts of*
fantastic gambols, bring MEPHISTOPHELES *a crown with loud*
acclamations).

> Oh, deign, with a flood
> Of sweat and of blood,
> The crown to belime!

> [*They handle the crown awkwardly, and break it into*
> *two pieces, with which they dance round and round.*

'Tis done! He! He!
We speak and we see,
We hear and we rhyme.

FAUST (*before the mirror*)

Woe's me!   As though I should go mad, I feel!

MEPHISTOPHELES (*pointing to the Apes*)

Why, even my head, too, begins to reel.

THE APES

And if we make a lucky hit,
And if the words fall in and fit,
Thought's begot, and with the jingle
Seems to interweave and mingle.

FAUST (*as before*)

My breast is all on fire!   Let us away!
Even now 'tis for my peace too late.

MEPHISTOPHELES (*still in the same position*)

Well, every one must own, that they
Are candid poets, at any rate.
[*The cauldron, which the She-Ape has neglected in the
interim, begins to boil over; a great flame shoots out
and rushes up the chimney. The* WITCH *comes
shooting down the chimney with a horrible shriek.*

THE WITCH

Au! Au! Au! Au!
Confounded beast! Accursèd sow!
Neglecting the cauldron and singeing your dame, you
Beast accursèd, I'll brain you, I'll lame you!
[*Espying* FAUST *and* MEPHISTOPHELES.

What do I see here?
Who may you be here?
What do you seek here?
How did you sneak here?
May fire-pangs fierce
Your marrow pierce!
[*She dips the skimming ladle into the cauldron, and
sprinkles flames on* FAUST, MEPHISTOPHELES, *and
the Apes. The Apes whimper.*

MEPHISTOPHELES (*inverting the whisk, which he holds in his hands,
and laying about with it among the glasses and pots*)

To smash! To smash,
With all your trash!
There goes your stew,
There goes your glass!
You see, we too
Our jest can pass!
You carrion, we
Can match your feat!
Good time, you see,
To your tune we beat!
[*As the* WITCH *recoils full of rage and amazement.*

Dost thou recognize me now?
Scarecrow! Atomy! Dost thou
Recognize thy lord and master?
What holds my hand, that I should not blast her?
Her and her monkey-sprites together?
Is all respect within thee dead
For me and for my doublet red?
Dost recognize not the cock's feather?
Have I so mask'd my face? My name
Must I on the house-top proclaim?

THE WITCH

Master, forgive my rough salute!
But yet I see no cloven foot:
And where may your two ravens be?

MEPHISTOPHELES

For this time that apology
May pass: for 'tis, I can't forget,
A long while now, since last we met.
Besides, the march of intellect,
Which into shape, as time runs on,
Is licking all the world, upon
The devil's self has had effect.
The northern goblin no more shocks the sense;
Horns, tails, and claws are things you never see;
As for the foot, with which I can't dispense,
That with society might injure me;
And therefore I for many years
Have, like young buckish cavaliers,
Among the upper circles gadded,
With calves most curiously padded.

THE WITCH (*dancing*)

I feel as if I were mad with sheer
Delight to see once more Dan Satan here!

MEPHISTOPHELES

Woman, that name offends my ear!

THE WITCH

Wherefore? What wrong has it done you?

MEPHISTOPHELES

                                  Tut!
It has been written down, for many a day,
With other things that men call fables; but
No whit the better off for that are they.
The Wicked One they certainly ignore,
But Wicked Ones are numerous as before.
If name I must have, call me Baron! That
Will do, although the title's somewhat flat.
A squire of quite as high degree
Am I, as any squire can be.
My gentle blood you doubt not; there
Is the escutcheon that I bear.

                         [Makes an obscene gesture.

THE WITCH (*laughs immoderately*)

Ha! Ha! That's just like you! So clever!
Always the same mad wag as ever.

MEPHISTOPHELES (*to* FAUST)

Mark this, my friend! Whate'er the hitch is,
This is the way to deal with witches.

THE WITCH

Now, gentlemen, what is 't you seek?

MEPHISTOPHELES

A bumper of your famous brew.
Your oldest, though, I must bespeak:
Years doubly efficacious make it.

THE WITCH

Right gladly! Here's a flask! I take it
Myself at times in little sips;
All trace of stink has left it, too.
I'll give it cheerfully to you.   [*Aside.*
But him there, if it touch his lips,
Unless he's season'd 'gainst its power,
You know, he cannot live an hour.

MEPHISTOPHELES

Oh, he is an especial friend,
'Tis just the thing to serve his end.
The best your kitchen can produce
I do not grudge him for his use.
So draw your circle, and unroll
Your spells, and hand him out a brimming bowl!

[*The* WITCH, *with weird gestures, draws a circle, and
places marvellous things within it; meanwhile the
glasses begin to ring, the cauldron to sound and make
music. Last of all she fetches a great book, places
the Apes within the circle, where she makes them
serve as a reading-desk, and hold the torches. She
beckons* FAUST *to approach.*

FAUST (*to* MEPHISTOPHELES)

What is all this to end in, say?
These mad paraphernalia,
These gestures and distortions frantic,
This mess of juggle and of antic,
I know them all too well of old,
And in profound aversion hold.

MEPHISTOPHELES

All humbug! stuff to laugh at merely!
But do not take things so severely!
Being a doctor in her way,
She must some hocus-pocus play,
In order that on you her juice
May the desired effect produce.

[*He forces* FAUST *to enter the circle.*

THE WITCH (*with great emphasis declaims from
her book*)

This must ye ken!
From one make ten,
Drop two, and then
Make three square, which
Will make you rich;
Skip o'er the four!
From five and six—
In that the trick's—
Make seven and eight,
And all is straight;
And nine is one,
And ten is none.
This is the witch's One Time's One!

FAUST

The beldame's babble seems as it
Were ravings of a fever fit.

MEPHISTOPHELES

Oh, there's a deal more yet to follow,
And just as solid, and as hollow;
The whole book clinks the selfsame chime.
I know it well; and much good time
Have I lost o'er it, good and serious.
For downright contradiction pulls
As hard on wise men's brains, as fools'!
And unto both remains alike mysterious.
The trick's both old and new.   The way
At all times was, and 'tis to-day,
By three and one, and one and three,
To preach up lies as simple sooth,
And sow broadcast by land and sea
Delusions in the place of truth.

So men talk on the nonsense, they
Have ground into them in the schools;
And no one cares to say them nay,
For who'd perplex himself with fools?
Men, for the most part, when they hear
Words smite with vigour on their ear,
Believe that thought an entrance finds
Into the things they call their minds.

THE WITCH (*continues*)

Science is light!
But from the sight
Of all the world 'tis hidden.
Who seeks it not,
To him 'tis brought,
Unnoticed and unbidden.

FAUST

What is this nonsense she is spouting?
My head will split anon.   I seem to hear
A hundred thousand maniacs shouting
Their lunacies full chorus in mine ear.

MEPHISTOPHELES

Enough!   Enough! most admirable Sybil!
Dispense thy drink, and, mind, no paltry dribble!
Fill up the cup, ay, fill it to the brim!
My friend is safe, 'twill do no harm to him.
He's taken honours 'mongst us, ay, and quaff'd
Full many a deep and most potential draught.
   [*The* WITCH *with many ceremonies pours the drink into a
        goblet.   As* FAUST *raises it to his lips, a film of flame
        shoots out from it.*

MEPHISTOPHELES

Off with it!   Leave no drop above!
'Twill warm the cockles of your heart!
What! with the devil hand and glove,
And yet at flame recoil and start?
                [*The* WITCH *dissolves the circle.*   FAUST *steps out.*

MEPHISTOPHELES

Now, forth at once!   To rest would mar all quite!

THE WITCH

Your little drop will do you good, I trust.

MEPHISTOPHELES (*to the* WITCH)

And, if in aught I can oblige you, just
Remind me of it on Walpurgis Night.

THE WITCH

Here is a song!   If you at times
Will sing it, you will find the rhymes
Produce upon you an effect
More singular than you expect.

MEPHISTOPHELES (*to* FAUST)

Come!   Come!   Be guided for your good!
'Tis indispensable you should
Perspire, that so its influence may
Through all your vitals find its way.
Hereafter I will teach you, how to prize
That prime distinction of noblesse,
Sheer lounging, listless idleness;
And soon you'll feel, with sweet surprise,
How Cupid gambols in the breast,
And flits and flutters there with exquisite unrest.

FAUST

One glance into the mirror there!
That woman's form was all too fair!

MEPHISTOPHELES

Nay, nay!   Thou shalt ere long behold
The paragon of womankind,
In feature perfect, and in mould,
Warm, living, ay, and loving to your mind.   [*Aside.*
With this draught in his body, he
In every wench a Helena will see.

STREET

FAUST, MARGARET (*passing along*)

FAUST

My pretty lady, permit me, do,
My escort and arm to offer you!

MARGARET

I'm neither a lady, nor pretty, and so
Can home without an escort go.
                    [*Breaks away from him and exit.*

FAUST

By heaven, this child is lovely!   Ne'er
Have I seen anything so fair.
She is so pure, so void of guile,
Yet something snappish, too, the while.
Her lips' rich red, her cheeks' soft bloom,
Will haunt me to the day of doom!
The pretty way she droops her eyes
Has thrill'd my heart in wondrous wise;
Her short sharp manner, half in fright,
'Twas charming, fascinating quite!
                    (*To* MEPHISTOPHELES, *who enters*)
Hark, you must get that girl for me!

MEPHISTOPHELES

Get you that girl?   Which do you mean?

FAUST

She that went by but now.

MEPHISTOPHELES

                                   What!   She?
She has to her confessor been,
Who gave her—he could scarce do less—
Full absolution; I was there,
Lying ensconced behind his chair.
Though she had nothing to confess,
Nothing whatever, to him she went,
Poor thing, she is so innocent.
Over that girl I have no power.

FAUST

Yet is she fourteen, every hour.

MEPHISTOPHELES

Spoken like Sir Rake, who would make prize
Of every dainty flower he spies,
And thinks all honours, favours, may
Be had for taking any day!
But this won't do in every case.

FAUST

Ho, Master Graveairs, is it so?
Your sermonizing's out of place.
And, in a word, I'd have you know,
Unless this very night shall see
This sweet young thing in my embrace,
All's at an end 'twixt you and me!

MEPHISTOPHELES

Think of the obstacles! I should
Require at least a fortnight good,
To bring about a meeting merely.

FAUST

In half the time I'll undertake,
Without the devil's aid, to make
A chit like that adore me dearly.

MEPHISTOPHELES

Why, by your talk, now, one might swear,
That you almost a Frenchman were!
But, pray, don't lose your temper so!
For where's the good, I'd like to know,
Of rushing to enjoyment straight?
The pleasure's not by much so great,
As when you've first by every kind
Of foolish fondling to your mind
The doll contrived to knead and mould,
As many Italian tales have told.

FAUST

My appetite, I tell you, wants
No such fantastic stimulants.

MEPHISTOPHELES

That may be—but, apart all jest,
Or slight upon you, I protest,
With this young thing you'll ne'er succeed
By pushing on at racehorse speed.
We cannot storm the town, in short—
So must to stratagem resort.

FAUST

Fetch me some thing she's used to wear!
Her bedroom, introduce me there!
A kerchief from her bosom bring,
The darling's garter, anything!

MEPHISTOPHELES

That you may see my readiness
To find you ease in your distress,
We shall not lose one moment—nay,
We'll bring you to her room this very day.

FAUST

And shall I see—possess her?

MEPHISTOPHELES

No!
She will be with a neighbour.   So
You may, quite undisturb'd the while,
Within her atmosphere beguile
The time by dreaming, fancy free,
Of pleasures afterwards to be.

FAUST

Can we go there at once?

MEPHISTOPHELES

Oh no.
'Tis much too early yet to go.

FAUST

Provide me with some present straight,
Which may her fancy captivate!   [*Exit.*

MEPHISTOPHELES

Presents?   Oh, rare!   He's sure to make a hit.
Full many a famous place I know,
And treasures buried long ago.
Well!   I must look them up a bit.

EVENING

A tidily appointed little room

MARGARET (*braiding and binding up her hair*)

THAT gentleman to-day, who was he?   Oh,
I would give something, now, to know.
He look'd so frank and handsome, he
Of noble blood must surely be.
That much, at least, his forehead told;
He ne'er had ventured else to be so bold.   [*Exit.*

MEPHISTOPHELES *and* FAUST *enter*

MEPHISTOPHELES

Come in as softly as you may!

FAUST (*after a pause*)

Leave me alone—alone, I pray!

MEPHISTOPHELES (*peering about the room*)

It is not every girl keeps things so neat.   [*Exit.*

FAUST (*casting his eyes around*)

Welcome, thou twilight glimmer sweet,
Throughout this sanctuary shed!
Oh, love's delicious pain, that art
By dews of hope sustain'd and fed,
Take absolute possession of my heart!
How, all around, there breathes a sense
Of calm, of order, and content!
What plenty in this indigence!
In this low cell what ravishment!
    [*Casts himself down upon a leathern arm-chair by the
        bedside.*
Receive me, thou, that hast with open arm
Held generations past in joy and moan!
Ah me, how often has a rosy swarm
Of children clung to this paternal throne!
Here did my love, perhaps, with grateful breast
For gifts the holy Christ-child brought her, stand,
Her chubby childish cheeks devoutly press'd
Against her aged grandsire's wither'd hand.

I feel thy spirit, maiden sweet,
Of order and contentment round me play,
That like a mother schools thee day by day,
Upon the table bids thee lay
The cover folded fresh and neat,
And strew the sand that crackles 'neath the feet.
Dear hand, that dost all things with beauty leaven,
Thou makest, like a god, this lowly home a heaven!
And here!   [*Raises one of the curtains of the bed.*
                What rapturous tremor shakes me now?
Here could I linger hours untold.
Here the incarnate angel thou,
O Nature, didst in airy visions mould;
Here lay the child, its gentle breast
Fill'd with warm life; and, hour by hour,
The bud, by hands divine caress'd,
Expanded to the perfect flower!

And thou!   What brings thee hither?   I
Am stirr'd with strange emotion.   Why?
What wouldst thou here?   What weight so sore
Is this that presses on thy heart?
Oh, hapless Faust, so changed thou art,
I know thee now no more, no more!

Is 't some enchanted atmosphere,
Encompasses, and charms me here?
Upon possession's bliss supreme
My soul till now was madly bent,
And now in a delicious dream
Of love I melt away content.
Is man, with all his powers so rare,
The sport of every gust of air?

And if she were to enter now,
How would your guilty soul her glances meet?
The mighty braggart, ah, how small! would bow,
Dissolved in abject terror, at her feet.

MEPHISTOPHELES
Dispatch!   She's coming to the door.

FAUST
Hence!   Hence!   Here I return no more.

MEPHISTOPHELES

Here is a casket, laden well;
I got it, where? no need to tell.
If you will only place it there
Within the press—quick, quick!—I swear
She'll be beside herself with joy.
Some baubles there I've stow'd away
I'd meant for different employ.
Pah!   Child is child, and play is play.

FAUST

I know not—shall I?

MEPHISTOPHELES

                          Can you ask it?
Perhaps you'd like to keep the casket?
In that case, friend, I would advise
Your lechery to economize
The precious hours—give up the bubble,
And save myself all further trouble.
You avaricious? You? Oh no!
I won't believe that this is so.
I scratch my head—toil might and main—
[He places the casket in the press and closes the lock.
Let us be off! Psha! lingering still?—
The sweet young thing for you to gain,
And bend her to your wish and will;
And here are you, with face of gloom,
For all the world, as if you were
Just entering your lecture room,
And saw before you Physics there,
And Metaphysics grimly stare!
Come!   Start!   [Exeunt.

MARGARET (enters with a lamp)

It is so close, so sultry here!   [Opens the window.
And yet outside 'twas rather chilly.
I feel, I can't tell how; oh dear!
I wish that mother would come in.
I have a creeping all over my skin.
I'm such a frighten'd thing—so silly!
              [Begins to sing as she undresses herself.

In Thule dwelt a King, and he
    Was leal unto the grave;
A cup to him of the red red gold
    His leman dying gave.

He quaff'd it to the dregs, whene'er
    He drank among his peers,
And ever, as he drain'd it down,
    His eyes would brim with tears.

And when his end drew near, he told
    His kingdom's cities up,
Gave all his wealth unto his heir,
    But with it not the cup.

He sat and feasted at the board,
    His knights around his knee,
Within the palace of his sires,
    Hard by the roaring sea.

Then up he rose, that toper old,
    A long last breath he drew,
And down the cup he loved so well
    Into the ocean threw.

He saw it flash, then settle down,
    Down, down into the sea,
And, as he gazed, his eyes grew dim,
    Nor ever again drank he.

[*She opens the press to put away her clothes, and discovers
    the casket.*

What's here?   How comes this lovely casket thus?
I'm very confident I lock'd the press.
'Tis surely most mysterious!
What it contains I cannot guess.
In pledge for money lent, maybe,
'Tis with my mother left to keep?
A ribbon and a little key—
I've half a mind to take a peep.
What's this?   Great Heavens!   All my days
The like of this I've never seen—
Jewels and trinkets!   Such a blaze
Might grace a duchess, ay, a queen!
On me how would the necklace sit?
Whose can they be, these braveries fine?
[*Puts on the trinkets, and walks before the looking-glass.*

Oh, if the earrings were but mine!
In them one doesn't look the same a bit.
You may be young, you may be pretty;
All very nice and fine to view,
But nobody cares a straw for you,
And, if folks praise, 'tis half in pity.
For gold all strive,
For gold all wive,
'Tis gold rules all things 'neath the sun.
Alas!   We poor folks that have none!

PUBLIC PROMENADE

FAUST *walking up and down wrapped in thought*

To him enter MEPHISTOPHELES

MEPHISTOPHELES

By love despised and its tortures fell!
By all the elements of hell!
Oh, would I only knew something worse,
That I might cram it into a curse!

FAUST

What's wrong?   What puts you in such case?
In all my life I ne'er saw such a face.

MEPHISTOPHELES

I could give myself up immediately
To the very devil, if that wasn't me!

FAUST

What has befallen to rob you of your wits?
How well on you this maniac fury sits!

MEPHISTOPHELES

Just think—'tis not to be endured—
The set of jewels I procured
For Margaret, a rascal priest
Has swept clean off—he has, the beast!
Her mother of them got an inkling,
And fell to quaking in a twinkling.

The nose that woman has, you'd ne'er
Believe, for scenting all that's wrong,
Over her Book of Common Prayer
She snuffles, snuffles, all day long.
With sanctimonious scowl demure
At every stick of furniture
She drops her nose to ascertain,
If it be holy or profane.
So in the trinkets soon she spies,
That not much of a blessing lies.
Quoth she, 'All such unrighteous gear
Corrupts both body and soul, my dear.
So let us, then, this devil's bait
To Mary Mother consecrate,
And she, as recompense instead,
Will gladden us with heavenly bread.'
Poor Gretchen pull'd a long wry face.
'Gift horse!' thought she, 'in any case!
And very godless he cannot be,
Who brought it here so handsomely.'
The mother for the parson sent,
Who heard her nonsense, and his eyes,
Be sure, they gleam'd with a rare content,
When he beheld the glistening prize.
Quoth he, 'Your views are sound and sane.
Who conquers self, the more will gain.
The church, for whom your gift is meant,
A stomach has most excellent.
Whole countries, land, and grange, and town,
She at a meal has swallow'd down,
Yet ne'er, however gorged with pelf,
Was known to over-eat herself.
The church, my dears, alone with zest
Can such unrighteous gear digest.'

FAUST

That power it shares with not a few;
Your king, now, has it, eke your Jew.

MEPHISTOPHELES

So saying, he swept off amain
Ring, necklace, bracelet, brooch, and chain,
With quite as unconcern'd an air,
As if they merely mushrooms were,
Treating my precious gems and casket
Like nuts so many in a basket;

And, promising that heaven no end
Of fair rewards to them would send,
He took his leave, and there they sat,
Immensely edified by that.

FAUST

And Gretchen?

MEPHISTOPHELES

She is all unrest,
And scarce knows what she'd like the best,
Thinks of the trinkets night and day,
And more of him that brought them—hey!

FAUST

It pains me that my love should fret.
Fetch her at once another set!
The first were no great things—

MEPHISTOPHELES

Heyday!
All things are to my lord child's play.

FAUST

Do what I wish, and quickly!   Go!
Stick to her neighbour close.   Be no
Mere milk-and-water devil, and get
Of these gewgaws another set.

MEPHISTOPHELES

That you desire it is enough.   [*Exit* FAUST.
Such lovesick fools away will puff
Sun, moon, and stars into the air,
And all to please their lady fair.

THE NEIGHBOUR'S HOUSE

MARTHA (*alone*)

My good man, God forgive him, he
Has acted scurvily by me,
To start away, the Lord knows where,
And leave me widow'd, lone, and bare.
I never plagued him—God forbid!—
I loved him dearly, that I did.   [*Weeps.*
Perhaps he's dead, though?   Cruel fate!
If I'd only a death-certificate!

Enter MARGARET

MARGARET

Martha!

MARTHA

What ails my pretty dear?

MARGARET

I feel just like to drop.   See here
Another casket—nothing less—
Of ebony left in my press!
And things, so grand and fine, I feel,
They're costlier than the first a deal.

MARTHA

You must not let your mother know,
Or to the priest they, too, will go.

MARGARET

Oh, see, now, see!   Look at them, do!

MARTHA

You lucky, lucky creature you!

MARGARET

Alas!   I never dare appear
In the street or at church in such fine gear.

MARTHA

But why not come in here, my lass?
You can put them on, and nobody know;
Parade a good hour before the glass,
We'll have our own enjoyment so.
And then, if you'll but wait, no doubt
You're sure somehow to get a chance,
Little by little to bring them out,
On holidays, or at a dance.
We'll manage it so as to make no stir;
A necklace first, and then the pearl
Earrings—your mother won't notice, girl;
We can always make out some story for her.

MARGARET

But who could both the caskets bring?
There's something wrong about the thing.
                              [*A knock at the door.*
Good heavens!   Can that be mother!

MARTHA (*peeping through the curtain*)
                                        Nay,
A strange gentleman.   Come in!

MEPHISTOPHELES (*entering*)
                              I pray
Your pardon, ladies, for intruding thus,
'Tis most unceremonious.
               [*Advances with a low bow to* MARGARET.
Which may Dame Martha Schwerdtlein be?

MARTHA

What is your pleasure?   I am she.

MEPHISTOPHELES (*aside to her*)

Now that I know you, that will do.
You've a visitor of mark with you.
Excuse my taking this liberty.
I'll look in later in the day.

MARTHA (*aloud*)

Why, fancy, child, our caller here,
He thinks you're a fine lady, dear!

MARGARET

A simple girl am I, and poor.
The gentleman's too kind, I'm sure.
These ornaments are not my own.

MEPHISTOPHELES

'Tis not the ornaments alone;
The piercing glance, the air urbane—
How glad I am, I may remain!

MARTHA

Well, sir, what news have you for us?

MEPHISTOPHELES

I would my tale were less distressing,
And hope you won't make too much fuss.
Your husband's dead, and sends his blessing.

MARTHA

Is dead?   Poor darling! lack a day!
My husband's dead.   I faint away!

MARGARET

Oh, keep your heart up, dearest friend!

MEPHISTOPHELES

Hear the sad story to the end!

MARGARET

Such things make me wish to stay unwed.
If I lost my love,
I'd as soon be dead.

MEPHISTOPHELES

Ah, joy goes hand in hand with care.

MARTHA

But tell me, how he died and where?

MEPHISTOPHELES

In Padua his bones repose.
There, ma'am, in Saint Antonio's—
The best of consecrated ground—
A quiet corner he has found.

MARTHA

But have you nought for me beside?

MEPHISTOPHELES

Yes, one most weighty, huge request—
Three hundred masses to provide,
To sing his poor soul into rest.
Of all but this my pocket's bare.

MARTHA

What! Not a luck-penny? What! Ne'er
A trinket—token? Why, there's not
A handicraftsman but has got,
Somewhere within his wallet stored,
However bare, some little hoard,
Something to touch a body's heart with,
He'd sooner starve, or beg, than part with.

MEPHISTOPHELES

I feel for you, but let me say,
His money was not fool'd away.
Besides, he did his sins deplore,
But mourn'd his evil luck considerably more.

MARGARET

Alas! That men should be so wretched! He
Shall for his soul's repose have many a prayer from me.

MEPHISTOPHELES

You are so good, so charming, you
Deserve a husband, ay, and quickly too.

MARGARET

Ah no! Too soon for that! I can't—

MEPHISTOPHELES

Well, till the husband comes, then, a gallant!
Heaven has no boon more sweet, more rare,
Than in one's arms to fold a thing so fair.

MARGARET

That's not our country's usage, sir.

MEPHISTOPHELES

Usage or not, such things occur.

MARTHA

Go on, sir!

MEPHISTOPHELES

I was at his side,
There by the bed on which he died,
A sorrier eyes never saw,
A mere dung-heap of rotten straw.
Yet still he made a Christian ending,
And found, that, what with drink and spending,
He had run up a great deal more
Than he had thought for on his score.
'How I detest myself!' cried he,
'For having so disgracefully
Deserted both my wife and calling.
The very thought on 't is appalling!
It saps my life.   Could I but know,
That she forgives me, ere I die!'

MARTHA (*weeping*)

Dear heart!   I—I forgave him long ago.

MEPHISTOPHELES

'Still, God knows, she was more to blame than I.'

MARTHA

He lied there!   What!   To lie, the knave,
Upon the threshold of the grave!

MEPHISTOPHELES

His latest gasps were spent in fiction,
That is my most profound conviction.
'Small time for idling had I,' he said,
'First getting children, then getting them bread,
And clothing their backs, yet never had yet
A moment's quiet to eat my crust.'

MARTHA

Did he thus all my truth, my love forget,
My drudging early and late?

MEPHISTOPHELES

                                     Be just!
Not so. Of that in his dejection
He show'd a touching recollection.
'When I,' he said, 'was leaving Malta, I
Pray'd for my wife and children most devoutly.
Heaven so far bless'd my prayers, that by and by
We met a Turkish galley, took it stoutly.
It carried treasure for the Sultan.   There
Valour for once had its reward, 'tis true,
And I received—and 'twas my simple due—
Of what we took a very handsome share.'

MARTHA

What?   How?   He hid it somewhere, I suppose?

MEPHISTOPHELES

Where the four winds have blown it now, who knows?
Strolling forlorn in Naples through the city,
A damsel on his loneliness took pity,
And such warm tenderness between them pass'd,
He bore its marks, poor saint, about him to the last.

MARTHA

Wretch!   To his children play the thief?
Not all his want, not all his grief,
Could check his shameless life.

MEPHISTOPHELES

                                  Ay, ma'am, but surely
'Twas this that kill'd him prematurely.
Now, were I in your place, I would
Mourn one chaste year of widowhood;
And look about meanwhile to find
A second husband to my mind.

MARTHA

Ah me!   With all his faults I durst
Not hope to find one like the first.
A kinder-hearted fool than he
'Twas scarcely possible to be.
His only fault was, that from home
He was too much inclined to roam,
Loved foreign women—filthy vice!—
And foreign wine, and those curst dice.

E 335

MEPHISTOPHELES

How different might have been his state,
Had he, poor wretch, been equally
Forbearing and affectionate!
Treat me as well, and, I protest,
I'd ask you to change rings with me.

MARTHA

Oh, Lord, sir, you are pleased to jest!

MEPHISTOPHELES (*aside*)

I'd best be off now!   This absurd
Old fool would take the devil at his word.
[*To* MARGARET.
How is it with your heart?—Content?

MARGARET

What mean you, sir?

MEPHISTOPHELES (*aside*)

                        Sweet innocent!
(*Aloud*).   Ladies, farewell!

MARGARET

                        Farewell!

MARTHA

                                    Before
You go, sir, give me one word more.
I'd like to have some proof to show
Where, how, and when my darling died,
And was interr'd.   I've always tried
To be methodical, and so
'Twould comfort me, it would indeed,
Could I his death but in the papers read.

MEPHISTOPHELES

Oh, certainly, good madam, I
Your wish at once can gratify.
One witness by another back'd,
All the world over, proves a fact.
I have a friend in town here, who will state
What you require before the Magistrate.
I'll bring him here with me.

MARTHA

                              Oh do, sir, pray!

MEPHISTOPHELES

And this young lady will be with you, eh?
A fine young fellow!   A great traveller!   Quite
A ladies' man—especially polite.

MARGARET

I'd sink with shame before him, sir.

MEPHISTOPHELES

No!   Not before an emperor.

MARTHA

At dusk in my back garden we
You and your friend will hope to see.

STREET

FAUST, MEPHISTOPHELES

FAUST

WHAT speed?   Will 't work?   What of my dear?

MEPHISTOPHELES

Bravo!   So hot?   You'll shortly bring
Your quarry down.   This evening
At neighbour Martha's shall you see her!
That is a woman made express
To play the pimp and procuress.

FAUST

Good!   Good!

MEPHISTOPHELES

                              But there is something, too,
That she requires of us to do.

FAUST

Well, one good turn deserves another.

MEPHISTOPHELES

                                        We
Have to depone—a mere formality—
That stiff and stark her husband's carcase lies
In Padua in holy ground.

FAUST

                    Most wise!
Why, we must make the journey first, of course?

MEPHISTOPHELES

Sancta simplicitas! No need of that! You just
Speak to the facts and take them upon trust.

FAUST

All's at an end, if that's the sole resource.

MEPHISTOPHELES

Oh, holy man, is this your cue?
Is this the first time in your life, that you
Have borne false witness?   Have you not
In language the most positive defined
God, the world, all that moves therein, mankind,
His capabilities of feeling, thought,
Ay, done it with a breast undash'd
By faintest fear, a forehead unabash'd?
Yet tax yourself, and you must own, that you
As much in truth about these matters knew,
As of Herr Schwerdtlein's death you do.

FAUST

Liar and sophist, thou wilt be
Liar and sophist to the close!

MEPHISTOPHELES

Oh, certainly, could one not see
A little farther before one's nose.
To-morrow will not you—of course,
In all integrity!—beguile
Poor Margaret, and your suit enforce
By swearing all your soul hangs on her smile?

FAUST

And from my heart I'd speak.

MEPHISTOPHELES

Oh, specious art!
You'll talk about eternal truth and love,
Of passion, all command, all change above,
Will this, too, come quite purely from the heart?

FAUST

Peace, fiend! it will!   What!   If I feel,
And for that feeling, frenzy, flame,
I seek, but cannot find a name,
Then through the round of nature reel
With every sense at fever heat,
Snatching at all sublimest phrases,
And call this fire, that in me blazes,
Endless, eternal, ay, eternal,
Is this mere devilish deceit,
Devised to dazzle, and to cheat?

MEPHISTOPHELES

Yet am I right.

FAUST

Thou fiend infernal!
Hear me!   And mark, too, what I say,
So spare these lungs of mine, I pray.
He that's resolved he's in the right,
And has but tongue enough, is quite
Secure to gain his point.   But come,
This babblement grows wearisome.
Right, then, thou art.   I grant it, just
Because I cannot choose but must.

GARDEN

MARGARET *on* FAUST'S *arm*.   MARTHA *with*
MEPHISTOPHELES *walking up and down*.

MARGARET

You only bear with me, I'm sure you do,
You stoop, to shame me, you so wise.
You travellers are so used to view
All things you come across with kindly eyes.
I know, my poor talk can but weary such
A man as you, that must have known so much.

FAUST

One glance, one word of yours, to me is more
Than all this world's best wisdom—all its lore.

[*Kisses her hand*.

MARGARET

Oh no, sir, no!   How can you kiss it?   'Tis
So coarse, so hard—it is not fit—
The things I've had to do with it!
Mother's too niggardly—indeed she is.

[*They pass on*.

MARTHA

And are you always travelling like this, good sir?

MEPHISTOPHELES

Business, alas! and duty force us.   Ah, what pain
It costs a man from many a place to stir,
Where yet his fate forbids him to remain.

MARTHA

'Tis very well to rove this way
About the world when young, and strong, and brave.
But soon or later comes the evil day,
And to go crawling on into the grave
A stiff old lonely bachelor—that can
Never be good for any man.

MEPHISTOPHELES

I shudder, thinking such may be my fate.

MARTHA

Then, sir, be wise, before it is too late.   [*They pass on.*

MARGARET

Yes!   Out of sight is out of mind!
Politeness costs you nothing.   Why,
You've friends in plenty, good and kind,
And they have far more sense than I.

FAUST

Oh, best of creatures, trust me, the pretence
Of that which passes with the world for sense,
More frequently is neither more nor less
Than self-conceit and narrow-mindedness.

MARGARET

How so?

FAUST

Ah!   That simplicity
And innocence will never recognize
Themselves, and all their worth so holy!
That meekness and a spirit lowly,
The highest gifts, that Nature's free
And loving bounty can devise—

MARGARET

A little moment only think of me;
I shall have time enough to think of you.

FAUST

You're much alone, then?

MARGARET

Yes!   'Tis true,
Our household's small, but still, you see,
It wants no little looking to.
We have no maid; so I've to do
The cooking, sewing, knitting, sweeping;
I'm on my feet from morn till night,
And mother's so exacting, and so tight
In her housekeeping.

Not that she needs to pinch so close.   We might
Much more at ease than other people be.
My father left us, when he died,
A cottage with some garden ground, outside
The town, a tidy bit of property.
But now I am not near so sore bestead.
My brother is away—a soldier he.
My little sister's dead.
Ah! with the child I had a world of trouble,
And yet, and yet, I'd gladly undergo
It all again, though it were double,
I loved the darling so.

FAUST

An angel, sweet, if it resembled you!

MARGARET

I brought it up, and, do you know,
It loved me with a love so true!
My father died, before 'twas born,
We gave up mother for lost; her fit
Left her so wasted, and so forlorn,
And very very slow she mended, bit by bit.
She could not, therefore, dream herself
Of suckling the poor little elf;
And so I nursed it all alone,
On milk and water, till at last
It grew my very own.
Upon my arm, within my breast
It smiled, and crow'd, and grew so fast.

FAUST

You must have felt most purely blest.

MARGARET

Oh yes!   Still I had many things to try me.
The baby's cradle stood at night
Beside my bed: if it but stirr'd, I would
Awake in fright.
One time I had to give it drink or food,
Another time to lay it by me;
Then, if it had a crying fit,
Out of my bed I needs must get,
And up and down the room go dandling it;
And yet

Be standing at the wash-tub by daybreak,
Then do the marketing, set the house to rights:
And so it went on, mornings, middays, nights,
With ne'er a pause!   Such things will make
One's spirits not at all times of the best,
Still they give relish to our food, our rest.

[They pass on.

MARTHA

Poor women get the worst on 't, though.   A dry
Old bachelor's not easy to convert.

MEPHISTOPHELES

Would one like you but make the trial, I
My wicked ways might soon desert.

MARTHA

Frankly, now!   Is there no one you have met?
Has not your heart form'd some attachment yet?

MEPHISTOPHELES

What says the proverb?   A hearth of one's own,
And a housewife good, it is well known,
Are better than gold or precious stone.

MARTHA

I mean, sir, have you never had a liking?

MEPHISTOPHELES

The favour shown me everywhere is striking.

MARTHA

I wish'd to say; your heart, has it
Never been conscious of a serious feeling?

MEPHISTOPHELES

Madam, a jesting mood were most unfit,
Not to say, dangerous, when with ladies dealing.

MARTHA

Ah, you don't understand what I'd be at.

MEPHISTOPHELES

I'm grieved most heartily for that.
But this is quite clear to my mind,
That you are very, very kind.   [*They pass on.*

FAUST

When I came in, you little angel, then,
You knew me at a glance again?

MARGARET

Did you not see?   I could not meet your look.

FAUST

And you forgive the liberty I took,
The mad impertinence, which prompted me
To stop you on the street the other day,
As you came out from the cathedral door?

MARGARET

It took me quite aback.   What could it be?
Nothing like this had e'er occurr'd before.
No one of me an evil word could say.
And then it cross'd my thoughts: 'Alas, the day!
Can he about me anything have seen,
Bold or unmaidenly in look or mien?'
It seem'd as if the thought had struck you—She
Is just the girl with whom one can make free!
Let me confess the truth!   Not then I knew,
What in your favour here began to stir;
But with myself I was right angry, sir,
That I could not be angrier with you.

FAUST

Sweet love!

MARGARET

Stay!
[*She plucks a star-flower, and picks off the petals, one
after the other.*

FAUST

What is this?   A nosegay?

MARGARET

No!
Only a game.

FAUST

A game?

MARGARET

You'll mock me—Go!

FAUST

What is it you are murmuring?   What?

MARGARET

He loves me, loves me not.

FAUST

I guess.

Angelic creature!

MARGARET

Loves me not,
Loves me—not—he loves me!

FAUST

Yes!
Let what this flower has told you be
An oracle from heaven.   He loves you!
Do you know what that means?   He loves you!
[*Seizes both her hands.*

MARGARET

I am all a-tremble!

FAUST

Oh, do not tremble!   Let this look,
This pressure of the hand, proclaim to you
What words can never speak; what bids us now
Surrender soul and sense to feel
A rapture which must be eternal?
Eternal, for its end would be despair!
No, no, no end!   No end!
[MARGARET *presses his hands, breaks from him, and
    runs off.   He stands for a moment in thought, then
    follows her.*

MARTHA (*advancing*)

'Tis growing dark!

MEPHISTOPHELES

Yes, and we must away.

MARTHA

I'd ask you, longer here to stay,
Were this not such a wicked place.
Folks seem to have nought else to do, I vow,
Or think about, except to play
The spy upon their neighbours—how
They rise, lie down, come in, go out;
And, take what heed one may, in any case
One's certain to get talk'd about.
But our young couple?

MEPHISTOPHELES

They have flown
Up yonder walk.   The giddy butterflies!

MARTHA

Quite fond of her, methinks, he's grown.

MEPHISTOPHELES

And she of him.   Could it be otherwise?

A SUMMERHOUSE

MARGARET *runs in, places herself behind the door, holds the tip
of her finger to her lips, and peeps through the crevice*

MARGARET

HE's coming!

FAUST

Did you fancy, you
Could give me so the slip?   Ah then,
I've caught you, rogue!   [*Kisses her.*

MARGARET (*embracing him and returning the kiss*)
                    Oh, best of men,
I love you, from my heart I do.
                              [MEPHISTOPHELES *knocks.*

FAUST (*stamping his foot*)
Who's there?

MEPHISTOPHELES
Your friend!

FAUST
                              Beast, beast!

MEPHISTOPHELES
                                        'Tis time to go.

MARTHA (*comes up*)
Yes, sir, 'tis late.

FAUST
                    Mayn't I escort you?

MARTHA
                                        No!
My mother would—Farewell!

FAUST
                              Must I begone?
Farewell!

MARTHA
          Adieu!

FAUST
          To meet again anon!
                              [*Exeunt* FAUST *and* MEPHISTOPHELES.

MARGARET
Dear God!   The things of every kind
A man like this has in his mind!
I stand before him dash'd and shy,
And say to all he speaks of, yes.
In such a simple child as I
What he should see, I cannot guess.

FOREST AND CAVERN [1]

FAUST *alone*

MAJESTIC spirit, thou hast given me all
For which I pray'd.   Thou not in vain didst turn
Thy countenance to me in fire and flame.
Thou glorious Nature for my realm hast given,
With power to feel, and to enjoy her.   Thou
No mere cold glance of wonder hast vouchsafed,
But let'st me peer deep down into her breast,
Even as into the bosom of a friend.
Before me thou in long procession lead'st
All things that live, and teachest me to know
My kindred in still grove, in air, and stream.
And, when the storm sweeps roaring through the woods,
Upwrenching by the roots the giant pines,
Whose neighbouring trunks, and intertangled boughs,
In crashing ruin tear each other down,
And shake with roar of thunder all the hills,
Then dost thou guide me to some sheltering cave,
There show'st me to myself, and mine own soul
Teems marvels forth I ween'd not of before.
And when the pure moon, with her mellowing light,
Mounts as I gaze, then from the rocky walls,
And out from the dank underwood, ascend
Forms silvery-clad of ages long ago,
And soften the austere delight of thought.

Oh, now I feel no perfect boon is e'er
Achieved by man.   With this ecstatic power,
Which brings me hourly nearer to the gods,
A yokemate thou hast given me, whom even now
I can no more dispense with, though his cold
Insulting scorn degrades me to myself,
And turns thy gifts to nothing with a breath.
Within my breast he fans unceasingly
A raging fire for that bewitching form.
So to fruition from desire I reel,
And 'midst fruition languish for desire.

[1] The 'majestic spirit' can only be the Earth Spirit, but if so, Goethe has again allowed two successive conceptions to remain side by side.   According to Faust's words at the end of this speech, as also in his second speech in the scene 'A gloomy day,' Mephistopheles has been sent to him by the Earth Spirit, but the Prologue in Heaven has led us to expect that Mephistopheles will seek out Faust of his own accord, following the wager with the Lord.

Enter MEPHISTOPHELES

MEPHISTOPHELES

What!　Not yet weary of this life of quiet?
How can it charm you such a while?　Pooh, pooh!
'Tis very well once in a way to try it;
And then away again to something new!

FAUST

Would thou hadst something else to do,
Than tease me when I would be still!

MEPHISTOPHELES

Oh, I will leave you, if you will,
And leave you very gladly, too.
No need to be so very cross.
A surly peevish mate like you
Is truly little of a loss.
My hands are full from morn till night,
And yet by look or sign you won't
Let me divine what's wrong or right,
What things you like, and what you don't.

FAUST

The true tone hit exactly!　He
Wants to be thank'd for boring me.

MEPHISTOPHELES

Why, without me, poor son of clay,
What sort of life would you have led?
I've cured that brain of yours this many a day
Of the whim-whams your sickly fancy bred;
And from this ball of earth you clean away
Had, but for me, long long ago been sped.
Is it for you, to mope and scowl
In clefts and caverns, like an owl?
Or, like a toad, lap nourishment
From oozy moss, and dripping stones?
Oh, pastime rare and excellent!
The Doctor still sticks in your bones.

FAUST

Dost comprehend, what stores of fresh life-force
I gain in roaming thus by wold and waste?
Ay, couldst thou but divine it, thou, of course,
Art too much fiend such bliss to let me taste.

MEPHISTOPHELES

A super-earthly ecstasy!   To camp
On mountains in the dark, and dews, and damp!
In transports to embrace the earth and sky,
Yourself into a deity inflate,
Pierce the earth's marrow by the light of high,
Unreasoning presentiments innate,
Feel in your breast the whole six days' creation,
And, in the pride of conscious power, to glow
With quite incomprehensible elation,
Anon with lover's raptures to o'erflow
Into the Universal All, with now
No vestige left to mark the child of clay,
This trance ecstatic, glorious in its way,
All winding up at last—   [With a gesture.
              I sha'n't say how!

FAUST

Shame on thee!

MEPHISTOPHELES

              Oh, that shocks you!   You have so
Much right with moral horror to cry shame!
One must not dare to squeamish ears to name
What, natheless, squeamish hearts will not forgo.
Well, well, I grudge you not the satisfaction
Of lying to yourself upon occasion:
That sort of thing soon loses its attraction;
You'll tire of it, and without my persuasion.
To your old whims you're falling back again,
And 'tis most certain, if I let you,
They'll into madness lash your brain,
Or into spasms and horrors fret you.
Enough of this!   At home your darling sits,
And all with her's vacuity and sadness.
She cannot get you from her mind.   Her wit's
Bewitch'd; she dotes on you to madness.
At first your passion, like a little brook,
Swoll'n by the melted snows, all barriers overbore;
Into her heart you've pour'd it all, and, look!
That little brook of yours is dry once more.
Methinks, instead of playing king
Among the woods, your lordship might
Be doing better to requite
The poor young monkey's hankering.
Time drags with her so sadly; she, poor wight,

Stands at her window, marks with listless eye
The clouds o'er the old city walls go sweeping by.
'Oh, if a birdie I might be!'   So runs her song
Half through the night, and all day long;
One while she's gay, more commonly downcast,
At other times she's drown'd in tears,
Then to appearance calm again, but first and last
In love o'er head and ears.

FAUST

You snake!   You snake!

MEPHISTOPHELES (*aside*)

Got him, and no mistake!

FAUST

Out of my sight!   Accursèd thing!
Dare not to name her!   Nor before
My half-distracted senses bring
Desire for her sweet body more.

MEPHISTOPHELES

What's to be done?   She thinks you gone for ever!
And in a manner so you are.

FAUST

I'm near her, ay, but were I ne'er so far,
I never can forget, can lose her never.
I envy even the Host itself, whene'er
'Tis touch'd by those sweet lips of hers!

MEPHISTOPHELES

Indeed!
Well, friend, I've often envied you the pair
Of dainty twins, that 'midst the roses [1] feed.

FAUST

Hence, pimp!

MEPHISTOPHELES

Oh, rare!   You rail, and I must laugh.
The God, who fashion'd lad and wench,
Knew what He meant too well by half,
His noble purpose not to clench,

[1] See Song of Solomon iv. 5.   Luther used 'roses' where our version has
'lilies.'

By fashioning occasion due
For bringing them together, too.
Away! 'Tis such a cruel case!
'Tis to your mistress' chamber, man, you go,
And not, methinks, to your undoing.

FAUST

What were heaven's bliss itself in her embrace?
Though on her bosom I should glow,
Must I not feel her pangs, her ruin?
What am I but an outcast, without home,
Or human tie, or aim, or resting-place,
That like a torrent raved along in foam,
From rock to rock, with ravening fury wild,
Down to the precipice below?   And she,
In unsuspecting innocence a child,
Hard by that torrent's banks, in tiny cot,
Upon her little patch of mountain lea,
With all her homely joys and cares, begot
And bounded in that little world.
And I the abhorr'd of God—'twas not
Enough that down with me I whirl'd
The rifted rocks, and shatter'd them!   I must
Drag her, her and her peace into the dust!
Thou, Hell, must have this sacrifice perforce!
Help, devil, then to abridge my torturing throes.
Let that which must be swiftly take its course,
Bring her doom down on me to crown my woes,
And o'er us both one whelming ruin close!

MEPHISTOPHELES

Ho, up at boiling point again!
Get in, fool, and console her!   When
Such silly pates no outlet can descry,
They think the very crash of doom is nigh.
Give me the man, that on will go,
Not to be sway'd or shaken from his level!
And yet at other times you show
A tolerable spice, too, of the devil.
Go to!   The devil that despairs I deem
Of all poor creatures poor in the extreme.

MARGARET'S ROOM

MARGARET (*at her spinning-wheel alone*)

My peace is gone,
  My heart is sore;
'Tis gone for ever
  And evermore.

Where he is not,
  Is the grave to me,
The whole world's changed,
  Ah, bitterly.

I sit and I ponder
  One only thought,
My senses wander,
  My brain's distraught.

My peace is gone,
  My heart is sore;
'Tis gone for ever
  And evermore.

From my window to greet him
  I gaze all day,
I stir out, if meet him
  I only may.

His noble form,
  His bearing high,
His mouth's sweet smile,
  His mastering eye;

And the magic flow
  Of his talk, the bliss
In the clasp of his hand,
  And oh! his kiss!

My peace is gone,
  My heart is sore;
'Tis gone for ever
  And evermore.

For him doth my bosom
  Cry out and pine;
Oh, if I might clasp him,
  And keep him mine!

And kiss him, kiss him,
  As fain would I,
I'd faint on his kisses,
  Yes, faint and die!

MARTHA'S GARDEN

MARGARET, FAUST

MARGARET

PROMISE me, Henry!

FAUST

           What I can, I will.

MARGARET

How do you stand about religion, say?
You are a thoroughly good man, but still
I fear, you don't think much about it any way.

FAUST

Hush, hush, my child!   You feel I love you.   Good!
For those I love could lay down life, and would.
No man would I of creed or church bereave.

MARGARET

That is not right; we must ourselves believe.

FAUST

Must we?

MARGARET

         Ah, could I but persuade you, dear!
You do not even the sacraments revere.

FAUST

Revere I do.

MARGARET

But seek them not, alas!
For long you've never gone to shrift or mass.
Do you believe in God?

FAUST

Love, who dare say,
I do believe in God?   You may
Ask priest or sage, and their reply
Will only seem to mystify,
And mock you.

MARGARET

Then you don't believe?

FAUST

My meaning, darling, do not misconceive.
Him who dare name?
Or who proclaim,
Him I believe?
Who feel,
Yet steel
Himself to say; Him I do not believe?
The All-Embracer,
The All-Sustainer,
Embraces and sustains He not
You, me, Himself?
Rears not the heaven its arch above?
Doth not the firm-set earth beneath us lie?
And with the tender gaze of love
Climb not the everlasting stars on high?
Do I not gaze upon you, eye to eye?
And all the world of sight and sense and sound,
Bears it not in upon your heart and brain,
And mystically weave around
Your being influences that never wane?
Fill your heart thence even unto overflowing,
And when with thrill ecstatic you are glowing,
Then call it whatsoe'er you will,
Bliss!   Heart!   Love!   God!
Name for it have I none!
Feeling is all in all;
Name is but sound and smoke,
Shrouding heaven's golden glow!

MARGARET

All this is beautiful and good; just so
The priest, too, speaks to us at times,
In words, though, somewhat different.

FAUST

So speak the hearts of all men in all climes,
O'er which the blessèd sky is bent,
On which the blessèd light of heaven doth shine,
Each in a language that is his;
Then why not I in mine?

MARGARET

To hear you speak, it looks not much amiss,
But still there's something, love, about it wrong;
For Christian you are not, I see.

FAUST

Dear child!

MARGARET

My heart has ached for long,
To see you in such company.

FAUST

How so?

MARGARET

The man, that is your mate,
Wakes in my inmost soul the deepest hate.
In all my life not anything
Has given my heart so sharp a sting,
As that man's loathsome visage grim.

FAUST

Nay, dearest, have no fear of him.

MARGARET

His presence makes my blood congeal.
Kindly to all men else I feel;
But howsoe'er for you I long,
From that man with strange dread I shrink;
That he's a knave I needs must think.
God pardon me, if I do him wrong!

FAUST

Such odd fish there must always be.

MARGARET

I would not live with such as he.
Whenever he comes, he's sure to peer
In at the door with such a sneer,
And looks of stifled rage to dart;
One sees, that he in no one thing takes part;
On his brow 'tis written, as on a scroll,
That he can love no human soul.
I feel so happy within your arms,
So free, so glowing, so fearless of harms,
But in his presence my heart shuts to.

FAUST

You sweet, foreboding angel, you!

MARGARET

It masters me in such a way,
I even think, when he comes near,
That I no longer love you, dear.
If he were by, I never could pray,
And that eats into my heart; you, too,
Must feel, my Henry, as I do.

FAUST

'Tis mere antipathy you bear.

MARGARET

Now I must go.

FAUST

Oh, can I ne'er
Hang one short hour in quiet on your breast,
Bosom by bosom, soul in soul caress'd?

MARGARET

Ah, if I only slept alone!   To-night
I'd leave the door upon the latch, I would.
But mother sleeps so very light,
And, were we caught by her, I should
Drop dead upon the spot, I vow.

FAUST

She need not know, you angel, though!
Here is a phial!   Let her but take
Three drops of this, and it will steep
Nature in deep and pleasing sleep.

MARGARET

What would I not do for your sake?
You're sure it will not do her harm?

FAUST

Would I advise it, else?

MARGARET

                    There's some strange charm,
When I but look on you, that still
Constrains me, love, to do your will.
I have already done so much for you,
That scarce aught else is left for me to do.   [*Exit.*

Enter MEPHISTOPHELES

MEPHISTOPHELES

The silly ape!   Is 't gone?

FAUST

                    So, then,
You have been playing spy again?

MEPHISTOPHELES

I heard distinctly all that pass'd.
You had, Sir Doctor, first and last,
A stiffish dose of catechizing.
I'm sure, I hope 'twill do you good!
It certainly is not surprising,
These silly-pated wenches should
Be always anxious to discover,
If in his prayers and pace their lover
Jogs on the good old humdrum way.
'If pliable in that,' think they,
'Us too he'll placidly obey.'

FAUST

You monster, you do not perceive,
How such a loving faithful soul,
Full of her faith, which is
To her the one sole pledge of endless bliss,
Is rack'd by holy anguish, to believe
Him that she dotes on doom'd to everlasting dole.

MEPHISTOPHELES

You supersensual sensual squire,
A chit of a girl has you firm by the nose.

FAUST

You vile abortion out of filth and fire!

MEPHISTOPHELES

What skill in physiognomy she shows!
She turns she can't tell how, when I am present;
This little mask of mine, it seems, reveals
Meanings conceal'd, but certainly unpleasant;
That I'm a genius, past mistake she feels,
The devil's self, perhaps, for aught she knows.
Well, well, to-night!

FAUST

What's that to you?

MEPHISTOPHELES

Oho!   In that I have my pleasure, too.

AT THE WELL

MARGARET *and* BESSY *with pitchers*

BESSY

WHAT!   Barbara?   Not heard the news of her?

MARGARET

Not I.   Across the door I rarely stir.

BESSY

Oh, never doubt it!
To-day Sibylla told me all about it!
She's made a rare fool of herself at last.
This comes of her fine airs and flighty jinks!

MARGARET

How so?

BESSY

     It won't keep down.   That's long, long past.
She feeds for two now, when she eats and drinks.

MARGARET

Alas!

BESSY

     She's rightly served, the jade!
For all the fuss she with the fellow made!
Such gadding here, such gadding there,
At village wake, at dance, and fair;
Must be first fiddle, too, everywhere;
He was treating her always with tarts and wine;
Set up for a beauty, she did, so fine,
And yet was so mean, and so lost to shame,
As to take his presents, though, all the same.
And then the hugging, and the kissing!
So the upshot is, her rose is missing.

MARGARET

Poor thing!

BESSY

     What!   Pity her, and her sinning!
When any of us was at the spinning,
Mother kept us indoors after dark.
But she was so sweet upon her spark,
On the bench by the door, and in the dark walk,
No hour was too long for their toying and talk.
So her fine fal-lals now my lady may dock,
And do penance at church in the sinner's smock.

MARGARET

But he will make her his wife, of course!

BESSY

A fool if he did!   A lad of mettle
Can have lots of choice, or ever he settle.
Besides, he's off.

MARGARET

How could he do it?

BESSY

If she should get him, she's sure to rue it.
The boys will tear her garland, and we
Strew chopp'd straw at her door, you'll see.   [*Exit.*

MARGARET (*going home*)

What railing once rose to my lip,
If any poor girl made a slip!
My tongue hard words could scarcely frame
Enough to brand another's shame.
It look'd so black, that blacken it
Howe'er I might, they seem'd unfit
To stamp its blackness infinite.
I bless'd myself and my nose up toss'd,
And now I, too, in sin am lost.
And yet—and yet—alas! the cause,
God knows, so good, so dear, it was!

ZWINGER

In the niche of the wall a devotional image of the Mater Dolorosa,
and in front of it pots of flowers

MARGARET (*placing fresh flowers in the pots*)

O thou, the sorest
Pangs that borest,
On mine look down with face benign!

With anguish eyeing
Thy dear Son dying,
The sword that pierced His heart in thine,

¹ The 'Zwinger' is the unfrequented passage between the city wall, the inner side of which contains occasional shrines in niches, and an inner wall or possibly the nearest buildings of the town.

Thou to the Father gazest,
And signs upraisest
For His and for thy mortal pine.

Oh, who can feel, as thou,
The agony, that now
Tears me and wears me to the bone!
How this poor heart is choked with tears,
All that it yearns for, all it fears,
Thou knowest, thou, and thou alone!

Still wheresoe'er I go,
What woe, what woe, what woe
Is in my bosom aching!
When to my room I creep,
I weep, I weep, I weep,
My heart is breaking.

The bow-pots at my window
I with my tears bedew'd,
When over them at morn to pluck
These flowers for thee I stood.

Brightly into my chamber shone
The sun, when dawn grew red;
Already there, all woebegone,
I sat upon my bed.

Help, sufferer divine!
Save me, oh save
From shame and from the grave!
And thou, the sorest
Pangs that borest,
On mine look down with countenance benign!

NIGHT

Street in front of MARGARET'S *door*

VALENTINE

AT drinking bouts, when tongues will wag,
And many are given to boast and brag,
When praises of their own pet dears
Were dinn'd by comrades in my ears,

And drown'd in bumpers, I was able,
My elbow planted on the table,
To bide my time, and calmly stay'd,
Listening to all their gasconade.
Then with a smile my beard I'd stroke,
And take a full glass in my hand;
'Each to his fancy!' up I spoke,
'But who is there in all the land,
To match with my dear Gretel—who
Is fit to tie my sister's shoe?'
All round about there went a hum,
Hob, nob! Kling! Klang! 'He's right!' they cried,
'Of her whole sex she is the pride.'
Then all the boasters, they sat dumb.
And now—oh, I could tear my hair,
And dash my brains out in despair!—
Now every knave will think, he's free
To have his gibe and sneer at me!
And, like a bankrupt debtor, I
At each chance word must sit and fry.
Smash them all up I might: what though?
I could not call them liars—no!

What's here? Ha! skulking out of view?
If I mistake not, there are two.
If it be he, at him I'll drive,
He shall not quit this spot alive!

Enter FAUST *and* MEPHISTOPHELES

FAUST

How from the window of yon Sacristy
The little lamp's undying flame doth glimmer,
While at the sides it flickers dim and dimmer,
And thicks the darkness round! Ah me!
Such midnight is it in my breast.

MEPHISTOPHELES

And I feel like a tom-cat, love-distress'd,
That up fire-ladders slyly crawls,
And steals on tiptoe round the walls;
I burn with quite a virtuous glow,
Half thievish joy, half concupiscence, so
Does the superb Walpurgis Night
Already thrill me with delight.
Just one night more, 'tis here, and then
One gets some real fun again.

FAUST

Look! What is that is glimmering there?
The treasure rising to the upper air?

MEPHISTOPHELES

Thou shalt ere long the pleasure test
Of digging up the little chest.
I took a squint at it to-night.
Such lion-dollars broad and bright!

FAUST

How! Not a trinket? Not a ring,
To deck her out, my love, my sweet?

MEPHISTOPHELES

I think I saw with them a string
Of pearls, or something just as neat.

FAUST

'Tis well! It vexes me to go
To her without some gift to show.

MEPHISTOPHELES

'Tis not a thing to feel dismay for,
To have some pleasure you don't pay for!
Now heaven with stars is all aglow.
A genuine titbit you shall hear;
A moral song I'll sing her, so
More thoroughly to befool the dear.

(*Sings to the lute*)

Katrina, say,
What makes you stay,
Ere dawn of day,
Before your sweetheart's door so?
Away, away!
The springald gay
Lets in a May,
Goes out a May no more so!

Walk still upright!
If once you're light,
Why then, Good night!

Poor things, 'twill ill bestead you.
Refrain, refrain!
Let no false swain,
Your jewel gain,
Till with the ring he wed you!

VALENTINE (*coming forward*)

For whom are you caterwauling?   Curst
Ratcatcher you!   Out, trusty whinger!
To the devil with the jingler first,
Then packing after it to send the singer!

MEPHISTOPHELES

The lute is crack'd!   'Tis ruin'd for the nonce.

VALENTINE

Have at you!   Now to crack your sconce!

MEPHISTOPHELES (*to* FAUST)

Tackle him, doctor!   Courage, hey!
Stick close, and, as I bid you, do.
Out with your duster!   Thrust away!
I'll do the parrying for you.

VALENTINE

Then parry that!

MEPHISTOPHELES

                And wherefore not?

VALENTINE

That too!

MEPHISTOPHELES

                Just so.

VALENTINE

                I'd swear, the devil fought!
What say you, then, to that?   My hand's benumb'd.

MEPHISTOPHELES (*to* FAUST)

Thrust home!

VALENTINE

                Oh, oh!

MEPHISTOPHELES

                    The bumpkin has succumb'd.
Let us be off!   We must evaporate!
The hue and cry is up!   Hark!   What a clatter!
With the police I might make things all straight,
But with the courts 'tis quite another matter!   [*Exeunt.*

MARTHA (*at window*)

Help!   Murder!

MARGARET (*at window*)

               Help!   A light!   A light!

MARTHA (*as before*)

They brawl and scuffle, shout and fight.

PEOPLE

Here's one of them already dead.

MARTHA (*coming out*)

The murdering villains!   Have they fled?

MARGARET (*coming out*)

Who's this lies here?

PEOPLE

               Your mother's son.

MARGARET

Almighty God!   I am undone.

VALENTINE

I'm dying!   Sooner done, than said.
Why, women, why do ye
Stand howling, whimpering there?   I'm sped!
Come close, and list to me!   [*All come round him.*
Look, Gretchen!   You're but young—by far
Too shy and simple yet!   You are
A bungler in your trade.
Soft in your ear a friendly hint!
You are a whore; so never stint,
But be right out a jade.

MARGARET

My brother!   God!   What mean you?

VALENTINE

Shame!
Out of your antics leave God's name!
What's done, alas the day! is done,
And you must run the course of sin.
You on the sly begin with one,
But several soon come trooping in,
And, once you to a dozen fall so,
Then all the town will have you also!

When shame is born, she's to the light
Brought stealthily 'mid grief and fears,
And she is in the veil of night
Wrapp'd over head and ears.
Yea, folks would kill her an' they might,
But grown, as grow she will apace,
She flaunts it in the broad daylight,
And yet she wears no fairer face,
Nay, it grows uglier every way,
The more she seeks the light of day.

I see the time—'tis coming—when
Each honest-hearted citizen,
As from a plague-infected corpse,
Will turn aside from you, you whore!
Your heart will fail you with remorse,
When people look you in the face.
No more you'll wear a golden chain;
Nor stand in church by the altar floor,
Nor in a collar of dainty lace
Shine foremost at the dance again.
In some dark wretched nook you'll hide,
With cripples and beggars and nought beside,
And even though God forgiveness grant you,
My curse upon the earth will haunt you!

MARTHA

Commend your soul to God! Would you
Lay on it the sin of slander, too?

VALENTINE

You shameless bawd, could I but smite
Your wizen'd carcase, then I might
For all my sins of every kind
Full absolution hope to find.

MARGARET

Oh, brother! Rack me not, oh, pray!

VALENTINE

Have done with tears!   Have done, I say!
To honour when you bade farewell,
You dealt my heart its heaviest blow.
Now like a soldier, stout and fell,
Through Death's long sleep to God I go.

CATHEDRAL

SERVICE.[1] ORGAN AND ANTHEM

MARGARET *amongst a number of people.*
EVIL SPIRIT *behind her*

EVIL SPIRIT

How different, Margaret, was 't with thee,
When thou, still, still all innocence,
Camest to the altar here,
And from the well-thumb'd little book
Didst prattle prayers, that were
Half childish playfulness,
Half God within the heart,
Margaret!
How is it with thy head?
Within thy heart
What guiltiness?
Art praying for thy mother's soul, that slept
Away to long, long agonies through thee?
Upon thy threshold whose the blood?
—And 'neath thy heart stirs not
What now is quickening there,
And with its boding presence racks
Itself and thee?

MARGARET

Woe!   Woe!
Oh, could I rid me of the thoughts,
That, spite of me,
Come rushing o'er my brain!

CHOIR

Dies irae, dies illa
Solvet saeclum in favilla!   [*Organ plays.*

[1] In the *Urfaust* the service is a funeral service for Gretchen's mother.
Here it is presumably one for Valentine, and Gretchen is the sole survivor
of the family present.

EVIL SPIRIT

Horror lays hold on thee!
The judgment trumpet sounds!
The graves rock to and fro!
And thy heart, from
Its ashy rest
Incorporate anew
For fiery pangs,
Quakes into life!

MARGARET

Would I were out of this!
I feel as though
The organ choked my breath,
As though the anthem drew
The life-blood from my heart!

CHOIR

Judex ergo cum sedebit,
Quidquid latet adparebit,
Nil inultum remanebit.

MARGARET

It feels so close!
The pillars of the wall
Press in upon me,
The arches of the roof
They weigh me down!—Air!

EVIL SPIRIT

Hide thyself!   Sin and shame
Will not be hidden—
Air?   Light?
Woe to thee!

CHOIR

Quid sum miser tunc dicturus?
Quem patronum rogaturus?
Cum vix justus sit securus?

EVIL SPIRIT

From thee the saints in bliss
Their faces turn away.
To reach their hands to thee
Makes the pure shudder!   Woe!

CHOIR

Quid sum miser tunc dicturus?

MARGARET

Neighbour!   Your smelling-bottle!   [*Swoons.*

WALPURGIS NIGHT [1]

THE HARZ MOUNTAINS.   DISTRICT OF SCHIERKE AND ELEND

FAUST, MEPHISTOPHELES

MEPHISTOPHELES

Do you not wish you had a broomstick, friend?
Oh, for a he-goat, rough and tough and strong!
We're still a long way from our journey's end.

[1] Walpurgis Night is the eve of Mayday.   According to popular superstition, German witches held a party on the Brocken mountain in the Harz
on this night, a riot of sensuality.   Goethe made out of this a symbolic
representation of further erotic adventures provided by Mephistopheles for
Faust, in the midst of which his conscience pricks him about the abandoned
Gretchen.   He imagines he sees her, and her approaching execution is
hinted at in the mention of the 'thin red line.'   He insists on returning to
her, although he has been outlawed after the murder of Valentine.
   It is disconcerting to find generals, ministers, authors, etc., present at this
gathering, but it is represented as a kind of devil's court, where his courtiers
include types of public figures and scholars whom Goethe has often wished
'to the devil.'   The idea was perhaps suggested by a seventeenth-century
work (by Praetorius) about Walpurgis Night, which Goethe read, and which
mentioned the presence of people of rank and learning.   Except for their
external form, these verses are already very like the *Xenien* (Parting Gifts),
the satirical epigrams on contemporary art and life with which Goethe and
Schiller caused such a stir in 1796.   They were all in couplets made up of a
hexameter and a pentameter, but Goethe wrote a number of others in
rhyming stanzas, and as Schiller had had rather too much of this kind of
thing for his *Muses' Almanach*, Goethe made out of these short satires the
'Intermezzo' or 'Walpurgis Night's Dream,' a kind of review arranged by
the elves in honour of Oberon and Titania, here newly reconciled with each
other, as in Shakespeare's more famous 'Dream.'   We are reminded of
contemporary dramatic satires by Tieck, like his *Puss in Boots*, but Tieck's
romantic ideas about destroying the dramatic illusion are hard for other
times to accept, and the inclusion of this scene is generally deplored by the
critics.   If Goethe saw no incongruity here, it is not likely that he was
troubled by the much smaller ones which German commentators have tried
so hard to explain away.
   The allusions in the scene are of little interest now, but the reference to a
'Proktophantasmist' shows that Goethe sided with the Romantics in their
opposition to the hide-bound rationalist Nicolai, the Berlin publisher.
When ghosts were reported to have been seen near Humboldt's home at
Tegel, Nicolai read a paper to the Berlin Academy about how leeches, applied
to his fleshy parts (Greek '*prōktos*'), had cured him of seeing *phantasms*.

FAUST

This knotted staff 's enough for me, so long
As I feel fresh upon my legs.   What boots
To cut our journey short, howe'er it lags?
To thread this maze of valleys all at rest,
And then to clamber up to yonder crags,
From which the fountain ever-babbling shoots,
'Tis this which gives our journey all its zest.
The birchen spray is kindling with the Spring,
And even the dull pines feel its quickening;
Shall it not also make our limbs more brisk?

MEPHISTOPHELES

Of that I feel no trace, nor will.
My body is all winter-chill.
Would that our path lay over frost and snow!
How sadly the red moon's imperfect disk
Moves up the sky with her belated glow,
And gives so bad a light, that we run bump
At every step against some rock or stump!
By your permission, I will hail
A Will-o'-Wisp.   Out there I see
One burning merrily.   So ho,
My friend!   Will you before us sail?
Why will you waste your lustre so?
Pray be so kind, as light us upward here.

WILL-O'-THE-WISP

Out of respect I'll struggle to repress,
And hope I may, my natural flightiness.
A zigzag course we're apt to steer.

MEPHISTOPHELES

Ha, ha!   He fain would imitate mankind.
Hold, in the devil's name, straight on, or, mind,
I'll blow your flickering life out!

WILL-O'-THE-WISP

'T would appear,
That you are master of the household here,
So I'll essay to do your bidding rightly.
But mind! the mountain's magic-mad to-day,
And if a Will-o'-Wisp's to light the way,
You must not deal with him too tightly.

FAUST, MEPHISTOPHELES, *and* WILL-O'-THE-WISP

(In alternating song)

Now we're in the sphere, I deem,
Of enchantment and of dream.
Lead us on, thou meteor-gleam,
Lead us rightly, and apace,
To the deserts vast of space!
See, only see, tree after tree,
How thick and swift behind they drift,
And crag and cliff make mop and mow,
And the long-snouted crags below,
Hark, how they snort, and how they blow!

Over moss and over stone,
Brook and brooklet race along.
What noise is that, around, above?
Hark, again!   The sounds of song,
Lovers lamenting and making moan,
Loosing their laden hearts in sighs,
Voices we knew in the days that are flown,
When to live and to love were paradise?
All that we hope for, all that we love,
Throbs in the heart and thrills in the brain,
And Echo, Echo, like the tale
Of ancient days, o'er hill and dale
Reverberates the strain!

Tu-whit! Tu-whoo!   More near, more near!
The jargon rises shrill and clear.
The owl, the peewit, and the jay,
All awake and abroad are they.
Can those be salamanders there,
Long in leg, and huge in paunch,
Striding onwards through the brakes?
Lo, the great roots gaunt and bare,
How from rock and sand they branch,
Wreathed fantastical like snakes,
In weirdest coils, which through the air
They stretch to scare and to ensnare us,
From wart-like knots, with life instinct,
Darting polyp-fibres, link'd
To enmesh and overbear us!
And see! the mice of every hue,
How they crowd, and how they speed
Through the moss and through the heather!
Up and down the fireflies, too,
Flit and flicker, throng'd together,
To bewilder and mislead!

But, tell me, are we standing?   Say,
Which is moving, we or they?
All about us seems to spin,
Rocks and trees grimace and grin,
And, swollen and puff'd, on every side,
Will-o'-the-Wisps are multiplied.

MEPHISTOPHELES

Grasp my skirt, and hold it tight,
Here's a central peak, where we
May with eyes of wonder see
The mountain all with Mammon bright.

FAUST

Through chasm and cleft how strangely gleams
A dull red light as of the dawn!
Down to the very depths it streams,
Where gloomiest abysses yawn.
There clouds and exhalations rise,
Here from the mists light glimmers soft,
Now like fine threads it winds and plies,
Then like a fountain leaps aloft.
Here in a hundred veins it coils
For many a rood the valley through,
There, shut within yon gorge's toils,
In sparkles scatters out of view.
Near us, like sprinkled sand of gold,
Are flame-sparks strewn upon the air,
And now, through all its height, behold,
The wall of rocks is kindling there!

MEPHISTOPHELES

Doth not Sir Mammon rarely light
His halls up for our sports to-night?
Lucky, you've seen it!   I can hear
Even now his boisterous guests are near.

FAUST

How through the air the storm-blast raves and hisses!
It smites my neck, shock after shock.

MEPHISTOPHELES

You'll have to clutch the old ribs of the rock,
Or it will hurl you down to yon abysses.
O'er the midnight a thick mist broods.
Hark to the crashing through the woods!

To and fro, the boughs between,
The affrighted owlets flit.
Hark, the columns, how they split,
Of the palaces evergreen!
Hear to the branches straining, snapping,
The giant tree-stems' mighty moaning,
The huge roots yawning, creaking, groaning;
Each across the other clapping,
Down they crash, and thunder all,
In mad and intertangled fall:
And through the cliffs with ruin strewn
The wild winds whiz, and howl, and moan.
Voices o'er us dost thou hear?
Voices far, and voices near?
All the mountain-range along
Streams a raving Witches' song.

WITCHES (*in chorus*)

The Witches are for the Brocken bound—
The stubble is yellow, the blade is green—
There shall a mighty throng be found,
Sir Urian seated aloft between.
Right over stock and stone they go,
Beldame and buck-goat, hilloah, hilloah!

A VOICE

Old Baubo comes alone; astride
A farrow-sow behold her ride!

CHORUS

To whom is honour due be honour!
Dame Baubo, advance, and lead the way!
A sturdy sow with a dame upon her
Is guide full meet for our troop so gay.

A VOICE

What road came you by?

A VOICE

By Ilsenstein.
I peep'd, as I pass'd on my midnight prowl,
Into the nest of the hornèd owl!
And didn't she open her eyes on mine?

A VOICE

To hell with you, old weason-face!
Why are ye riding at such a pace?

A VOICE

She grazed me as she pass'd.   Just see,
The jade, how she has wounded me!

WITCHES' CHORUS

The way is wide, the way is long.
Is this not a jolly bedlam throng?
The pitchfork pricks, and the broom it scratches,
The babe is stifled, the mother she hatches.

WIZARDS. SEMI-CHORUS

We crawl like snails; the womenkind
Have left us far and far behind;
For woman, when to hell she rides,
Outstrips us by a thousand strides.

SECOND SEMI-CHORUS

That's not at all the way we view it.
She takes a thousand strides to do it,
But, post howe'er she may, the man
Does it at once in a single span.

A VOICE (*above*)

From Felsensee, come away, come away!

VOICES (*from below*)

Up through the sky we fain would fly.
We've washed, and we're clean, as clean may be,
But barren for evermore are we.

BOTH CHORUSES

The wind is down, and the stars are flown,
The wan moon hides her woe-worn face,
Along the dark shoot flame and spark,
To mark the wizards' roaring chase.

A VOICE (*from below*)

Hold hard!   Hold hard!   Behind I'm left.

A VOICE (*from above*)

Who is calling there from the rocky cleft?

A VOICE (*from below*)

Oh, take me with you!   Three hundred year
Have I been climbing, climbing here,
But never can I the summit gain.
To be with my fellows I were fain.

BOTH CHORUSES

Besom and broomstick, he-goat and prong,
All are good to whisk you along;
And surely the wight is in doleful plight
Who cannot mount in the air to-night.

DEMI-WITCH (*from below*)

I've been tottering after this many a day,
And the rest are already so far away!
No peace have I at home, and here
I'm likely to light on no better cheer.

CHORUS OF WITCHES

'Tis ointment puts heart in the witches' crew.
Any fluttering rag for a sail will do.
Any trough make a stout ship to scud through the sky,
Who flies not to-night, he will never fly.

BOTH CHORUSES

And when you have got to the mountain's crest,
Drop to the ground, where it likes you best.
And cover the moorland all round about
With the weltering swarm of your wizard rout!

[*They descend.*

MEPHISTOPHELES

Here's jamming, jolting, jabbering, justling,
Here's whizzing, whirling, babbling, bustling!
Here's flashing, sparkling, stinking, burning,
All things topsy-turvy turning!
The real hurly-burly, which is
Very meat and drink to witches!
Stick close by me, or we shall be
Swept asunder presently.
Where art thou?

FAUST (*in the distance*)

Here!

MEPHISTOPHELES

                              Ha!   Steady, steady!
What! torn away so far already?
Then is it time I should make clear
My right as lord and master here.
Room for Sir Voland, room, I say!
My most sweet people, please, make way!
Here, doctor, here, take hold of me,
And let us at a bound get free
Of this wild rabble, and its din there.
'Tis too mad even for such as I.
There's something shining there hard by,
With lustre quite peculiar.   Look!
Yon bushes seem a quiet nook.
Come, come along!   Let us slip in there!

FAUST

Spirit of contradiction!   Well, well, lead the way!
Yet 'tis a splendid notion, I must say;
To Brocken we on Mayday night repair,
To keep aloof from all, when we get there.

MEPHISTOPHELES

What many-coloured flames!   Just see,
There is a jovial company!
One's not alone, however few the folk.

FAUST

Up yonder I would rather be.
Already flames and whirling smoke
I see ascending, and the throng,
That to the Evil Spirit's lair
Tumultuously sweeps along!
There would I be, for surely there
Will many a riddle be untied.

MEPHISTOPHELES

And many a riddle be knotted, too.
Let the great world go brawling on!   *Aside*
We'll tarry here in quiet out of view.
With men the custom is of ancient date,
To make themselves small worlds within the great.

Young witches yonder I espy,
As naked as their mother bore 'em,
And old ones, too, that, wisely shy,
Have veil'd their charms with true decorum.
For my sake, now, be civil to them all.
The pastime's great, the trouble small.
Hark! Instruments a-tuning! Curse
Upon their blowing and their scraping!
Come on, come on! There's no escaping;
We must submit, or suffer worse.
I'll step before and introduce you; so
Will under further obligation lay you.
Look here, look here, my friend! How say you?
No cramp'd up shabby ball-room this, no, no!
Look onward there! You scarce can see the end.
A hundred fires are burning, row on row.
They dance, they chat, cook, drink, make love. In short,
Where, let me ask, will you find better sport?

FAUST

Will you, in ushering us into their revel,
Present yourself as wizard, or as devil?

MEPHISTOPHELES

My general rule's to play incognito.
On gala days, however, one may show
One's orders. With no garter am I deck'd,
But here the horse hoof 's held in high respect.
Dost see yon snail come crawling up? 'Tis clear,
Her tentacles already have found out,
There's something more than common hereabout.
Even if I would forswear myself, I could not here.
But come along! From fire to fire we'll go:
The pander I will be, and you the beau.
[*To some, who are seated round expiring embers.*
Old gentlemen, what is the reason, pray,
You sit so far from all the mirth away?
I'd think, you show'd more wisdom, if I found you
Right in the thick of it in jovial mood,
With lots of brisk young wenches dancing round you.
At home one has enough of solitude.

GENERAL

Who can trust a nation's truth,
   Though from ruin he may save her?
For, just as with the women, youth
   With them stands always high in favour.

MINISTER

Folks now have all gone far astray.
  The good old times! that is my creed.
For when we had things all our way,
  That was the golden age indeed.

PARVENU

No fools were we, yet I allow,
  We often did the things we should not.
But all's turn'd topsy-turvy now,
  Just when we most desired it would not.

AUTHOR

Who, as a rule, will now read aught,
  That has the least pretence to thought?
And, as for the young people, they
  Grow sillier, perter, every day.

MEPHISTOPHELES (*who all at once appears very old*)

Mankind, I feel I may assume,
Are ripen'd for the day of doom,
Now that I here for the last time
The Mountain of the Witches climb:
My cask runs muddy, and one sees
The world is also on the lees.

A WITCH (*who traffics in old odds and ends*)

Come, gentle folks, don't pass me so!
Why throw a chance like this away?
Observe my wares; so choice a show
Is what you don't see every day.
Within my shop, sirs, there is nought—
A shop like it you'll nowhere find—
But has its proper mischief wrought
Unto the world and to mankind.
Here is no dagger, but has run with gore;
No chalice, but from it has flow'd
Hot shrivelling poison through each pore,
Which, till it came, with health had glow'd:
No trinket, but to shame it has betray'd
Some woman born to be beloved; no blade,
But has been drawn for treasons fell and black,
Or stabb'd a foe, perchance, behind his back.

MEPHISTOPHELES

Coz, coz, you're quite behind the age.
For what it wants you have no feeling.
Now novelties are all the rage;
In these, then, you should take to dealing!

FAUST

Grant that I may not lose my wits!   Was e'er
In all the universe so strange a Fair?

MEPHISTOPHELES

To reach the top the whole mad throng are striving.
'Tis you are driven, and yet you think you're driving.

FAUST

Who, who is that?

MEPHISTOPHELES

                    Observe her well.
'Tis Lilith.

FAUST

        Who?

MEPHISTOPHELES

                    Adam's first wife.   Beware
Of her and of her beauteous hair!
Wherein she doth all women else excel.
A young man once let her with that ensnare,
It is a mesh he'll find it hard to tear.

FAUST

Yonder sit two, an old witch and a young;
But now they danced like mad, and wheel'd, and flung.

MEPHISTOPHELES

No rest from that to-night!   They start anew.
Come, take a partner!   We must foot it, too.

FAUST (*dancing with the young witch*)

I dream'd a dream, was sweet to see;
In it I saw an apple-tree,
And on it shone fair apples two,
I climb'd to pluck them, where they grew.

THE FAIR ONE

From Eden downwards, you've, in sooth,
For pippins had a liquorish tooth.
It glads my very heart to know,
That such within my garden grow.

MEPHISTOPHELES (*with the old one*)

I dream'd a dream, was wild to see;
In it I saw a cloven tree.
It had a   *   *   *   *   *
*   *   as it was, I fancied it.

THE OLD ONE

With deepest reverence I salute
The cavalier of the horse's foot.
If at a   *   * he does not scare,
Let him   *   *   * straight prepare.

PROKTOPHANTASMIST

Confound your impudence!   Have we to you
Not proved long since by reasons most complete,
That spirits never stand on ordinary feet?
Yet here you dance, as common mortals do.

THE FAIR ONE (*dancing*)

What brings him to our ball, now?

FAUST (*dancing*)

Oh!
He's everywhere, and always so.
What others dance he must apprise.
Each step he cannot criticise
In his conceit's no step at all.
The thing that most excites his gall,
Is onward motion.   If you would
In circles keep revolving still,
As he does in his ancient mill,
No doubt he'd say, all right and good!
And that especially, provided
You own'd you were by his opinion guided.

PROKTOPHANTASMIST

Still at it!   'Tis past bearing!   Vanish hence!
What! in these days of high intelligence!
This devilish crew despise all rule.   We boast
Our great good sense, yet Tegel has its ghost.

The years, heaven knows how many, I have been
Sweeping out such delusions piece by piece!
But never will the human mind be clean.
'Tis labour lost—such follies never cease.

THE FAIR ONE

Then cease to bore us here.   Give place!

PROKTOPHANTASMIST

I tell you, spirits, to your face,
I'll not endure this spirit-thrall!
My spirit cannot manage it at all.
                              [*The dancing proceeds.*
No one to-night, I see, my word regards.
My journey for my pains have I;
And still I hope, before I die,
To put a curb on devils and on bards.

MEPHISTOPHELES

Straight in a puddle he will squat;
He always soothes himself with that.
And when the leeches have grown plump
Upon the juices of his rump,
He's cured, and without more ado,
Of spirits, and of spirit, too.
                    [*To* FAUST, *who has left the dance.*
Why have you left the pretty wench, that sang
So sweetly to you in the dance?

FAUST

Ugh! from her mouth a red mouse sprang,
Even while she sang.

MEPHISTOPHELES

                    A lucky chance!
About such things we're not too nice.
It was not grey, let that suffice.
Who cares for trifles such as this,
When on the very brink of bliss?

FAUST

Then I saw—

MEPHISTOPHELES

What?

FAUST

Mephisto, see'st thou there,
Far off, alone, a girl pale, pale and sweet?
She drags herself along, and with the air
Of one that makes her way with shackled feet.
It cannot, cannot be; and yet
She minds me of sweet Margaret.

MEPHISTOPHELES

Don't look that way! It can do nought but scathe.
'Tis but a magic shape, a lifeless wraith.
It is not well to meet such anywhere.
It curdles up man's blood by its cold stare,
And he is turn'd by it to stone wellnigh.
Thou'st heard, of course, of the Medusa.

FAUST

Ay.
The eyes of one that's dead, in sooth, are those,
Which there has been no loving hand to close.
That is the breast, Margaret gave up to me,
Those the sweet limbs, whose touch was ecstasy.

MEPHISTOPHELES

Thou ready gull, therein the sorcery lies.
To all that love she wears the loved one's guise.

FAUST

What bliss! What torture! From that stare
Myself away I cannot tear.
How strangely does a thin red line,
No thicker than a knife's back, deck
The marble of her lovely neck!

MEPHISTOPHELES

Right! I too see it, thin and fine!
Beneath her arm, too, she can carry
Her head, for Perseus cut it off, poor soul.
Pshaw! Evermore the visionary!
Come on with me to yonder knoll;
The Prater's self is not more gay,
And, if I'm not bewitch'd, I see
A real theatre. What's doing, hey?

SERVIBILIS

They recommence immediately.
'Tis a new piece, the last of seven.   To play
That number is the custom here.
The piece was written by an amateur,
And amateurs perform it.   You'll, I'm sure,
Forgive me, if I disappear;
It is my office, on these days,
The curtain, sirs, *en amateur* to raise.

MEPHISTOPHELES

I'm truly charm'd to see you here:
The Blocksberg's just your proper sphere.

WALPURGIS NIGHT'S DREAM; OR, OBERON AND TITANIA'S GOLDEN WEDDING

INTERMEZZO

MANAGER OF THE THEATRE

CARNIVAL to-day we hold,
  Mieding's children true we,
All our scenery, mountain old,
  Valley dank and dewy!

HERALD

Golden is the wedding, when
  Fifty years have roll'd on,
But, the feud once over, then
  Golden it will hold on.

OBERON

Fairies, if ye haunt this ground,
  Here do homage duly,
For your king and queen are bound
  In love's fetters newly.

PUCK

Puck, when he begins to spin,
  And foot it in the dingle,
After him troop hundreds in,
  With his mirth to mingle.

ARIEL

Ariel with his silver song
    Divine fills all the air, too,
Many frights to hear it throng,
    Many that are fair, too.

OBERON

Learn ye, whom the marriage-bond
    Has not made one-hearted,
If you would make a couple fond,
    You've but to have them parted.

TITANIA

Is he all snarl, and she all whim,
    Upon them seize instanter,
Away to the South Pole with him,
    And at the North Pole plant her!

ORCHESTRA (*tutti fortissimo*)

Fly's proboscis, midge's nose,
    And what to these akin are,
Frog and shrilling cricket, those
    Purveyors of our din are.

SOLO

See where, a soap-bubble sack,
    The bag-pipe, it is coming!
Hark the Schnecke-Schnicke-Schnack,
    Through its snub-nose humming!

SPIRIT (*that is fashioning itself*)

Paunch of toad and spider's foot,
    With little wings below 'em,
Make not, 'tis true, a little brute,
    But make a little poem.

A PAIR OF LOVERS

Tiny step and lofty leap
    Through honeydew and vapours;
Yet up in air you do not sweep,
    Despite of all your capers.

INQUISITIVE TRAVELLER

Is this glamour, to fade anon?
    Shall I believe my sight, to
See the fair god Oberon
    Here with us to-night, too?

ORTHODOX

No claws! No tail! And yet, I wis,
    Undoubtedly the fact is,
That, like the gods of Greece, he is
    A devil in his practice.

NORTHERN ARTIST

My things at present, to be sure,
    Are sketchy and unsteady,
Still I for the Italian tour
    Betimes am getting ready.

PURIST

'Tis ill luck brings me here; this crew,
    Their din grows loud and louder,
And of the whole witch-medley two,
    And only two wear powder.

YOUNG WITCH

Powder is, like petticoat,
    For beldames old and ugly,
So I sit naked on my goat,
    And show my body smugly.

MATRON

With you we're too well bred by far
    To squabble on the spot, Miss;
But, young and tender as you are,
    I hope that you may rot, Miss.

LEADER OF THE BAND

Fly's proboscis, midge's nose,
    These nude folk buzz not round so,
Frog and shrilling cricket, close
    In, keep time, and sound so!

WEATHERCOCK (*towards one side*)

More brilliant throng could heart desire?
    All brides, young, fresh, and active!
And younkers, full of blood and fire,
    A medley most attractive.

WEATHERCOCK (*towards the other side*)

Well, if the ground here shall not gape,
    These all to swallow plump down,
Right off, their antics to escape,
    Into hell-pit I'll jump down.

XENIEN

See us here as insects! Ha!
  With nebs small, sharp, and slitting,
To render Satan, our papa,
  High homage, as befitting.

HENNINGS

See, how they crowd, and cheer the fun
  Of every kind that's started!
They'll even say, ere all is done,
  That they are kindly-hearted!

MUSAGET

Itself among this witches' rout
  My fancy gladly loses;
For I could manage them, no doubt,
  More readily than the Muses.

CI-DEVANT GENIUS OF THE TIME

Cling to my skirts! Whate'er betide,
  Our worth will somewhere class us;
The Blocksberg's summit's broad and wide,
  Like Germany's Parnassus.

INQUISITIVE TRAVELLER

Who is yon stiff starch'd fellow, say,
  With stride so pompous walking!
He sniffs and sniffs where'er he may,
  ''Tis Jesuits he is stalking!'

CRANE

In troubled streams as well as clear
  'Tis my delight to angle;
So you see pious people here
  With devils mingle-mangle.

WORLDLING

Yes, nothing can the pious daunt,
  This place is good as any;
Upon the Blocksberg here they plant
  Conventicles a-many.

DANCER

Hark, far-off drums! Sure, some new throng
  Is in the distance looming!
Oh, never mind! It is among
  The reeds the bitterns booming!

DANCING MASTER

Oh, how they fling, and jig, and flop,
  Each capering as he best can,
The crooked skip, the clumsy hop,
  To foot it, as the rest can.

FIDDLER

Though mingling thus, this rabble crew
  For hate would like to rend them;
As Orpheus' lyre together drew
  The beasts, the bagpipes blend them.

DOGMATIST

Critic or sceptic shall not throw
  A doubt on my ideals;
The devil must be something, though,
  Or how could devils be else?

IDEALIST

The fancy that doth work in me
  For once much too intense is;
In sooth, if I be all I see,
  To-night I've lost my senses.

REALIST

Oh, entities a world of strife
  And torment do entail me;
Here for the first time in my life
  I find my footing fail me.

SUPERNATURALIST

I'm quite enchanted with this scene,
  Its babble and confusions,
For as to angels I can e'en
  From devils draw conclusions.

SCEPTIC

Upon the flamelet's track they roam,
  And think the treasure near is;
Here I am perfectly at home,
  For doubt the devil's fere is.

LEADER OF THE BAND

Frog and shrilling cricket, those
  Confounded dilettanti!
Fly's proboscis, midge's nose,
  You're fine musicanti!

THE KNOWING ONES

Sans souci, they call us so,
   Us jolly dogs, that troll out;
To walk on foot is now no go,
   So on our heads we stroll out.

THE MALADROIT ONES

Ah, many rare good things, 'tis true,
   We had of yore a hand in;
But, oh! our pumps are danced quite through,
   And we're on bare soles standing!

WILL-O'-THE-WISPS

We come fresh from our native haunts,
   From bogs and from morasses,
But who, of all these gay gallants,
   In glitter can surpass us?

STARFLAKE

I shot down hither from on high,
   A star-fire sheen all o'er me;
Now prostrate on the ground I lie,
   Who'll to my legs restore me?

THE MASSIVE ONES

Room! Room! A lane there! Clear the way!
   The grass snaps, where we jump once:
Lo! Spirits come; but spirits they
   With bodies, ay, and plump ones!

PUCK

Tread not, I beg, so heavily,
   Like young calves elephantine;
And let stout Puck the plumpest be
   To-night our fairy haunt in!

ARIEL

If you have wings, boon Nature's gift,
   Then, ere our revel closes,
Away with me by grove and clift
   Up to yon hill of roses!

ORCHESTRA (*Pianissimo*)

On trailing cloud, and wreathed mist,
   A sudden light has kindled;
Trees, sedges whist, a breeze has kiss'd,
   And all to air have dwindled!

A GLOOMY DAY. OPEN COUNTRY

FAUST, MEPHISTOPHELES

FAUST

IN misery! In despair! After long wandering wretched to and fro, to be now in prison! She, that gentle ill starred being, immured as a malefactor in a dungeon, to wait a frightful doom! And it has come to this! to this! Treacherous, worthless Spirit, and thou hast kept this from me!—Ay stand there, stand! Roll thy fiendish eyes in savage wrath! Stand and defy me by thy intolerable presence! A prisoner! in irremediable misery! Given over to wicked spirits, and to the merciless judgment of men! And me, me wert thou all the while lulling into forgetfulness, with vapid dissipations hiding her hourly increasing wretchedness from me, and leaving her to perish without help.

MEPHISTOPHELES

She is not the first.

FAUST

Hound! Detestable monster! Change him, thou infinite Spirit, change the reptile once more into that semblance of a dog, in which he often delighted to gambol before me at night, to double himself up at the feet of the harmless wayfarer, and, if he fell, to fasten upon his shoulders. Change him again into his favourite shape, that he may crawl on his belly in the dust before me, that I may spurn him with my feet, accursèd as he is!—Not the first!—Woe! Woe! Not by the soul of man is it to be comprehended, how more than one human creature has sunk to such a depth of misery—how the first did not in its writhing death-agony make satisfaction for all the rest before the eyes of Him that evermore forgives! The misery of this single soul pierces my very marrow, eats into my life; thou grinnest complacently at the fate of thousands!

MEPHISTOPHELES

Now are we once more at our wit's end, strung to that pitch, at which the reason of your mortals snaps. Why do you make fellowship with us, if you cannot be one of us out and out? Will you fly, yet are not proof against dizziness? Did we force ourselves on you, or you on us?

FAUST

Gnash not thy ravening teeth against me thus! I'm sick of it!—Great and sublime Spirit, thou who didst deign to reveal thyself to me, thou who knowest my heart and my soul, why link me to this infamous yoke-fellow, who feeds on mischief, and battens on destruction?

MEPHISTOPHELES

Hast done?

FAUST

Save her! Or woe to thee! The awfullest of curses smite thee for myriads of years!

MEPHISTOPHELES

I cannot loose the bonds of the avenger, nor undo his bolts. —Save her!—Who caused her ruin? I or thou? [FAUST *looks wildly round.*] Would'st grasp the thunder? 'Tis well, it was not given to you miserable mortals. To crush the first innocent man he comes across, that is just the tyrant's way of making a clearance for himself out of a difficulty.

FAUST

Take me where she is! She shall be free!

MEPHISTOPHELES

And the danger which you run? Remember the guilt of blood, shed by your hand, still lies upon the town. Avenging spirits hover over the spot where the victim fell, and lie in wait for the returning murderer!

FAUST

This too from thee? A world's murder and death upon thee, Monster! Conduct me thither, I say, and set her free!

MEPHISTOPHELES

I will conduct thee; hear what I can do! Have I all power in heaven and on earth? I will cast a glamour over the gaoler's senses; do you possess yourself of his keys, and bear her off with mortal hands. I shall watch outside. My magic horses shall be ready to carry you away. This much I can do.

FAUST

Up and away!

NIGHT.   OPEN COUNTRY [1]

FAUST, MEPHISTOPHELES, *sweeping along on black horses*

FAUST

WHAT are they about yonder around the gallows-tree?

MEPHISTOPHELES

Can't tell what mess they have in hand.

FAUST

They wave up, they wave down, they are swaying and stooping.

MEPHISTOPHELES

A Witches' Guild.

FAUST

They strew and make libation.

MEPHISTOPHELES

Push on!   Push on!

[1] The Ravenstone is the raised place of execution, round which spirits were believed to perform mysterious rites (as in Bürger's *Lenore*); here a further reminder of Gretchen's doom.   Goethe liked the illustration by Eugène Delacroix to this highly evocative little scene.

A DUNGEON [1]

FAUST *with a bundle of keys, before a small iron door*

FAUST

LONG unaccustomed dread, the woe of all
Mankind possesses me.　This is her cell!
Here does she lie behind this cold dank wall,
And all her crime was having loved too well.
Why do I hang back thus?　Is 't fear
To think how I again shall see her?
Onward!　Each moment's pause brings nearer her death-
　　knell.
　　　　[*Opening the lock.　A voice is heard within singing.*

> My mother, the wanton,
> She took my life,
> My father, the rogue,
> Ate me up with his knife!
> My wee little sister
> She pick'd up my bones,
> And laid them to cool
> All under the stones.
> Then I turn'd to a woodbird
> So bonnie to see;
> Fly away, fly away
> To the woodland with me!

FAUST (*opens the door*)

She little dreams that her beloved is near,
The rattling chains, the rustling straw can hear.
　　　　　　　　　　　　　　　　　　　　[*He enters.*

MARGARET (*hiding her face on her pallet*)

They come!　Oh, bitter death!　Oh, woe is me!

---

[1] Gretchen's mad song reminds us of Ophelia, whose own song in *Hamlet*
iv. 5 became Mephisto's serenade in the Valentine scene.　Gretchen's own
actions are translated as in dream into symbols, taken from the German
folk-tale of the Juniper Tree, later included in the Grimms' collection.　A
wicked stepmother kills her stepson and serves him up as a meal to the
father.　A little sister buries the bones under a juniper-tree.　They become
a little bird which sings 'My mother who killed me,' etc.　Gretchen's
speeches reflect the jumble in her head of tragic memories and fears, folk
beliefs, and thoughts of religion.　As the piety ingrained in her gradually
prevails, Faust himself becomes a stranger to her and her sole aim is to
make her peace with God.

FAUST (*softly*)

Hush! hush! I come to set you free!

MARGARET (*throwing herself at his feet*)

Oh, pity me, if you know fear!

FAUST

Hush! not so loud! The guards will hear.
[*Takes hold of her fetters to unlock them.*

MARGARET (*on her knees*)

Who, hangman, who has given you right
To treat me thus—or who could give?
You fetch me, while 'tis yet midnight.
Be merciful and let me live!
Is daybreak to-morrow not soon enough? [*Rises.*
Oh, I am still so young, so young,
And yet must die!
Fair, too, they told me, once was I,
And that was my undoing. He was nigh,
My own dear love, in those sweet hours.
But now he's far away from me.
My wreath is torn, and scatter'd are its flowers.
Seize me not with a grasp so rough!
What have I done to you? Let me be!
Oh, let me not in vain implore!
I never saw you all my days before.

FAUST

Can I survive this miserable hour?

MARGARET

Now I am wholly in your power,
To do with me whatever you think best;
But to the babe first let me give the breast!
All through the night I coax'd and still'd it:
They took it from me to vex my brain,
And now they say that I have kill'd it,
And never shall I be blithe again.
The people, they sing songs about me,
To sting me, and flout me.
Ah, they mean me unkindly by it,
An old tale ends so. Who bade them apply it?

FAUST (*flings himself on the ground*)

Your lover here lies prostrate at your feet,
To rend these miserable bonds, my sweet!

MARGARET (*throws herself by his side*)

Oh, let us kneel to call upon the saints!
Look! Look! Under the stair!
Under the door there,
The fires of hell,
They seethe, and they roar there!
The fiend within,
Furious and fell,
Is making a din!

FAUST

Margaret! Margaret!

MARGARET (*listening*)

That was my loved one's voice!
                 [*She springs up—her fetters fall off.*
Where is he? Where? I heard him call.
I'm free! I'm free! Let no one try
To stay me! On his neck I'll fall,
Upon his bosom lie!
He call'd on Margaret! stood there at the door!
Through all hell's howling and its roar,
Through devilish scoff, and gibe, and groan,
I recognized the sweet, the loving tone!

FAUST

'Tis I!

MARGARET

You, you! Oh, say it once again!
                         [*Clasping him.*
'Tis he, 'tis he! Where now are all my pains?
The anguish of the dungeon? Of the chains?
'Tis you! You come to rescue me! Oh, then,
Then I am saved. Oh, now again
Along the street I wander free,
Where first I heard you speak to me;
Am in the cheerful garden, by the gate,
Where for you I and Martha wait.

FAUST (*trying to force her away*)

Come with me! Come!

MARGARET

Oh, stay!
I like so much to stay, love, where you do.

FAUST

Quick, quick, away!
If you will not hurry, oh
We shall rue dearly the delay!

MARGARET

How's this?
You can no longer kiss?
Parted from me so short a time, and yet
You could the way to kiss forget?
Why do I grow so sad upon your breast,
When, from your words, your looks, in other days
Heaven flooded in upon me, and you pressed
Me close and smothered me in your embrace.
Kiss me, or I'll kiss thee!   [*Embraces him.*
Oh, woe is me!
Your lips are cold, they chill me through.
How! not one word!   Where have you left
Your love?   Oh, who
Has your poor Margaret of that bereft?
                              [*Turns away from him.*

FAUST

Come, follow me!   Take courage, oh my sweet!
I'll clasp you to my heart, when this is o'er,
A thousand times more fondly than before,
So you'll but follow me.   Hence, I entreat!

MARGARET (*turning to him*)

And is it you, then, you?   And is this true?

FAUST

Oh yes!   Come!   Come!

MARGARET

My chains you will undo,
Take me again into your breast!—So, so!
How comes it, that you do not shrink from me?
Oh, my sweet love, do you, then, know
Whom you are setting free?

FAUST

Come!   Come!   The night's already on the wane!

MARGARET

My mother I have slain,
And drown'd my child!   Yours too.
Was it not given to me and you?
To you, love, too!   'Tis you!   Oh, can it be?
Give me your hand!   Yes!   Yes! these are no dreams—
Your own dear hand.   But, woe is me! 'tis wet!
How! dripping, dripping yet?
How it doth run!
Oh, wipe it off!   Meseems,
There's blood upon 't!   Ah God! what have you done?
Put up your sword!   Oh, sheathe it, I implore!

FAUST

Let what is past be past!   I can no more.
Each word you speak is death to me.

MARGARET

No, I must go, but you must stay.
I'll tell you how the graves must be:
To-morrow see to them all three
By break of day.
For mother the best place provide.
Then to her lay my brother nearest;
Me a little to one side,
But not too far off, dearest!
And the little one on my breast to the right!
No one else shall lie by me now.
Ah, love, to nestle up to you,
It was a sweet, a dear delight!
But that I never again shall know.
I have a feeling as if I must
Force myself near you, and as if you thrust
Me back—back—back!   Yet, wherefore so?
It is you, and you look so good, so kind!

FAUST

If such you feel I am, come, come, love!

MARGARET

                                        Where?

Out yonder?

FAUST

Out to the open air!

MARGARET

If the grave is there,
If death is waiting, come! 'Tis best.
From here into the bed of everlasting rest,
And not a step beyond! No, no!
You are going? Henry, if I too might go!

FAUST

You can! Decide! See, open stands the door!

MARGARET

I dare not go. For me all hope is o'er.
They'll follow on my heels. Why should I try?
It is so hard to have to beg your way,
And with an evil conscience harder still;
It is so hard in a strange land to stray,
And they will catch me, do whate'er I will.

FAUST

Then I remain with you!

MARGARET

Fly, fly!
Your child will die!
Save it, oh, save it!
Away! away!
Keep to the path,
Up by the brook,
And into the wood beyond!
Strike to the left
By the fence near the pond!
Quick! Seize it, seize it!
It tries to rise!
It is struggling yet.
Help! Help!

FAUST

Be calm! be still!
Only one step, and you are free!

MARGARET

Oh, were we only past the hill!
There sits my mother upon a stone;
My temples throb with an icy dread.
There sits my mother upon a stone,
And to and fro she wags her head:
Her eyes are set, she makes no moan,
Her hand is heavy as lead.
She slept so long, no more she'll wake;
She slept, that we our delight might take;
What happy days those were!

FAUST

You are deaf to all remonstrance, prayer,
And I perforce must bear you hence.

MARGARET

No, let me be!   No violence!
Do not drag at me so murderously.
I did everything you asked of me.

FAUST

The day is breaking!   Darling!   Darling!

MARGARET

                                        Ay!
The day, indeed!   The last of my days draws nigh,
It should have been my wedding day.   Let no one know,
That you have been with Margaret before.
Woe to my garland, woe!
Already all is o'er.
Love, we shall meet once more,
But not in the dance, ah, no!
The multitude, they come!
So hush'd, you cannot hear the hum.
The lanes, the streets, the square
Scarce hold the thousands there.
The bell!   Hark to its boom!
The staff of doom
Is broken.   How they bind me, blind me!
Now to the seat of blood they drag me off;
And every neck doth feel
The quiver of the steel,
That's quivering for mine!
Now lies the world all silent as the grave.

G 335

FAUST

Oh, that I never had been born!

MEPHISTOPHELES (*appears at the door*)
                                        Away!
Away!   Or you are lost for ever!
Truce to this waiting and prating, this bootless delay!
My horses shiver!
The morning is dawning grey!

MARGARET

What's that sprang from the ground?   I know its face.
Send him away! 'tis he! 'tis he!
What should he do in a holy place?
He comes for me.

FAUST

You shall—must live!

MARGARET

Judgment of God!   I give
Myself unto Thine everlasting grace!

MEPHISTOPHELES (*to* FAUST)

Come!   Come!   How's this?   You will not stir?
I'll leave you in the lurch with her.

MARGARET

Thine am I, Father, thine!
Save me!   Ye angels!   Ministers of light,
Compass me round with your protecting might!
Henry, I shudder as I think of you.

MEPHISTOPHELES

She's judged.

A VOICE (*from above*)
                She is saved.

MEPHISTOPHELES (*to* FAUST)
                        Away with me!
                        [*Disappears with* FAUST.

A VOICE (*from within, dying away*)
Henry!   Henry!

FAUST: A TRAGEDY

THE SECOND PART

ACT I

A BEAUTIFUL LANDSCAPE [1]

FAUST *reclining in a flowery meadow, wearied,
restless, trying to sleep*

TWILIGHT
(*A troop of elves flitting round him, graceful little forms*)

ARIEL

(*Song, accompanied by Aeolian harps*)

WHEN the springtime, scattering flowers,
   Robes in verdure hill and glen,
When green meadows, bright with showers,
   Gladden all the sons of men,
Little elves, where spirits languish,
   Haste their troubled fears to still;
They are grieved by mortal's anguish,
   Be the mourner good or ill.

[1] The Second Part opens with a scene which is poetically in no way inferior
to the opening monologue of the First Part. The fairy music is as enchanting as in *A Midsummer Night's Dream* or *The Tempest*, and behind Ariel
we seem to hear Prospero-Goethe, with the increased trust in nature of the
Romantic age, calling up for the restoration of his hero's spirit, distraught
from his experiences of the 'little world,' all the healing forces of time and
natural beauty. On this Alpine meadow, inspired by sunrise in the mountains, Faust again expresses the highest aspirations, as earlier in his narrow
Gothic chamber, with books of magic before him. Between the two scenes
he has brought tragedy on others and on himself in his pursuit of 'glowing
passions,' and many critics have asked whether he is any wiser for it all.
The 'bitter arrows of self-reproach,' they think, are removed too easily, and
no moral struggles are revealed to us. Goethe's chief concern is to fit his
hero for further vigorous life. As in other works of his, it is only in sleep,
by the slow action of unconscious processes, that the most grievous wounds
of the soul are healed. In his monologue at the close, Faust gives magnificent utterance to Goethe's ripest wisdom, but in the rest of the act he can
hardly be said to 'scale life's topmost heights.' Until the final act, our
attention is focused on the unfolding of a cultural panorama rather than of
an individual character.

Ye, who in airy circles round him float,
Here show that ye are elves of noble note.
Soothe into calm his heart's distressful fray,
Pluck out the burning arrows of remorse,
Wash from his spirit all its past dismay;
Night hath four periods in her solemn course,
Now fill them kindly up without delay!
Pillow his head on yon cool bank, and then
Bathe him in dew from Lethe's stream; anon
Will his cramp-stiffened limbs relax again,
When all refreshed he wakens with the dawn.
Do the elves' fairest 'hest aright,
Restore him to the blessèd light!

CHORUS

When across the emerald meadows
   Warm and fragrant breezes play,
Closing round in misty shadows,
   Softly falls the twilight grey;
Whispers gently peace to mortals,
   Rocks the heart to childlike rest;
Closes up the daylight's portals
   To those wearied eyes unblest.

Now the night is deeply darkling,
   Gleams out hallowed star on star,
Lights of power, or faintly sparkling,
   Twinkle near, and gleam afar.
In the lake they sparkle tender,
   Gleam in yon clear vault profound;
Reigns the moon in full-orbed splendour,
   Perfecting the peace around.

See, the hours of night have vanished,
   Joy and grief have passed away.
Wake! rejoice! thy pain is banished,
   Trust the new-advancing day.
Vales grow green, hills steep and steeper,
   Shadows deepen thick with leaves,
And the harvest to the reaper
   In long silvery billows heaves.

Fix thy gaze in yonder glory,
   Wouldst thou win thy wish and keep,
Frail the spell that resteth o'er thee,
   Fling away the husk of sleep!

Though the crowd grow pale and waver,
  Onward thou with dauntless soul!
Gallant heart is baffled never,
  Striving to a noble goal!

[*A tremendous clangour indicates the approach of the Sun.*

ARIEL

Hark, the ringing hours of morn!
Pealing unto spirit ears,
Lo, another day is born,
Lo, another dawn appears!
Adamantine gates are crashing,
Phoebus' car-wheels rattling, clashing—
What clang harbingers the sun!
Trump and clarion pealing clear,
Dazzling eye and stunning ear!
Hence! Our elfin reign is done.
Slip into your flowery cells,
Couch in lone, untrodden dells,
To the clefts and thickets come!
Day will all your powers benumb.

FAUST (*awaking*)

Life's pulses dance with fresh and bounding pace,
The ethereal splendours of the dawn to greet;
Thou, earth, thou this night too didst hold thy place,
And breathest with new vigour at my feet,
Bid'st joy even now within my breast grow rife,
And high resolves dost stir with kindling heat,
To scale life's topmost heights through toil and strife!
Now lies the world in morning's twilight beam,
The woodland rings with thousand-voicèd life,
All through the valley misty hazes stream,
Yet to its depths doth heaven's clear radiance creep,
And, bathed in freshness, wood and thicket gleam,
From dewy clefts where late they lay asleep;
The glades are dappled with a thousand dyes,
Where flower and leaflet trembling pearls do weep,
And all around grows fair as Paradise!

Aloft the giant peaks, far-gleaming bright,
Proclaim the hour at hand, that fires the skies;
They feel the first flush of the eternal light,
That finds its way betimes to us below.
Now o'er the green slopes of yon Alpine height

The advancing splendour spreads a livelier glow,
And, step by step, it gains the lower ground.
Lo, the broad sun!   And blinded with the flow,
That stings the shrinking sight, I turn me round.

So when a hope, by long devotion fanned,
Hath won the height of its desire and found
Fulfilment's portals wing-like wide expand,
But now from yonder depths eternal leaps
A whelming burst of flame, amazed we stand;
Life's torch we'd fain illumine there, when sweeps
A sea of fire around us, eddying fast—
Is 't love? is't hate? that round us hotly creeps,
With joy and pain, in alternation vast—
So that once more to earth we turn our gaze,
And shrinking childhood's mantle round us cast.

So then behind me let the sunbeams blaze!
The waterfall, that down yon chasm is roaring,
I view with deepening rapture and amaze.
Now, in a myriad broken runlets pouring,
It bounds from ledge to ledge, and, shattering there,
Shoots up, in spray and filmy vapour soaring.
Yet o'er this turmoil how divinely fair
The rainbow's many-tinted arch is wound,
Now pencilled clear, now melting into air,
A dewy cool diffusing far around.
A mirror this of mortal coil and strife,
Wherein is darkly writ this truth profound:
In its reflected glory we have life.

IMPERIAL PALACE.   THRONE ROOM

PRIVY COUNCIL MET IN EXPECTATION OF THE EMPEROR

TRUMPETS

Enter courtiers of every rank in magnificent dresses.   The EM-
PEROR *ascends the throne.   On his right hand The* ASTRO-
LOGER.

EMPEROR

I greet the liegemen true and dear,
Met here from near and distant lands;
My sage, I see, beside me stands,
But where's my fool, is he not here?

PAGE

Sir, on your royal train he stumbled
As we came up the stair, and tumbled;
They bore Sir Corpulence away—
Or dead or drunk, who is to say?

SECOND PAGE

And what was passing strange, apace
Another steps into his place;
The dress he wore is rich and rare,
But so grotesque, it makes folks stare.
The guards their halberds crossed before
The fellow, as he reached the door,
As coming contrary to rule;
But see! he's here, the forward fool!

MEPHISTOPHELES (*kneeling before the throne*)

What is accursed, yet welcome ever;
What is desired, yet kept at bay;
What do men turn their backs on never,
Yet's banned and railed at day by day;
Whom dost thou dare not summon here,
Whose name in all men's ears is sweet,
Who to the very throne draws near,
Yet is self-banished to retreat?

EMPEROR

Friend, for the nonce your jargon spare!
Here riddles out of place are sadly;
They are these gentlemen's affair.
Resolve them, and I'll listen gladly.
My former fool, I fear, has lost his head:
You, take his place, and come up here instead.

[MEPHISTOPHELES *goes up and places himself on the*
   EMPEROR'S *left.*

MURMUR OF THE CROWD

A new fool—so new plagues begin.
Where comes he from?—how come he in?
The old one tripped—used up, past saving:
He was a vat—here now's a shaving.

EMPEROR

So now, my liegemen, whom I love,
Be welcome all, from far and near!
Beneath auspicious stars ye're gathered here;
For us are joy and weal writ there above!
But say, why at a time, when we
From every care would fain be free,
In mumming, mask and revelry
To take our fill of pure delights,
Should we be plagued with setting state affairs to rights?
But since you're clear they will not brook delay,
Then be it so, and have it your own way.

CHANCELLOR

Virtue supreme, that, like an aureole bright,
Circles the Emperor's brows, his royal hand
Alone can exercise by sovereign right.
Justice!   What all men love, what all demand,
All long for, and without it scarce may live—
This to his people 'tis his part to give.
But what avails clear head, or kindly heart,
Or ready hand to play the patriot's part,
When the state's torn by feverish disquiet,
And mischief runs in breeding mischief riot?
The whole broad realm below to us doth seem
From our high vantage ground a nightmare dream,
Where forms misshapen are in chaos blent,
Where lawlessness makes law its instrument,
And error and delusion everywhere
Are rampant, and infect the very air.
One steals a flock, a woman one,
Cross, chalice, candles from the altar,
Brags through the years of what he's done,
Nor gets his neck into a halter.
Now to the court the accusers throng,
The judge in cushioned state sits proud,
In surging eddies rolls along
Tumultuously the clamorous crowd.
Yet dreads the criminal no ill,
Who in accomplices has friends,
And 'Guilty!' is the sentence still,
Where innocence on itself depends.
So will the world in time be wrecked,
Truth, honour, virtue perish quite;
How should we there the sense expect,
Alone can guide us to what's right?

A man, not ill-disposed, in time
To flattery or to bribes will fall,
A judge, who cannot punish crime,
Go partner with the criminal.
My sketch I've drawn of blackest hue,
Yet fain had kept it from the view.   [*Pause.*
Steps must be taken, and ere long;
When all or do or suffer wrong,
There's danger even to the throne.

FIELD-MARSHAL

Oh, the mad days wherein we're living!
All men are taking blows or giving—
Obedience is a thing unknown.
The cit behind his moated wall,
The noble in his rocky nest,
Combine at bay to keep us all,
Each holding stoutly by the rest.
Our mercenaries restive grow,
Demand their hire with angry cry,
Yet, if 'twere all paid up, we know
They'd bolt, and never say 'Good-bye!'
To say what all men want's debarred,
Is to disturb a hornet's nest;
The kingdom they should shield and guard
Is ravaged, plundered, and oppressed.
None try to curb the rabble rout;
Already half the world's undone;
Kings still there be, a few, about,
But not one thinks 'tis his affair, not one.

TREASURER

Who'd pin his faith upon allies?
Our funds, they say, they'll subsidize,
But at the source their bounties stop,
And leak through to us drop by drop.
Again, sir, who, your wide realms through,
Keeps what his fathers left him, who?
Where'er we turn, some new man's in the ascendant,
And will, forsooth, be independent.
Do what he may, howe'er absurd
Or wrong, we must not say a word.
We have surrendered rights so many,
We have not left ourselves with any.
On so-called parties in the state
There's no dependence nowadays;

Whether they rail at us, or praise,
We prize alike their love and hate.
Your Ghibelline, so too your Guelph,
Greedy of ease, gets out of reach.
What man now helps his neighbour?   Each
Is only thinking of himself.
The golden gates are barred; men screw,
And scrape, and snatch, and hoard, and pile,
And our exchequer's empty all the while.

STEWARD

What plagues beset my office too!
We're trying day by day to save,
Yet each day brings me calls for more,
And cares and worries new and grave.
The kitchen never lacks good store:
Stags, wild boars, leverets, hinds, and hares,
Fowls, turkeys, geese, and ducks in pairs—
Payment in kind—whate'er may hap,
Come duly in, to fill the gap.
But now our wine is running low.
Butts upon butts we once did own,
All the best growths, the finest years,
Piled in the cellar, tiers on tiers;
But our great nobles round the throne,
Slaking a thirst that knows no stop,
Are draining them to the last drop.
Even the Town Council are not able
To keep their stores untapped; they fly
To bowl and beaker, drain them dry,
Till the sots sink beneath the table.
Now I, perforce, must pay for all:
The Jew won't spare me: he presents
His bonds of credit, that forestall
The produce of the next year's rents.
Our very pigs we cannot fatten,
The pillow's pawned from off the bed,
And what to table comes is forehand-eaten bread.

EMPEROR (*reflects awhile, then says to* MEPHISTOPHELES)

Have you no grievance, fool, to bring us pat in?

MEPHISTOPHELES

Not I, indeed.   Viewing this grand display—
Thee and thy Court—full trust who must not feel,
Where kingship holds indisputable sway,
And, backed by ready force, makes foemen reel?

Where loyal hearts, strong through conviction clear,
And energy to act, are ever near,
Who could for wrong or purpose dark unite,
Where stars are shining so supremely bright?

MURMUR

He is a knave—a shrewd one too.
He lies—but with an end in view.
I'm sure there's something lurks behind—
Some what?—Some scheme to cheat the blind!

MEPHISTOPHELES

Where lacks not something in this earthly sphere?
Here this, there that: 'tis Coin is lacking here.
Not from the floor can it be scraped, no doubt;
Still wisdom draws what's hid most deeply out.
In mountain-lodes, in walls far under ground,
Gold, coined and uncoined too, is to be found.
And ask you, who can bring it to the light?
Some gifted man's Nature-and-Spirit might.

CHANCELLOR

Nature and Spirit?   No words for Christian men!
For this they burn your atheists now and then,
As such talk is extremely dangerous.
Nature is Sin, Spirit the devil; thus
They gender doubt betwixt them—that
Deformed hermaphroditic brat.
This sort of thing won't do with us!
Our Emperor's ancient kingdom through,
Two orders have sprung up, and only two—
The Clergy and the Nobles—and they make
A sure stay for his throne, and seemly guard,
Defying every tempest; so they take
The Church and State for their well-earned reward.
There's a rebellious spirit brewing
Amongst the vulgar and the bad;
All heretics' and wizards' doing,
Who're driving town and country mad.
And now with ribald jests you, you, begin
To assail the men who move in this high sphere!
Hearts rotten at the core to you are dear,
For they to fools are very nigh akin!

MEPHISTOPHELES

I see the scholar, sir, in what you say.
What you touch not, for you lies miles away;
What you grasp not, no being has for you;
What you count not, you're clear cannot be true;
What you weigh not, has neither weight nor size;
What you coin not, is worthless in your eyes.

EMPEROR

Our needs are nowise to be lightened thus.
Your Lenten Sermon, what is that to us?
I'm sick of the eternal How and When:
'Tis cash we want—hard cash! So get it, then!

MEPHISTOPHELES

All you desire I'll get, and more, so please ye;
The task is light, and yet, though light, not easy.
The gold is there; but how to haul it in?
That calls for skill: who knows how to begin?
Only reflect, in the dark days, when tides
Of men swamped countries and their folk besides,
How he and he, in the first panic scare,
Hid what he prized most dearly anywhere!
So was it under Rome's imperial sway—
So on to yesterday, ay, to-day.
It all lies hidden in the soil; the soil
The Emperor's is, and he shall have the spoil.

TREASURER

Well, for a fool, he does not talk amiss;
The Emperor's ancient right undoubted this!

CHANCELLOR

For you spreads Satan golden snares; you'll do
What is unrighteous and unholy too.

STEWARD

So that he only bring us gifts of price,
About unrighteousness I shan't be nice.

FIELD-MARSHAL

Shrewd fool, to promise what by all is sought!
The soldier won't inquire whence it was brought.

MEPHISTOPHELES

And if, belike, you think I'm talking fudge,
There's the Astrologer—let him be judge!
Cycle on Cycle, Hour and House he knows;
Say, sir, what do the heavenly signs disclose?

MURMUR

A pair of knaves—confederates clear,
Phantast and fool—the throne so near.
An old old story! stale with age—
As the fool prompts, so speaks the sage!

ASTROLOGER (*speaks*, MEPHISTOPHELES *prompting*)

Gold of the purest is the orb of day;
Mercury, the herald, serves for grace and pay;
Dame Venus hath bewitched you, one and all,
On you all hours her loving glances fall.
Chaste Luna's full of whims and fancies light;
Mars, though he strike not, awes you with his might;
And Jupiter shows the loveliest star of all.
Saturn is great, far to the eye and small;
Him lowliest 'mongst the metals do we rate,
Trivial in value, ponderous in weight.
But mark!   When Sol and Luna come together,
And gold mates silver, then 'tis finest weather;
Straightway one gets whatever else one seeks,
Parks, palaces, plump bosoms, rosy cheeks.
All this is wrought by that most learned man,
Who can achieve what none amongst us can.

EMPEROR

His words ring double in all they say;
But they convince me not, not they.

MURMUR

An idle tale—jest worn and stale!
Star-gazer's dreams—alchemists' schemes!
Things oft told to us—devised to do us!
For all his coaxing, merest hoaxing!

MEPHISTOPHELES

With foolish stare they stand around;
No faith have they in hidden prizes:
Kobold and gnome one man surmises,
Another prates of the coal-black hound.

What matter, if sorry jokes one crack,
Another at sorcerers' cantrips rail,
If gout his feet with its twinges rack,
And his legs beneath him quake and fail?
Ye all the secret working feel
Of nature's ever-predominant power,
And her living traces this very hour
Up from her nethermost regions steal.
When every bone in your body grows sick,
And a something uncanny stirs in the air,
Then courage! to work with spade and pick!
There lies the fiddler, the treasure is there!

MURMUR

My feet are heavy as lead—that's gout;
Cramps through my arms run in and out;
My great toe burns, and shoots, and twitches;
All over my back there are pains and stitches:
By all these signs it would appear,
There are heaps of richest treasure here.

EMPEROR

Look sharp! I brook no more delay!
Prove that your frothy flams are true,
And bare these famous piles to view!
Then sword and sceptre I'll put away,
And with my royal hands I will,
If you lie not, the work fulfil;
But if you lie, I'll pack you off to hell!

MEPHISTOPHELES

The road there I at least should know right well!
But, sir, words fail me, adequate to tell,
What unowned wealth lies waiting everywhere.
The boor, that through the furrow drives his share,
Turns up a crock of bullion with the mould;
He hopes saltpetre hidden in the clay,
And, half in ecstasy, half in dismay,
In his gaunt fingers finds rouleaux of gold.
But then the arches must be burst,
The chasms, the shafts, through which he must,
Who's treasure-wise, a passage thrust,
To reach the wondrous world below!
In spacious vaults, strong-barred, untold
Plates, goblets, salvers, all of gold,
He sees around him, row on row.

There ruby-studded beakers stand,
And, if he'd drink from them, at hand
Are fluids aged as the hills.
The casks have long been turned to dust.
But the wine-tartar—if you'll trust
One who knows well—their function fills.
The essences of noble wine,
As well as gold and jewels fine,
Themselves in gruesome night enshrine.
'Tis here the wise man—pray you, mark!—
Unweariedly pursues his quest.
To hunt by daylight were a jest;
The home for mysteries is the dark.

EMPEROR

That may be so.   Gloom!   What's the good of that?
Things of true worth are sure to come to light.
Who can detect a rascal in black night?
Your cow in the dark is black, and grey your cat.
These pitchers down below, crammed full of gold,
Do you with ploughshare to the light unfold!

MEPHISTOPHELES

Take spade and pickaxe, dig yourself!   The toil
Will make you great, mere peasant's though it be,
And presently, emerging from the soil,
A herd of golden calves will struggle free.
Then in your transports may you without check
Yourself and your fair lady-love bedeck,
For lustrous gems give lustre great
To beauty as well as to royal state.

EMPEROR

Dispatch, dispatch!   How long are we to wait?

ASTROLOGER

Such urgent longing, pray, sir, moderate.
First finish off the motley masquing show.
A mind distraught conducts not to the goal.
We must to settled calm compose our soul,
And earn by what's above what is below.
Who would have good things must himself be good.
Who would have joy must temper down his blood.
Who would have wine must lay ripe clusters by—
Who miracles, his faith must fortify.

EMPEROR

Then be the time in mirth and frolic spent,
And welcomer will be the coming Lent!
Meanwhile more merrily, whate'er befall,
We'll celebrate the roaring Carnival.

MEPHISTOPHELES

How merit's coupled with success,
Is what your fools can never guess;
If they the wise man's stone possessed,
With wisdom they would not be blest.

SPACIOUS HALL, *with apartments adjoining embellished for a
masquerade* [1]

HERALD

Expect not here old German fancies,
Devils' and fools' and dead men's dances;
A *fête* awaits you gay and bright.
Our master, when he went to Rome,
Has for his profit, your delight,
Crossed the high Alps, and thence brought home
To his fair realm a royal right.
There at the holy feet bowed down,
That right he first devoutly sought,
And, while he went to fetch away his crown,

---

[1] To enter into the spirit of this rather overgrown scene of carnival
pageantry, we must remember Goethe's delight in the carnival at Venice
and the large share he had in devising masquerades in Weimar itself.   Long
as the scene is, Goethe has recourse to summarizing rubrics in the middle of
it.
   After a section introducing picturesquely contrasted occupations and
classes we see figures from classical mythology, often in revised versions
(among the Parcae, for instance, Clotho and Atropos have exchanged
roles), and finally the main group, allegorical figures, headed by Fear, Hope,
and Prudence.   Mephistopheles as Zoilo-Thersites (a Greek disguise for
the spirit of negation, compounded of the Homeric Thersites, who allowed
no merit in any hero, and the critic Zoilos, who allowed none in Homer
himself) introduces unrehearsed features, the magic element, into the show.
The Boy-Charioteer is Poetry, whom Goethe thought of as identical with
the Euphorion of Act III.   Faust appears in the costume of Plutus,
Mephistopheles in the new role of the Starveling (Avarice) and finally the
Emperor as Pan.   We hear in the next scene that in the midst of the revelry
the Emperor unwittingly signed an authorization for the issue of paper
money, against treasure which, as Mephistopheles has assured him, lies
buried in his domains.   The point of this episode of the credit scheme, apart
from contemporary references (to the 'assignats' in the French Revolution,
etc.) is to be found in some earlier words of Mephistopheles.   If people
like these courtiers acquire the philosophers' stone itself, they will not have
the sense to use it rightly.

Away for us the fool's cap with him brought!
Now we are all new-born; and every man
To whom the world has been his school,
O'er head and ears the cap will snugly pull—
The air it gives him of a crack-brained fool,
And under it he plays sage, as best he can.
Already they break up, I see,
Some into pairs, some into groups;
And in and out unceasingly
The throng of choral singers troops.
Well!   With its fooleries untold,
The world is, as it was of old,
A big fool, not to be controlled!

FLOWER GIRLS (*sing, accompanied by mandolines*)

Maids of Florence, by the splendour
    Of your Court drawn here are we,
And our tribute thus we render,
    Decked in all our bravery.

Woven into our nut-brown tresses
    Bright flowers manifold we bear,
Silken streamers, silken jesses
    Join to prank it gaily there.

For we hold it meritorious,
    And a thing to make us dear,
That our flowers, by art made glorious,
    Bloom and blow through all the year.

Sprays of every hue commingle,
    In symmetric order placed;
You may slight them, taken single,
    But the mass contents your taste.

Comely are we to the eye, as
    Girls should be so gay and smart,
For the woman's native bias
    Closely is allied with art.

HERALD

Show your baskets richly freighted,
    Those that on your heads are pressed,
Those with which your arms are weighted;
    Let each choose what likes him best.
Quick!   Till all with leaf and alley
    Semblance of a garden bears.
Who but fain with such would dally,
    Dealers lovely as their wares?

GARDEN GIRLS

Choose, then, each at fancy gleaning—
    Freely choose, and huxter not!
Tell in few words, full of meaning,
    Every one what he hath got.

OLIVE-BRANCH (*with fruit upon it*)

Flowery blooms I envy none,
Strife of every kind I shun;
    It doth with my nature jar.
Yet earth holds no gem more fair,
Pledge and token everywhere
    Of peace, and what its blessings are.
To-night, I hope, 'twill be my place,
Some fair and worthy head to grace!

WHEAT-WREATH (*golden*)

Nought more winning-sweet attireth
    Than the gifts by Ceres sent;
What man most for use desireth,
    Be your fairest ornament!

FANCY-WREATH

Motley flowers, resembling mallows,
    Strangely peep from mosses green;
These are things that fashion hallows,
    Though in nature never seen.

FANCY-NOSEGAY

What my name is, to declare
Theophrastus would not dare;
Yet I have my hope I shall
Please a many, if not all.
She that in her hair will wind me,
She that on her breast will bind me,
Shall, if with a will she do it,
Find she has no cause to rue it.

CHALLENGE

Gaudy fancies, let them flower
For the fashion of the hour,
Form in guises wondrous moulded,
Such as nature ne'er unfolded!
Golden bells and sprays of green
Peer out flowing locks between.
But we——

ROSEBUDS

Shrink from sight.
Happy who on us doth light!
When the winds of summer blow,
Roses kindle then and glow;
Who such happiness would miss?
Promise, then fulfilment, this
Is in Flora's realm the rule!
Eye, and sense, and heart fed full!

[*The* GARDEN GIRLS *arrange their wares tastefully under green alleys.*

GARDENER (*song accompanied by theorbos*)

Flowery blooms, where you have placed them,
　　Charmingly your head adorn,
　　So our fruits you will not scorn;
They'll delight you, if you taste them.

Magnum bonums, cherries, peaches,
　　Dusky are of hue; but buy!
　　Worst of judges is the eye;
Trust what tongue or palate teaches.

Let all come where, gladdening eyes
　　And taste, the choicest fruits invite them;
Men on roses poetise,
　　Apples, they perforce must bite them.

To your bounteous bloom of youth
　　Grant us leave, then, to ally us,
And our ripest wares, in sooth,
　　Shall on you be lavished by us.

In alleys gay that wind about,
　　In the shade of pleachèd bowers,
You'll find all you want laid out,
　　Blossoms, foliage, fruit, and flowers.

[*Singing alternately, accompanied by guitars and theorbos, the two Choirs proceed to arrange their wares in rows one above the other, and to offer them for sale.*

MOTHER *and* DAUGHTER

MOTHER

O lass, when you first came to the light,
　　A bonny wee hood I made ye;
Your limbs were so lissom, your face so bright,
　　You were quite a dainty lady.

What a bride you'll make! to myself I said,
  With figure and face so sunny,
And already I pictured you wooed and wed
  By a suitor with heaps of money.

But years they have come, and have passed again,
  And, alas! you are left on my hands still;
For somehow or other the marrying men
  Sweep by you, and none of them stand still.
No fault of yours!   For with one you dance,
  And flirt it and foot it sprightly;
On another you smile with a coy kind glance,
  And cling to his elbow tightly.

Picnic or party, 'twas all the same,
  However we might devise them;
Forfeits, Third Man, no kind of game
  Could into an offer surprise them.
But all the fools are let loose to-day,
  And they're brimming with silly rapture;
So, dearest, your charms without stint display,
  And one of them you may capture!

[*Girl playfellows, young and beautiful, join the groups,
    and break out into a loud chatter of mutual confi-
    dences. Fishermen and bird-catchers with nets,
    fishing-rods, limed twigs, and other implements of
    their craft, enter and mingle with the girls. Mutual
    attempts to attract attention, to catch, to escape, and
    to hold fast, give occasion for pleasant interchange
    of talk and banter.*

WOODCUTTERS (*enter, boisterous and ungainly*)

  Room! room! give place!
  We must have space!
  Trees we fell;
  Down as we tear them,
  They crash in the dust!
  Off as we bear them,
  Come push and thrust.
  This to our praise,
  Look, that ye tell!
  Were no rough men
  To work in the land,
  Where, tell me, then,
  Would your fine folks stand?

This truth, forget it not,
Stretched at your ease,
For, if we sweated not,
You all would freeze!

PUNCHINELLOS (*awkward, almost silly*)

Fools are ye, hacks,
Born with bent backs!
We the wise, who
Burden ne'er knew!
For, look ye, our caps,
Our jackets and flaps,
We carry them lightly,
Gaily and sprightly—
We, ever idle,
Saunter and sidle,
Slippers on feet,
Through market and street,
There to stand gaping,
Crowing and japing;
Under the hubbub loud,
Through the thick thronging crowd,
Eel-like we slip off,
In a mass trip off,
A rumpus to raise.
Whether you praise,
Or whether you blame,
'Tis to us all the same!

PARASITES (*with a wheedling air*)

Ye porters, stout of thew,
And their own brothers, you
Charcoal that burn,
Are the men for our turn.
For bowing and scraping,
Assenting and smiling,
Fine phrases shaping,
Obscure and beguiling,
Framed to blow hot
Or cold, or what not,
Just the moment to please;
What profit all these?
Fire might be given
Straight out of heaven,
In volume enormous;
But how would it warm us,

Had we no billet,
No coal-heaps to throw
On our fire-place, and fill it
With gladdening glow?
Then the steaming and roasting,
The stewing and toasting!
The real gourmet,
The licker of dishes,
Scents the roast by the way,
And surmises the fishes.
This incites him to ply
A robust knife and fork
When his host says, Come, try!
And he tackles to work.

DRUNKEN MAN (*in a stupor*)

Oh, this day shall be happy beyond all measure,
 I feel so jolly and free!
Songs to delight you, and holiday leisure,
 I have brought you along with me.
And that's why I drink! Drink, drink!
Join glass to glass, boys! Clink, clink!
You behind there, come out to the light!
Strike your glass upon mine! All right!

My wife she jeered at this coat of motley,
 And railed as though she my ears would pull;
She fleered and sneered, till I felt it hotly,
 And called me a mumming masking fool.
But I drink for all that! Drink, drink!
Let every glass ring! Clink, clink!
Ye masking mummers, come, all unite!
When the glasses go clink, all's right!

Never say I'm cracked! for my boast is,
 I know, when I want, where to get my fill!
If my host won't trust me, why, there's the hostess;
 And if she won't do it, the maiden will.
So I drink at all times! Drink, drink!
You fellows there, up! Clink, clink!
Join glass to glass! Keep it up all night!
Things now, I've a notion, are perfectly right!

Leave things as they are! The joys they've made me,
 What better could mortal wish to his hand?
All right! let me lie here where I have laid me,
 For now on my legs I can no more stand!

CHORUS

Every good fellow, drink, drink!
Drain down your glasses, clink, clink!
To bench and to board stick while you are able;
He's done for, that fellow there under the table!

[*The* HERALD *announces poets of various kinds, Poets of
Nature, Court and Ritter Singers, bards sentimental
and gushing. In the throng of competitors no one
will allow the other to obtain a hearing. One of them
throws out a few words as he slips past.*

SATIRIST

Know ye what were the sweetest thing
    For me, a poet among poets here?
This! Were I free to say and sing
    What none of them all would wish to hear.

[*The* NIGHT *and* CHURCHYARD POETS *send apologies,
because they are just at that moment engaged in an
interesting conversation with a Vampyre that has
made its appearance recently, out of which a new
kind of poetry may perhaps be developed. The*
HERALD *has to accept their excuses, and in the mean-
time summons* GREEK MYTHOLOGY, *which, even in
modern masquerading costume, loses neither character
nor charm.*

The Graces

AGLAIA

Into life we carry grace!
In your givings give it place.

HEGEMONE

In receiving grace retain!
Sweet it is a wish to gain.

EUPHROSYNE

And in days of thoughtful mood,
Let grace sweeten gratitude.

THE PARCAE

ATROPOS

Me, the eldest, have they wooed on,
  Here among you all to spin;
Much to think of, much to brood on,
  Lies life's fragile thread within.

That it may be pliant, tender,
  Flax the finest still I choose;
Smooth to make it, even, and slender,
  I shall deftest fingers use.

Should the dance's joyous eddies
  Pulses all too quick awake,
Think, how very frail this thread is,
  And be wary!   It may break.

CLOTHO

Know, of late years they confided
  Unto me the shears of dread;
For the way our elder plied it
  Had its power discredited.

Spinnings worthless quite, she bore them
  Through long years of life and bloom;
Threads of promise rare, she shore them,
  Hurried to a timeless tomb!

I myself made many a blunder
  In my young and headstrong years;
Now to keep my rashness under,
  In its sheath I keep the shears.

Gladly then my hands I fetter;
  Kindly I your sports survey;
In these hours of ease what better,
  Than give mirth its fullest play?

LACHESIS

To me, whose judgment wavers never,
  Was the task of order given;
So my spindle, circling ever,
  Never has been over-driven.

Threads around and round it playing,
   I to each its path assign,
None I suffer to go straying,
   All into the ball I twine.

Could I pause, myself forgetting,
   For the world my heart would ache;
Days and years sink to their setting,
   She that weaves the skein will take.

HERALD

These that are coming now, you will not know,
   How versed soe'er in ancient lore ye be;
Gazing on these, who work such worlds of woe,
   Guests you would think them, men were glad to see.

The Furies they; none will believe us; kind,
   Of comely presence, fair withal, and young:
But fall into their hands, and you will find,
   How serpent-cruelly these doves have stung!

Crafty they are, 'tis true; but nowadays,
   When every fool for failings craves renown,
Even they, not coveting, as angels, praise,
   Own they're the plagues of country and of town.

ALECTO

What boots such talk? You'll trust us all the same:
   For we are pretty, young, sweet coaxing dears;
If you've a swain has set your heart aflame,
   We'll go on pouring flattery in his ears.

Till we dare tell him, eye to eye, his fair
   Has smiles for other men as well as him—
That, if he's pledged his troth, he'd best beware,
   For she's a fool, crook-backed, and halt of limb.

And we can make the lady wretched too;
   Some weeks ago her friend said slighting things
Of her to someone else.   They may, 'tis true,
   Be reconciled; still we have left our stings.

MEGAERA

That's but a joke!   I wait till they are wed,
   Then set to work, and poison—such my powers—
Bliss, when it seems more surely perfected;
   Men they are changeful as the changing hours.

Let what he yearned for once be won, all's o'er,
  His rapture cools, the prize its charm has lost;
For something else he madly yearns still more,
  Flies from the sun, and seeks to warm the frost.

Asmodi here I bring, my henchman true;
  Well does he work my will in such affairs,
Mischief broadcast at the right time to strew,
  And so destroy the human race in pairs.

TISIPHONE

Poison, dagger, not backbiting,
Mix I, whet I, for the traitor;
Lov'st thou others, sooner, later,
Shalt thou feel destruction smiting.

Turn to gall and wormwood must
What in sweetness was abounding;
Here no bargaining, no compounding!
Suffer as ye wrought! 'Tis just!

Let none say, 'Forgive, forgive!'
To the rocks my plaint I bring.
Hark! 'Revenge!' the echoes ring;
Who betrays, he shall not live!

HERALD

Please, step a little back, you there behind;
For what comes next is of no common kind.
Onward a mountain works its way, you see,
Swathed on its flanks in gorgeous tapestry.
Long tusks, a snake-like snout, its head are on;
A mystery! But I'll show the key anon.
Gracefully on its neck a fair girl rides,
And with a slender staff its movements guides;
Another stands above, of stately height,
Begirt with radiance dazzling to the sight.
Two noble dames walk, chained, on either side,
One blithe and bright, one sad and sober-eyed;
One yearns to be, one feels that she is, free.
Let each of these declare, who, what is she.

FEAR

Through this revel wild the light
  Of lamps and torches flares around;
Traitor faces throng my sight,
  And I, alas! in chains am bound.

Hence, ye laughers, brainless, loud,
  From your grins I shrink in fear;
All that mean me mischief crowd
  Close to-night around me here.

Here a friend has grown a foe;
  Read him through his mask I may:
There is one would kill me; lo!
  Now, found out, he slinks away!

Ah, how gladly would I fly
  Through the wide world anywhere!
But destruction dogs me—I
  Hang 'twixt darkness and despair.

HOPE

Hail, beloved sisters, hail!
If these mumming sports prevail
Here to-night, as yester-e'en,
Yet to-morrow, well I ween,
You will doff your masking gear.
If we find no special pleasure
In the torches' flare, we shall
Anon in days of sunny leisure,
And with none to thwart us near,
Now with others, now alone,
Roam at will, by waters clear,
Meads with bright flowers overgrown.
Living lives exempt from care,
With nor want nor idlesse there.
Welcome guests where'er we go,
In we pass with easy mind;
For the best of cheer, we know,
Somewhere we are sure to find.

PRUDENCE

Two of men's worst foes are these;
  In chains I hold them—Hope and Fear—
From the crowd they else would seize.
  You are saved.   A pathway clear!

I this live Colossus lead;
  Though a tower is on his back,
Unfatigued, with steady speed,
  See, he climbs the steepest track!

But upon its summit, lo!
  A goddess, with wings swift and wide
Waving lightly to and fro,
  As she turns to every side!

Light plays round her, pure and glorious,
  Sheds afar a wondrous sheen;
Victory is her name—victorious
  Goddess of great deeds, and queen!

ZOILO-THERSITES

Ugh! ugh!   I come, though no one call:
Fools that you are, I chide you all;
But what I chiefly will not spare
Is Madam Victory up there!
With her white wings, she fancies, she
An eagle at the least must be,
And that, where'er she looks or stirs,
Country and people both are hers.
But let some field of fame be won,
And straight my fighting gear I don.
When high turns low, and low turns high,
The crooked straight, the straight awry—
Then, only then, I feel aglow;
All through the globe I'd have things so.

HERALD

Then, thou vile cur, the swashing blow
Of my good staff on thee I lay!
Now crawl and wriggle as you may!
How quickly has the dwarfish elf
Up in a bundle rolled himself!
The ball becomes an egg!—oh, wonder!—
Puffs itself out, and bursts asunder!
Out comes a strange twin-growth quite pat,
An adder one, and one a bat.
One crawls off in the dust; his brother
Up to the roof flies like a bird:
Outside they'll shortly join each other,
There I've no wish to make a third.

MURMURS

Come on!   They're dancing there behind.
No!   To be off I have a mind.
Do you not feel, how all about
Us flits the ghost and goblin rout!

Now they go swish above my hair—
About my feet I feel them there!
None have been hurt in flesh or bone,
But all are into panic thrown.
The sport is wholly spoiled; but this
Was what these monsters wished, I wis.

HERALD

Since unto me the Herald's task
Has been intrusted for our mask,
I watch the door with anxious care,
Lest aught amiss should unaware
Into our festive circle steal.
No terror for myself I feel,
But much I fear, the airy crew
Of ghosts may slip the windows through;
Nor could I, if with you they mix,
Protect you from their wizard tricks.
The dwarf looked ominous to begin,
And now a swarm comes pouring in.
What every figure means, am I
In duty bound to signify;
But how may I expound to you
What is to me a mystery too?
To clear things up, assist me all!
What's this, winds yonder through the hall?
A gorgeous chariot sweeps along,
Drawn by a team of four-in-hand;
And yet it does not part the throng—
I see no crowd about it stand.
Far off with many-coloured beams
It shines, while flitting round it gleams
The light of many a starry zone,
As from a magic-lantern thrown.
On, on, it snorts with giant force!
Room there!   I shudder!

BOY-CHARIOTEER

Stay your course!
Ye coursers, fold your wings!   Obey
The bridle's well-accustomed sway.
Rein in yourselves, whilst you I rein;
When I incite, dash on amain.
Unto these halls due honour show.
Look how the people, row on row,
Keep gathering round with wondering eyes!
Speak, herald, speak, in proper wise,

Before we go, our name to tell,
And who and what we are as well;
For we are allegories—so
Us you are clearly bound to know!

HERALD

Name you I cannot.   Easier far
It were to paint you as you are.

BOY-CHARIOTEER

Essay it then.

HERALD

That you are fair
And young withal, one must declare;
A boy half grown; yet women fain
Would see you fully grown.   'Tis plain,
You'll prove in time a pretty rake,
And with the sex rare havoc make.

BOY-CHARIOTEER

Not badly said.   Proceed! and see,
If of the riddle you can find the key.

HERALD

Dark flashing eyes, locks black as night, and there
A jewelled circlet 'mid the blackness glowing;
A robe that falls in graceful folds you wear,
Down from the shoulders to the buskins flowing,
With purple hem, and fringe of tissue rare.
Rail at you for a girl one fairly might;
Yet even now, for weal or woe, you'd be
For girls themselves an object of delight;
They'd give you lessons in love's A B C.

BOY-CHARIOTEER

And he, this stately form, that gleams
Enthroned this car of mine within?

HERALD

A very king, rich, mild, he seems,
Whose grace it were rare luck to win.
Nought's left for him to wish for here;
Quick to descry, where aught is wanting,
Wealth, state, to him are far less dear
Than the pure joy of giving, granting.

BOY-CHARIOTEER

To stop with this will not avail;
You must describe in more detail.

HERALD

What's worthiest words never drew.
But the broad healthy visage, fine
Full mouth, the cheeks of ruddy hue,
That 'neath the jewelled turban shine,
His flowing vestments' rich array—
What of his bearing shall I say?
In him one used to rule I see.

BOY-CHARIOTEER

Plutus, the God of Wealth, is he.
He comes himself in regal state;
The Emperor's need of him is great.

HERALD

Now of yourself the What and How proclaim!

BOY-CHARIOTEER

I am Profusion, Poesy my name!
The poet I, who works to noblest ends,
When his best wealth he most profusely spends.
Rich beyond measure, too, I am; and dare
Myself in this with Plutus to compare.
To dance and revel I give charm and soul,
And what he lacks, dispense without control.

HERALD

This vaunt becomes you well; but we
Some of these arts of yours would see.

BOY-CHARIOTEER

I snap my fingers! There! And lo!
Around the car what gleam and glow!
Out leaps a string of pearls!
                              [*Goes on snapping his fingers.*
                   And here
Are golden clasps for throat and ear!
Combs, too, and heaps of diadems,
And rings ablaze with rarest gems!
Small flames, too, here and there I scatter;
Kindle or not, is no great matter.

HERALD

How these good people snatch and rush!
The giver's self they almost crush.
'Tis like a dream, the way gems fly
Off from his fingers, far and nigh.
But lo! another juggling sleight!
A sorry profit gets the wight
From what so eagerly he clutched;
The gift slips off as soon as touched!
The pearls unstring themselves, and all
About his hand cockchafers crawl.
He shakes them off, poor fool, and straight
They buzz and flutter round his pate.
What others thought a solid prize
Turns into flighty butterflies.
For all his promises so fine,
The knave gives only golden shine!

BOY-CHARIOTEER

Masks, I observe, you indicate full well,
But to proclaim what lives within the shell
Is no part of a herald's courtly task;
That doth a keener insight ask.
But wrangle I abhor; my lord, and king,
To thee I turn my speech and questioning.
                                   [*Turning to* PLUTUS.
Didst not to me, their course to guide,
This fourfold fiery team confide?
Drive I not well, thou standing o'er me?
Do I not reach the goals thou set'st before me?
Have I not known, with daring sweep
The palm for thee to win and keep?
Often for thee as I have fought,
When have I ever failed?   And now,
If the proud laurel decks thy brow,
Have not my brain and hand the chaplet wrought?

PLUTUS

If need there be that I my tribute pay,
'Soul of my soul art thou!' I gladly say.
Thy acts are echoes of my mind and heart;
Far, far more wealthy than myself thou art.
As guerdon for thy services, I rate
The bays more high than all my crowns of state.
Then hear me all aloud declare my mind,
'My darling son, in thee great joy I find!'

BOY-CHARIOTEER (*to the crowd*)

The greatest gifts my hand shakes out;
See! I have sent them all about.
On this, and now on yonder head
A flamelet glows, which I have shed;
From one it to another leaps,
Slips off from this, by that it keeps;
Now here and there it shoots on high,
And flames with short-lived brilliancy,
But, with the most, burns sad and low,
And then goes out before they know.

CHATTER OF WOMEN

The man, up yonder on his feet,
Beyond all question is a cheat.
Crouching behind is Hanswurst, so
By thirst and hunger wasted low,
As never Hanswurst was before.
Pinch him, he will not feel it sore.

THE STARVELING

Avaunt, ye odious womenkind!
I know I'm never to your mind.
Whilst dames their households overhauled,
Then I was AVARITIA called:
Then flourished in our homes content,
For much came in, out nothing went!
My care was all for chest and bin:
Folks tell us now, this was a sin!
But as the wife in these last days
Has quite given up those saving ways,
And, as all evil payers are,
Has more desires than cash by far,
Her husband has a deal to bear;
Debts crowd upon him everywhere.
All that she earns by spinning goes
In treating swains, or in fine clothes;
Richly she feeds, drinks largely too
With paramours, a baneful crew.
So on gold's charms I fondlier feed;
And now, turned masculine, I am GREED.

LEADER OF THE WOMEN

Dragon with dragon may pinch and spare;
This is all lying juggling stuff!
He comes to rouse the men, and they're
Already troublesome enough.

WOMEN (*en masse*)

The scarecrow!   Box his ears!   What, dare
To threaten us!   As if he could
Grown women with his rubbish scare!
The dragons are but paste and wood:
Come, let's go at him, squeeze and tear!

HERALD

Now, by my staff! keep order there!
Yet for my help there scarce is need;
See how the monsters grim unfurl—
As swift the flying crowds recede—
Great wings, that round them wave and swirl!
The dragons snort, and gnash in ire
Their scaly jaws, out-belching fire:
The crowd has fled, the place is clear.
                    [PLUTUS *descends from the chariot.*
How kingly all his movements are!
The dragons at his nod draw near;
They lift the coffer from the car,
And Gold and Greed on it appear.
There at his feet it stands; but how
The thing was done, I marvel now.

PLUTUS (*to the Charioteer*)

Now from the charge, that all too heavy lay
On thee, thou'rt free: to thine own sphere away!
Here it is not; wild, tawdry, full of din,
Is the fantastic world here hems us in.
Only where thou through clear untroubled air
Look'st with untroubled eye—there, only there,
Where nought delights thee but the good, the fair,
Art thou thyself, canst move with soul elate.
To solitude then go!   There thine own world create!

BOY-CHARIOTEER

So as an envoy still myself I prize,
Charged with a noble mission from above;
So thee, as bound to me by nearest ties
Of kindred and of sympathy, I love.
Where thou art, there is plenty; and where I,
All feel their souls enriched, their pulse beat high.
Ofttime from side to side men's thoughts incline;
Shall they to thee or me themselves resign?
Thy votaries may in idlesse rest, 'tis true,
But mine have always endless work to do.

Nor may I work in secret and in shade;
Let me but breathe, at once I am betrayed.
Farewell!   Thou grantest what is bliss to me;
But back again I at a word will be.   [*Exit as he came.*

PLUTUS

Now it is time to set the treasures free.
With the Herald's rod I strike the bolts, and lo!
The chest flies open!   In steel caldrons, see,
Red golden blood heaves, bubbling, to and fro!
Hard by are ornaments, ring, chain, and crown;
It swells as 'twould engulf and melt them down.

ALTERNATING EXCLAMATIONS OF THE CROWD

See here! see there!   How treasures brim!
The chest is full up to the rim!
Vessels of gold melt down, and whole
Rouleaux of gold by dozens roll.
Ducats leap out, new-minted, bright—
Oh, how my heart leaps at the sight!
All it desired I see, and more;
There they go sprawling on the floor!
They're offered you.   Quick!   On them swoop!
If you'd be rich, you've but to stoop.
We, quick as lightning, shall the great
Chest to ourselves appropriate.

HERALD

What would ye, fools?   Are you possessed?
'Tis but a masquerading jest:
To-night we looked for nothing more.
Think you, we'd give you gold galore?
Why truly, on occasions such
Counters for you are quite too much.
Blockheads! with you a quaint device
Grows fact substantial in a trice.
What's fact to you—you, always fain
To flounder in delusions vain?
O Plutus, send this rabble rout,
I pray thee, to the right about!

PLUTUS

Handy for that your staff would be;
For some few moments lend it me.
I dip it in the red heat; there!
And now, ye maskers, have a care!

What sparkling, sputtering, in the pot!
The staff's already fiery hot.
Whoever comes too near shall be
Scorched by it quite remorselessly,
Look out!   Now is my round begun!

CRIES AND TUMULT

Oh, woe! oh, woe! we're all undone!
Let him escape, escape who may.
You there behind, back, back, I say!
Hot sparks fly out into my face.
On me the red-hot staff falls heavy:
We're all and each in piteous case!
Back, back, ye masquerading bevy!
Back, back!   'Tis madness to come nigh!
Oh, had I wings, away I'd fly!

PLUTUS

Back has the surging throng been thrust;
And no one has been hurt, I trust.
In sheer dismay
The crowd give way:
Still, as a guarantee for order, we
Will draw a circle none can see.

HERALD

'Twas nobly done!   A power so sage
As thine must my best thanks engage.

PLUTUS

Still, friend, be patient.   There will be
Tumult in plenty presently.

GREED

A man may round him here with pleasure glance,
If meetings of this kind his fancy suit,
For women always are well in advance,
When there be shows or junketings on foot.
I'm not yet quite used up, not quite pumped dry
I like a pretty woman with the best;
And, as to-night it costs me nothing, I
Will go a-wooing with especial zest.
Yet as, in such a crowd as we have here,
All that one says may fail to reach the ear,
I'll try, and, as I hope too, with success,
In pantomime my meaning to express.

Hand, foot, and gesture will not do alone,
So I must try some cantrip of my own.
I'll treat the gold as though 'twere moistened clay,
For we may turn this metal any way.

HERALD

The meagre fool, what is he at?
Humour in a scarecrow like that!
The gold, he kneads it into dough;
Soft 'neath his fingers it doth grow,
But, squeeze and turn it how he will,
The mass remains quite shapeless still.
He to the women turns, but they
All scream, and try to get away,
And show he'll ne'er be in their books.
There's mischief in the rascal's looks.
I fear, his lickerish tooth he'll sate,
Though he decorum violate.
Not to speak out were sore offence;
Give me my staff to drive him hence!

PLUTUS

He dreams not of what coming dangers loom.
Let him pursue his pranks a little longer;
For his mad capers there will be no room;
Though law be strong, necessity is stronger.
    [*Enter Fauns, Satyrs, Nymphs, etc., in attendance upon
    Pan, and heralding his approach.*

TUMULT AND SONG

From mountain-height and forest-dell
The savage crew with shout and yell
Sweep on, and stay them no one can;
They celebrate their mighty Pan.
They know what none else know, and fling
Themselves into the vacant ring.

PLUTUS

You and your mighty Pan, I know you well,
How bold the step you've taken here can tell:
Full well I know what's known to none beside,
So throw our narrow bounds here open wide.
Good luck attend you, even to overflowing!
Great marvels may anon befall.
They know not whither they are going;
They have not looked ahead at all.

WILD SONG

Ye butterflies, with gewgaws decked,
A rough and rugged hand expect.
With leaps and bounds they come apace,
A stalwart and a sturdy race.

FAUNS

We are Fauns, and we
Dance merrily;
Oak-wreaths we wear
In our crispèd hair,
And out from our curly head an ear,
Sharpened to finest point, doth peer;
Our noses are stumpy, our faces flat,
But we lose not woman's goodwill for that;
The fairest she, if a Faun advance
His paw, will scarcely refuse to dance.

SATYR

The Satyr next comes bounding in,
With hoof of goat and wizened shin—
Both sinewy, of course, and thin!
To gaze around from mountain-heights,
Like the wild chamois, him delights.
There in the free air bounding wild,
He views with scorn man, woman, child,
Who, 'mid the low vales' smoke and steam,
Deem fondly they are living too;
Whilst he, unfettered and supreme,
Reigns sole that upper region through.

GNOMES

A pigmy troop comes tripping now,
Not two by two, but anyhow;
In mossy garb, with lamplets lit,
Swiftly they each through other flit,
Each working for himself, and so
They swarm like fireflies to and fro—
Now here, now there, and all intent
Upon the task whereto they're bent.
To the 'Good People' near related,
As rock-chirurgeons celebrated,
We cup the lofty hills, we drain
The ore from every teeming vein;

'Good luck!' as greeting cheers us, while
The metals up in heaps we pile.
'Tis all meant for a worthy end.
All truly good men we befriend;
Yet gold we to the light reveal,
That men may pimp with it and steal,
And steel to tyrants proud be lent,
Who are on wholesale murder bent.
These three commandments who shall slight,
Of all the rest makes very light.
But this is not our fault; so you
Should have, like us, forbearance too.

GIANTS

The Wild Men we are called, and strange
To none who know the Harzberg range;
Of giant bulk, unclad, and strong
As men of yore, we tramp along,
A pine-tree stem in our right hand,
Around our loins a padded band.
With leaf and bough for apron barred;
The Pope has no such bodyguard.

CHORUS OF NYMPHS

(They surround the great Pan)

He too comes here!
All unto man
In this earth's sphere
Is imaged clear
In mighty Pan.
Ye merriest of heart, advance,
And around him wheel in joyous dance;
For, being grave, but also good,
He'd have men be of cheerful mood.
Even 'neath the azure-vaulted sky
He watches with unsleeping eye:
But brooks for him low murmurs keep,
And soft winds cradle him to sleep,
And, when at noon he 'gins to drowse,
Stirs not a leaf upon the boughs;
Plants, breathing health from fairest blooms,
On the hushed air exhale perfumes;
The Nymph disports no more, but, where
She stood, drops off in slumber there.

But if, by sudden anger stirred,
His voice, his mighty voice, is heard
Like thunder, or wild ocean's swell,
Which way to fly, no man can tell;
Brave hosts are scattered in dismay,
And heroes quail in mid *mêlée*.
Then honour give where honour's due;
Hail him who led us here to you!

DEPUTATION OF GNOMES
(*To the great Pan*)

Where rich ore lies, and, brightly shining,
  Through rocky fissures thread-like steals,
The rod alone, by its divining,
  The labyrinthine maze reveals.

In troglodytic fashion now
  Our home in sunless caves we make,
And in the sunshine pure dost thou
  Deal treasures forth for us to take.

Hard by to us has been revealed
  A vein of wondrous breadth and scope,
Which promises with ease to yield
  What to attain we scarce might hope.

To make it sure thou hast the power—
  Then subject it to thy commands;
To all mankind a priceless dower
  Grows every treasure in thy hands.

PLUTUS (*to the* HERALD)

All base misgivings we must cast away,
And with composure meet come what come may.
Erst thou hast shown a firm courageous soul.
But something terrible will soon fall out,
That present time and after-time will doubt;
So write it duly in thy protocol.

HERALD
(*Grasping the staff, which* PLUTUS *holds in his hand.*)

The dwarfs lead great Pan soft and slow
To where the fount of fire doth glow;
It seethes up from the abyss below,

Then down to depths unseen sinks back,
And grim the wide mouth stands and black.
Again fierce flames flash out on high—
The great Pan stands complacent by,
Joying to see such wondrous sight—
And pearl-foam sparkles left and right.
How can he trust himself so near?
He stoops, into the chasm to peer—
And now his beard falls in: and he,
With chin so smooth, who may he be?
His hand conceals his face from view.
Now doth a great mishap ensue.
The beard takes fire, flies back again,
And wreath, head, breast, all blaze up too;
So joy is turned to fear and pain!
The crowd rush to his aid, but none
Escapes the spreading flames, not one;
And, as they flash and dart about,
Fresh fire on every hand breaks out;
While, netted in the burning maze,
A troop of maskers is ablaze.
But hark! a cry, that scatters fear
From mouth to mouth, from ear to ear!
O night, with endless sorrow fraught,
On us what anguish hast thou brought!
To-morrow's dawn will tidings bring,
That every heart with grief shall wring.
Still from all sides I hear the cry,
'The Emperor is in agony!'
Too true, alas! the news unmeet!
The Emperor's burning, and his suite.
Accursed be they beguiled him, wound
With leaves and resinous branches round,
In roistering guise to brawl it here,
And spread disaster far and near!
O youth, youth, wilt thou never draw
Around thy joys a prudent line?
O greatness, wilt thou ne'er with law
And reason boundless power combine?
Now to the wood the flames have spread,
Their forkèd tongues shoot high o'erhead,
And round the wooden rafters play;
Nought can the conflagration stay!
Brimmed is the measure of our grief;
I know not who may bring relief.
Imperial splendour, rich and bright,
Sinks down to ashes in a night.

PLUTUS

Enough of terror and dismay!
Now let help come into play.
Strike, staff of power, until the ground
Quake and reverberate the sound!
Thou wide and mantling air, fill full
Thyself with breezes blowing cool!
Teeming streaks of vaporous mist,
Come, and round us coil and twist;
Close the fiery ferment over!
Cloudlets, drizzling, dropping, drenching,
Dew-distilling, gently hover,
Everywhere the danger quenching,
Turning by your soothing might
Flames now laden with affright,
Into harmless rosy light!
When spirits threaten us with ill,
'Tis time to use our magic skill.

PLEASURE-GARDEN. MORNING SUN

The EMPEROR, *his Court, male and female.* FAUST, MEPHISTO-
PHELES, *dressed quietly and becomingly in the prevailing
fashion. Both kneel.*

FAUST

Dost thou forgive our trick, sir, with the fire?

EMPEROR (*beckoning to him to rise*)

Such jests, and many too, I much desire.
Sudden I found me in a sphere of flame;
Pluto himself, methought, I then became.
Girt by thick night a cavern round me lay,
Red-hot with fire. From many a chasm and bay
Wild whirling flames by myriads ascended,
And in an arching vault their flashing blended.
Up to the topmost dome they rose, and crossed,
For ever kindling and for ever lost.
Far far along, 'midst columns all aglow,
I saw long lines of people moving slow.
In a wide circle round me then they drew,
And made obeisance, as they always do:
Some of my Court I spied within the ring,
And seemed of thousand Salamanders king.

MEPHISTOPHELES

And so you are; for every element
To own your sovereignty is well content.
Fire thou hast proved obedient; in the sea
Plunge, where its billows wildest, maddest be,
And scarcely shalt thou tread the pearl-strewn floor,
Ere springs a stately dome to arch it o'er;
Waves of pale green, with purple edged, shall there
Sway up and down, to rear a mansion fair
Round thee, the central point.   A palace home
Attends on thee wherever thou dost roam.
The very walls are all alive, and flow
With swiftness as of arrows to and fro.
Up to the strange soft sheen sea-wonders throng—
They dare not enter in, but shoot along;
Bright gold-scaled dragons round thee sport and swim;
Gapes the grim shark, and thou canst laugh at him.
Gay as thy present Court may be, and bright,
No throng like this has ever met thy sight.
Yet art thou not cut off from beauty there:
To that superb abode, so fresh, so fair,
The Nereids, peering curiously, draw nigh—
The young ones, amorous as fish, and shy,
The old ones sage: soon Thetis learns thy haunts,
And hand and lip to her new Peleus grants.
Anon thy seat on high Olympus' crest——

EMPEROR

Those airy regions, you may let them rest.
Quite soon enough one has to mount that throne.

MEPHISTOPHELES

And earth, my liege, already is thine own.

EMPEROR

What lucky chance has brought thee hither straight
From the Arabian Nights?   If thou canst mate
With Scheherezade in inventive skill,
Take this, the highest proof of my goodwill—
Be still at hand, when worries of the day
Pain and dispirit me, as oft they may.

MARSHAL (*entering hurriedly*)

Your Highness, never did I think to live,
Tidings of such supreme good luck to give

As these, which to thy presence thus
Send me in transports rapturous.
Every outstanding bill is squared,
The usurer's ruthless claws are pared.
I from the pangs of hell am free;
In heaven things could not brighter be.

COMMANDER-IN-CHIEF (*follows hurriedly*)

Arrears paid off to the last sou,
The army's all sworn in of new;
The trooper feels his blood aflame,
And wench and tapster make their game.

EMPEROR

How is't you breathe so freely now?
Furrows no longer seam your brow.
What makes you here so swiftly run?

TREASURER (*entering*)

Ask those, sir, who the work have done!

FAUST

'Tis meet, the Chancellor the facts should state.

CHANCELLOR

In my old days my happiness how great!
Hear, then, and see this fateful scroll, for this
Has turned our woe and wailing into bliss.   [*Reads.*
'Be it to all whom it concerneth known,
This note is worth a thousand crowns alone,
And, for a guarantee, the wealth untold,
Throughout the empire buried, it doth hold.
Means are on foot this treasure bare to lay,
And out of it the guarantee to pay.'

EMPEROR

Crime I surmise, some monstrous fraud.   Oh, shame!
Who dared to counterfeit the Emperor's name?
Has he been brought to punishment condign?

TREASURER

Reflect!   That note, sir, thou thyself didst sign
Only last night.   Thou didst as Pan appear;
The Chancellor said to thee—we standing near—
'A few strokes of thy pen, and so thou'lt seal—
This revel's crowning joy—thy people's weal!'

These strokes thou mad'st, which were ere morning-tide
By thousand hands in thousands multiplied.
That all alike the benefit might reap,
We stamped the whole impression in a heap;
Tens, thirties, fifties, hundreds, off they flew—
You can't conceive the good they were to do.
Look at your town—'twas mouldering and half dead—
Now all alive, and full of lustihead!
High as thy name stood with the world, somehow
'Twas never looked so kindly on as now.
The lists of applicants fill to excess;
This scrip is rushed at as a thing to bless.

EMPEROR

My people take it for good gold, you say?
In Court, in camp, it passes for full pay?
Strange! strange!   Yet I must let the matter drop.

MARSHAL

'Twere hopeless now the flying leaves to stop;
With lightning speed they spread throughout the land.
The money-changers' doors wide open stand;
They cash the notes with silver and with gold,
And even allow a premium, I am told.
Thence they reach vendors of meat, bread, and drinks:
One-half the world of feasting only thinks;
Whilst in its bran-new clothes the other struts—
Briskly the tailor sews, the mercer cuts.
Toasting thy health in taverns never bates,
And all is roast and boil and clattering plates.

MEPHISTOPHELES

Who on the terraced walks alone shall stray,
Drops on some fair one, clad in rich array,
Who from behind proud peacock-fan will smile
On him, with eye on these same notes the while,
Which quickly will love's crowning favours gain,
Whilst wit and eloquence may plead in vain.
Men won't be teased with purse or scrip, when they
Can in their bosoms slip a note away,
To mate there snugly with a billet-doux.
Priests lodge them in their breviaries, too;
Soldiers, to move more freely, turn their coins
To notes, and of the waist-belt ease their loins.
Pardon, your Majesty, if what I state
From this great work may seem to derogate.

FAUST

The superflux of wealth that, heap on heap,
All o'er thy realm in earth lies buried deep,
Is practically lost.   Thought cannot cast
A limit wide enough for wealth so vast,
And fancy in her wildest flight may strain
To picture it, yet find the effort vain;
But spirits, meet enigmas dark to face,
Dare on the boundless boundless faith to place.

MEPHISTOPHELES

Paper like this, instead of pearls and gold,
Is handy, for we know then what we hold;
No need to change or chaffer!   Men at will
In love may revel, drink of wine their fill:
If coin they lack, the changer's prompt with it;
And when coin fails, you've but to dig a bit.
Chalice and chain to auction must be brought;
But this good paper, cashed upon the spot,
Puts sceptics, who dared scoff at us, to shame.
People, once used to it, nought else will name.
So henceforth, all the imperial regions round,
Will jewels, gold, and paper-cash abound.

EMPEROR

This mighty boon our empire owes to you;
Great as the service, be the guerdon too!
Our kingdom's nether soil, be that your care.
Who may so well protect the treasures there?
That vast well-tended hoard you understand,
And, if men dig, 'tis you must give command.
Now, masters of our Treasury, embrace;
Wear, and with pride, the honours of your place,
Where, linked in happy union, all shall know,
The world above blends with the world below.

TREASURER

'Twixt us no strife, however slight, shall stir:
I for a colleague love your sorcerer. [*Exit with* FAUST.

EMPEROR

As I dispense my gifts among you now,
Let each the use he'll put them to avow.

PAGE (*as he takes the gift*)
I am for sports, and mirth, and junketings.

ANOTHER PAGE (*même jeu*)
Straightway I'll buy my sweetheart chains and rings.

LORD OF THE BEDCHAMBER (*même jeu*)
My cellar, with the choicest wine I'll stock it.

SECOND LORD (*même jeu*)
The dice already rattle in my pocket.

BANNERET (*musingly*)
I'll free my castle and my grounds from debt.

ANOTHER BANNERET (*même jeu*)
Aside with other treasures this I'll set.

EMPEROR

I hoped for joy, brave heart, fresh enterprise;
But, knowing you, one might your course surmise.
Full well I note, howe'er your coffers fill,
What you have been, you will continue still.

FOOL (*advancing*)
You're scattering favours; give me some, I pray.

EMPEROR
Alive again!   You'll drink them all away.

FOOL
These magic leaves, I cannot make them out.

EMPEROR
Quite so; you'll make bad use of them, no doubt.

FOOL
There others drop; what, sir, am I to do?

EMPEROR
Just pick them up.   They're what were meant for you.
[*Exit.*

FOOL

Five thousand crowns! and all for me?

MEPHISTOPHELES

                                        How then!
Thou paunch upon two legs, got up again?

FOOL

Not the first time, but ne'er such luck I've met.

MEPHISTOPHELES

So great your joy, it puts you in a sweat.

FOOL

Look here!   And is this money's worth?

MEPHISTOPHELES

                                        Yes, knave!
You'll get for it what throat and belly crave.

FOOL

Can I buy farm, house, cattle, then, with this?

MEPHISTOPHELES

Of course!   Just bid!   'Twill never come amiss.

FOOL

What! castle, forest-chase, and fish-stream?

MEPHISTOPHELES

                                        Good!
I'd like to see you a great lord, I would!

FOOL

This night I'll sleep within my own domain!   [*Exit.*

MEPHISTOPHELES (*solus*)

Who still can doubt, our fool doth bear a brain?

A DARK GALLERY [1]

FAUST, MEPHISTOPHELES

MEPHISTOPHELES

Why drag me to this gloomy corridor?
Within there is there not enough of sport,
For jest and trick not ample scope, and more,
Among the motley butterflies of court?

FAUST

Tush, tush!   Time was when you were cap in hand,
Ready to come and go at my command;
But now your only aim, I see,
Is how to break your faith with me.
To act, however, I am pressed.
Marshal and Chamberlain won't let me rest:
The Emperor wants, and that with haste,
Paris and Helena before him placed.
These paragons of man and woman he
Has set his mind just as they lived to see.
Quick, to the task!   My word I dare not break.

MEPHISTOPHELES

Such promise you were worse than mad to make.

FAUST

You have forgotten, mate, to what
Your clever sleights conduct us; we
Have made him rich, and after that
We must amuse him *à tout prix.*

[1] Commentators never tire of the 'Mothers,' a piece of mystification probably meant to baffle us. The name (but only that) comes from Plutarch. To call up the shade of Helena, the ideal of beauty, Faust must descend to the realm of the Mothers and touch a tripod there with a key provided for him by Mephistopheles. It will then follow him and enable him to produce Paris and Helena as the Emperor requires. What Goethe had principally in mind was no doubt the Platonic realm of ideas, the eternal patterns of all things. He was probably also thinking of his own notion of 'Urphenomene,' the archetypal forms which nature seemed to him to elaborate in plants and animals. It has been suggested that his own experience of poetic creation is also referred to. To write genuine poetry, the poet must reach down to the depths of the mind, an unfathomable region like this realm of the Mothers. There is something mysterious about the process, it is a kind of magic too. What Faust succeeds in calling up on his return has only the appearance of life. He cannot clasp this Helena in his arms and keep her. The function of Act II in the plot, so far as this Second Part has a plot, is to explain the appearance in Act III of a Helena who is apparently of flesh and blood.

MEPHISTOPHELES

No sooner said, you think, than done?
This task is a much harder one,
Than ever we ventured on before.
You would pierce to a region of wonders vast,
And recklessly run up a further score
Of debts you'll be forced to pay off at last.
You think 'tis as easy a task for me
To conjure up Helena, at my will,
As it was the imperial treasury
With flimsy, fairy bank-notes to fill.
Witches, imps, goitred dwarfs, and sprites,
I can turn to all uses, and place in all plights,
But, though not to be sneezed at, our ladies below
As heroines never will do to show.

FAUST

The same old song!   The same old introduction!
There's nothing but uncertainties with you:
You are the sire of all sorts of obstruction,
And must at every turn be bribed anew!
You grumble.   Still you'll do it, I know well,
And fetch them here, ere we ten words can say.

MEPHISTOPHELES

These heathen gentry are not in my way;
They live within their own peculiar hell;
And yet there is a way!

FAUST

On with your tale!

MEPHISTOPHELES

I'm loath the higher mysteries to unveil.
There are goddesses, beings of might supernal,
That sit alone, each on a throne,
In the solitudes eternal.
Round them space is not, and time still less;
To speak of them even embarrasses.
These are THE MOTHERS!

FAUST (*starting*)

The Mothers!

MEPHISTOPHELES

Afeared?

FAUST

The Mothers! the Mothers!   That sounds so weird!

MEPHISTOPHELES

And weird it is.   Divinities, to you
Mortals unknown—we're loath to name them, too.
Through depths unplumbed you may their haunts invade:
'Tis all your fault, that we require their aid.

FAUST

And whither lies the road?

MEPHISTOPHELES

Road there is none
To what has been, and must untrodden still be;
There is no road to what was never won
By mortal prayer or vow, nor ever will be.
Art ready?   Neither bolt nor bar is there,
To hinder thy advance, but everywhere
Shalt thou be drifted by the empty air.
Canst thou conceive and fully comprehend
A void and isolation without end?

FAUST

Such speeches 'tis idle with me to try!
They're of the Witches-Kitchen kind,
And smack of a time that is long gone by.
Was I not doomed to mingle with mankind?
To learn and teach, that all that they possess
Is mere vacuity and emptiness?
By reason schooled, if as I saw I spoke,
Strife and denial round me roared and broke.
Turn where I might, still baffled, thwarted, I
To wilds and solitudes was forced to fly,
Till, at my very loneliness aghast,
I gave myself up to the devil at last.

MEPHISTOPHELES

And with the ocean if thou wert contending,
And round thee heaved a limitless expanse,
Yet there, though death were in each wave impending,
Thou'dst see before thee wave on wave advance.

There something thou shouldst see; see dolphins leap
O'er the green hollows of the glassy deep,
See clouds sweep on, and sun, and moon, and star,
But nothing shalt thou see in that great void afar;
Thou shalt not hear thy very footfall pace,
Nor light on one substantial resting-place.

FAUST

The best of mystagogues you rival quite,
That e'er deluded trustful neophyte!
But you reverse the rule, dismissing me
To gain both strength and skill from blank vacuity.
You use me like the cat, to scratch for you
The chestnuts from the coals.   Well, well, go to!
We'll probe this business; and I hope I shall
In what you say is Nought discover All.

MEPHISTOPHELES

Before we part, your courage I commend!
The devil, I see, you fully comprehend.
Here, take this key!

FAUST

Thin tiny bauble?   No!

MEPHISTOPHELES

Take hold of it, before you slight it so.

FAUST

It grows within my hand!   It flames, it lightens!

MEPHISTOPHELES

Mark it but well, you'll find its virtue brightens!
This key will how to shape your course instruct you.
Follow it, and to THE MOTHERS 'twill conduct you.

FAUST (shudders)

Again that word!   It strikes me like a blow.
What is there in that word to thrill me so?

MEPHISTOPHELES

Art thou a pedant, at new words to scare?
Familiar phrases only canst thou bear?
Nothing, however weird or strange, should make
One so long used to mightiest marvels quake.

FAUST

I covet not an adamantine heart.
This shuddering awe is man's divinest part.
Howe'er the world may dull our feelings, still
At what is vast and mystical we thrill.

MEPHISTOPHELES

Sink, then!   I might as well say, Mount!   'Tis quite
The same.   From all that is take flight
Into the void and viewless Infinite
Of visionary dreams, and revel so
'Midst phantoms of the ages long ago!
Like clouds they flit and waver.   In thy hand
Swing high the key!   Thy body must not touch it.

FAUST (*with enthusiasm*)

'Tis well!   I feel new strength, as thus I clutch it,
And for the mighty task my breast expand.

MEPHISTOPHELES

A flaming tripod shall proclaim, thou hast
Into the nethermost abysses passed.
Its gleam THE MOTHERS unto thee will show.
Some sit, some stand, some wander to and fro;
Each as it haps; strange shapes of every kind,
The eternal pastime of the eternal mind,
Circle them round with every form of being.
Thee they behold not, phantasms only seeing.
See that thou quail not, for the peril's great,
But to the tripod go thou forward straight,
And touch it with the key!
    [FAUST *assumes a resolute and commanding attitude
        with the key.*
                                    Ay, that will do!
It will attend thee like a servant true,
And with it thou, if fortunate, shalt rise
To earth again, ay, fast as fancy flies.
And, it once here, thou mayest by its might
Evoke those famed heroic forms from Night:
The foremost who has e'er achieved such feat;
And when it is done, and thy task complete,
Forthwith, by sleights of magic, timely suited,
The incense smoke to gods will be transmuted.

FAUST

And now what else?

MEPHISTOPHELES

              Thy spirit downward bend;
Sink with a stamp, and, stamping, reascend!
             [FAUST *stamps, and sinks into the ground.*
Now, if the key its power with him should lack?
I'm curious to see if he comes back.

A HALL BRILLIANTLY ILLUMINATED

EMPEROR, PRINCES, COURTIERS, *moving up and down*

CHAMBERLAIN (*to* MEPHISTOPHELES)

You still are owing us the phantom-play.
The Emperor grows impatient.   Quick, I pray!

MARSHAL

He asked about it not an hour ago.
You must not keep his Majesty waiting so.

MEPHISTOPHELES

My comrade is upon this business gone;
He knows the way to set about it;
This very moment, never doubt it,
He's hard at work to push it on.
Shut in his room from vulgar gaze,
No ordinary sleights he tries,
For he that would such peerless beauty raise,
Must use the highest art, the magic of the wise.

MARSHAL

What arts he uses we don't care a pin—
Sir, sir, the Emperor wants you to begin.

BLONDE (*to* MEPHISTOPHELES)

One word, sir!   My complexion now is clear,
But in the tiresome summer 'tis not so!
A hundred freckles then from ear to ear,
Quite horrid, tawny things, begin to show.
A remedy!

MEPHISTOPHELES

That such a blonde—'tis hard!—
Should every May be spotted like the pard!
Take spawn of frogs, and tongues of toads new killed,
At the moon's fullest craftily distilled;
This lotion, when she wanes, apply: the spring
May come, you'll find the spots have taken wing.

BRUNETTE

You're in request.   Here's quite a mob advancing.
Oh, sir, a remedy!   A frost-bit foot
Prevents me both from walking and from dancing;
I can't even curtsey gracefully, to boot.

MEPHISTOPHELES

Allow me, child, to press you with my foot!

BRUNETTE

That's very well 'twixt lovers in their sports.

MEPHISTOPHELES

A vast deal more a tread from me imports.
Like draws to like, as web combines with woof,
Thus foot heals foot, limb limb.   Come close!   And, mind!
You need not think of answering in kind.

BRUNETTE

Oh! oh!   It burns!   'Twas like a horse's hoof,
It stamped so hard.

MEPHISTOPHELES

You of my cure have proof.
Now you may dance as much as e'er you please,
And your swain's foot beneath the table squeeze.

LADY (*pushing forward*)

Make way for me!   Too heavy are my woes.
My inmost heart is racked by maddening throes!
He lived but in my looks till yesterday,
Now he woos her, and turns from me away.

MEPHISTOPHELES

'Tis very sad! But I will set you right.
Up to his side you must contrive to steal.
This charcoal take, and draw it, as you may,
Across his sleeves, cloak, shoulder, and the wight
Shall sweet remorse within his bosom feel.
Then swallow off the charcoal—but no sips
Of water or of wine must cross your lips—
And at your door he sighs this very night.

LADY

It is not poison?

MEPHISTOPHELES (offended)

Honour where 'tis due!
For such charcoal you must go many a mile.
'Twas gathered from a certain funeral pile,
Of which we raked the ashes through and through.

PAGE

I'm mad in love; they say, I'm not full grown.

MEPHISTOPHELES (aside)

This sort of thing how am I to endure?   [To the PAGE.
The very young ones you must let alone.
You'll find admirers 'mong the more mature.
                                      [Others press round him.
Still others coming! Here's a fine to-do!
I must resort to truth, to help me through.
The worst of helps! But no escape I see.
O Mothers, Mothers! set but Faustus free!   [Looks round.
Already they are lighting up the hall.
The whole Court is upon the move; and all
The motley stream in graceful order pours
Through far arcades and lengthened corridors.
Now to the old baronial hall they throng,
Scarce holds them all, wide though it be and long.
Its spacious walls are hung with tapestries rich,
And armour old on bracket and in niche.
No need of magic here, or spell, I wis:
Ghosts of themselves must haunt a place like this.

BARONIAL HALL DIMLY ILLUMINATED

The Emperor *and* Court *assembled*

HERALD

My old vocation, to announce the play,
Is by strange ghostly influence much perplexed;
I can't pretend to make things out, or say,
In such a ravelled business, what comes next.
There stand the couches ready, chairs and all,
The Emperor seated right before the wall;
Upon the tapestry he can behold
At ease the fights of the great times of old.
Round him are lords and gentlefolks reclined,
While common benches throng the space behind;
The lover, too, though ghosts are hovering near,
Has found a pleasant seat beside his dear;
And so, as all are comfortably placed,
The phantoms may appear with all convenient haste!

                                                     [Trumpets.

ASTROLOGER

Now to begin the business of the play!
Our liege lord so commands.   Ye walls, give way!
The spell and magic work to our desire,
The tapestry fades as 'twere devoured by fire;
The walls divide, and, as they backwards bend,
A stage and ample theatre disclose,
Where we shall be regaled with mystic shows;
And I to the proscenium ascend.

MEPHISTOPHELES (*popping up from the
                prompter's box*)

My skill, I trust, all here will duly prize;
The devil's rhetoric all in prompting lies,
                                [To the ASTROLOGER.
Thou, who the courses of the stars canst tell,
My whispers wilt interpret passing well.

ASTROLOGER

By magic sleight, behold before your eyes
In massive bulk an ancient temple rise!
Like Atlas, who erewhile the heavens upbore,
Stand pillars ranged in rows, a goodly store;
Lightly they hold the rocky load in air,
Two shafts like these a structure vast could bear.

ARCHITECT

That's your antique!   I don't admire the style.
'Tis a great, clumsy, over-weighted pile.
The rude's called noble, and the unwieldy grand;
Give me small shafts that far in air expand.
The pointed style exalts the soul, and nought
With such instructive influence is fraught.

ASTROLOGER

The hours the stars concede accept with awe;
Be reason chained by the magician's saw;
But keep your fancy's wing unfettered still,
To roam with noble daring where it will.
Look with your eyes at what you long to see;
It is impossible, and cannot be,
And therefore merits your credulity.
          [Faust *rises at the other side of the proscenium.*
In priestly robes, and wreathed, a wondrous man,
Who now completes what boldly he began!
A tripod rises with him from the ground,
I scent the incense shed its fumes around;
See, he prepares the noble work to bless,
And for our pageant here ensure success!

FAUST (*in a majestic style*)

In your name, Mothers, yours, who have your throne
In the infinite, and evermore alone,
Yet in communion dwell!   The forms of life
Float round you, lifeless, yet with motion rife.
What once has been, in seeming as of yore,
Flits there, for 'twill exist for evermore;
And ye apportion them, ye powers of might,
'Twixt the day's canopy and the vault of night;
Some upon life's glad stream are borne away,
While others bend to the bold wizard's sway,
Who doth to you with hand profuse unfold
What marvels each is yearning to behold!

ASTROLOGER

Scarce on the dish the golden key he lays,
When the air thickens to a dusky haze;
It coils and curls, now spreads, like clouds, about,
Contracts, expands, divides, shifts in and out.
Phantoms of power, be sure, are stirring there!
Hark! as they move, what music in the air!

With a weird charm the tones aërial thrill,
From every cloud soft melodies distil,
Each pillared shaft, the very triglyph rings,
Yea, I could swear, that all the temple sings.
The mists subside, and from the filmy air
Comes graceful forth a youth surpassing fair.

[PARIS *appears.*

Mute let me be; what need his name to show?
Paris the Fair, who, who could fail to know?

FIRST LADY

What youthful fire!   What bloom upon his brow!

SECOND LADY

As fresh and juicy as a peach, I vow!

THIRD LADY

The finely chiselled, sweetly pouting lip!

FOURTH LADY

At such a chalice you were fain to sip?

FIFTH LADY

Handsome, no doubt, but not a noble face!

SIXTH LADY

He's well enough, but sadly wanting grace.

FIRST KNIGHT

The shepherd boy, and nothing more, 'tis plain;
Of prince and courtly breeding not a grain.

SECOND KNIGHT

The lad's half naked, still he has his charms;
To judge, though, we must see him clad in arms.

FIRST LADY

He sits him down with such a gentle grace,

FIRST KNIGHT

Were not his breast a dainty resting-place?

ANOTHER LADY

He bends his arm so prettily o'er his head.

CHAMBERLAIN

Oh, shocking!   Fie!   Where was the fellow bred?

FIRST LADY

You men always find out defective points.

CHAMBERLAIN

What!   In the Emperor's presence, stretch his joints?

FIRST LADY

It's in the play.   He thinks himself alone.

CHAMBERLAIN

Even in a play good manners should be shown.

FIRST LADY

Sweet youth!   Soft slumber steals his senses o'er.

CHAMBERLAIN

'Tis perfect!   To the life!   Is that a snore?

YOUNG LADY (*in raptures*)

What perfume's this, that, with the incense mingling,
Right to the centre of my heart goes tingling?

OLDER LADY

A breath steals deep into your soul, forsooth!
It comes from him.

OLDEST LADY

It is the bloom of youth,
A rare ambrosia, bred within the boy,
Which sheds around an atmosphere of joy.

[HELENA *advances*.

MEPHISTOPHELES

So! such she was!   Yet I am fancy-free.
She's pretty, hum! but not the style for me.

ASTROLOGER

My task is ended.   Frankly I avow,
What well I feel, my task is ended now.
She comes, the ideal Fair, and though a tongue
Of fire were mine, of yore her charms were sung.
Who sees her, thenceforth is her slave confessed,
Who should possess her were too highly blessed.

FAUST

Have I still eyes?   I see, in trancèd thought,
Fair Beauty's fountain welling like a sea.
My voyage dread a glorious gain hath brought;
How blank, how dreary was the world to me!
And since my priesthood what hath it become?
Fleeting no more, nor void and wearisome!
May palsy's blight my every sense benumb,
If e'er I long for other love than thine!
The gracious form for which of old I panted,
Which in the magic glass my soul enchanted,
Was but a phantom of thy charms divine!
For thee, for thee I would expend my whole
Pent passion's force, my energies of soul,
The love, devotion, madness of my heart!

MEPHISTOPHELES

Be calm, be calm, and don't forget your part!

ELDERLY LADY

Tall, well proportioned, but her head's too small.

YOUNG LADY

Look at her foot! that's clumsiest of all!

DIPLOMATIST

Princesses just like this I've seen and know,
Methinks she's beautiful from top to toe!

COURTIER

Now to the sleeper softly doth she glide.

FIRST LADY

He young and pure—she's hideous by his side!

POET

Her beauty seems to bathe his form in light.

SECOND LADY

Endymion and Luna, pictures quite.

POET

Yes! As from heaven she comes, the goddess pale,
O'er him she bends, his breathing to inhale;
O happy boy! A kiss! Oh, bliss untold!

DUENNA

Before us all! 'Tis really too bold!

FAUST

Oh! dreadful boon for one so young!

MEPHISTOPHELES

Be still!

Let the fair phantom do whate'er it will!

COURTIER

She glides away on tiptoe; does he wake?

FIRST LADY

She looks behind; I thought she would, the snake!

COURTIER

He starts!   He's lost in wonder and amaze!

FIRST LADY

No wonder 'tis to her, that fills her gaze!

COURTIER

She turns to greet him with enchanting grace.

FIRST LADY

She teaches him his lesson, what and how.
All men are stupid dolts in such a case.
He thinks, no doubt, she never loved till now.

KNIGHT

She's perfect!   So majestic, form and face.

FIRST LADY

The wanton minx!   Her conduct's a disgrace!

PAGE

I would give worlds to occupy his place!

COURTIER

In such a coil who'd not be netted fast?

FIRST LADY

The jewel through so many hands has passed,
The setting's lost a lot of gilt since then.

ANOTHER LADY

She's been a baggage since the age of ten.

KNIGHT

Each to his taste!   But, have it if I might,
This lovely ruin would content me quite.

LITERATUS

I see her plainly, yet I don't feel clear,
That we have got the real Helen here.
Our eyes are apt to carry us astray;
To trust to what is written is my way.
There, then, I read, that she enchanted all
Troy's greybeards as she stood upon the wall;
And that is just, methinks, what here I see:
I am not young, and she enchanted me.

ASTROLOGER

A boy no more, he clasps her with a bound!
In vain she strives his ecstasy to school.
With stalwart arm he lifts her from the ground,
And now he bears her off.

FAUST

                    Audacious fool!
Thou darest?   What?   Not hear me?   Hold, I say!

MEPHISTOPHELES

It is yourself who make this phantom play!

ASTROLOGER

A word, one only! After this, we may
This pageant call—'The Rape of Helena.'

FAUST

The Rape! Do I then count for nothing here?
This key, do I not hold it in my hand?
It was my guide through the wide ocean drear
Of the dread Solitudes to solid land.
Here is firm footing! here Realities!
Here spirit may with spirits cope at ease,
And give the mighty phantom-world command.
And she who dwelt afar in grace divine,
How can she e'er be nearer to my hand?
I'll rescue her, then is she doubly mine.
The venture shall be made. Ye Mothers! ye
Must compass it! I charge ye, aid me! He,
Who her unmatched perfection once has known,
Must die, or win and wear it for his own.

ASTROLOGER

Hold, Faustus, hold! He clasps her in his arm.
A cloudy dimness gathers o'er her form.
The key, he points it to the youth, and lo!
He touches him. We're all undone. Woe, woe!
    [*Explosion.* FAUST *is dashed to the ground. The
    phantoms melt into air.*

MEPHISTOPHELES (*takes* FAUST *upon his shoulders*)

You've caught it now! With fools his lot to cast,
To trouble brings the devil's self at last!
                                    [*Darkness. Tumult.*

END OF ACT FIRST

ACT II

A HIGH-VAULTED, NARROW GOTHIC CHAMBER, FORMERLY
FAUST'S; UNALTERED [1]

MEPHISTOPHELES (*stepping out from behind a curtain. As he
lifts it up and looks back,* FAUST *is seen stretched out upon an
old-fashioned bed*).

LIE there, poor wretch! Yours is a crisis,
Will last you for a while, be sure!
The man whom Helen paralyses
Takes many a long day to cure.   [*Looks round.*
Where'er I look, amid the glimmer,
There's nothing changed the very least.
The stained-glass panes, methinks, are rather dimmer,
The cobwebs round the room somewhat increased.
The ink's dried up; the paper yellow. There
Stands everything just where it did—yes, all!
There lies the very pen, too, I declare,
Faust to the devil signed himself withal.
And of his blood a tiny droplet still
Lingers within the hollow of the quill.
The very greatest of collectors might
In so unique a specimen delight.
Ha! On the old hook, too, the old furred cloak!
Of the old time it 'minds me, when, in joke,
Of solemn saws I gave the boy his fill,
At which the youth, perhaps, is mumbling still.
Warm, cosy robe, I feel as then,
And long to get inside of you,
And play the teacher once again,
As everybody thinks he's fit to do.
How to accomplish it your scholars know;
The devil lost the trick long, long ago.

   [*Takes down the furred pelisse; crickets, moths, and
      chafers fly out from it.*

---

[1] In the first scene we return to Faust's university, where Wagner is con-
tinuing Faust's alchemical researches, while the one-time freshman advised
by Mephistopheles has grown into the Baccalaureus, who, as Goethe said to
Eckermann, like all young people thinks the world began with him and
exists for his sake. He speaks the philosophical language of the Germany
of Goethe's later years, and some lines caricature Fichte's idealism in
particular.

CHORUS OF INSECTS

We welcome thy coming,
Old patron and friend;
With buzz and with humming
On thee we attend.
Singly, in silence,
Thou plantedst us here,
Skipping by thousands,
Behold, we appear!
The rogue in the bosom
Hides close in his lair;
Our fur-bed we gladly
Forsake for the air.

MEPHISTOPHELES

'Tis quite a treat to hear these young fry cheep!
Let one but sow, in time he's sure to reap.
Again I shake the old tag-rag, and out
The creatures fly and flutter all about.
Up and away!   In nooks on every side,
My little darlings, quickly hide.
In yon old boxes, chests, and bins,
Here in these yellow parchment skins,
In dusty pots, retorts, and bowls,
In yonder skulls' grim eyelet-holes.
Enjoy yourselves you surely must,
Among such maggots, dirt, and dust.

[Slips into the pelisse.

Come! and once more my back array!
I'm Principal again to-day:
But what avails to bear the name!
Where are the people, to admit my claim?

*[Pulls the bell, which emits a shrill, penetrating sound,
at which the halls shake and the doors burst open.*

FAMULUS (*stumbling along the dark passage*)

What a clamour! what a quaking!
Walls and staircase rocking, shaking!
Ugh! the lightning, how it flashes
Through the coloured window-sashes!
From the ceiling, fast and faster,
Rattle stucco, lath, and plaster;
And, by wizard cantrip parted,
From the doors the bolts have started!
Yonder—horrors ne'er will cease!—
A giant in Faust's old pelisse!

He so stares and nods at me,
I shall drop down presently.
Shall I fly, or shall I stay?
I'm undone!   Oh! well-a-day!

MEPHISTOPHELES

Come hither, friend!   Your name is Nicodemus.

FAMULUS

Most worthy sir, that is my name.   Oremus!

MEPHISTOPHELES
Some other time!

FAMULUS
            You know me, it appears!

MEPHISTOPHELES

Right well!   A student still, though up in years!
Well, well, the learnedest, my moss-grown friend,
Can't choose but go on studying to the end.
A card-house so he builds him, small and neat;
But not even greatest minds their house complete.
Your master, though, he has indeed a name;
Who has not heard of Dr Wagner's fame?
Wagner, the learned world's acknowledged head,
Which, but for him, indeed, might go to bed!
Daily from him new flashes burst
Of wisdom, science, and of knowledge,
And pupils, in and out of college,
For pure omniscience athirst,
In crowds surround this wondrous teacher.
He is your only brilliant preacher;
He like Saint Peter wields the keys,
And opens Hell's or Heaven's gates at his ease.
All other doctors' fame has faded
Before the brilliancy of his;
Even Faustus' name is overshaded;
The great inventor he, he only, is.

FAMULUS

Fair sir, forgive me, if I may
Your dictum venture to gainsay;
Trust me, 'tis quite the other way.
The doctor would such praises spurn,

For he is modest to a flaw;
To Faustus he looks up with awe,
And may indeed be said to burn
For that distinguished man's return,
Whose absence, ever since he went,
Has caused him sore bewilderment.
This room, and everything that's in it,
Awaits its former master, just
As when he left it, even the dust.
I scarcely dare set foot within it.
What must the astral hour be—what?
The walls, methinks, have somehow parted,
The door-posts sprung, the ring-bolts started,
Else in here you had never got.

MEPHISTOPHELES

Well then, your master, where is he?
Bring me to him, or him to me.

FAMULUS

His order's strict, to let none enter;
I scarcely know if I may venture.
On his stupendous task intent,
For months on months he has been pent
Within his room, in strict seclusion,
And will not brook the least intrusion.
The meekest of all learned men,
He looks like demon in his den,
Begrimed from ears to nose, his eyes
With blowing up the furnace red;
So day and night his tongs he plies,
And never thinks to go to bed.

MEPHISTOPHELES

Refuse to me admittance?   Why,
The very man his ends to forward, I.
[*Exit* FAMULUS.   MEPHISTOPHELES *sits down with a very
        solemn air.*
Scarce seated at my post, when—hark! oh rare!
A visitor comes clattering up the stair;
But this time he is of the latest school;
Not to be bound by dogma or by rule.

BACCALAUREUS (*swaggering along the passage*)

Gate and doors wide open cast!
Good! So we may hope at last,
That the living man no more
Grubs in dust, as heretofore,
Like a dead man—moping, sighing,
And, though living, truly dying.

This old fabric, roof and wall,
Bends and totters to its fall;
Scarce if soon we do not make us,
Crash and wreck will overtake us:
I, though not a man to flinch,
Go no farther, not an inch.

Was it not here? It was, I know,
That I, so many years ago,
A freshman came, in deep concern,
And full of foolish fears, to learn;
And in these greybeards did confide,
By their cold morsels edified.
Out of their musty volumes old
All sorts of lies they did unfold;
Believing not the things they knew,
Wasting their own lives, and mine too.
How? In yon cell there's one, I'm sure,
Still sitting in the clear-obscure!

How odd! Yes, in the very gown,
Turned up with fur of dingy brown!
In look or garb no sort of change!
Just as I left him. This is strange!
Then with an awe profound I scanned him,
Because I did not understand him;
To-day he'll find I'm up to trap.
Here goes! So now look out, old chap!
                              [*To* MEPHISTOPHELES.
Old gentleman, if Lethe's muddy tide
Have not o'erflowed your bald skew-dropping pate,
Here an old scholar see with grateful pride,
From academic thrall emancipate.
You are the same as then in every feature,
But I am quite another creature.

MEPHISTOPHELES

I'm glad you've answered to my bell!
Even then your merits I could see;
As in the chrysalis one can foretell
The brilliant butterfly to be.
In collar laced, and curls well dressed,
You then felt quite a childish zest.
You never wore a pigtail, eh?
A crop, I see, you wear to-day.
You have a bold and dashing air,
Pray, don't too hard upon me bear!

BACCALAUREUS

Old gentleman, this place may be the same,
But things have not been at a stop,
So your ambiguous phrases drop:
We're fly to all that sort of game.
You once could trot the simple youth;
It needed no great skill, to do
What now would puzzle more than you.

MEPHISTOPHELES

If to the young one speaks unvarnished truth,
Their yellow beaks the precious food eschew;
But when, in course of time and tide,
They've learned it dearly through their hide,
They fancy, then, they found it out at once,
And so exclaim, 'Our master was a dunce!'

BACCALAUREUS

A knave, perhaps! For which of them has grace,
To speak the plain truth plumply to our face?
They treat us like good children—here caress,
There threaten, letting out now more, now less.

MEPHISTOPHELES

There is a time to learn; but, by your speech,
You are, I see, yourself prepared to teach.
Through many moons, and suns some few,
Profound experience, doubtless, has been gained by you.

BACCALAUREUS

Experience! Psha! Mere dust and scum!
Mind, mind's the thing! Mind free and growing!
Of what man's always known the sum
Is not, confess it, worth the knowing.

MEPHISTOPHELES (*after a pause*)

I've long surmised I was a fool. Alas!
It strikes me now, I am an utter ass.

BACCALAUREUS

Delightful! There's some reason in you yet!
The first old man of sense I ever met!

MEPHISTOPHELES

I sought for hidden golden store, and lit
On merest cinder-rubbish everywhere.

BACCALAUREUS

Your bald old pate is not, you'd best admit,
Worth more than yonder hollow skulls up there.

MEPHISTOPHELES (*good-humouredly*)

How rude you are, you're not aware, friend, quite.

BACCALAUREUS

In German one must lie, to be polite.

MEPHISTOPHELES (*who has been throughout the dialogue rolling his chair nearer the proscenium—to the pit*)

I'm choked up here! Nor air nor light I've got.
You'll find me quarters 'mongst you, will you not?

BACCALAUREUS

It's quite preposterous, that men will try
To cut a figure, when their day's gone by.
Man's life lives in his blood; and where, forsooth,
Does blood so course and pulsate as in youth?
That's the true thing, with glow and vigour rife,
Which out of its own life creates new life.
There all is stir, there something's done and sped;
The weak fall out, the stalwart go ahead.
Whilst we have made one half the world our own,
What have you done? Why, napped and mused alone,

Dreamed, pondered, planned, still planned, and that is all!
Old age a shivering ague is—no more!—
Of whims and frosty fancies bred;
When once his thirtieth year is o'er,
A man is just as good as dead.
'Twere best yourself betimes to slay.

MEPHISTOPHELES

The Devil here has nothing more to say.

BACCALAUREUS

Save through my will, no Devil can exist.

MEPHISTOPHELES (aside)

The Devil, though, some day your neck shall twist.

BACCALAUREUS

This is youth's noblest calling and most fit!
The world was not, till I created it.
Out of the ocean I evoked the sun,
With me the moon began its course to run,
To light my path the day its splendour wore,
For me the earth her flowers and verdure bore.
At my command, on yonder primal night,
Did all the stars pour forth their glorious light.
Who but myself for you deliverance wrought
From the harsh fetters of pedantic thought?
I with free soul, ecstatical and bright,
Walk in the radiance of my inward light,
With fearless step and joy-illumined mind.
Before me brightness, darkness far behind.   [Exit.

MEPHISTOPHELES

Well, go in pride, original, thy ways!
Insight would make thee melancholy:
What thought of wisdom or of folly
Has not been often thought in bygone days?
Yet in good time all will come safely round—
A few more years, this folly will have passed;
Even where the must ferments beyond all bound,
It yields a wine of some kind at the last.
    [To the younger occupants of the pit, who do not applaud.
You to my words are deaf and cold.
Well, well!   Good boys like you in time will mend 'em.
Reflect! the Devil, he is old;
Then grow you old, to comprehend him!

LABORATORY, *after the fashion of the Middle Ages; a quantity of
bulky, cumbrous apparatus, for fantastic purposes* [1]

WAGNER (*at the furnace*)

The bell rings; at its clangour drear
The mouldy walls with horror thrill;
This dread suspense of hope and fear
Must soon be solved, for good or ill.
Joy, joy!   The gloom begins to clear!
Now is the phial's core below
As with a living coal aglow;
Yea, like a fine carbuncle, mark,
It flashes lightnings through the dark!
And now a light, pellucid, white!
Oh, let me, let me fail no more!
Great heavens! a rustling the door?

MEPHISTOPHELES (*entering*)

Pray, don't alarm yourself! all's right.

WAGNER (*anxiously*)

Welcome!   The stars my purpose aid!   [*In a low voice.*
But not a word.   Breathe lightly, for a grand
Conception's consummation is at hand.

MEPHISTOPHELES (*in a whisper*)

What is afoot?

WAGNER (*also in a whisper*)

A man is being made.

MEPHISTOPHELES

A man!   What pair of amorous tools
In the alembic there are sweating?

---

[1] Wagner's attempt to make life from the inorganic succeeds only because
Mephistopheles lends a helping hand, as we see from the words Mephistopheles speaks as the Famulus leaves him, and to the spectators at the end.
Homunculus, this strange creation of Goethe's fancy, owes nothing but his
name to Paracelsus and the alchemists.   He seems to have only the higher
attributes of man, mind, and the power of speech, he is all ironical quips and
witty sallies, but he has no body, and that is the one thing he wants.   As
pure spirit, he can read Faust's thoughts, and we learn that he is dreaming of
Leda and the Swan, that is, of the conception of Helena—these fine lines
read like a description of Correggio's picture of the incident.   As a master
of psychology he can prescribe a cure for Faust, that he be taken to Greek
soil, and through his encyclopaedic knowledge he is aware that it is just the
time of year for the Classical Walpurgis Night.

* I 335

WAGNER

Nay, heaven forfend! 'Tis only fit for fools,
That ancient method of begetting.
The tender point, which was life's source,
That subtle, springing, inward force,
Which, to impress its image bent,
Did something take, and something lent,
And to its ends essayed to win
Both what was foreign, what akin,
Is now from its high honours thrust.
If brutes this way still sate their lust,
Man, with his mighty gifts, henceforth, I wis,
Must have a source more high, more pure than this.
                    [*Turns to the furnace.*
It flashes! Look! My hopes were not unfounded.
I knew, and now the proof behold,
That when, from substance hundredfold,
From every source and quarter singled,
And all—for there's the art, I hold—
In suitable proportion mingled,
Man's substance we had thus compounded,
And in alembic then confounded,
In proper combination, we
The work in silence perfected should see.
                    [*Again turns to the furnace.*
Yes, yes! Behold! the mass grows clearer.
The demonstration nearer, nearer!
What men call Nature's mystery, we dare
By mind to probe and analyse,
And what she organized whilere,
We now contrive to crystallize.

MEPHISTOPHELES

He that lives long learns much, as time goes by;
The world can nothing new before him set.
Already in my early travels I
Of mortals crystallized not few have met.

WAGNER (*who has meanwhile been watching the phial intently*)

It flashes, mounts, the atoms blend!
One moment, and we reach the end!
A grand design mere madness seems at first;
But in the end with us will be the laughter,
And thus a brain, which living thought has nursed,
Shall breed a living thinker, too, hereafter.
                    [*Contemplates the phial with rapture.*

The glass rings piercingly and sweet.
It clouds, it clears!　All, all, as it should be!
Settling into proportion meet,
A comely manikin I see.
More can the world or can I wish for?　No!
The mystery lies unveiled within our reach;
Just mark that sound, and you will find it grow
To perfect voice, to most articulate speech.

HOMUNCULUS (*in the phial, to* WAGNER)

How goes it, daddy mine!　It was no jest.
Come, press me very gently to your breast.
But not too hard, else will the crystal shatter.
Remember, 'tis the law of matter,
That all the universe doth scarce suffice
For Nature's procreations grand,
While things produced by Art's device
A bounded space and well enclosed demand.
　　　　　　　　　　　　　　　[*To* MEPHISTOPHELES.
Ha, rogue!　That's you, sir kinsman, is it?
Thanks, thanks!　Most aptly have you timed your visit.
Rare chance for us that brought you here!　And I,
Whilst I exist, my task must briskly ply.
I long to tackle to my work, and you
Are just the man to show me what to do.

WAGNER

One word, just one, to screen my credit, pray,
And save my reputation many a slight!
With problems I am pelted every day,
By young and old, which baffle me outright.
For instance, nobody can comprehend,
How body and soul so exquisitely blend,
Sticking as close as though they ne'er would part,
Yet every day embroiled in conflict tart.
Then——

MEPHISTOPHELES

　　　　Stop!　Ask rather, how it comes about,
That man and wife so constantly fall out?
Such problems, friend, you never will see through.
The little one wants work; here's work to do.

HOMUNCULUS

What's to be done?

MEPHISTOPHELES (*pointing to a side-door*)
            Yonder thy gifts employ!

WAGNER (*still gazing into the phial*)
In sooth, thou art a darling of a boy!
      [*The side-door opens.* FAUST *is seen lying upon the
      couch.*

HOMUNCULUS (*amazed*)
Strange!
      [*The phial bounds out of* WAGNER'S *hands, hovers over*
      FAUST, *and sheds a light upon him.*
            What a gorgeous garniture of dream!
Deep in the umbrage of a wood, a stream
Lucent as crystal—women, oh, how fair!
Their limbs unrobing in the sunlit air;
And one, who o'er them all asserts her place,
Supreme in beauty, and supreme in grace,
Sprung of heroic, yea, Olympian race!
She dips her foot in the transparent tide,
Cooling the glow of her majestic frame
In waves that leap and sparkle up her side,
In loving dalliance with the fragrant flame.
But hark! a rushing as of wings in flight!
What plash and plunging mar the mirror bright!
Her maidens fly in terror: she, their queen,
Gazes around her, smiling and serene,
And with a thrill of pride and pleasure sees
The foremost swan come fondling to her knees,
Importunate, yet gentle. Now, at ease,
With the coy beauty he disports and plays.
But lo! at once a mist begins to rise,
And veils in an impenetrable haze
The loveliest of all visions from my eyes.

MEPHISTOPHELES
A very exquisite romance, I vow;
Small though thou art, a mighty phantast thou.
I can see nothing.

HOMUNCULUS
            I believe it.   How
Should you, a creature of the northern clime,
Bred 'mid the frippery of priests and knights,
Have your eyes open to such glorious sights?
You never are at home but where
Darkness and gloom infect the air.   [*Looking round.*

Grey stone walls, moss-grown, ugly, groins,
High-pointed arches, volutes, coigns!
If here he wake, 'twill ruin all,
Dead on the spot he'd surely fall!
Swans, naked beauties, woodland, stream,
These made up his prophetic dream.
How should he ever reconcile
Himself to breathe in den so vile?
Though little caring where I be,
I find it rather much for me.
So hence with him!

MEPHISTOPHELES

Your wish shall be obeyed.

HOMUNCULUS

Command the warrior to the fight,
To dance and roundel lead the maid,
And then their joy is at its height.
This is—ha, ha! the thought is bright—
The Classical Walpurgis Night.
The very thing to nurse his bent!
He'll there be in his element.

MEPHISTOPHELES

Of such a thing I never heard.

HOMUNCULUS

                              Oh! good!
And was it probable you should?
You only know romantic spectres; but
The genuine spectre's of a classic cut.

MEPHISTOPHELES

In what direction shall we ride?
Antique companions, mind, I can't abide.

HOMUNCULUS

Your pleasure-grounds north-westward, Satan, lie,
But south and eastward we to-night must hie.
O'er a broad flat doth fair Peneios wind,
By many an oozy bay, green woodlands through:
The mountain cliffs close in the plain behind,
And far up lies Pharsalus old and new.

MEPHISTOPHELES

Out and away! No longer let me hear
Of slaves and tyrants waging conflict drear!
They bore me; for one war is scarcely done,
When out of hand another is begun;
And not a man of them can see, that they
Only the game of Asmodeus play.
For Freedom's rights they battle, that's the cry;
Slaves murder slaves, were nearer truth, say I.

HOMUNCULUS

Oh, to their strife and wrangling leave mankind.
Each must protect himself as best he can,
From boyhood up; so grows at last a man.
The cure for him (*pointing to* FAUST) is what we have to find.
If you've a panacea, prove it now;
If not, give way, and leave the task to me.

MEPHISTOPHELES

The bolts of heathendom, I must avow,
Defy my Brocken spells to find the key.
These Greeks were never good for much. Yet stay!
They charm men's senses with external show.
Their sins look bright, and beautiful, and gay;
While ours seem always dreary, dull, and slow.
And now what else?

HOMUNCULUS

        You used not to be shy.
I think I've something I can tempt you by.
What say you to Thessalian witches, eh?

MEPHISTOPHELES (*kindling up*)

Thessalian witches? Good! A gentry these
I've been inquiring for this many a day.
I have a notion, though, that they
My taste will not exactly please—
Night after night, at least, with them to stay.
But we shall see. Away!

HOMUNCULUS

        The cloak once more!
And in it wrap yon sleeping cavalier!
'Twill bear you both, as it has done before.
I go ahead, you by my light to steer.

WAGNER (*alarmed*)

And I?

HOMUNCULUS

Why, you—stay here at home, and those
Researches most momentous close!
Turn your old parchments o'er and o'er—collect
The elements of life, as they direct,
Then piece them warily; and, look ye now,
Consider well the WHAT, but more the How!
I o'er a slice of earth the while will hie,
And should I find the dot upon the I,
Why, this your mighty enterprise will cap.
The prize is more than worth the effort—wealth,
Honour, renown, long life, unfailing health,
Knowledge withal, and virtue too—mayhap.
Farewell!

WAGNER

Farewell!   My heart is sad and sore,
For much I fear I ne'er shall see thee more.

MEPHISTOPHELES

Now for Peneios!   My small friend,
I'm not ashamed to claim his aid.
                                    [*Ad spectatores.*

We in the long-run all depend
Upon the creatures we have made.

CLASSICAL WALPURGIS NIGHT [1]

PHARSALIAN FIELDS—DARKNESS

ERICHTHO

To this night's ghastly revel, as full oft before,
I hither come, Erichtho I, the sad of mien,
Yet not so loathly, as with calumny's gross tongue
The libellous poets paint me.   They, in praise or blame
No stint nor measure know.   The vale through all its length

---

[1] Erichtho, the witch consulted by Pompey before he fought Caesar at
Pharsalus in 48 B.C., introduces the scene in the rhymeless six-footed iambic
metre (trimeter) used in Greek tragedy for the dialogue.   At the other end
of these two acts concerned with things classical, in Faust's first speech in
Act IV, the same metre is used for the last time.   In the dialogue of the

Is white as with a sea of tents, all ashy grey,
An after-reflex of that awful, ghastly night.
How oft already has it been repeated!   'Twill
Be through all time repeated!   Empire no one yields
To another; no, not even to him, by whom 'twas won
By force, by force is swayed.   For who, though powerless
To rule his inner self, is not intent to rule
His neighbour's will, at the proud dictates of his own?
But here a signal proof to bitter end was fought,
How power arrays itself against a mightier power;
Rends freedom's chaplet fair, with all its thousand flowers,
And stubborn laurels round the victor's brows entwines.
Here Magnus of the days of his first greatness dreamed.
There Caesar watched the wavering balance shake.
Here shall they grapple!   Well the world the victor knows.
With tongues of ruddy flame the watch-fires glow, the ground
A semblance of the blood, that dyed it erst, exhales,
And, by the night's most strange and weird-like sheen allured,
The beings of Hellenic legend 'gin to throng.
The fabled forms of ancient days unstably flit
Around the fires, or sit in circles at their ease.
The moon, though only half her orb, resplendent, clear,
Climbs up the sky, and fills the vale with mellow light.
The phantom tents fade out, and bluely burn the fires.
But lo! what meteor strange comes sailing through the air!
Itself illumed, a ball corporeal it illumes.
I scent life near at hand.   Destructive as I am
To all that lives, 'twill not beseem me to remain;
'Twould bring me ill repute, advantage none at all.
Now it descends to earth!   'Tis best that I retire.

[*Withdraws.*

---

first half of Act III it is used in conjunction with a lyrical chorus in the Greek manner.

To find the thread which holds the following scenes together, it is helpful first to follow the action as it concerns each of the three Aerial Travellers separately.   Faust, who recovers consciousness when he touches the soil of Greece, and his inner and outer world are to this extent brought into harmony, is led by his inquiries after Helena to the entrance to the under-world, where like a second Orpheus he will plead for his beloved's return. The projected scene between Faust and Persephone, the mistress of the underworld, was not carried out, but we must imagine his quest as successful, for Helena duly appears in Act III.   We see nothing more of Faust after the first third of Act II, when he has been referred by the Sphinxes to Chiron, has seen again with waking eyes the vision of his dreams ('On the lower Peneios'), and been taken by Chiron to Manto, the prophetess, to begin with her his descent into the underworld.

Meanwhile Mephistopheles, on pleasure bent, has been having his leg pulled, as a mere northerner, by creatures from the lower ranks of Greek mythology, Griffins, Sphinxes, Sirens, Lamiae, and so forth.   He ends up by borrowing the shape of one of the ugly Phorkyads, in which form he

The AERIAL TRAVELLERS *above*

HOMUNCULUS

Hover, hover in the air,
  O'er these flames and phantoms dreary;
Down within the valley there
  Things look spectral, wild, and eerie.

MEPHISTOPHELES

As a-north, through casements old
  Ghastly shapes and horrors rare,
Hideous ghosts I now behold;
  Here I'll be at home, as there!

HOMUNCULUS

See yon figure, long and gaunt,
  Swift away before us gliding!

---

appears in Act III. Evil takes the form of ugliness in this apotheosis of beauty.

The search of Homunculus for a body loosely links together the rest of the act. In the scene 'On the Upper Peneios' he overhears two philosophers, Anaxagoras a Plutonist, and Thales a Neptunist, arguing their different hypotheses about the history of the earth's surface, the one ascribing primary importance to cataclysms brought about by fire, the other to gradual changes wrought by water, in which, he insists, life began. All this reflects rather dimly Goethe's interest in the scientific controversies of his time. Thales takes Homunculus to his sea friend Nereus, and Proteus, dear to the 'morphologist' Goethe, tells him he must begin life in the sea and gradually work up the scale of creation. He takes the first step by dashing himself against the chariot of the fairest daughter of Nereus, Galatea, here thought of as a sea-born incarnation of beauty like Aphrodite. As he does so, fire and water seem to be mingled and all the elements work together to bring forth a new form of life, a new creation of Eros, 'the beginner of all.' Here again, in one of its Greek manifestations, love, the 'eternally feminine' principle celebrated in the closing verses of the play, leads on Faust's counterpart, Homunculus, to higher forms of existence.

The connection of events in this most difficult section of the work is obscured by what clearly interested Goethe much more at the age of eighty, the significant arrangement of figures and situations according to their symbolic fitness. The five scenes show a progression from utmost gloom to brightest light, from semi-grotesque creatures (Griffins, Sphinxes) in a bare, rocky landscape to more and more attractive mythical figures (Nymphs, Chiron, finally Nereus and his daughters, Proteus, Galatea and her train) by a broader river amidst lush growth and at last by the seashore, lit by the full moon. The gradual growth of ideas of beauty and higher religion in Greek civilization is thus suggested by the selection and presentation of the mythical material. Even the scientific philosophizing is not an excrescence, for it conveys Goethe's idea that the great achievement of the Greeks, their conception of the divine in human shape, was a product not only of mind but of nature, through a process of what Goethe the scientist called 'Steigerung,' raising to a higher potential.

MEPHISTOPHELES

She looks troubled, to her haunt
  Through the air to see us sliding.

HOMUNCULUS

Let her go! Set down thy freight,
  That paladin of dreams unstable,
And life will come back to him straight:
  He seeks it in the realm of fable.

FAUST (*as he touches the ground*)

Where is she?

HOMUNCULUS

              Cannot say, good sir;
But here you may get news of her.
From fire to fire till dawn do you
Unceasingly your quest pursue.
Should anything his courage daunt,
Who dared invade The Mothers' haunt?

MEPHISTOPHELES

I too have here a part to play;
And there can be no better way,
Than for us each to seek his own
Adventures 'mongst these fires alone.
And thou, small friend, to reunite us,
Shalt ring, and with thy radiance light us.

HOMUNCULUS

Thus shall I blaze, thus ring for you!
            [*The glass booms and flashes vehemently.*
Now, haste away to marvels new!

FAUST (*alone*)

Where is she? Wherefore now inquire?
If this were not the land that bore her,
These not the waves that paddled o'er her,
This is, at least, the air that did her speech inspire.
Here! here in Greece! Here, by a marvel swept,
I knew at once the soil on which I stood:
A spirit fired my life-blood as I slept;
Antaeus-like I feel a giant's mood,
And though my path be thronged with visions dire,
I will explore this labyrinth of fire.   [*Goes off.*

ON THE UPPER PENEIOS

MEPHISTOPHELES (*peering about*)

As in and out among these flames I flirt,
I'm quite put out, for almost all I view
Is naked, only here and there a shirt;
The Sphinxes lost to shame, the Griffins too,
And all those long-tressed things of wingèd kind,
Bare to the eye in front, and bare behind.
We relish rarely what is gross and free,
But, really, the antique's too lively even for me.
On it we must our modern views impress,
And clothe it in the latest style of dress.
A hideous crew! Yet must I not neglect
To greet them, as a stranger, with respect.
Hail, lovely females—hail, ye grizzled sages!

GRIFFIN (*snarling*)

Not grizzled! Griffins! No one likes to hear
Himself called grizzled. Every word betrays
Its lineage by the sound which it conveys.
Grey, gruesome, grizzled, graves, grim, grizzly, all
Of the same root etymological,
Grate on our ears.

MEPHISTOPHELES

                    And yet it cannot be,
That in the Griffin you dislike the Gri?

GRIFFIN

Of course not! Kindred as it is with what,
If sometimes censured, oftener praise has got:
A man should grasp at Beauty, Empire, Gold,
Fortune the grasping favours and the bold.

ANTS (*of colossal size*)

You speak of gold; we had collected heaps,
And stored them close in caves and rocky keeps;
The Arimaspians, they found out the place,
Hid all away, and mock us to our face.

GRIFFIN

We'll force them to acknowledge where it lies.

ARIMASPIAN

Not on this night of jubilee.
Until to-morrow all are free.
This time we're certain of our prize.

MEPHISTOPHELES (*has stationed himself between the Sphinxes*)

Quite comfortable here I feel,
For you I comprehend and know.

SPHINX

Then what our spirit-tones reveal
Clothe thou with shape, if this be so.
That we may know thee, let thy name be told.

MEPHISTOPHELES

The names men call me by are manifold.
Say, are there any Britons here?
They're always roaming far and near,
To spy out battle-fields, old crumbling walls,
Drear spots of classic fame, rocks, waterfalls.
Meet goal were this for them!   And they,
If here, would testify, in the old play ·
They talked of me as Old Iniquity.

SPHINX

And why?

MEPHISTOPHELES

That's just what puzzles me.

SPHINX

Perhaps! perhaps!   Canst read the starry book?
What say'st thou to its aspect, then, to-night?

MEPHISTOPHELES

Star courses star, the shaven moon shines bright,
And I'm delighted with this cosy nook,
And warm me rarely 'gainst thy lion's skin.
To go up higher were a loss to win.
Come now, enigmas or charades propound.

SPHINX

Propound thyself; enigma more profound
Than thou 'twere scarcely possible to start.
So, then, essay to fathom what thou art.

'What to the pious and the heedful,
Or wicked man alike is needful,
To that a butt, to try his foil on,
To this a chum, to folly to beguile on,
And every way a thing for Zeus to smile on?'

FIRST GRIFFIN (*snarling*)

I can't abide him.

SECOND GRIFFIN (*snarling more vehemently*)
What does he want here?

BOTH

Such scum why should we suffer near?

MEPHISTOPHELES

You think, perhaps, my nails are not a match
For your sharp talons, should we come to scratch.
Try then, just try!

SPHINX (*mildly*)

Remain, if you desire;
Ere long you will be anxious to retire.
At home you can do anything you please:
Here, if I err not, you are ill at ease.

MEPHISTOPHELES

Above, no daintier bit of flesh I know,
But, ugh! I shudder at the beast below.

SPHINX

False churl, beware, or dearly shall ye rue:
These claws of ours are sharp and fell!
Lord of the shrunken hoof, no place for you
Our circle holds, and that ye know full well.

[SIRENS *prelude above.*

MEPHISTOPHELES

What birds are these on yonder bough,
Among the river-willows there?

SPHINX

The best have fallen a prey, ere now,
To such sing-song, so thou beware!

SIRENS

Ah, why wilt thou linger long
'Midst the wondrous, the unsightly?
Hark, we come, a chorus sprightly,
Carolling melodious song,
As beseems the siren throng!

SPHINX (*mocking them in the same melody*)

Force them to come down, for they
Hide among the leafy spray
Their long talons, hooked and hideous,
Which on thee will fall perfidious,
Shouldst thou listen to their lay.

SIRENS

Hatred, envy, hence take wing!
We the purest pleasures bring,
Which beneath the welkin be.
Best of water, best of earth,
Shapes of beauty, shapes of mirth,
Shall combine to welcome thee.

MEPHISTOPHELES

These are the new vagaries fine,
Where note round note is made to twine,
From throat or strings with curious art.
On me the caterwauling's lost;
It titillates my ears at most,
But fails to penetrate the heart.

SPHINX

Speak not of heart!   What heart hast thou?
A shrivelled leathern flask, I vow,
For face like thine were heart enow.

FAUST (*enters*)

How wondrous! yet how fine!   Where'er I gaze,
Even in the loathly grand impressive traits!
There's something tells me, this way fortune lies;
Where do they bear me, these calm earnest eyes?
                                        [*Indicating the Sphinxes.*
Ha!   Before such stood Oedipus of yore.
                                        [*Indicating the Sirens.*
Even such Ulysses crouched in hempen cords before.
                                        [*Indicating the Ants.*

By such, a priceless treasure was amassed.

[*Indicating the Griffins.*

By these 'twas guarded safely to the last.
With new-born life I feel my soul expand.
Grand are the forms, the recollections grand.

MEPHISTOPHELES

Time was, you would have banned these creatures here,
But now, it seems, to them you're well inclined;
For where a man is hunting for his dear,
Monsters themselves a ready welcome find.

FAUST (*to the Sphinxes*)

Ye female forms must answer me!   Who e'er
Among you hath seen Helena the Fair?

SPHINX

Not to her age did we pertain.
The last of us by Hercules was slain.
From Chiron thou mayst tidings gain.
He will be roaming hereabout to-night.
Much mayst thou hope, if thou canst stay his flight.

SIRENS

Thou, too, shouldst not lack for glory. . . .
As Ulysses stayed beside us,
Neither mocked us, nor defied us,
Much he learned for after-story.
Come unto the bright green sea,
Come and dwell with us, and we,
All we know will tell to thee.

SPHINX

Noble child of earth, away!
Heed not their delusive lay.
Let our counsels bind thee fast
As Ulysses to the mast.
Find great Chiron, he will show
All thy heart desires to know.   [FAUST *retires.*

MEPHISTOPHELES (*peevishly*)

What are these unsightly things?
How they croak and flap their wings!
Scarce visible, so swift they go,
And one by one, all in a row.
They would tire a sportsman, these.

SPHINX

Like the wintry storm-blast flying,
Alcides' shafts almost defying,
These are the fleet Stymphalides;
Though in hoarsest croakings sent,
Yet their greeting's kindly meant:
With their vulture beaks, and feet
Webbed like geese, they fain would win
Footing here in our retreat,
As being to ourselves akin.

MEPHISTOPHELES (*scared*)

More monsters still among them hiss and play!

SPHINX

These are the heads—nay, dread no ill!—
Of the Lernean snake, that think they're something still,
Though from the trunk dissevered many a day.
But what's the matter with you, say?
You look uneasy, twist awry.
Where would you wish to go? Away!
Yon group, I see, has caught your eye.
Do not constrain yourself to stay.
Be gone to them! You'll stumble there
On many a visage passing fair.
They are the Lamiae, wantons rare,
With smiling lips and foreheads bold,
Revel with satyrs fit to hold;
With them what may not Goatfoot dare?

MEPHISTOPHELES

You'll stay, then, here or hereabout,
That I again may find you out?

SPHINX

Go, mingle with the revel rout!
Long has our native Egypt known
Our kith and kindred keep their throne
Thousands of years; we shall not weary soon.
Ours is no fickle fleeting state;
Moveless ourselves, we regulate
The periods of the sun and moon.
Before the Pyramids we sit:
The nations dree their doom before us—
War, peace, or deluge—and no whit
Of change or turning passes o'er us.

ON THE LOWER PENEIOS

PENEIOS (*surrounded by streams and Nymphs*)

Stir, ye sedges, swaying slowly;
Breathe, ye tangled rushes, lowly;
Wave, ye willows, softly sighing,
To the aspens' thrill replying,
'Midst the pauses of my dreams!
But a thund'rous murmur dread
Scares me from my slumb'rous bed
'Neath the ever-flowing streams.

FAUST (*advancing to the stream*)

Hear I rightly, then I ween
In behind the leafy screen
Of these woven boughs are noises,
Like the sound of human voices,
Yea, each wavelet seems to be
Brattling, prattling merrily.

NYMPHS (*to* FAUST)

Lay thee down lowly,
Thy joy will be full!
Rest thy o'erwearied
Limbs in the cool.
The peace shall come o'er thee,
That evermore flees thee;
We'll lisp, or we'll whisper,
Or murmur to please thee.

FAUST

I wake indeed!   I see them well,
These forms of grace unmatchable,
    In beauty palpable to sight!
What transports strange my spirit seize!
Can these be dreams, or memories,
    The shadows of an old delight?
The limpid waters, as they stray
Through bushes green, that gently sway
    Above them, scarce a murmur make;
An hundred rills together meet,
In one broad, clear, unruffled sheet
    Of waters deep—a crystal lake:
Young female forms, plump, debonair,
That fill the eye with rapture, there

Are in the liquid mirror glassed!
In merry groups to bathe they come,
Some stoutly swim, wade shyly some,
    Shout, splash in sportive fray at last.
Could these content, mine eye should find
Enjoyment here; but no, my mind
    Looks farther, and with vision keen
Would pierce yon thick embowering roof
Of clustering leaves, whose tangled woof
    Conceals the glory of their queen.

Oh, wonderful!   Swans bright of hue,
From leaf-screened nooks swim into view
    With slow majestic pace,
All side by side serenely steering,
Their neck and crest right proudly rearing,
    As conscious of their grace.
Yet one that breasts the glassy tide,
Outstripping all, a statelier pride
    And bearing seems to vaunt:
With pinions all blown proudly out,
He cleaves the waves that curl about,
    And nears the sacred haunt.
The rest glide softly to and fro,
With feathers smooth and white as snow;
    But lo! their crests in wrath they set,
And put to flight the fearful maids,
Who, seeking safety in the glades,
    Their mistress-queen forget.

NYMPHS

Sisters, sisters, lay your ear
    To the shore's green brink, and say,
If, like me, the beats you hear
    Of horses' hooves that come this way.
Much I marvel, who to-night
Message bears in stormy flight!

FAUST

The earth rings with a hollow sound,
As from a flying courser's bound!
There, there, see there!
Should fate so rare
Be mine, then, then would all be well,
Oh, marvel without parallel!
A horseman on a snowy steed—
High mettle in his looks I read—

Comes trampling on and on to me.
I do not err—'tis he, the son
Of Philyra, the far-famed one!
Stop, Chiron, stop!   I'd speak with thee.

CHIRON

How now?   What wouldst thou?

FAUST

Pause, I prithee.

CHIRON

I may not rest.

FAUST

Then take me with thee!

CHIRON

Mount!   And I then may question thee at will.
Whither wouldst go?   Thou stand'st here on the banks—
Wouldst cross the stream?   I'll take thee.   Pausing still?

FAUST (*mounting*)

Where'er thou wilt—and win my endless thanks.
The great man thou, the teacher rich in glory,
Who reared a race of heroes high and bold,
Those gallant Argonauts renowned in story,
And all who made the poet's world of old.

CHIRON

Best speak no more of that!   E'en Pallas hath
Not always honour as a Mentor gained;
Men will be men, and hold their wayward path,
Do what we will, as though they'd ne'er been trained.

FAUST

The leech who gives a name to every plant,
Knows every root, its virtue, and its haunt,
Has balm for every wound, and physic for each pain,
With mind and body's force here to my heart I strain.

CHIRON

Were hero stricken down, I still could find
All needful aid and skill his hurt requires,
But I my leechcraft long long since resigned
To simple-culling beldames and to friars.

FAUST

The truly great art thou, whose ear
His proper praise is loath to hear,
Who shrinks from view, and seems to be
But one of many great as he.

CHIRON

And thou, methinks, hast flattering wile,
Both prince and people to beguile.

FAUST

At least confess, thou hast stood face to face
With all the best and greatest of thy time,
With noblest spirits vied in virtue's race,
And lived the strenuous life of demigods sublime.
Then tell me, 'midst these grand heroic forms,
Which of them all possessed the goodliest charms?

CHIRON

In that brave Argonautic circle shone
Each hero with a lustre of his own,
And by the force that in his soul prevailed,
Supplied the void wherein his comrades failed,
Ever where youth and manly grace held sway,
The Dioscuri bore the palm away.
Resolve and speed to act for others' ease
The glory was of the Boreades.
Far-seeing, wary, firm, in council wise,
So lorded Jason, dear to woman's eyes.
Then Orpheus, gentle, given to muse apart,
Whene'er he swept the lyre, subdued each heart.
Keen-sighted Lynceus, he, by shine and dark,
Steered on o'er rock and shoal the sacred bark.
The danger many share we scarcely fear,
And toil grows light, with others by to cheer.

FAUST

But wilt thou tell me now of Hercules?

CHIRON

Oh, woe!   Awaken not sad memories!
    Nor Mars, nor Phoebus had I viewed,
       Nor Hermes, born of Maia's line,
    When on a day before me stood
       What all men worship as divine.

A monarch born was he, in all
    Youth's noblest graces past compare?
And yet his elder brother's thrall,
    And thrall of women passing fair.
Not earth shall yield his like again,
    Nor Hebe to the gods present;
Men weave for him their lays in vain,
    In vain the sculptured stone torment.

FAUST

So then, not all the sculptor's cunning can
    Embody charms so superhuman!
Thou'st told me of the finest man,
    Now tell me of the finest woman.

CHIRON

What!   Woman's beauty to portray,
    I deem it but a bootless task;
Too oft it is, alas the day!
    An icy-chill and moveless mask.
But her alone can I account
    As lovely, be she maid or wife,
From whom doth flow, as from a fount,
    A stream of bright and gladsome life.
Self-blest is beauty, look who list,
Grace has a charm none may resist,
Like Helena, whom once I bore.

FAUST

Whom once you bore?

CHIRON

        Ay, on my back.

FAUST

Was I not crazed enough before,
But I must light on such a track?

CHIRON

She twined her hand into my hair,
As thou dost now.

FAUST

        Oh, joy most rare!
My senses reel!   Say how, I pray.
She only is my soul's desire!
Whence, whither didst thou bear her, say?

CHIRON

Soon told is what you thus require!
The Dioscuri had—it happened then—
Freed their young sister from some thievish men,
Who, little used to yield, took heart of grace,
And, mad with fury, gave their victors chase.
On sped the fugitives, but the morass
Hard by Eleusis checked them as they flew;
The brothers, wading o'er, contrived to pass,
I caught her up, and, swimming, bore her through.
Then she leapt down, and, in a childlike vein,
Playing and fondling with my dripping mane,
Thanked me in tones so sweet, yet calm and sage.
Oh, what a charm she had!   Young, yet the joy of age!

FAUST

Scarce seven years old.

CHIRON

The philologues, I see,
Self-mystified themselves, have cheated thee.
Your mythologic woman's of a kind
Unlike all other members of her sex;
Each poet paints her after his own mind,
And with his own peculiar fancies decks.
Never too young, nor ever old, her form
Wears at all times a soul-enkindling charm,
When young, she's ravished—old, she's courted still;
Enough!   Time cannot bind the poet's will.

FAUST

Then why by time should Helena be bound?
At Pherae she was by Achilles found,
Beyond the verge of Time.   Oh, rare delight,
To triumph where he loved, in fate's despite!
And should not I on this wild heart of mine
Bear back to life that perfect form divine;
That peer of gods, that soul of endless time,
As grand as gentle, winning as sublime?
Thou long ago, but I to-day have seen
That shape of light, and dignity serene,
Fair to the eye, as in her grace most rare,
And loved, desired, adored as she is fair!
Now am I bound her slave, sense, soul, and thought;
Come death, and welcome, if I win her not!

CHIRON

Strange being!   Men would call you rapturous,
We spirits simply mad, in doting thus.
But by good luck the fit has seized you here;
For 'tis my usage, once in every year,
To call on Manto, Æsculapius' daughter,
Who doth in silent prayer her sire implore,
Even for the love and reverence which he taught her,
Some rays of light on leeches' minds to pour,
And turn them from their headlong course of slaughter.
I love her most of all the Sibyl guild.
Not given to fancies she, nor fond pretence,
But meek and gentle, yet profoundly skilled,
Unwearied in a wise beneficence.
Stay some short space with her, and, trust me, she
With potent roots will cure thee utterly.

FAUST

Cured?   I will not be cured!   My soul is strong!
It will not grovel with the vulgar throng.

CHIRON

Slight not the virtues of the noble fount!
But see, we're at the place.   Be quick, dismount!

FAUST

Whither to land through the grim dark hast thou
Across the pebbly shallows brought me now?

CHIRON

Here by Peneios and Olympus too,
Rome grappled Greece in fight, and overthrew
The mightiest empire, e'er has known decay.
The burgher triumphs, and the king gives way.
Look up and see, above thee, close at hand,
The eternal temple in the moonshine stand!

MANTO (*muttering in a dream*)

Hoof-beats there,
Ring on the steps of the sacred stair!
Some demigods are nigh!

CHIRON

Right! right!   Arouse thee!   Wake!   'Tis I, 'tis I!

MANTO (*awakening*)

Welcome!   I see thou still art true.

CHIRON

And still thy temple-home is standing, too.

MANTO

Dost thou still wander, tiring never?

CHIRON

Thou liv'st in calm contentment ever,
Whilst I go circling round the sphere.

MANTO

Time circles me, I tarry here.
But he?

CHIRON

This night of eldritch glee
Hath whirled him hitherward with me.
Helen hath set his brains a-spin—
Helen he is intent to win,
But weets not how he shall begin.
A patient he, of all men best,
Thine Æsculapian skill to test.

MANTO

Me do such spirits chiefly please,
As crave impossibilities.

[CHIRON *is already far away.*

MANTO (*to* FAUST)

On, daring heart!   Bliss shall be thine!
This dusky path conducts to Proserpine.
Deep in Olympus caverned base sits she,
And waits forbidden greetings secretly.
I once sped Orpheus on this murky way—
Push on, be bold, and wiser heed display!

[*They descend.*

ON THE UPPER PENEIOS AS BEFORE

SIRENS

Plunge into Peneios!   There,
Oh, what joy, as on we swim
And plash about, our songs to hymn,
For these poor mortals all too fair!
Water is of health the spring!
Haste ye then, and, when we gain
The Aegean's azure main,
Rare shall be our revelling!   [*Earthquake.*

All afoam the wave runs back,
Flows no longer in its track;
Quakes the ground, the waters shiver,
Bank and gravel smoke and quiver.
Let us fly!   Come, sisters all,
Lest disaster worse befall!

Away, and let our pastime be
In bright ocean's Jubilee,
Where the billows, rippling o'er,
Break in sparkles on the shore;
Where Selene o'er our heads
Her serenest lustre spreads,
And, mirrored in the ocean blue,
Moistens all with holy dew.
There is gladsome life and free,
Earthquake here and agony.
Haste, then, hence, if ye be wise!
On this region horror lies.

SEISMOS (*growling and grumbling underground*)

One more thrust with might and main,
Set the shoulders to the strain,
So shall we the surface gain,
Where all must give way before us!

SPHINX

What a tremor's here, what rumbling,
What a gruesome grating, grumbling,
What a reeling, quaking, ho!
Oscillation to and fro!
'Tis a most provoking pinch,
Yet shall we not move an inch,
Though all hell itself broke o'er us!

Now in wondrous wise a mound
Swells and rises from the ground.
'Tis that very old man hoar,
Built up Delos' isle of yore,
Heaving it from ocean's deep,
Safe a teeming dame to keep.
Thrusting, squeezing, straining thew,
Stretching arms, and bending shoulders,
He, like Atlas to the view,
Heaves up earth and turf and boulders,
Sand and gravel, shale and clay,
Tranquil strata of our bay.
So a section up he rends,
Right across the vale extends.
Though waist-deep in earth still squatted,
The colossal Caryatid
Bears unmoved, without a groan,
A tremendous bulk of stone.
Nearer it shall not approach,
Nor upon our haunt encroach.

SEISMOS

Alone, alone I did it!   Truly
Men will this at last allow.
Had I not shaken it up so throughly,
This world, would it be fair as now?
How should yon mountain-ridges cleave
The gorgeous depths of ether blue,
Had I not thrust them forth, to weave
A beauty picturesque to view?
When, whilst my primal sires looked on—
Night and old Chaos—I my force displayed,
And, of the Titans the companion,
With Pelion, as at ball, and Ossa played.
Wildly we plied our youthful freaks,
Until, to crown them all, at last,
Like a twin cap two mountain-peaks
We on Parnassus madly cast,
Where now, for sport and joyance, meet
Apollo and the Muses' choir.
I even upheaved the glorious seat
Of Jove, and all his bolts of fire.
So now with stress stupendous I
Have struggled up from depths profound,
And for inhabitants I cry,
To spread new life and stir around.

SPHINX

This for birth of primal eld
We assuredly had taken,
Had we not ourselves beheld
How it from the ground was shaken.
Still upward brake and forest spread,
And rocks on rocks still forwards tread;
But not for things like these shall Sphinx retreat:
They shall not drive us from our sacred seat.

GRIFFINS

Gold in specks and veins I spy
    Gleam in fissures all about:
Let not such a prize slip by;
    Emmets, up, and pick it out!

CHORUS OF ANTS

Fast as the giant ones
Yonder upheave it,
Seize it, ye pliant ones,
And never leave it.
Quick! Every cranny in
Ranging and rifling;
None that there's any in
Can be too trifling.
Murkiest, shiniest,
Look ye explore it;
Each speck, the tiniest,
Seize it and store it.
Work away with a will,
Till it's all rolled out:
Move the hill how it will,
Do you get its gold out!

GRIFFIN

Pile the gold up! Pile away!
We on it our claws will lay.
Be the treasure what it may,
Surest of all bolts are they!

PIGMIES

We have found a footing here;
How, a puzzle is would task us.
That we've come, is very clear;
Whence we come, then, do not ask us!
Every country, where life glows,
Finds a master soon to guide it;

So no rock a fissure shows,
But a dwarf is straight beside it.
There his busy toil he plies,
Model spouse with model mate;
If 'twas so in Paradise,
That is more than I can state.
But we like this for a nest,
Bless the stars that hither sent us,
In the East as in the West
Mother Earth yields foison plenteous.

DACTYLS

If she in a night these small
Imps did into being call,
Smaller still she will create,
And with kindred creatures mate.

THE OLDEST OF THE PIGMIES

Hasten, and fit ye
Stoutly to quit ye.
Get to work quickly!
Strike your strokes thickly!
In force though they fail,
Let their swiftness prevail.
Peace still is with ye!
Up with the stithy,
Buckler and glaive
To forge for the brave.

And you, ye emmets, ho,
Swarming there to and fro,
Metals with swiftest speed
Fetch for our need!
Ye dactyls slumberless,
Tiny, but numberless,
Quick, from the brake
Fetch faggot and stake!
Pile the fire, heap it up,
Feed it, and keep it up,
Charcoal to make!

GENERALISSIMO

With arrow and bow
Away! Hillio, ho!
Shoot me those herons
Down by the marsh there,

Clustering numberless,
Croaking so harsh there!
Quick, let me see them
Slain altogether!
So shall we prank it
In helmet and feather!

ANTS AND DACTYLS

Iron we bring them—
Ah, who is to save us?—
Which into fetters
They forge to enslave us.
Not yet is the hour come
To rise up defiant;
Then be to your tyrants
Submissive and pliant.

THE CRANES OF IBYCUS

Shrieks of murder, dying groans,
Wings that flutter in dismay,
Oh, what outcry and what moans
To our peaks here pierce their way!
They are all already slain,
All the lake their blood doth stain.
Wanton passion for display
Shore the heron's plumes away.
See it on the helmet wave
Of each bow-legged pot-bellied knave!
Ye companions of our host,
That in troops o'er ocean post,
We to vengeance call you, in
A cause so near your own akin.
Death, so we avenge their fate!
To this rabble deathless hate!

                              [*Disperse, croaking in the air.*

MEPHISTOPHELES (*on the plain*)

The northern witches I could manage featly,
But those strange phantoms baffle me completely;
And then the Blocksberg's such a handy site,
Go anywhere you will, you're always right.
DAME ILSA on her stone keeps watch and ward;
HENRY upon his peak holds cheery guard;
Then to DESPAIR the SNORERS snort and blow
All as they did a thousand years ago.

But here, stand still or walk, who's he can say,
If under him the ground will not give way?
Through a smooth dell as pleasantly I stroll,
Up all at once behind me starts a whole
Hillside, yet scarcely to be called a hill,
And yet quite high enough to part me still
From my pet Sphinxes. Down the valley here
Fires flicker, flashing round strange shapes and drear.
Dancing and wheeling see yon winsome crew
With becks and wiles enticing to pursue.
Soho, then! We, who're used to toothsome fare,
Must still be hankering, no matter where.

LAMIAE (*luring* MEPHISTOPHELES *after them*)

Onward, still onward,
Faster and faster!
Then with a spiteful
Coyness delaying,
Prattling and playing,
He'll think he's the winner.
'Tis so delightful,
Thus the old sinner
To lure and o'ermaster!
Fretting and groaning,
His stiff foot bemoaning,
Hark, he comes grumbling,
Stumbling and tumbling!
Do what he will,
While before him we fly,
Be it far, be it nigh,
He must follow us still!

MEPHISTOPHELES (*stands still*)

Curst fate! Born but to be made fools of!
From Adam made mere dolts and tools of!
We all grow old, but who grows steady?
Wert thou not fooled enough already?
We know they're good for nothing, all the race.
Pinched at the girdle, painted in the face;
No bit about them wholesome, firm, and sound,
They fall to pieces if you clasp them round;
We know it, feel it, see it at a glance—
Yet let them pipe, and after them we dance.

LAMIAE (*stopping*)

Stay! he reflects—he pauses—lingers.
Advance, or he'll slip through your fingers!

MEPHISTOPHELES (*striding on*)

Push on!   Let no uneasy twitches
Of foolish doubting stay your revel:
Good gracious! if there were no witches,
Who, who the deuce would be the devil?

LAMIAE (*in coaxing tones*)

Round this hero, round we run;
Soon within his heart for one
Of us, full sure, will love ensue.

MEPHISTOPHELES

Truly in this twilight gleam
Damsels fair to view ye seem,
So I can't be wroth with you.

EMPUSA (*pressing forward*)

Not yet with me!   Me too admit,
As for your company most fit.

LAMIAE

She amongst us is too many;
Always spoils our sport, the zany!

EMPUSA (*to* MEPHISTOPHELES)

From your dear cousin hold aloof,
Empusa with the ass's hoof?
You've but a horse's hoof; yet still,
Sir Kinsman, hail, with right good will!

MEPHISTOPHELES

I fancied no one knew me here,
Yet find relations—that's severe!
The old, old tale—Go where you will,
From Harz to Hellas, kinsfolk still!

EMPUSA

With much decision I can act;
Can take what shape I please in fact,
But in your honour, for the nonce,
I've donned just now this ass's sconce.

MEPHISTOPHELES

These folk, they set great store, I see,
By being of the family;
Yet come what will—disaster, shame—
The ass's head I will disclaim!

LAMIAE

Avoid this hag! who puts to flight
All that is most fair and bright:
What was fair and bright before,
When she comes, is so no more.

MEPHISTOPHELES

These cousins, too, so smooth of speech,
I'm doubtful of them, all and each,
Behind their cheeks so rosy red
Some metamorphosis I dread.

LAMIAE

Come set to work now! We are many.
Essay your luck—if you have any,
The first prize you may win. Come, try!
What means this pitiful to-do?
A miserable wooer you,
To strut and bear your head so high!
And now amongst us see him skip;
Your masks off slow and slyly slip,
And be your true selves by and by.

MEPHISTOPHELES

I've caught the prettiest and most lissom—
                    [*Embracing her.*
Ugh, ugh! The dry old withered besom!
                    [*Seizing another.*
And this one? The disgusting fright!

LAMIAE

Ha! have we caught you? Serves you right!

MEPHISTOPHELES

I had the short one in my grips—
A lizard from my finger slips,
With poll most serpent-like and smooth!
Anon the taller jade I clasp—
A Thyrsus-staff is in my grasp,
With pine-cone for a head, forsooth!
What means it all? The stout one there,
Better with her perchance I'll fare.

One venture more—the last—here goes!
Juicy and plump, just of the size
The Orientals highly prize.
Ugh!   The puff-ball bursts beneath my nose!

LAMIAE

Away, and round him flit, now like
The lightning, now all blackness!   Strike
The witch's baffled son with fear!
On silent wings, a ghastly crew,
Wheel round like bats!   We'll make him rue
The hour he thought of coming here.

MEPHISTOPHELES (*shaking himself*)

I have not grown much wiser, 'twould appear.
They're idiots in the north, they're idiots here.
They're humbugs here as there, the ghostly crew,
And bores the bards and people too.
Here has been precious mumming, and
Sense has, as usual, had the upper hand.
At features fair a clutch I made,
And in my grasp found what appalled me;
Yet had it only longer stayed,
Even that delusion had enthralled me.
                    [*Losing his way among the rocks.*
Where am I?   What is this, and how?
This was a path, 'tis chaos now.
The road was smooth; but boulders, lo!
At every turn perplex my feet.
Vainly I clamber to and fro—
Nowhere can I my Sphinxes meet.
One night a hill like this to breed!
Who could have dreamt so mad a thing?
A jolly witches' ride, indeed,
When they with them their Blocksberg bring!

OREAD (*from the natural rock*)

Up here!   My mountain's old as time;
Its shape the same as in its prime.
My precipices jagged and sheer,
Pindus' extremest spur, revere!
Unshaken here I lift my head,
As when across me Pompey fled.
That dream-begotten phantasm there
At cock-crow will dissolve in air.
Such fabled forms I ofttimes see
Arise, then vanish suddenly.

* K 335

MEPHISTOPHELES

Be honour thine, thou reverend head,
With sturdy oaks engarlanded!
To thy recesses dark and deep
The brightest moonshine cannot creep.
But down by yonder brushwood strays
A light that glows with modest rays.
What strange coincidence is this?
Homunculus?   It is, it is!
Whither away, my little friend?

HOMUNCULUS

Thus on from spot to spot I wend.
Much do I long to burst my glassy screen,
And in the best sense into life to enter;
Only from all that I as yet have seen,
I can't find courage for the venture.
But hearken in your ear!   On two
Philosophers I've stumbled, who
Are wrapt in deep debate, and all their talk
Is 'Nature, Nature,' as they walk.
I'll keep by them; for they, I wis,
Must know what earthly being is.
And I at last am sure to learn,
Whither 'tis best for me to turn.

MEPHISTOPHELES

What your own instinct prompts pursue.
For where ghosts find a lodgment, your
Philosopher is welcome too.
And be they many, be they few,
To show his skill off, he is sure
To conjure up a dozen new.
Make no mistakes, and you will ne'er be wise.
By your own doings into being rise!

HOMUNCULUS

Still, good advice it were not wise to miss.

MEPHISTOPHELES

Go your own way!   We shall see more of this.
                                    [*They separate.*

ANAXAGORAS (*to* THALES)

Will not your stubborn mind the truth concede,
Or do you further demonstration need?

THALES

The wave is stirred by every breeze that creeps,
But from the beetling crags far off it keeps.

ANAXAGORAS

This mountain-ridge to fire its being owes.

THALES

From moisture all that lives to being rose.

HOMUNCULUS

Let me go side by side with you.
I yearn to rise to being too.

ANAXAGORAS

Could you, O Thales, in one night produce
A mountain such as this from mud and ooze?

THALES

Nature, has she with her creative powers
E'er had regard to days, and nights, and hours?
Calm and serene she plies her shaping hand;
It is not violence makes even what is grand.

ANAXAGORAS

But here it did!   Raging Plutonic fire,
Steam pent for ages, with explosion dire
Burst through the ancient crusts of earth, and threw
A mountain in a moment into view.

THALES

What boots it to continue this debate?
The mountain's there; that's well, at any rate.
In such disputes no one step we advance,
Yet lead the patient crowd a precious dance.

ANAXAGORAS

See, from the mountain how in bevies
They stream to fill each chasm and crevice!
With pigmies, ants, and gnomes it rings,
And other bustling tiny things.   [*To* HOMUNCULUS.
Within your hermit cell retired,
To greatness you have ne'er aspired.
To rule if you your mind can bring,
I'll have you straightway crowned their king.

HOMUNCULUS

What says my Thales?

THALES

I say no!
With little people, little deeds;
With great ones even the little grow
To size, and greatness greatness breeds.
Look at these cranes, a dusky cloud!
They threaten yon excited crowd,
And so would threaten, too, the king.
Downward they swoop on rushing wing,
With bony claw and pointed beak,
Their vengeance on the dwarfs to wreak.
The very air is charged with doom,
And tempest hurtles through the gloom.
A wicked elf the herons slew,
As round their quiet mere they drew.
But that death-laden arrowy sleet
Arouses vengeance fell and meet,
And in their kin such ire doth wake,
As blood, and blood alone can slake.
What now avail shield, helm, or spear?
Their heron-plumes, what boot they?   See,
How ant and dactyl disappear!
The hosts, they reel, they turn, they flee.

ANAXAGORAS (*after a pause, solemnly*)

If hitherto my praise
Has to the subterranean powers been given,
In this conjuncture I uplift my gaze
To those that have their seat in heaven.

Oh, Throned above, through endless time
Wearing the freshness of thy prime,
Thee I invoke, thee now as then the same,
Threefold in form, threefold in name,
My people in their woe to free,
Diana, Luna, Hecate!
Thou the bosom that expandest,
Thou of thinkers deepest, grandest,
Thou aspect serene that wearest,
Thou a soul of fire that bearest,
Open the abysses drear
Of thy shadowy glooms—and here,
With no necromancer's aid,
Be thine ancient power displayed!   [*Pause.*
Is my prayer too quickly heard?
By its force
Has the course
Of nature been disturbed and marred?
And larger, ever larger, and more near
The goddess' orbèd throne wheels down the sphere!
Fearful to the eye and dread
Turns its fire to dusky red.
No nearer!   Mighty threatening ball,
Thou'lt crush us, land and sea, and all!
Was it then true, that hags Thessalian by
Dark incantations from the sky
Drew thee down, and wrung from thee
Blight and bane and misery?
The shining disk's o'ercast.   It crashes!
And now it lightens and it flashes!
What din, what rushing, whizzing, pouring;
What gusts of wind through thunder roaring!
Behold me fall, abased and prone,
Down at the footstool of thy throne!
'Twas I invoked thee, I!   Do thou
Forgive, forgive my madness now!

[*Throws himself on his face.*

THALES

What things this man has heard and seen!
They may or they may not have been;
But I felt nothing, ne'ertheless.
Mad hours are these, we must confess,
And Luna sails along the blue,
As smoothly as she used to do.

HOMUNCULUS

Look at the pigmies' haunt! See, how
The hill, once round, is pointed now!
I felt a hideous crash and shock:
   Down from the moon had fallen a rock;
And in an instant made an end,
No warning given, of foe and friend.
Yet arts like these I must revere,
Which in one single night could so
This mighty mountain structure rear,
Both from above and from below.

THALES

Tush, tush! 'Twas all a dream.   That brood
So vile is gone, then let them go!
That thou wert not their king is good.
But now away, away with me,
To Ocean's glorious Jubilee!
There guests of wondrous kind, like thee,
Expected, ay, and honoured be.   [*They withdraw.*

MEPHISTOPHELES (*clambering up on the opposite side*)

Here I go clambering over crags and rocks,
Among the gnarlèd roots of ancient oaks.
The vapours on my own Harz have a flavour
Of pitch, that much commends them to my favour.
'Tis next to brimstone!   Here, among the Greeks,
In vain for even one sulphurous whiff one seeks.
Still, I should like to find out what the spell,
By which they feed the pangs and fires of hell.

DRYAD

In your own land you for a sage may pass,
Abroad you're little better than an ass.
'Tis not of home you should be thinking here,
But how you should the sacred oaks revere!

MEPHISTOPHELES

We harp on what we've lost—a feeble vice!
What we've been used to's always Paradise.
But say, what three are those in yonder den,
Who squat and cower in the glimmering shade?

DRYADS

They are the Phorkyads.   Go forward, then,
And speak to them, if you be not afraid.

MEPHISTOPHELES

And wherefore not?   I am bewildered vastly!
Proud as I am, even I must needs avow,
I ne'er have looked upon their like till now,
Our hell's worst hags are not one half so ghastly!
Who shall this hideous Triad see,
Yet think there's aught repulsive in
The deadliest of old deadly sin?
We should not suffer them, not we,
To cross the threshold of the worst
And eeriest of our hells accurst.
Yet in the land of beauty, here,
This antique land to glory dear,
They children of the soil appear!
They move, they scent me, it would see,
Twitter like vampire bats, and pipe and scream.

PHORKYADS

Sisters! the eye, quick, give it me to spy,
Who to our temple dares approach so nigh!

MEPHISTOPHELES

O most revered! permit me to draw near,
And beg your triple benediction here!
I am not quite a stranger—so, forgive!
Indeed, I am a distant relative.
Gods of old standing in my time I've known,
To Ops and Rhea made my bow of yore,
The Parcae, Chaos' sisters, and your own,
I saw them last night, or the night before;
But such as you have never crossed my sight.
I'm positively dumb with sheer delight!

PHORKYADS

There seems some sense in what this spirit says.

MEPHISTOPHELES

My only wonder is, no bard has sung your praise!
In statues I have never seen you.   Say,
How comes this so, most honoured ones, if you know?
Yours are the forms the chisel should portray,
And not such things as Venus, Pallas, Juno.

PHORKYADS

In solitude, and silent night inurned,
Our thoughts have never on such matters turned.

MEPHISTOPHELES

How should they? Living from the world retired,
By none can you be seen, or, seen, admired.
For that you must a residence command,
Where art and luxury rule hand in hand;
Where from a block of marble—presto, hey!—
Starts into life a hero every day;
Where——

PHORKYADS

Peace! And wake in us no yearnings fond!
What should we gain, by knowing aught beyond?
In Night begot, and kin to things of Night,
To ourselves almost unknown, to others quite.

MEPHISTOPHELES

This being so, there is not much to say;
But you to others may yourselves convey.
One eye suffices for the three, one tooth,
And 'twill comport with mythologic truth,
To merge in two the essence of the three,
And lend the semblance of the third to me
For some brief space.

ONE OF THE PHORKYADS

How think ye? Speaks he sooth?

THE OTHERS

Let's try it. But without the eye and tooth.

MEPHISTOPHELES

Take these away, and you the essence take,
For these are what the perfect picture make.

ONE OF THE PHORKYADS

Press one eye close! 'Tis very simply done;
That's well! Now of your dog-teeth show but one!
And you will instantly in profile show
Our sister perfectly from top to toe!

MEPHISTOPHELES

I'm honoured—much! So be it!

PHORKYADS

So be it!

MEPHISTOPHELES (*as a* PHORKYAD *in profile*)
                                          Done!

Behold in me old Chaos' darling son!

PHORKYADS

Chaos' undoubted daughters we.

MEPHISTOPHELES
                                  Oh, spite!
They'll scoff at me as an hermaphrodite!

PHORKYADS

Our new third sister is surpassing fair!
Of eyes we have, and eke of teeth a pair.

MEPHISTOPHELES

I must get out of sight, or I know well
I'll scare the devils of the nether hell!   [*Exit.*

ROCKY BAYS OF THE AEGEAN SEA
—*The Moon pausing in the Zenith*

SIRENS (*lying on the cliffs around, fluting and singing*)

Thou whom hags Thessalian erst,
By unholy spells rehearsed,
Drew from heaven, serenely bright,
Looking from the vault of night,
With thy silvery radiance lave
Every bright and rippling wave,
And illume yon wondrous throng
Rising now the waves along.
Thy devoted vassals we;
Luna fair, propitious be!

NEREIDS AND TRITONS (*as wonders of the deep*)

Loud with shriller voices sing,
Let them o'er broad ocean ring,
All its people summoning!
As we lay within our caves,
Fathom deep beneath the waves,

Safe from wind and stormy weather,
Your sweet song has drawn us hither.
In our transports we, behold!
Deck ourselves with chains of gold,
Brooch and clasp and diadem,
Rich with jewel and with gem.
All your fruitage, all are these!
Treasures plucked from argosies,
That now wrecked and rotting lie,
Lured to their destruction by
You, the demons of our bay.

SIRENS

Well we know, that in the sea
Fish live well and merrily,
Without pain, or care, or wish!
Still, ye throng so brisk and gay,
Fain we'd like to know to-day,
If ye're something more than fish.

NEREIDS AND TRITONS

Ere we hither came, did we
Ponder well how things should be.
Brothers, sisters, come!   Not far
Is it needful we should go,
Most conclusively to show
That we more than fishes are.   [*They retire.*

SIRENS

In a twinkling they
To Samothrace have sped away,
And fair for them the breezes blow!
What can they expect to gain
Where the high Cabiri reign?
Gods of wondrous kind are they,
Who beget themselves alway,
And what they are they never know.
Deign to linger on thy heights,
Gentle Luna!   So the night's
Veil will tarry, and the day
Chase us not from hence away!

THALES (*on the shore to* HOMUNCULUS)

Fain would I lead you to old Nereus!   See,
His cavern must be somewhere hereabout:
But such a cross-grained sour old carle is he,
It is no easy thing to draw him out.

Churl that he is, in his distorted sight
No mortal man is ever in the right.
But unto him the future is unveiled,
So he with reverence deep is hailed,
And bears a highly honoured name.
To many, too, he has been kind.

HOMUNCULUS

Let's knock and try him!   I don't mind.
It will not cost me both my glass and flame.

NEREUS

Men's voices could they be, my ear that met?
With wrath they stir my heart down to its core:
Forms striving to attain to gods, and yet
Doomed to be like themselves for evermore.
Long years ago, had I like others felt,
In ease I might, even like a god, have dwelt;
But I was ever by the wish possessed,
To benefit the men I deemed the best;
And ever when I looked, in hopes to know,
My counsels into goodly acts had thriven,
I found that matters were the same, as though
My counsels never had been given.

THALES

Yet people trust thee, man of ocean old.
Most sage of sages, turn us not away!
This flame, that bears a human shape, behold!
Whate'er you counsel him, he will obey.

NEREUS

Counsel!   Has counsel e'er availed with men?
The sagest saw falls dead on stubborn ears.
Oft as men's folly has been mourned in tears,
Wilful as ever they will be again.
Warned I not Paris like a father, ere
His passion did another's wife ensnare?
As bold he trod the Grecian shore, with awe
I told him all that I in vision saw—
Clouds steaming up, with lurid light aglow,
Charred rafters, massacre and death below,
Troy's day of doom, immortalized in song,
Beaconing through time the curse that waits on wrong.

He mocked the old man's words, the ribald boy,
Obeyed the impulse of his lust, and Troy,
A giant corpse, fell, worn with many a fray,
To Pindus' eagles a right welcome prey.
Ulysses, too, foretold I not to him
Circe's dark wiles, the Cyclops' horrors grim?
His own delays, the follies of his train,
What not, besides!   Yet where to him the gain?
Till at long last the favouring billows bore
The weary wanderer to a friendly shore.

THALES

Such conduct to the sage is fraught with pain,
Yet his heart prompts him on to fresh essay.
Of thanks that glad his soul, one little grain
Will bushels of ingratitude outweigh.
For we are here to ask no trivial boon:
The boy there wishes to attain, and soon,
To being, and as sagely as he may.

NEREUS

Mar not my mood—'tis of no common kind;
Far other matters now possess my mind.
My daughters I have summoned here to me,
The Dorides, the Graces of the Sea.
Not on Olympus, nor on earth you'll meet
With forms so beautiful, so moving sweet.
From water dragons, with a bending sweep
Of subtlest charm, on Neptune's steeds they leap,
And with the element so softly blend,
The foam-flakes scarce beneath them seem to bend.
'Mid rainbow splendours in her shelly car
Comes Galatea, of them all the star,
Of Paphos hailed the goddess, since the day
When Aphrodite turned from us away;
And so for many a year, she as her own
The Temple town has claimed, and chariot throne.
Begone!   Nor by your questionings eclipse
The solemn transports of a father's bliss;
I would not have, in such an hour as this,
Hate in my heart, nor fury on my lips.
Away to Proteus!   Ask that being strange—
He will your purpose better serve than me—
How yonder boy may pass from change to change,
And come at length to be.   [Retires towards the sea.

THALES

We have gained nothing by this step; for, say
We light on Proteus, straight he melts away.
And, after all, he'll only, if he stays,
Give answers that bewilder and amaze.
Still, such advice you lack; so, come what may,
Let's make the trial.   Onward, then, away!

[*They retire.*

SIRENS (*above, on the rocks*)

See, what are these that glide
Far o'er the billowy tide?
'Tis as white sails were nearing,
By gentle breezes steering,
So radiantly they shine,
These ocean-nymphs divine!
Let us descend!   You hear
Their voices sweet and clear.

NEREIDS AND TRITONS

What we bring with us to-night
Shall content you and delight.
Flames a dread form from the field
Of Chelone's giant shield;
Gods they be, whom here we bring:
Hymns ye must of glory sing!

SIRENS

Great in might, though small in form,
Such as shipwrecked are ye save,
When in thunder and in storm
Ships go down beneath the wave;
Gods in deepest reverence held
From the days of primal eld!

NEREIDS AND TRITONS

We bring the Cabiri hither, to keep
Peace, while we revel it over the deep;
For in their presence, so holy be they,
Neptune will gently exert his sway.

SIRENS

Yield we must to you:
If a vessel's wrecked,
Ever ye her crew
Resistlessly protect.

NEREIDS AND TRITONS

Three we have transported thus;
The fourth refused to come with us.
He declared he was the best,
And had to think for all the rest.

SIRENS

So one god, it would appear,
Likes at other gods to sneer.
All that gracious are revere,
All that are malignant fear!

NEREIDS AND TRITONS

Seven of them by rights there be.

SIRENS

Where, then, are the other three?

NEREIDS AND TRITONS

To answer that were no easy task.
For them you may in Olympus ask.
There the Eighth, too, you may find,
Who was never in anybody's mind.
Their grace we have and hope to get,
But they are not all complete as yet.
These Incomparables still
    On and on aspire,
For the Unattainable
    Hungering with desire.

SIRENS

'Tis our custom, evermore
Every throne to bow before,
In the Sun and in the Moon,
There to worship and adore;
It repays us late or soon.

NEREIDS AND TRITONS

How must our fame transcendent be,
The leaders of this Jubilee!

SIRENS

The heroes of the olden time
Reached not a glory so sublime,
How high soe'er their fame may run.
If they the Golden Fleece have won,
You, you have the Cabiri!

UNIVERSAL CHORUS

If they the Golden Fleece have won,
You, you⎫
We, we ⎭ have the Cabiri!

HOMUNCULUS

To me these uncouth shapes are like
Vile earthen pots: by token,
Sages their heads against them strike,
And, though hard, get them broken.

THALES

That's just the thing they long for!   Just
As coin takes value from the rust.

PROTEUS (*invisible*)

Such shows delight a fabler old like me;
More prized the more preposterous they be.

THALES

Where art thou, Proteus?

PROTEUS (*ventriloquially, now near, now far off*)
                                        Here, and here!

THALES

I pardon you the stale old joke.
I am a friend—no mocking insincere!
I know you sham the place from which you spoke.

PROTEUS (*as from a distance*)
Farewell!

THALES (*whispers to the* HOMUNCULUS)

     He's close at hand!   Flame out now!   Whish!
He is as curious as a fish,
And, wheresoever he may hide,
Your blaze will lure him to your side.

HOMUNCULUS

I'll pour a flood of light—but gently though,
Or into splinters, crack! my glass will go.

PROTEUS (*in the form of a gigantic tortoise*)

What sheds a light so soft and bright?

THALES (*concealing the* HOMUNCULUS)

Good! good!   Come nearer, if you'd see't.
Don't grudge the trouble, 'tis but slight!
And show yourself upon two human feet.
'Tis by our grace and leave alone,
That what we've hidden will be shown.

PROTEUS

You have not lost your skill in dodges clever.

THALES

Of changing shapes you're quite as fond as ever.
               [*Uncovers the* HOMUNCULUS.

PROTEUS (*amazed*)

A luminous dwarf!   Was never such sight?   Never!

THALES

He wants advice from you, for he would fain
To being real and complete attain.
He came into the world, I've heard him say,
Only by half in some mysterious way.
With gifts of spirit he is dowried well,
But sorely lacks in what is tangible.
As now the glass there only gives him weight,
He with all speed would be incorporate.

PROTEUS

A real virgin's son art thou;
Thou art before thou ought to be, somehow.

THALES (*in a whisper*)

In other ways, methinks, all is not right.
He is, I fancy, an hermaphrodite.

PROTEUS

So much the better, since in every case
He's sure to find himself not out of place.
But much reflection here no good will do,
In the wide sea you must begin anew!
There in the little things commence,
And on the less delight to feed:
So by degrees you grow, and thence
To higher excellence succeed.

HOMUNCULUS

The air blows sweet and softly here.   The dew
Thrills me with rapture through and through.

PROTEUS

Right, right, my pretty youth!   And you,
As you go on, will find it sweeter still.
On this small tongue of land the dew
Exhales a vapour more ineffable.
See, right in front yon wondrous train,
That's wafted hither o'er the main!
Come with me to them!

THALES

Take me too!

HOMUNCULUS

A wondrous ghostly three are we to view.

TELCHINES OF RHODES (*upon Hippocampi and Sea-dragons,
bearing Neptune's Trident*)

CHORUS

The trident of Neptune we forged, that at will
The angriest waves of the ocean can still.
If the Thund'rer his storm-clouds unrolls overhead,
Straight Neptune opposes their armament dread;

And as down from above lightning quivers and flashes,
So up from below wave after wave dashes;
And the bark, that in anguish 'twixt billow and blast
Has been tossed to and fro, is sucked down at the last;
Then as he has lent us his sceptre to-day,
Serene and at ease let us gambol and play!

SIRENS

Hail, ye priests of Helios, hail,
Blest ones of the cheerful day,
Now whilst we to Luna pale
Our devoted homage pay!

TELCHINES

Fair queen of the bow that shines o'er us so bright,
Thou hearest thy brother extolled with delight!
To Rhodes the high-favoured thine ear thou dost lend,
Whence unto him Paeans eternal ascend.
He begins the day's course, and on us at its close
A long level glance keen and fiery he throws.
The mountains, the cities, the shore, and the wave,
Give delight to the god, and are beauteous and brave.
No mist hangs around us, and if one comes near,
A zephyr, a beam, and our island is clear!
In manifold shapes he beholds himself there,
As stripling, as giant, as mighty, as fair.
We, we were the first, did such beings divine
In the forms, not unworthy, of mortals enshrine!

PROTEUS

Let them sing, and let them boast!
Dead works are a jest, at most,
Beside the sun's life-giving rays;
They melt and mould, and when at last
Their handiwork in brass is cast,
Straightway they riot in its praise.
But what's the end of all their vaunted show!
These images of gods renowned,
An earthquake hurled them to the ground;
And they've been melted down long, long ago.

The throes of earth, or past or present,
Are always anything but pleasant.
Life in the billows better fares;
Thee to the eternal waters bears

The Dolphin Proteus.   (*Transforms himself.*)   See, 'tis done!
There will you thrive in all you try:
So leap upon my back, and I
Will wed you to the deep anon!

THALES

Yield to the noble aspiration
Of new-commencing your creation.
Prepare for mighty effort now!
By laws eternal move, and thou,
Through countless changes having passed,
Shalt rise into a man at last.

[HOMUNCULUS *mounts the Proteus-dolphin.*

PROTEUS

In spirit hence to ocean wide!
Unfettered there shalt thou abide,
There roam as blithe as free;
But yearn not for a higher state,
For, once as man incorporate,
All's over then with thee.

THALES

That's as things chance: it is a fine thing, too,
To be a proper man in season due.

PROTEUS (*to* THALES)

If of your stamp he be, perchance it may.
You are no fleeting creature of a day;
For 'tis now many hundred years, since I
'Mongst the pale ghosts first saw you trooping by.

SIRENS (*on the rocks*)

Lo, what clouds are yonder streaming
  Round the moon in circlet bright!
Doves they are, love-kindled, gleaming,
  Pinioned as with purest light.
Paphos forth has sent them, glowing
  Harbingers of love and joy;
Perfect is our feast, o'erflowing
  Full with bliss without alloy!

NEREUS (*advancing to* THALES)

Roamers through the night might deem
Yonder halo merely haze,
But we spirits know the gleam,
Hail it with a wiser gaze.
They are doves, that round my child
In her shelly chariot fly,
Wondrous is their flight and wild,
Learned in ages long gone by.

THALES

I too look on that as best,
Which to good men pleasure gives,
When in warm and cosy nest
Something holy haunts and lives.

PSYLLI AND MARSI (*on sea-bulls, sea-calves, and rams*)

In Cyprus' wild cave-recesses,
Where the god of the sea annoys not,
Where Seismos shakes and destroys not,
Where the breeze evermore wafts caresses,
There Cypris's chariot, the golden,
We watch, as we watched in the olden
Days, in contentment serene;
And our fairest we bring in the hushing
Of night, o'er the rippling waves rushing,
In the bloom of her loveliness flushing,
By the new race of mortals unseen.

Our duty thus silently plying,
Nor eagle, nor yet wingèd lion,
Dismays us, nor cross, no, nor crescent;
However, through changes incessant,
On earth they may fool it, and rule it,
Now hither, now thitherward swaying,
Pursuing, and smiting, and slaying,
Waste cities and harvest-fields laying.
'Tis ever our care,
To herald our mistress, the matchlessly fair.

SIRENS

Through the waves serenely cleaving,
  Circling round the car divine,
And like serpents interweaving,
  Row on row, and line on line,

Speed ye, nereids, stately gliding,
  Ocean's daughters, pleasing wild,
With you Galatea guiding,
  And the graceful Dorids mild.
Grave is she, of godlike seeming,
  As of an immortal race,
Yet, like gentle human women,
  Sweet, and of alluring grace.

DORIDES (*passing in chorus before* NEREUS, *riding
                  upon dolphins*)

Luna, shine, thy radiance pouring
  Round this flower of youth, for here
To our sire we bring, imploring
  His goodwill, our bridegrooms dear!   [*To* NEREUS.
Boys we rescued, when the billow
  Whelmed them in the tempest's wrack;
Couching them on rushy pillow,
  We to life caressed them back!
Now with kisses to delight us,
  Kisses all of fire, must they
For the life we gave requite us:
  View them, then, with grace, we pray!

NEREUS

The twofold gain who would not highly treasure,
In doing others grace, to do himself a pleasure?

DORIDES

Father, did we well?   To hold them,
  Grant us, so shall we be blest:
All undying let us fold them
  To our ever-youthful breast.

NEREUS

Would you enjoy your lovely prey,
  Then mould each stripling to a man;
But, children, know, I never may
  Bestow what Zeus, Zeus only can.
The wave, on which you're swept and tossed,
  Makes love, too, changeful evermore:
If on their hearts your hold be lost,
  Best set them quietly on shore!

DORIDES

Sweet boys, we love ye well, but soon
    From you, alas! must sever;
The gods deny the wished-for boon,
    A love that lives for ever.

THE YOUTHS

Still love and tend us, and your own
    Stout ship-boys will not falter;
Such goodly cheer we ne'er have known,
    Nor would for better alter.
                    [GALATEA *approaches in the shell chariot.*

NEREUS

My darling!

GALATEA

    O father, what ecstasy!
Stay, dolphins, stay!   My gaze is riveted by thee!

NEREUS

Already are they passed, already gone,
In sweeping circles steering o'er the ocean;
What is to them the yearning heart's emotion?
Oh, would that I with them were sailing on!
Yet in that one brief glance is such delight,
As doth the long year's yearning well requite!

THALES

Hail! hail! hail evermore!
With joy I am brimming o'er,
Each fibre and nerve, through and through
By the Beautiful pierced, and the True!
From water sprang all things, and all
Are by water upheld or must fall.
Then, ocean, grant thou for our aiding
Thine influence ever-pervading!
If by thee the clouds were disspread not,
If by thee the rich brooklets were shed not,
If by thee the streams all ways were sped not,
And the rush of the torrents were fed not,
What then were the universe, mountain and plain?
'Tis thou dost all life that is freshest maintain!

ECHO

Chorus of the whole circle

'Tis from thee flows all life that is freshest amain.

NEREUS

Already they are far from shore,
Meet me eye to eye no more!
On they speed, a countless train,
All in festival array,
In a long extended chain,
Winding, circling on their way.
But my Galatea's car,
Still I see it sharp and bright!
It is shining like a star
Through them all upon the sight!
That dear cynosure is steeped in light!
Though it be removed so far,
Still it shimmers bright and clear,
Ever true and ever near!

HOMUNCULUS

'Mid these waters soft and bright,
All whereon I flash my light
Is bewitching fair!

PROTEUS

'Mid these waters living bright,
For the first time gleams thy light
With a music rare!

NEREUS

But lo! what fresh mystery yonder between
The groups of the children of ocean is seen?
What flames round the car, round my darling one's feet?
Now wildly it flashes, now softly, now sweet,
As if with love's passionate pulses it beat!

THALES

'Tis Homunculus, ferried by Proteus so fleet.
The symptoms are these of a yearning intense;
Soon the cry shall be heard of an agonized moan:
He will shatter his glass on the radiant throne.
Now it flames, now it lightens, now pours forth immense.

SIRENS

What fiery marvel illumines the sea,
Where wave breaks on wave in sparkles of light?
It so lightens, and brightens, and flashes, that we
See their forms all aglow as they move through the night,
And flames round them eddy and glimmer and gleam.
Then be Eros, of all the Beginner, supreme!

Hail, ye ocean billows, bound
With zone of holy fire around!
Water, hail!   Hail, fire!   Hail, all
Doings strange that here befall!

GENERAL CHORUS

Hail, ye breezes, blowing free!
Hail, ye caves of mystery!
You we praise, and you adore
Mighty elemental Four!

ACT III [1]

IN FRONT OF THE PALACE OF MENELAUS AT SPARTA

Enter HELEN, *with a Chorus of Captive Trojan Women*
—PANTHALIS *leader of the Chorus*

HELENA

I, HELENA, of men much famed, and much reviled,
From yonder shore, where we but now have landed, come
Still reeling with the heave, and ever-restless roll
Of ocean billows wild, whose high and foamy crests,
By Euros' might and great Poseidon's grace, have borne
Us back from Phrygia's plains to these our native bays.
Now on the sea-beach joys King Menelaus, thus
Returning safe with all his bravest warriors back.
But do thou bid me welcome home, thou mansion fair,
Which Tyndarus, my sire, when home returning, reared,
Hard by the broad incline of Pallas' sacred hill;
And, when I here with Clytemnestra, sisterly,
With Castor, Pollux too, grew up in gladsome play,
That in its trappings rich all Sparta's homes excelled!

---

[1] This act was first published separately, in 1827, and was then described as a 'classical romantic phantasmagoria.' In the completed Second Part it is, however, no more of a dream picture than the carnival scene, the Classical Walpurgis Night and much else, and it is no interlude, but an integral part of the whole. The modern reader may think of it as an elaborate 'imaginary interview.' An episode in the old Faust legend suggested it, but it has been given an altogether new interpretation. This Faust does not think of Helena as a kind of siren, the tool of the devil, but as the embodiment of all that is best in Greek civilization. His 'love' for her is obviously symbolic, 'not that of a man for a woman, but of a humanist for an ideal' (Lowes Dickinson). Goethe's and Schiller's enthusiastic Hellenism inspired its beginning, in 1800, but in the final version, written over twenty years after Schiller's death, Goethe seems to be conscious of the romantic nature of their longing for a beauty no longer capable of being realized in its ancient form, yet he sees a positive value in this longing, for it has inspired memorable poetry, and even heroic action in such a poet as Byron, the 'familiar form' whom Euphorion resembles.

Goethe had at one time laid the scene on the Rhine, but in the end he takes Faust towards Helena, as it were, in space, and Helena towards him in time, and they meet in a castle like many that were built by European knights in northern Greece after the Crusades. To begin with Helena appears as if she were returning, after the fall of Troy, to her original home, the palace of Menelaus at Sparta, but with great skill Goethe reminds us through her own words that she is the creation of a modern mind, giving her a 'ghostly semi-consciousness and glassy beauty' (Santayana).

Ye portal's brazen wings, lo, here I bid you hail!
Through you, wide open flung with hospitable sweep,
Did Menelaus first, of many chosen the chief,
Upon my vision beam in bridegroom guise of yore.
Expand to me again, that, as doth spouse beseem,
My lord's high urgent 'hest I rightly may fulfil!
Let me go in, and oh! may all the storms of fate,
Which round my path have swept till now, remain behind!
For since I parted hence, a stranger then to care,
To offer homage due at Cytherea's shrine,
And there was by a spoiler seized, the Phrygian boy,
Hath misadventure much befallen, which men are fain
To babble of, but which offends his ear, whose tale,
Expanding as it spread, to gossip fable grew.

CHORUS

Fairest of women, despise not thou
The treasure, supreme in honour, is thine!
For to thee, thee alone, has the chief boon been given,
The fame of a beauty unmatched in the world.
Before the hero his name resounds,
And therefore his port is proud,
But even the stubbornest veils his pride
In the presence of beauty, the lord of all.

HELENA

Enough said!　With my lord I hitherward have sailed,
And now before him I am to his city sent;
Yet what his purpose is, defies me to divine.
Come I as consort back?　Or come I as a queen?
Or as a victim for the princes' direful woes,
And for the years of loss and shame the Greeks endured?
A captive, or a friend recaptured, which am I?
For the Immortals marked a doubtful fame, belike,
And destiny for me—companions dread that wait
On beauty, and upon the very threshold here
Stand at my side with dark and threatening mien.
For even within the hollow ship my husband scarce
Vouchsafed to me one look, nor word of comfort spoke,
As brooding some fell purpose, fronting me he sat.
But when Eurotas' deep-indented bay we gained,
Scarce of our vessels' prows the foremost kissed the land,
When, starting up, he spake, as by the God inspired.
'My warriors troop by troop shall from the ships descend,
And I will marshal them in order on the beach;
But thou, go on at once, still keeping by the banks,
Wealthy in fruit, that bound Eurotas' sacred stream,

Driving the steeds across the moist bloom-dappled meads,
Until thou shalt arrive on the delightsome plain,
Where Lacedemon, once a broad and fertile field,
Close girdled by the solemn mountains, lifts its roofs.
There enter straight the lofty tower-crowned royal house,
And round thee call the maids whom there I left behind,
Also the Stewardess, that matron old and sage.
Bid her to thee the pile of hoarded treasures show,
Was by thy sire bequeathed, and which, in war and peace
Augmenting evermore, I have myself amassed.
In order duly ranged thou'lt find them all; for 'tis
The prince's privilege to find, on his return,
The things preserved with care, in their appointed place,
Even as he left them, when he parted from his home.
For nothing of himself the slave hath power to change.'

CHORUS

Now gladden thine eye and thy heart by viewing
The glorious treasures, the spoils of years!
For the armlet fair, and the jewelled crown
Rest haughtily there, of their lustre proud;
But enter and challenge them all, right soon
Shall they 'quip them for war.
I joy in the conflict where beauty vies
With gold and with pearl and with luminous gem.

HELENA

Thereafter from my lord there followed this command:
'Now when in order all thou thoroughly hast viewed,
As many tripods take, as thou shalt needful deem,
And vessels of all kinds, which he at hand requires,
Who to the gods performs high sacrificial rites—
The caldrons, salvers too, and patera withal;
Pure water crystal clear from the sacred fount be by,
In lofty pitchers—well-dried faggots furthermore,
That quickly kindle into flame, have ready there;
And, last of all, fail not a knife of keenest edge;
What other things may lack I trust thy care to find.'
So spake he, urging my departure straight; but nought
That breathes the breath of life did his injunctions show,
Which he, in honour of the Olympians, wished to slay.
'Tis very strange; yet I will nurse that thought no more,
But leave all to the will of the great gods on high,
Who bring to pass whate'er they in their minds decree;
And seem it good to man, or seem it ill, it must
Be borne; for mortal man, his duty is to bear.

The ministering priest full many a time hath raised
The ponderous axe above the earth-bowed victim's neck,
Yet could not strike the blow, for suddenly his hand
By intervening foe or deity was stayed.

CHORUS

The fate of the future thou canst not divine.
Enter, queen, enter,
Be of good cheer!
Good and ill cometh
To man without warning;
E'en when foretold us we credit it not.
What saw we, when Troy was in flames, before us?
Death, death only, a death of shame!
Yet are we not here,
Mated with thee, serving thee joyfully,
Beholding the sun in heaven resplendent,
Beholding what is on the earth most fair,
Thee, to us happy ones gracious and kind!

HELENA

A truce to fear!   Whate'er betide, 'tis meet that I,
No longer lingering, should ascend the royal house,
Which, long lost, sighed for much, and wellnigh forfeited,
Stands once again before my eyes, I know not how.
With weak and tottering tread I mount its lofty steps,
Up which erewhile I sprang, a light and frolic child.

CHORUS

Fling, O ye sisters, that
Mourn your captivity,
Grief to the winds!
Share in the bliss
Of your mistress,
Share in Helena's bliss,
Who joyfully neareth
The hearth of her fathers
With step that, though late
To return, is more firm
For the years that have flown.

Praise ye the holy,
Happy-restoring
And home-bringing gods!

Over fate's rudest shocks,
As upon pinions,
Floats the enfranchised one, the while
The captive, vainly his arms outspreading
Over his dungeon's ramparts,
Pines dejected away.

But a god caught her up
In her exile afar;
And from Ilion's ruins
Transported her back
To the old, newly decorate
Home of her sires,
After unspeakable
Pleasures and pains,
On the days of her childhood
To ponder anew.

PANTHALIS (as leader of the Chorus)

Forsake we now the joy-environed path of song,
And turn our gaze awhile upon the portal's wings.
What see I, sisters?   Lo, the queen returning here,
And flying too with wild and agitated step?
What is it, mighty queen?   What sight or sound of dread
Could greet thee in thy halls, instead of welcoming
From thine own people?   This expect not to conceal;
For plainly can I read displeasure on thy brow,
A wrath of noble sort, that struggles with surprise.

HELENA (who has entered in great agitation, leaving
the folding-doors open)

Beseemeth not Jove's child to own a vulgar dread,
Nor fleeting touch of fear hath power to move her soul.
But Horror grim, that, in the womb of ancient Night
And Chaos old begot, in form and shape diverse,
As clouds of lurid smoke from the volcano's throat,
Comes whirling forth, doth even the hero's breast appal.
In such appalling wise the Stygian gods to-day
My entrance to my home have signalized, that fain
I would, like guest dismissed, for ever bid farewell
To that dear threshold, ofttime trod, and yearned for long.
But no! I have retreated hither to the light,
Nor shall ye drive me further, Powers, whate'er ye be!
Some expiation I'll devise, then, purged from blame,
The hearth-fire may bid hail the consort like her lord.

PANTHALIS

Disclose, O noble queen, to thy handmaidens, who
In reverence and in love attend thee, what hath chanced!

HELENA

The thing that I have seen your eyes shall also see,
If ancient Night hath not within her murky womb
With sudden close engulfed the creature which she bred.
That ye may know it, list!   My words its form shall paint.
As I, my thoughts intent upon my mission, passed
With solemn tread along the inmost palace halls,
I marvelled at the hushed and vacant corridors.
No sound fell on the ear of moving to and fro,
Nor met the eye the sweep of quick and busy haste.
No maid was to be seen, nor stewardess, who erst
With friendly welcome wont all strangers to salute.
But to the inner hearth when I had made my way,
There, by the embers of the smouldering fire, I saw,
Crouched on the ground, a woman thickly muffled, huge;
Asleep she seemed not, but like one in reverie wrapt.
With voice of stern command I bade her 'Up, to work!'
Not doubting 'twas the aged stewardess, the same
My lord had sagely left behind to guard his home;
Yet moveless as a stone, still muffled there she sits.
Stirred by my threats, at length she raises her right arm,
As though from hearth and hall to beckon me away.
In wrath I turn away from her, and presently
Speed to the steps whereon towers high the thalamus,
Magnificently decked, the treasure-room hard by;
But swiftly from the ground up springs the wondrous shape,
Imperiously obstructs my passage, and displays,
In long and meagre bulk, with hollow bloodshot eyes,
A form so wild and weird, might eye and soul confound.
But to the winds I speak; for impotent are words,
To body forth to life such images as these.
There!   See her for yourselves!   She dares confront the light!
Here we bear sway, until our royal lord arrives.
The ghastly births of Night doth Phoebus, Beauty's friend,
Chase to their native dens, or fetter fast in chains.

[PHORKYAS *appears on the threshold between the door-posts.*

CHORUS

Much have I seen and known, though my tresses
Youthfully undulate still round my temples,
Horrors I've witnessed full many, the woeful
Havoc of warfare, Ilion, the night
When it fell!

Over the cloud-covered, dust-thickened din of
Death-grappling warriors, heard I the gods
Shouting, dread clamour! heard I the brazen
Voices of Discord clang through the field
To the walls.

Ah, they yet towered high, Ilion's
Walls!   But the merciless
Flame shot from roof to roof,
Spreading and broadening,
Hitherward, thitherward,
Fanned by the fury
Itself had engendered,
Over the city by night.

Flying I saw, through smoke and glare,
And tongues of eddying flame,
Deities grimly stalk in wrath,
Figures wonderful, gigantic,
Striding through the dusky
Fire-illumined gloom.

Did I see, or was it fancy,
Shaped amid my spirit's anguish
Phantoms so confused and wild?
That I ne'er may tell.
Yet that with my eyes I gaze on
This revolting thing before me,
Of a verity I know.
Yea, my very hands might grasp it,
Did not terror hold me back
From the venture dread.

Which of the daughters
Of Phorkys art thou?
For of her kindred
Surely thou art.
Art thou, perchance, sprung of the Graiae,
Sisters appalling, of Darkness engendered,
Alternately using
One eye and one tooth?

Darest thou, monster,
Sidelong with beauty,
Thyself unto Phoebus'
Keen glances unveil?
Yet come thou out boldly, it recks not,
For on ugliness looketh he never,

Even as his blessèd eye never
The gloom of a shadow beholds.

But alas! we mortals are fated
By a woeful doom to endure
The unspeakable anguish of eye,
Which the monstrous, the evermore loathly,
In lovers of beauty awake.

Hear then, hear, if unblushingly
Thou wilt confront us, curses,
Threatenings of manifold ill
From the ban-laden lips of the blest ones,
Who are moulded and made by the gods!

PHORKYAS

Old is the saw, but true its meaning and profound,
That modesty doth ne'er with beauty, hand in hand,
One common path along the verdant earth pursue.
Enrooted deep in both hate from of old abides,
And thus where'er, whene'er, they cross each other's track,
Each doth her back upon her adversary turn,
Then speedeth on her way with quickened tread again;
Coy modesty perplexed, but beauty proud and fierce,
Till Orcus' hollow night at length devours her up,
If Age hath not before subdued her haughty pride.
Ye wantons, now I find you, wafted from afar,
Wagging your saucy tongues, like flight of clangorous cranes,
Hoarse-screaming as they wing above our heads, a long
And sable cloud, and send a croaking clamour down,
Which lures the wanderer, pacing silent on his way,
To raise his eyes aloft; but they hold on their course,
And so goes he on his: so will it be with us.
Who, then, are ye, that thus with Maenad fury wild,
Like drunken brawlers, dare these royal gates assail?
Who are ye, I would know, that howl your wrath against
The house's stewardess, like dogs that bay the moon?
Think ye, I know not well the kith whereof ye come?
Thou callow brood, begot of war, in battle nursed,
Lascivious crew, at once seducing and seduced,
That sap the warrior's strength, the burgher's too as well!
Thus huddled here, to me ye seem a locust swarm,
Alighted like a cloud upon the early grain.
Consumers ye of others' industry!   Smooth-lipped
Destroyers of the fruits of year-long wary thrift!
And thou, thou ravished, huckstered, fingered piece of goods!

HELENA

Who, with the mistress by, the handmaids dares to chide,
Audaciously usurps her privilege of rule;
For unto her alone pertains it to extol
Whoso be worthy praise, as to chastise the ill.
Full well content am I with the good service they
Did at my bidding, when great Ilion's mighty strength
That lengthened leaguer stood, and fell, and low was laid;
Nor less throughout our travel's drear vicissitudes,
Where people commonly think only of themselves.
Here from the busy train like conduct I expect;
Not what the servant is, but how he serves, the lord
Inquires.   Then silence, thou! and rail on them no more!
If thou the royal house hast duly kept till now,
The mistress' place supplying, be it to thy praise.
But now herself is come, step back into thy sphere,
Lest chastisement, not guerdon, follow as thy due!

PHORKYAS

To chide the household is a high prerogative,
Which the heaven-favoured lord's illustrious spouse, by years
Of management discreet, most rightfully doth earn.
As thou, whom now I know, dost here again resume
Thy whilom place of queen, and mistress of the house,
Seize thou the reins, that long have hung relaxed, rule now,
The treasures take in charge, and take us too with them;
But, chief of all, shield me, that oldest am in years
From this pert band, who near thy swan-like loveliness
Are but a flock of cackling poorly feathered geese.

PANTHALIS

How hideous showeth hideousness by beauty's side!

PHORKYAS

How foolish by the side of wisdom foolishness!

*(The following repartees are spoken by the Choretides, stepping
out individually from the Chorus:)*

CHORETIDE 1

Tell us of father Erebus, of mother Night!

PHORKYAS

Then speak of Scylla thou, thy sister uterine!

* L 335

CHORETIDE 2

From thy ancestral stock hath many a monster sprung.

PHORKYAS

Away to Orcus, seek thy kith and kindred there!

CHORETIDE 3

Who have their dwelling there are much too young for thee.

PHORKYAS

Tiresias, hoar with eld, go wooing unto him!

CHORETIDE 4

Thy great-granddaughter was Orion's nurse, I trow,

PHORKYAS

By Harpies thou, I ween, wert fattened up in filth.

CHORETIDE 5

Such scragginess supreme, how dost thou nourish that?

PHORKYAS

Not with the blood which thou art ever keen to lap.

CHORETIDE 6

Thy teeth for corpses long, a loathly corpse thyself.

PHORKYAS

Pah! in thy saucy chops a vampire's grinders gleam.

LEADER OF THE CHORUS

Thine should be closed, were I to mention who thou art.

PHORKYAS

Name thou thine own name first, then is the riddle solved.

HELENA

In sorrow, not in wrath, I interpose to place
My ban upon this wild and stormy war of words.
For to the master nought more mischievous befalls,
Than rancours by his trusty serfs in secret nursed.
His mandates' echo then returns to him no more

Harmoniously in deeds with ready zeal performed;
No! gusts of wilful brawl buzz evermore around
His 'wildered head, while he commands and chides in vain;
Nor this alone.　Ye have in your unmannered wrath
Evoked and conjured forth dread forms, of mould unblest,
That throng upon me so, I feel as I were dragged
To Orcus down, despite the natal soil I tread.
Is't memory, or fancy, thus lays hold on me?
Was I all this? or am I?　Or am I to be
The phantom dire to scare yon town-destroying crew?
My maidens quail; but thou, the oldest of them all,
Thou art unmoved—then speak, resolve me of my fears.

PHORKYAS

Who on long years of joy diversified looks back,
To him heaven's choicest gifts appear at last a dream.
But thou, high-favoured far beyond all bound or stint,
Along thy way of life didst only suitors see,
With souls on fire to dare all perils for thy love.
Thee Theseus, fired with passion, early carried off,
A man of glorious mould, and stout as Hercules.

HELENA

He bore me off by force, a ten years' timorous doe,
And in Aphidnus' keep in Attica immured.

PHORKYAS

But thence by Castor and by Pollux soon set free,
A rare heroic band came wooing to thy feet.

HELENA

But my heart's secret love, I willingly avow,
Patroclus won, that was Pelides' other self.

PHORKYAS

Yet thee thy father did to Menelaus plight,
The ocean-rover bold, the house-sustainer too.

HELENA

His daughter and with her his sceptre too he gave;
And from these nuptials sprang Hermione my child.

PHORKYAS

Yet whilst afar for Crete, his heritage, he fought,
Stole on thy solitude a guest was all too fair.

HELENA

Wherefore remind me thus of that half widowhood,
And all the train of ills which had from it their birth?

PHORKYAS

That voyage caused to me, a free-born child of Crete,
Captivity—a doom of lifelong slavery.

HELENA

His stewardess wert thou appointed here full soon,
With much intrusted—house and treasure stoutly won,

PHORKYAS

All which didst thou desert for Ilion's tower-girt town,
And for the joys of love that perish not, nor pall.

HELENA

Speak not to me of joys!   No!   Anguish, bitter woe
Have 'whelmed me, heart and brain, like an unending sea!

PHORKYAS

Yet is it said, that thou a twofold form didst wear,
In Ilion seen, and seen in Egypt too the while.

HELENA

My weak and wandering mind confound not utterly.
Who, what I truly am, even now I cannot tell.

PHORKYAS

And furthermore they say, that from the phantom-world
Achilles rose heart-fired, and linked himself with thee!
Thee loving from of yore, despite all Fate's resolves.

HELENA

A phantom I to him a phantom was allied.
It was a dream, the words themselves proclaim as much.
I faint away, and grow a phantom to myself.
                    [*Sinks into the arms of the Semi-chorus.*

CHORUS

Silence! silence!
Thou of the evil eye,
Thou of the evil tongue!

Through lips of such ghastliness,
Grim with one tooth, what
Fell exhalations
Rise from a gulf so revolting and dread!

For the malignant that masks him in kindness,
Heart of a wolf 'neath the fleece of a sheep,
Strikes me with terror, far more than three-headed
Cerberus' throat.

Fearfully watching we stand
When? How? Where will it burst,
The deep-brooding storm
Of a malice so vile?

And thou, too, instead of words freighted with comfort,
Tempered with kindness, and lulling as Lethe,
Summonest forth from the past recollections
Of all that is evil, ignoring the good,
Nor only the sheen of the Present
Darken'st with shadows, but also
The delicate dawn of a future,
Illumed with the sunshine of Hope.

Silence! silence!
That the soul of our mistress,
Even now in the act to take flight,
May linger, still firmly may cleave to
That form, of all forms the divinest,
Which ever the sunshine beheld.

[HELENA *revives, and again stands up in the midst of her attendants.*

PHORKYAS

Forth from clouds of fleeting vapour come, this day's resplendent sun,
Veiled, thy glories woke our rapture, dazzling now thy radiance shines!
As the world before thee kindles, look forth thou with gracious eyes.
Though they rail on me as hideous, what is beauty well I know.

HELENA

Heart-sick from the void I totter, which possessed my swimming brain.
Oh, how gladly would I rest me—for my limbs are weary-sore!
Yet beseems it queens, yea, truly, it beseems all mortals well,
With a bold and tranquil spirit to abide all threatened ill.

PHORKYAS

Standing in thy might before us, standing in thy beauty there,
Tells thine eye, command befits thee.   What dost thou command
    me?   Speak!

HELENA

To retrieve the moments wasted in your wrangling straight
    prepare!
Haste! arrange a sacrifice, as the King commanded me.

PHORKYAS

All within the house is ready, patera, tripod, hatchet keen,
For besprinkling, for befuming; say, what shall the victim be?

HELENA

That the King disclosed not.

PHORKYAS

                Spake he not of that?   Oh, word of woe!

HELENA

Why this grief, that overcomes thee?

PHORKYAS

                       Queen, thou art the victim meant.

HELENA

I?

PHORKYAS

And these.

CHORUS

                Oh, woe and wailing!

PHORKYAS

                  Thou shalt fall beneath the axe.

HELENA

Fearful!   Yet my heart foretold it!

PHORKYAS

                  No escape can I descry.

CHORUS

Oh!   And we!   What will befall us?

PHORKYAS

She shall die a noble death;
But upon the lofty rafter that supports the roof within,
Ye, like thrushes in the birding-time, shall flutter in a row.

[HELENA *and* CHORUS *stand astounded and horror-struck
in an expressive and well-studied group.*

Poor spectres!   There ye stand like images of stone,
Afeared to quit the day, the day which is not yours.
Mankind, that are no more than spectres, even as you,
Bid to the sun, like you, reluctantly farewell;
Yet prayer nor mortal might can wrest them from their doom:
All know, the end must come; yet few can welcome it.
Enough!   Your fate is sealed.   So to the task at once!

[*Claps her hands; thereupon masked dwarfish figures
appear at the portal, who actively carry into execution her orders as they are delivered.*

Approach, ye dusky, round, unsightly atomies,
Trundle yourselves along, here's mischief rare afoot.
The altar horned with gold, a place for it prepare,
Upon the silver rim the gleaming hatchet lay;
The water-pitchers fill, of them we shall have need,
To wash the pitchy gore's unsightly stains away.
Spread here upon the dust the tissued carpet fine,
That so the victim down right royally may kneel,
And coiled within its folds, head shorn from trunk, but still
With all due grace, may to the sepulchre be borne!

LEADER OF THE CHORUS

Absorbed in thought, apart my royal mistress stands,
Her maidens droop and blench like meadow-grass that's mown;
Yet seemeth it to me the eldest not unmeet,
With thee to parley, that in primal eld wert born.
Experienced, sage thou art, to us seem'st well disposed,
Though yonder brainless crew assailed thee with contempt.
Then say, if chance of rescue any thou dost know.

PHORKYAS

Not hard is that to say; but with the queen it rests,
To liberate herself, and you her train with her.
But then decision lacks, and of the promptest too.

CHORUS

Most to be revered of Parcae, wisest of the Sibyls thou,
Folded keep the golden shears, and life and weal to us proclaim,
For we feel already wavering, swinging, dangling, undelightsome,
Our poor little limbs, that rather in the dance of yore delighted,
And in lover's soft embrace.

HELENA

Leave these to their laments!   Grief do I feel—no fear!
Yet if escape thou know'st, my gratitude be thine!
To wise far-seeing souls even the impossible
Oft possible appears.   Then speak—thy plan reveal!

CHORUS

Speak, and tell us, tell us quickly; how shall we eschew the dismal
Loathsome noose, that waits, oh horror, like a carcanet detested
Round our necks to coil?   Already, luckless wretches, we can
      feel it,
Twisting, stifling, choking, if thou, Rhea, mother high and
      mighty
Of the Gods, relentest not.

PHORKYAS

Have ye the patience then, in peace to list a plan
Of somewhat tedious length?   Its turns are manifold.

CHORUS

Abundant patience!   So that listening we shall live.

PHORKYAS

The man who keeps at home, guarding great store of wealth,
And pargetting his mansion's walls from time to time,
With him it shall go well through length of many days;
His roof securing too against the battering rain,
But he that overleaps with mad and fickle haste
His threshold's sacred bounds, nor ever stays to think,
On his return will find the ancient place, indeed,
But topsy-turvy all, even if not wholly wrecked.

HELENA

Why these trite saws at such a time as this?   Thou wert
To tell thy tale.   Stir not what only serves to gall!

PHORKYAS

I mentioned facts.　Reproach was never in my thought.
King Menelaus swept the seas from bay to bay;
Mainland and isles, on all he swooped, and spoiled their wealth,
Which hither he brought back, and yonder is it stored.
Ten tedious years before the walls of Troy he spent,
How many to come home it passeth me to tell.
But how stand matters here the while at Tyndarus'
High mansion?　How with all his territories round?

HELENA

Is sarcasm, then, in thee so thoroughly ingrained,
Thou canst not ope thy lips, unless to gibe and rail?

PHORKYAS

Thus many a long year was the mountain-glen forlorn,
Which north from Sparta to the upper lands extends
Behind Taygetus, where rolls Eurotas down,
A merry prattling brook, and thence along our vale
Spreads out among the reeds, which shield your favourite swans.
Among the mountains there, a bold and stalwart race,
Forth issuing from Cimmerian night, their quarters fixed,
And there a tower-girt keep impregnable have reared,
From which they harry land and people when they list.

HELENA

How could they so?　That were impossible, methinks.

PHORKYAS

Most ample time they had, some twenty years, or so.

HELENA

Is there one chief?　Or a confederate robber-band?

PHORKYAS

No robbers they, yet one they as their chief obey.
I blame him not, not I, though hither once he came.
He might have plundered all, yet was content with some
Few things, free gifts he called them, tribute not at all.

HELENA

How looks he?

PHORKYAS

Not amiss!   Agreeable, say I.
A man he is of parts, quick-witted, handsome, bold,
Endowed with gifts of soul, like few among the Greeks.
They call the race Barbarians, yet of them, methinks,
Not one so savage is, as at beleaguered Troy
Heaps of your man-devouring heroes proved themselves.
He's truly great; myself I trusted in his hands.
And then his castle, that you for yourself should see!
Far other thing it is than that rude boulder-work,
Your ancestors, poor botchers, crudely huddled up
Like Cyclops, Cyclop fashion, rude amorphous crag
On crag amorphous heaving; there, believe me, there
Is all symmetrical, and shaped by square and rule.
Look on it from without!   High up to heaven it soars,
So straight, so closely jointed, mirror-smooth as steel.
To clamber there—why even the very thought slides down.
Within, again, are halls and spacious courts, begirt
With mason-work substantial, every sort and kind.
Pilaster, pillar, arch, and spandrel there you see,
Balconies, galleries, for looking out and in,
And scutcheons.

HELENA

Scutcheons!   What are scutcheons?

PHORKYAS

Ajax bore
A wreathèd snake, yourselves have seen it, on his shield.
The Seven that 'leaguered Thebes bore carved devices too,
Each on his shield had one, of sense symbolical.
There moon and stars were seen in the great vault of heaven,
There goddess, hero, ladder, torches, swords withal,
And whatsoever else threats cities far with doom.
Even such devices, too, our band of heroes bears,
In colours bright, from their great-grandsires handed down.
There lions, eagles, claws and beaks ye may behold,
The horns of buffaloes, wings, roses, peacocks' tails,
With bandelets of gold, black, silver, blue, and red;
Such matters, row on row, are on the walls uphung,
In never-ending halls, as spacious as the world.
Rare places these to dance!

CHORUS

Say, be there dancers there?

PHORKYAS

Ay, of the best!   A gay and gold-locked buxom crew;
All redolent of youth!   Such as was Paris, when
He came too near our queen.

HELENA

                              Again thou fallest quite
Out of thy part; proceed, and bring it to a close!

PHORKYAS

That thou shalt do, so thou pronounce a serious 'Yes!'
Then with that castle straight will I surround thee.

CHORUS

                                         Speak,
Oh, speak the little word, and save thyself and us!

HELENA

What cause have I to fear, King Menelaus should
With cruelty so fell desire to work me woe?

PHORKYAS

Hast thou forgot, how thy Deiphobus of yore,
The slaughtered Paris' brother, in unheard-of wise
He mangled, him that made thy widowhood his prey,
And rifled all thy charms; his nose and ears he slit,
And maimed him so beside, 'twas dismal to behold.

HELENA

This to that churl he did; for my sake was it done.

PHORKYAS

Because of that same churl he'll do the same to thee.
Beauty may not be shared; who once hath owned it all,
He sooner than participate, will end it quite.
          [*Trumpets in the distance.   The* CHORUS *huddle together.*
As the shrill trumpet's blast doth ear and bowels pierce
With shattering shock, even so strikes jealousy its claws
Into the bosom of the man, who ne'er forgets
What on a time was his, and now is his no more.

CHORUS

Heard'st thou not the trumpets pealing?   Saw'st thou not the
    armour gleam?

PHORKYAS

Welcome, welcome, Lord and Monarch, gladly I will give
    account!

CHORUS

Ay, but we?

PHORKYAS

                You know full surely, you shall here her death
    behold.
There within your own must follow; no, there is no help for you.
                                                    [*Pause.*

HELENA

I have resolved the course, befits me to pursue.
That thou a demon art of power unblest, I feel,
And fear thou canst convert e'en good itself to ill.
Yet first of all I will go with thee to this keep;
What rests beyond I know; but what of after plans
The queen within her breast in mystery may veil,
Be undivulged to all.   Now, beldame, lead the way!

CHORUS

    Oh, how gladly we go hence, with
    Hurrying foot!
    Behind us is Death,
    Once more before us
    A fortress's high
    And impregnable walls.
    Oh, may they shield us well,
    As well as Ilion's ramparts,
    Which only by grovelling cunning
    At length in the dust were laid low!
        [*Mists arise and conceal, first the background, then the
            front of the scene.*
    How!   How is this!
    Sisters, look round!
    Was it not radiant day?
    Trailing vapours are rising
    From the sacred stream of Eurotas;
    Already hath faded its beautiful
    Rush-covered margin from view,
    And the sportive, the gracefully haughty
    Swans, that swim hither and thither,
    Moving in soft undulation,
    Ah, I behold them no more!

Yet, yet there
Singing I hear them,
Singing a shrill song afar!
Omen of death, says the legend,
Oh, grant that it may not betoken,
Instead of the rescue was promised,
To us, too, only destruction,
To us that are swan-like and tall,
Fair and white-throated, and ah!
To her, too, our swan-born mistress!
Woe, and disaster! woe, woe!

Everything now
Around us is shrouded in mist.
Yet we see not each other!   Oh, what,
What will befall?   Are we moving?
Or are we hovering only
With stumbling footsteps on earth?
See'st thou nought?   Is that Hermes flits yonder
Before us?   Is that not his golden
Staff waving, commanding us back,
To Hades, the joyless, the dusky,
That teemeth with bodiless phantoms,
O'erthronged, yet evermore void?

Yes, at once the darkness thickens, not a ray illumes the vapour,
Grey and dusky, dungeon-gloomy.   Walls before our gaze are
    rising,
Stark before our open gaze.   A courtyard is't, or yawning
    cavern?
Whether this or that, 'tis fearful!   Sisters, sisters, we are captives,
Captives as we were before.

INNER COURT OF THE CASTLE

*Surrounded by rich fantastic structures in the style of
the Middle Ages* [1]

LEADER OF THE CHORUS

Foolish and over-swift, true woman as ye are!
Dependent on the instant, sport of every gust
Of good or evil fortune, neither have ye wit
To await with even mind.   One evermore gainsays
The other, and the other her with fiery heat.
In joy and woe alike you only laugh and wail.
Now silence!   And await attentive what our queen's
High soul may here resolve both for herself and us.

HELENA

Where art thou, Pythoness?   Whatever be thy name,
Come forth, I say, from this grim castle's gloomy vaults!
Mayhap thou'rt gone to tell this wondrous hero-lord,
That I am here, and my reception fair bespeak.
Then take my thanks, and lead me to him with all haste.
Oh, for a period to my wanderings!—oh, for peace!

LEADER OF THE CHORUS

In vain thou look'st, O queen, around on every side;
The uncouth shape has vanished, or perchance remained
In yonder mist, from forth whose bosom we came here,
I wist not how, swiftly, yet never stirring foot.
Or else perchance she roams the labyrinthine maze
Of this strange castle framed of many blent in one,
Seeking fair princely greeting for us from its lord.
Yet see, above there stirs, on busy errands bent,
At casements, and through corridors and portals wide,
A throng of servants moving swiftly to and fro.
Reception cordial this, and courteous doth portend.

---

[1] To avoid becoming herself the victim for the sacrifice commanded by
Menelaus, Helena allows herself to be transported by the magic of Phorkyas-
Mephistopheles to Faust's castle.   She is addressed by Faust in five-footed
iambics and replies in the same metre, but the rhyme used by Lynceus
attracts her attention, she questions Faust about it, and her quick response
to rhyme with rhyme symbolizes the marriage of their minds and hearts.

CHORUS

My heart bounds within me!   Oh, only look yonder,
How gracefully downwards, with hurrying footsteps,
Yon bevy of loveliest youths are advancing
In measured array!   By whose order, I marvel,
Appear they thus early, all decked in their trim,
This glorious muster of beautiful youths?
What most claims my wonder?   Their bearing so graceful,
The tresses that curl round their foreheads of snow,
Or the bloom of their cheeks that outrival the peach,
And are clothed like the peach with a delicate down?
Full fain would I bite, did I shrink not with fear,
For lips that aforetime such morsel attempted,
Oh, fearful to think on, with ashes were filled!

> But lo! now the fairest
> Approach to our feet.
> What is it they bear?
> Steps for a throne.
> Carpets and seat,
> Curtain, and hangings,
> In tent-like array,
> Like clouds interlacing,
> That circle and wave o'er
> The head of our queen:
> For already hath she
> On their invitation
> Ascended the gorgeous throne.
> Forward!   And round her,
> Stepping in measure,
> Range in a row!

Worthy, oh worthy, trebly worthy,
Be blest such a welcome as this!

> [*After the pages and squires have descended in long
> procession,* FAUST *appears at the top of the staircase
> in a knight's court-dress of the Middle Ages, and
> descends slowly and with dignity.*

PANTHALIS (*regarding him attentively*)

If that the gods have not, as ofttimes they have done,
For but some little space, a form of wondrous mould,
A gracious presence, and an air of lofty grace,
Unto this mortal lent, he will be prosperous
In all that he essays—or battling man with man,
Or in that puny war, with beauteous woman waged;

In sooth to all men else he is superior far,
However dear to fame, whom e'er mine eyes beheld.
Majestical and slow, with reverential air,
The prince approaches; turn, and greet him, O my queen!

FAUST (*advances with a man in chains at his side*)

Instead of stateliest greeting, as were meet,
Instead of reverent welcome, lo, I bring,
In gyves fast bound, a varlet who, remiss
Himself, hath made me fail in duty too.
Kneel down, and here at this sweet lady's feet
Lay the confession of thy heavy guilt.
This, O most puissant empress, is the man
Of lynx-keen eye, appointed to keep watch
Upon our topmost turret, thence to scan
The canopy of heaven, the earth's expanse,
And note whate'er is to be noted there—
What from the mountains to our castle here
May cross the valley, be they jostling herds,
Or banded hosts in arms; we guard the one,
The other we oppose. To-day, oh shame!
He noted not thy coming; so there lacks
The welcome stately, and the homage due
To guest so noble. Forfeit is his life,
A double forfeit; he had lain ere this
In his most guilty blood, but only thou
Mayst punish or forgive, as likes thee best.

HELENA

The lofty honour thou accordest me,
As judge and mistress absolute, belike
Is meant to test how far I dare presume.
Thus, then, the judge's foremost duty I
Will exercise, and hear the culprit! Speak!

LYNCEUS, THE TOWER-WATCHER

Let me kneel, and let me view thee,
    Live or die, I reck not how!
For, O godlike woman, to thee
    All my soul is bondslave now.

Watching for the morning's blushing,
    Looking eastward, where it glows,
All at once with magic flushing
    In the south the sun arose.

To itself my gaze it rooted:
  Rocky pass, and valley green,
Earth and heaven, were all unnoted,
  All save her, that peerless queen.

I with eyesight keen am dowered,
  Keen as any lynx on tree,
But in vain I strove, o'erpowered
  By that vision fair to see.

What to me portcullised gateway,
  What if roof or tower be kept?
Mists arise, fade off, and straightway
  Forth a radiant goddess stept!

Eye and soul I straight surrender,
  Drinking in the blissfull light;
Dazzling all, her beauty's splendour
  Dazzles me, poor minion, quite!

I forgot the warder's duty,
  Quite forgot the trumpet call;
Menace, yet oh spare me!   Beauty
  Holds all angry thought in thrall.

HELENA

The evil to chastise myself have caused
Were most unmeet.   Woe's me, what ruthless fate
Pursues me, that where'er I go I thus
Befool men's senses, so they not respect
Themselves, nor aught that's worthy!   Now by force,
Now by seductive arts, by warfare now,
Now dragging me about from land to land,
Gods, heroes, demigods, yea, demons too
Have made my life one wild and errant maze.
I sowed confusion o'er the world—it grew,
And now it spreads, confounded worse and worse.
Remove this worthy man and set him free;
Light never harm on him the gods have crazed.

FAUST

Lost in amazement I behold, O queen,
The smiter and the smitten here together.
I see the bow that sped the arrow forth,
And him it struck.   Shaft follows thick on shaft,
And me they pierce.   Methinks, they seem to whizz
Around in hall and tower on every hand.

What am I now?   Thou in a moment mak'st
My trustiest vassals rebels, insecure
My very walls; so now I fear my hosts
Obey the conquering and unconquered fair.
What's left me then, save to resign to thee
Myself and all I fondly dreamed was mine.
Here let me at thy feet, thy liegeman true,
Proclaim thee queen, whose presence, only seen,
Won thee at once my throne and its domains.

LYNCEUS (*returns with a chest, followed by men
                carrying other chests*)

See me, once more, O queen, advance!
The rich man begs one little glance;
He looks on thee, and feels, be sure,
As monarch rich, as beggar poor.

What was I erst?   What am I now?
What shall I do or wish or vow?
What boots the eye's most piercing ken?
Back from thy throne it shrinks again.

Out from the East our course we pressed,
And soon were masters of the West;
A throng of warriors long and vast,
The first knew nothing of the last.

The first was slain, the second stood,
The third struck in, a spearman good;
And still their numbers waxed amain,
Unnoted were the myriads slain.

We rushed, we crushed, we stormed apace,
We were the lords from place to place;
And where to-day I bore control,
Ere morn another sacked and stole.

We looked, and rapid was the look,
And one the fairest damsel took,
Another seized the sturdy steer,
The horses all were lifted clear.

But I in peering took delight
For all that rarest is to sight,
And what another's too might be
Was only withered grass to me.

I tracked where treasures lay concealed,
And all my piercing glance revealed;
To all recesses I could spy,
No coffers might exclude mine eye.

And heaps of gold were piled by me,
And gems most glorious to see.
But none of all were fit to shine,
Save emerald, on that breast of thine.

From each fair ear let pearls be hung,
That grew the ocean's caves among;
The ruby's fire grows faint and weak
Beside the crimson of thy cheek.

And so these treasures rich and rare
Unto thy throne I proudly bear,
And at thy feet the harvest lay
Of many a long and bloody fray.

And many though these coffers be,
Yet coffers many more have we;
Deign but to speak thy gracious will,
And treasure-vaults for thee I'll fill.

For scarce dost thou the throne ascend,
When instantly in homage bend
Our reason, wealth, and all that's ours,
Before thy beauty's matchless powers.

All this I deemed securely mine,
But now surrender, it is thine—
All this high-worthy once I thought,
But now I see that it was nought.

What I possessed away hath flown,
Like withered grass that hath been mown.
Oh, with one gracious look restore
The virtue that it owned before!

FAUST

Hence with the burden by your valour won,
Unchid indeed, but unrewarded too!
Already hers is all this castle holds,
'Tis bootless to present particular gifts.

Away!   And pile in orderly array
Treasure on treasure!   Rear a structure grand
Of pomp till now unseen!   Let every arch
Shine like the heavens at morning-break!   Create
From lifeless life a paradise around!
Let carpet heaped on carpet, thick with flowers,
Unroll before her; all that meets her tread
Be delicate, and splendours so divine,
Might dazzle all but gods, allure her eye!

LYNCEUS

Poor and trivial is at best
This our gracious lord's behest:
Greeting such to work for thee
Will the servant's pastime be;
For our life and goods and all
Thy resistless charms enthrall.
Is not every warrior tame,
Every falchion blunt and lame?
Near that form of glorious mould,
Even the sun is dull and cold;
Near the wonders of that face
All is drear, and all is base.   [*Exit.*

HELENA (*to* FAUST)

I would hold converse with thee—come thou up,
And sit here by my side!   The vacant place
Invites its master, and secures me mine.

FAUST

First, kneeling, noble lady, let me crave
Thy grace for my true homage; let me kiss
The hand, which thus would raise me to thy side.
Confirm me as co-regent with thyself
Of realms whose bounds were never scanned, and win
Adorer, vassal, guardian all in one!

HELENA

Marvels so many do I see, and hear,
I'm all amaze, and fain would question much.
Prithee resolve me, wherefore rang the speech
Of yonder man so strangely—strange, yet sweet?
Each tone into the other seems to fit,
And, when one word is wedded to the ear,
A second comes to dally with the first.

FAUST

If that our people's speech delight thee, how
Their song will ravish, through their inmost depths
Steeping thine ear and spirit in content!
To make it ours, let us this art essay;
Converse invites, and calls it into play.

HELENA

Say, how to words such grace I may impart?

FAUST

'Tis easy; they must flow out from the heart.
And, when the soul is touched with passion's flame,
We look around and ask—

HELENA

                    Who burns the same?

FAUST

Nor past nor future now the soul employ,
The present only—

HELENA

                    Constitutes our joy.

FAUST

'Tis treasure, glorious gain, supreme command.
Who gives it confirmation?

HELENA

                    This—my hand.

CHORUS

Who shall taunt our mistress, that she
To this castle's lord demeans her
With a loving grace?
For what are we, every one,
What but captives, now and ofttime,
Since Troy's shameful overthrow,
And our labyrinthine roamings
Thence in woeful wise?

Women with men's love familiar
Dally never in their choice,
In such lore proficient;
And as to golden-locked shepherds,
It may be, to black-bearded fauns,
They, as it haps for the moment,
Over their delicate limbs,
The selfsame privilege yield.

Near and nearer already they sit,
Each on the other reclining,
Shoulder to shoulder, knee to knee;
Hand in hand they are swaying
Over the throne's
Deep-cushioned lordliness.
No scruple hath royalty, thus
Its secret delights
To the gaze of the people
With never a blush to reveal.

HELENA

I feel so far away, and yet so near,
And oh! how gladly say—Here am I—here.

FAUST

Scarce do I breathe. I tremble, heart and knee;
'Tis all a dream. Time, place, have ceased to be.

HELENA

Meseems as I had lived in olden time,
And yet were now new-budding in my prime;
Inwoven with thine my being seems to be,
Bound to thy stranger life eternally.

FAUST

Oh, ponder not! To quaff the present bliss,
Though death were at the gate, our duty is.

PHORKYAS (*running in*)

Prattle in Love's alphabet,
Billing, cooing, toying—yet
Time it is, aside were set
All such childish gear.

Feel ye not the tempest louring?
Hark the trumpet's bray!   O'erpowering
Ruin draweth near.
Menelaus, with his bands,
Storming at your portal stands.
Arm for conflict drear!
By these victors girdled, you
Like maimed Deiphobus shall rue
Your bondage to the sex.
These light goods shall swing in halter,
And for her upon the altar
Lies the new-ground axe!

FAUST

Accurst intrusion!   Most unseasonable now!
Nor even in peril can I senseless brawling brook.
Ill favour from ill news the goodliest bearer takes;
And these, vile hag! alone 'tis thy delight to bear.
Yet shall they stead thee nothing here—with empty breath
Thou dost assail the air.   No peril, none, is here,
And peril's self would seem but idle threat—no more.

> [*Signals, explosions from the turrets, trumpets and horns,
> warlike music.   A mighty host marches across the
> stage.*

No!   Straightway thou a throng of lances,
    Each by a hero borne, shalt see;
He only merits woman's glances,
    Who can protect her valiantly.
> [*To the leaders, who detach themselves from the columns,
> and advance towards him.*

With fiery, yet self-reinèd power,
    That makes your victory sure, go forth,
Ye of the East the prime and flower,
    Ye budding blossoms of the North.

In steel encased, where'er they enter,
    Empire on empire up they break,
They come, earth trembles to her centre,
    They pass, and thunders fill their wake.

It was at Pylos that we landed,
    The aged Nestor was no more!
And all the petty kinglets banded
    Our dauntless host to ruin bore.

Now from these walls with force of thunder
  Drive Menelaus back to sea!
There let him rove, and sack, and plunder,
  Such was his choice and destiny!

Dukes shall I hail you—grace's fountain,
  Great Sparta's queen, hath so decreed;
Now at her feet lay vale and mountain,
  . And you shall have a realm for meed.

With rampart piled, and high-banked galleys,
  Thou, German, Corinth's bays defend!
Achaia with its hundred valleys
  I to thy keeping, Goth, commend.

To Elis let the Franks betake them,
  The Saxon make Messene his,
Lord of the sea the Normans make them,
  And raise to glory Argolis!

Then each, in joy at home abiding,
  Shall wield an honoured rule abroad,
Yet Sparta shall, o'er all presiding,
  Be, as of yore, our queen's abode!

For each and all in long endurance
  One general weal is thus in store;
At *her* feet shall ye seek assurance,
  And light and justice evermore.
[FAUST *descends, the princes form a circle round him to
    receive his instructions and commands.*

CHORUS

The man, who the Fairest would win and keep,
Foremost of all should see,
That of weapons he has good store.
Though by fond arts he should make his own
What upon earth is the prize supreme,
Yet he possesseth it not in peace.
Fawning and flattery lure her from him,
Reivers audaciously snatch her away,
Against such wrong let him well provide!

Therefore do I our prince extol,
Prize him more highly than all men else,
Prudence with valour commingling so,
That stalwart vassals submissive stand,
Watching his every nod.

Faithfully they his behests fulfil,
And each his proper advantage finds,
They in their master's liberal guerdon,
Both in achievement of loftiest fame.

For who shall ravish her now
From her potent possessor?
To him she belongs—to him we resign her,
Resign her with twofold goodwill, for he
With her hath encompassed ourselves,
Within, with impregnable walls,
And with an invincible host, without.

FAUST

The gifts we here on these amass,
  To each a goodly kingdom's thrall,
Are great and glorious.   Let them pass!
  We hold our station 'midst them all.

With emulous pride they'll guard thee round,
  Half-island, girdled by the main,
To Europe's mountain-ridges bound
  By hills inwoven in slender chain.

Oh, may this land, of all the fairest,
  From age to age be ever blessed!
'Tis thine, my queen!   Again thou bearest
  The sway by thee of yore possessed.

When from the shell thou burst resplendent
  Amidst Eurotas' sedges green,
Thy mother and her maids attendant
Were dazzled by the radiant sheen.

This glorious land, intent to woo thee,
  With all its treasures courts thy hand;
Though all earth's round pertaineth to thee,
  Oh, tarry with thy fatherland!

And though the sunbeams coldly play, and drearly,
  Upon its jaggèd mountain-summits frore,
Though 'midst the green the rocks peer forth austerely,
  Where nibbling goats collect their scanty store:

Yet mingling brooklets brawl, and welling fountains,
  And dell and slope and meadow, green are they,
And o'er the verdure of a hundred mountains
  We see the fleecy herds far spreading stray;

See by the beetling cliffs the cattle marching,
  With measured pace and wary, one by one;
Yet doth the rock, in hundred caverns arching,
  From tempest yield them shelter or from sun.

Pan shields them there, and there, from moss-clefts peering,
  And boskage cool and dewy, wood-nymphs be,
And high in air their struggling branches rearing,
  As for the sun athirst, crowds tree on tree.

Primeval woods!   The oak, in strength excelling,
  In jags and knots its gnarlèd boughs distorts;
The gentle maple, with sweet juices swelling,
  Sweeps far aloft, and with its burden sports.

And milk in still and shady pastures floweth
  For child or lamb, maternal drink to them,
And fruit hard by, the plains' ripe bounty, groweth,
  And honey trickles from the hollowed stem.

Here cloudless bliss, from sire to son descending,
  Makes cheek and lip alike serene and clear,
Each owneth in his sphere a life unending,
  And health and sweet content dwell ever here.

And so, to all its father's strength expanding,
  The infant grows beneath the pure bright day,
And at the sight amazed we pause, demanding
  If these be gods, or men of mortal clay.

Thus 'mong the shepherds seemed the young Apollo
  A shepherd, only than the rest more fair,
For all created things one impulse follow,
  Where Nature doth untrammelled empire bear.
                        [Sits down beside HELENA.

So thou and I, our souls from bondage freeing,
  Shall dwell in peace, the past behind us thrown;
Oh, feel, 'twas Jove supreme, that gave thee being!
  Thou 'longst to earth's first golden age alone.

Thou shalt not be bound in by rock-built towers!
  Still in immortal youth Arcadia smiles
For us, and o'er us spreads her blissful bowers,
  Here neighbouring close on Sparta's household piles.

O'er this thrice happy land to reign its queen would
  Earth's brightest destiny to thee ensure!
Now be these thrones transformed to arching greenwood,
  And free our joys as Arcady's and pure!

> [*The scene is entirely changed.*[1] *A range of grottoes
> abuts upon arbours thickly covered with leaves.
> A shady grove extends to the base of the rocks which
> enclose the place.* FAUST *and* HELENA *are not seen.
> The Chorus lying asleep, dispersed up and down.*

PHORKYAS

How long these maidens here have slept, I cannot tell,
Or in their dreams if they have seen, what I beheld
Before my waking eyes, as little do I know.
I'll wake them, therefore.   These young folks shall be amazed;
You too, ye bearded ones, that sit beneath and wait,
To these strange goings-on in hopes to find the clue.
Up, up!   Arise, and shake your tresses from your brows,
And slumber from your eyes!   Blink not, but list to me!

CHORUS

Only speak!   Say on, and tell us all the marvels thou hast
    witnessed,
Gladliest would we list to legends, that would sorest tax our
    credence;
For our souls are very weary, gazing on these rocks around.

PHORKYAS

How!   Already weary, children, though you scarce have rubbed
    your eyes?
Hearken then!   Within these caverns, grots, and leafy bowers
    umbrageous,
To our lord and to our lady, as to two Idyllic lovers,
Shield and shelter have been granted.

CHORUS

How!   Within there?

---

[1] The scene changes to the timeless world of Arcadia, where Faust and
Helena, united, experience a new Golden Age.   Their son Euphorion,
endowed with the impulsive energy of Faust and Helena's self-surrender to
the beauty of the passing moment, lives through a whole life in one scene.

PHORKYAS

                         Yes—Sequestered
From the world, to secret tendance me and me alone they sum-
     moned.
Highly honoured stood I near them; yet, as confidante beseemeth,
I looked round at other matters; hither, thither I betook me,
Culling mosses, roots, and barks, in all their properties con-
     versant,
So that they were left alone.

CHORUS

Thou wouldst have us think, that in there quite a little world is
     hidden,
Wood and meadow, lake and river! Pretty fables thou dost
     weave!

PHORKYAS

Simple sooth, ye inexperienced! There be depths were never
     trodden:
Halls on halls, and courts on courts, enwrapt in musings deep I
     traversed,
When at once a peal of laughter echoed through the vaults
     cavernous.
I look in, a boy is bounding from a woman to a man,
From his father to his mother; the caressing and the fondling,
All love's silly play and banter, shouts of glee and sportive
     babbling,
Interchanging stun me quite.
He, a wingless genius, naked, faun-like save in what is bestial,
To the solid earth leaps down, but straight the earth reverberating
Up into the ether shoots him, till thus, twice or thrice rebounding,
He has touched the arching roof.
Full of terror calls the mother, 'Bound as much as e'er thou
     willest,
But forbear to think of flying—flying is to thee forbid.'
And the faithful father counsels—'In the earth the power
     abideth,
That impels thee upwards. Only with thy tiptoe touch its
     surface,
Like the son of Earth, Antaeus, straightway is thy strength
     renewed.'
So along the rocky ledges bounds he on from peak to ridge,
Hither, thither, back and forward, like a stricken ball in play!
But at once within the fissure of a chasm he sank and vanished,
And it seemed as we had lost him; mother moaneth, sire con-
     soleth,
I my shoulders shrugged in fear. When lo! again! what vision
     wondrous!

Treasures, were they hidden yonder?   Garments, all with flowers
    embroidered,
He with seemly grace hath donned.
Tassels dangle from his elbows, bow-knots flutter on his bosom,
In his hand the golden lyre, quite a little Phoebus, gaily
To the edge of the o'erhanging rock he stepped; we stood
    astonished,
And his parents fell in raptures into one another's arms.
For about his brows what radiance!   What gleams there is hard
    to tell.
Is it burnished gem, or is it flame of lordly might of soul?
And his port is high and noble, even as boy himself proclaiming
Lord to be of all that's lovely, whom the melodies eternal
Permeate through every fibre; and so ye anon shall hear him,
And so ye shall see him, and be in especial wonder wrapt!

CHORUS

Call'st thou this marvellous,
Daughter of Creta?
Has never thine ear been lulled by
The beautiful lore of the poets?
Hast thou heard never Ionia's,
Never been tutored in Hellas's
Legends primeval, that teem with
Achievements of heroes and gods?

All that befalleth in these
Our days is only an echo,
Wailing and sad, of the glorious
Days of our far-away sires.
Not to compare is thy tale with
That, which beautiful Fiction,
Than Truth more welcome to credence,
Hath chanted of Maia's son.

This gracefully moulded, yet lusty
Nursling, just newly begotten,
His bevy of gossiping nurses
Folds in pure fleecy swaddlings,
Decks with the richest adornings,
In their irrational way.
Sturdily, featly, however, the rogue
Slippeth his flexible
Body elastic
Out from the folds,
Craftily leaving the vesture of purple,
That round him close was encinctured,

Quietly there in his stead,
Like the consummated butterfly,
Which, from the chrysalis torpid
Its pinions untrammelling, soareth,
Boldly at wild will careering
Through air all aglow with the sun.

So he too, the lissomest, nimblest,
That he to thieves and to cozeners,
Yea, to all that on profit are bent,
The favouring genius would be,
Instantly proved by the practice
Of all the most dexterous arts.
Straight from the monarch of ocean he filches
His trident, yea, even from Ares
His falchion purloins from its sheath,
His arrows and bow from Apollo,
And eke from Hephaestos his pincers;
Even Jove's, the dread father's, own bolts he
Had ta'en, had the flashes not scared him;
Eros himself in the grapple
Of limbs interlacing he threw,
And from Cypria's bosom the Cestus,
The while she caressed him, he stole.

[*A delightful strain of pure melody, as if from a lyre, is
heard from the cavern; all are arrested by the sound,
and appear thrilled to the soul. From this point to
the pause, which is noted below, the progress of the
scene is accompanied by a full orchestra.*

PHORKYAS

Hark, the glorious tones! In fable
Old and faded trust no more!
Your old throng of gods unstable,
Let them pass, their reign is o'er!

Men again shall know them never,
Higher faith their souls must fill;
From the heart must well whatever
Is upon the heart to thrill.

[*Retires towards the cliffs.*

CHORUS

If, dread being, these soft-soothing
Strains can thus incline thine ears,
They create fresh-budding youth in
Us, dissolved in sweetest tears.

What though heaven's great sun be clouded,
　So within our soul it live?
In our own hearts lies enshrouded
　More than all the world can give.

HELENA, FAUST, EUPHORION, *in the costume
above described*

EUPHORION

Children's tones, their carols singing,
　Seem your own mirth's voice to be;
Seeing me in cadence springing,
　Leaps your heart in tune with me.

HELENA

Mortal life with bliss to flavour
　Love links Two in union sweet,
But, that it of heaven may savour,
　Makes with Three the bond complete.

FAUST

Thus is all we longed for ended,
　I am thine, and mine art thou;
And our beings so are blended,
　May we ever be as now!

CHORUS

For this pair long years of pleasure
　In this fair and gracious boy
Gathered are in golden measure;
　In their union how I joy!

EUPHORION

Now let me gambol,
Now let me spring!
Up to yon cloudland
I would take wing—
I would be soaring
Aloft on the gale.

FAUST

Oh, from these frantic
Flights let me call thee,
Lest misadventure
And ruin befall thee,
And our own darling
Plunge us in wail!

EUPHORION

Earth shall not fetter me
Longer from air.
Let go my hands now,
Let go my hair,
Let go my garments,
They're mine—let me free!

HELENA

Think, oh bethink thee,
To whom thou belongest—
Think how thou grievest us,
Grievest, and wrongest,
Bursting the bond unites
Him, thee, and me!

CHORUS

Soon sundered, I fear me,
The union will be.

FAUST *and* HELENA

For our love, who adore thee,
Restrain, oh, my child,
Restrain, we implore thee,
These impulses wild!
Orderly, tranquilly,
Trip o'er the plain,

EUPHORION

But to content ye,
Will I refrain.
[*Winding in and out among the* CHORUS, *and compelling
them to dance with him.*
Cheerily I foot it
Through this bevy bright!
Does the measure suit it,
Is the motion right?

HELENA

Yes—'tis bravely footed.   Twine
With these comely maidens mine
In the roundel gay!

FAUST

Would the end were come!   Oh, me!
All this madcap revelry
Fills me with dismay.
[EUPHORION *and* CHORUS, *dancing and singing, move
about in interlacing roundels.*

CHORUS

When thou thine arms in air
Gracefully crossest;
When thou thy sunny hair
Dancest and tossest;
When trips thy foot so light
Over the meadow bright;
When thy limbs come and go
Lightsomely to and fro—
Then thou thy goal hast gained,
Beautiful boy!
All hearts, to thee enchained,
Make thee their joy.   [*Pause.*

EUPHORION

Hinds ye resemble,
That frolic and speed,
Sportive and nimble,
Over the mead;
I am the huntsman,
Ye are the game.

CHORUS

Wouldst thou o'ertake us,
Make but the trial,
Blest would it make us—
Vain were denial—
Might we but fondle
Thy beautiful frame!

EUPHORION

Now o'er brake and bramble,
Rock and thicket ramble!
What's easy of capture, it
    Liketh not me,
To give me true rapture, it
    Fought for must be.

HELENA *and* FAUST

What waywardness!   What mad caprices!
Nought his headlong course can rein!
Hark!   Can these be hunting-horns,
Ringing over wood and plain?
Shrieks! and still the din increases!

CHORUS (*running in one by one*)

Shooting past us like the breezes,
Daffing us aside in scorn,
He our wildest sister seizes,
And by him she's hither borne.

EUPHORION (*enters, carrying a young girl in his arms*)

Here I bring the maiden coy,
To enforce my hard-won joy;
Now to make me fully blest,
Thus I clasp her struggling breast,
Kiss her shrinking lips, that she
Both my power and will may see.

GIRL

Let me go!   This frame of mine, too,
Holds a spirit bold and strong,
But it is not swept, like thine, too
Lightly by each gust along.
So! thou think'st thou hast me fairly!
Think'st thine arm has fixed its prey!
Hold me fast, fond boy, and rarely
I will scorch thee for my play.
                    [*She flames up, and vanishes into air.*
Follow me to realms supernal,
Follow me to caves infernal,
Win the prize, if win you may!

EUPHORION (*shaking off the last of the flames*)

Forest brake and greenwood tree
Stifle here, by crags o'erhung;
Are they to fetter me?
I am lusty yet, and young.
Yonder the wild wind raves,
Thundering roll the waves;
Both afar I hear them,
Would I were near them!
        [*He continues to spring upwards from rock to rock.*

HELENA, FAUST, *and* CHORUS

Wouldst thou match the mountain goat?
We are thrilled for fear of thee.

EUPHORION

Ever higher must I float,
Ever farther must I see.
Now where I am, I know;
There lie the isles below.
Yes, yes, I am in
The midst of the land
Of Pelops, akin
To both ocean and strand.

CHORUS

If rock and forest wold
Cannot allure thee,
Apples with cheeks of gold
We shall ensure thee,
Figs, and, in alleys spanned,
Vines on the mountain-side.
Oh, in this darling land,
Darling, abide!

EUPHORION

Dream ye of peace's day?
Dream on who may!
War is the signal-cry,
Conquer or die!

CHORUS

Who in peace would rekindle
War's terrible flame,
Shall see his hopes dwindle
In sorrow and shame.

EUPHORION

All whom this soil in peril bore
To bear their part in perils more,
With spirits soaring and unslavish,
Of their own blood like water lavish,
All who shall battle with a soul
Illumined by a heaven-sent ray,
Which nought can quench and nought control,
A glorious guerdon win shall they!

CHORUS

He mounts, he mounts!   Yet in the farness
He shows undwindled to our gaze,
Like conqueror in battle harness,
And all in brass and steel ablaze.

EUPHORION

Let not wall nor moat environ,
Each in self alone repose,
Ever is man's breast of iron
Surest stronghold 'gainst his foes.
Would ye live unvanquished ever,
Onwards to the battle-field,
Amazons your women, never
Child but bears a hero's shield!

CHORUS

Oh, sacred poesy,
Heavenward thy soaring be!
Shine on, thou brightest star,
Afar, and still more afar,
Yet doth thy glorious strain
Visit us still, and fain
To hail it we are.

EUPHORION

No, not like child's shall be my bearing,
The youth appears in armour dight,
Peer for the free, the strong, the daring,
His spirit braced to do the right.
            Forth fare!
            For there
The path to glory opens bright.

HELENA *and* FAUST

Ushered scarce to life and gladness,
    Scarce to day's resplendent beam,
Thou dost rush with giddy madness,
    Where dismay and danger teem.
            Are then we
            Nought to thee,
Is our gracious bond a dream?

EUPHORION

Hark, hark, what thunder on the ocean?
Its echoes roll from dale to dale,
Host grappling host in fierce commotion,
Dust, tempest, war, and woe, and wail!
Death our doom,
Not with gloom,
But with welcome let us hail.

HELENA, FAUST, *and* CHORUS

Oh, what horror!   Agonizing!
Is then death *thy* doom?   Despair!

EUPHORION

Should I hold back unsympathizing?
No, every pang and grief I'll share.

HELENA, FAUST, *and* CHORUS

Wilfulness peril brings,
Death-laden harms.

EUPHORION

Ha!   And a pair of wings
Shoots from my arms.
Away!   I must venture thus!
Lift me in air!
[*He casts himself into the air, his garments support him
for a moment; an aureola surrounds his head, and a
train of light follows him.*

CHORUS

Icarus!   Icarus!
Woe and despair!
[*A beautiful youth falls at the parents' feet, and you think
that in the dead young man you recognize a familiar
form;* [1] *when all at once the material part of his frame
disappears, the aureola mounts to heaven like a
comet, while the dress, mantle, and lyre remain upon
the ground.*

[1] For Goethe's admiration for Byron, compare J. G. Robertson, *Goethe
and Byron*, London, 1926. (Publications of the English Goethe Society,
New Series, II).

HELENA *and* FAUST

Soon mirth into anguish fades,
Joy into moan!

EUPHORION'S *voice from beneath*

Let me not, mother, to the Shades
Descend alone!   [*Pause.*

CHORUS.   (*Dirge*)

Not alone!   Where'er thou bidest;
    For to know thee still we trust.
Ah, though from the day thou glidest,
    Hearts, that loved thee, ever must.
Dirges none we'll sing in sadness,
    Enviously we chant thy fate!
Still thy song in grief or gladness,
    Like thy soul, was fair and great.

Born to earthly bliss, most rarely
    Gifted, of a race sublime,
Yet, alas! thy soul too early
    Dropped its blossoms in their prime.
Thine a vision was divine, too,
    Thine a heart that felt for all,
Noblest women's love was thine, too,
    And a song most magical.

Yet didst thou in wild defiance,
    Swayed by wayward impulse still,
Spurn at rule, and all compliance
    With the laws that curb the will.
But thy higher soul, victorious,
    Burst the bonds of passion through!
Thou didst seek the greatly glorious,
    But couldst not attain it too.

Ah, who *does*?   Forlorn inquiry,
    That from fate wrings no reply,
When, on their day of anguish fiery,
    The nations mute and gory lie.
Yet sing new songs in jocund measure,
    And droop, in sorrow sunk, no more!
For earth again will these untreasure,
    As she hath ever done of yore.
                              [*Full pause.   The music ceases.*

HELENA (*to* FAUST)

An ancient saw, alas! approves itself in me—
That Bliss and Beauty ne'er enduringly are twined.
The bond of life is riven, and riven the bond of love;
Bewailing both I say a bitter-sad farewell!
And fling myself once more, yet once, into your arms.
Persephoneia, now receive my boy and me!

[*She embraces* FAUST, *her corporeal part vanishes, her dress and veil remain in his arms.*

PHORKYAS (*to* FAUST)

Hold fast by all the residue is left,
Let not the dress escape thee!   Even now
Tug demons at its skirts, would sweep it fain
Off to the world below.   Hold fast, I say!
'Tis not indeed the goddess thou hast lost,
Yet is the thing divine.   Turn to account
Its priceless virtue, and ascend in air;
Swift o'er all common things 'twill bear thee on,
Wafted on ether, long as thou canst fly.
We meet again, far, very far from here.

[HELEN's *garments dissolve into clouds, envelope* FAUST, *lift him into the air, and move away with him.*

PHORKYAS (*lifts up* EUPHORION's *dress, mantle, and lyre, steps into the proscenium, and, holding up the exuviae, says:*)

Rare treasure-trove are these to view.
The flame has disappeared, 'tis true,
Yet is the world no whit the worse;
Here is enough to consecrate
A legion of the sons of verse,
To scatter envy, malice, hate,
Amongst the poetaster crew;
And if to give them genius, too,
Surpass my power, at least confess,
I can supply them with the dress.

[*She sits down upon the proscenium, leaning against the base of a column.*

PANTHALIS

Bestir ye, girls!   At length we from the spell are free,
The old Thessalian hag's weird sorceries are o'er,
The jargon ceased of yonder intertangled tones,
That did the ear, and, worse, the inner sense confound.

To Hades now away!   Our queen has hurried there
With sorrow-saddened tread.   Let us, her faithful maids,
Where she has led the way, attend upon her path.
We'll find her at the throne of the Inscrutable.

CHORUS

Queens, right royal, allwheres are they!
Even in Hades they fill the high places,
Haughtily with their peers consorting,
With Persephone mating as friends;
But we, in the far-away distance
Of slumbrous asphodel meadows,
Mated with long scraggy poplars,
With barren unbeautiful willows,
What pastime is ours or what pleasure?
Bat-like to pipe and to whistle,
Ungladsome, and ghost-like, and drear?

PANTHALIS

Who hath nor fame achieved, nor nobly doth aspire,[1]
Belongs but to the elements; so get ye gone!
My spirit burns to be with my dear queen once more;
'Tis not desert alone, but loyalty as well,
Perpetuates for us the individual life.   [*Exit.*

ALL

Back to the daylight given are we;
Persons, in sooth, no more,
We feel and we know it well,
But to Hades we never return.
Nature, the evermore-living,
Asserts on us spirits, as we do
On her, unimpeachable claim.

A PORTION OF THE CHORUS

In the whispering thrill, the breezy waving of these thousand
    branches,
From the roots by soft endearments we shall woo life's flowing
    currents,
Up into the boughs; and soon with foliage, soon with teeming
    blossoms,

[1] '*Who hath nor fame achieved. . . .*' On several occasions Goethe
expressed a belief in immortality, but only for a select few, e.g. in his words
to Eckermann (1st Sept. 1829): 'I do not doubt our survival after death, for
nature cannot dispense with the entelechy; but we are not all immortal in
the same way, and to manifest oneself as a great entelechy in the future, one
must really be one now.'   Hence the different fates of Helena and Panthalis, on the one hand, and the chorus, on the other.

Decked profusely, shake our flowing tresses to the amorous
　　breeze.
Falls the fruit, anon assemble swains and herds in throngs
　　exulting,
Pressing, crowding swift and eager, of our bounties to possess
　　them,
And they all bow down before us, as before the primal gods.

ANOTHER PORTION

Floating o'er the polished mirror of these rocky walls far-
　　gleaming,
Moving in soft undulations, we caressingly shall glide;
There to every sound we'll hearken, song of birds, or shepherd's
　　pipings;
If Pan's voice tremendous ringeth, straight we send an answer
　　back;
Rustling zephyrs we re-echo—thunders it, we roll our thunders,
Till the peals with doubling crash reverberate along the hills.

A THIRD PORTION

Sisters! Of more mobile spirit, onwards with the brooks we
　　hasten;
For the richly garnished ridges of yon distant mountains lure us;
Downwards ever, ever downwards, we meandering shall water
Now the uplands, now the meadows, now the garden round the
　　house.
There across the landscape, skyward soaring, the long tapering
　　summits
Of the cypress mark, where flows our crystal mirror 'twixt its
　　banks.

A FOURTH PORTION

Ye may roam where'er it lists you; we shall circle, we shall
　　murmur,
Round yon planted hill, where greenly on the vine-stock grows
　　the vine;
There from hour to hour the toil of him that with a feverish
　　passion,
Fearful for his labour's issues, trims the tendrils we shall note.
Now with hoe, and now with shovel, earthing now, now pruning,
　　binding,
All the gods he sends up prayers to, to the sun-god, chief of all.
Bacchus, listless dreamer, little recks he of his faithful vassal.
He in leafy cave reclineth, toying with the youngest Faun.
All that for the half-awakings of his fumy dreams he lacketh

Lies in leathern skins, and earthen crocks and pitchers stored
  already,
From the ancient days eternal, right and left his grotto cool.
But when all the gods combining, Helios still of all the chiefest,
Airing, moistening, warming, firing, have the plumpy berries
  filled,
Where the dresser worked in silence, straightway all is life and
  bustle,
Voices ring from every alley, ring along from stake to stake;
Baskets patter, pitchers clatter, butt and wagon groaning stagger
Onwards to the mighty wine-press, to the pressers' sturdy tread;
And the sacred fullness of the purely nurtured juicy berries
Is profanely crushed; it mingles, foaming, seething, loathly
  squashed.
And now peals the cymbal, mingling with the beaker's brazen
  clangour,
For the mighty Dionysos hath his awful front unveiled;
Forth with cloven-footed Satyrs, and with reeling Bacchants
  comes he;
And, amid the din, incessant brays Silenus' long-eared beast!
Nought is spared! By cloven clutches trodden down is all
  decorum;
All the senses whirling madly, hideous din the ear confounds.
Tipsily they grope for goblets, heads and paunches both o'er-
  laden;
Here and there some look dejected, still they swell the tumult
  higher;
For, the new-made must to garner, out they drain the wine-skin
  old!   [*The curtain falls.*

PHORKYAS *in the proscenium rises to a gigantic height, descends
  from the cothurnus, lifts back the mask and veil, and discovers
  herself to be* MEPHISTOPHELES, *in order, so far as necessary, to
  comment on the piece by way of epilogue.*

ACT IV

A HIGH MOUNTAINOUS REGION. STRONG, JAGGED, ROCKY PEAKS

A cloud comes sweeping across the peaks, and settles upon a projecting plateau. It divides, and FAUST *advances.*

FAUST

DOWN-GAZING on the lonely depths beneath my feet,
I on this high-peaked ridge have purposely stepped forth,
Leaving my cloudy car behind, that bore me well
Through days of sunshine over land and sea:
Slowly, but still compact, it draws from me away,
Trailing in volumed folds along towards the East.
The eye, in admiration lost, strains after it:
It parts, in wave-like motion swayed from change to change,
Yet working into shape the while. What's this I see?
On sun-illumined cushions statelily reclined,
Of more than mortal size, a godlike woman's form!
Majestically fair, she floats before my eyes,
Like unto Juno's self, like Leda, Helena!
Ah me! already gone! Broad, shapeless, high up-piled,
Like far-off peaks of ice, it settles in the East,
And flashes what they mean, the days that fleet and fade.
Still round my breast and brow there floats a film of mist,
Cool, tender, and caressing, filling me with cheer:
Now softly up and up, and lingeringly, it ascends,
Then draws together. Mocks me a witching form,
In semblance of youth's first, long-lost, supremest bliss?
From my heart's depths its earliest treasures well;
For me love, light of wing, in its first dawn it types;
The look, felt to the core, the first, scarce understood,
That, cherished in the heart, all treasures else outshone.
Like beauty of the soul, the sweet form is sublimed;
Still it dissolveth not, into the sky it soars,
And with it bears away whate'er is best in me.

A seven-league boot comes clamping in, followed presently by another. MEPHISTOPHELES *steps out. The boot strides rapidly away.*

MEPHISTOPHELES

We've come on at a rattling pace!
But what's your fancy now?   What drags
You down on this disgusting place,
All gaping chasms and gruesome crags?
Though not where now it is, I know it well;
For 'twas in very sooth the floor of hell.

FAUST

Your stock of silly legends never fails;
Again you'd mock me with these idle tales?

MEPHISTOPHELES (*gravely*)

When God the Lord (why, all too well I know)
Hurled us from out the sky to depths profound,
Where fires eterne shot from their central glow
Great sheets of flame that circled round and round,
We found ourselves, 'neath that too copious light,
Together jammed in most unpleasant plight.
The devils fell a-coughing, all of them,
Up hill, down dale, they spat and voided phlegm:
With acids and with sulphurous stench inflated—
That was a gas!—hell grew so much dilated,
That very soon the earth's crust, flat at first,
Thick though it was, with a great crash upburst!
So things are all reversed; and this is how,
What bottom was erewhile is summit now.
The good sound doctrine, too, on this they base,
To give what's undermost the topmost place.
For we escaped from fiery bondage there,
To lord it bravely in the upper air—
An open secret, warily concealed,
And only lately to mankind revealed.

FAUST

To me are mountain-masses nobly dumb;
I neither ask them whence, nor why, they come.
When Nature in herself herself had grounded,
Deftly the earthly ball she shaped and rounded,
With crested peak and rifted gorge she played,
Mountain with mountain, cliff with cliff arrayed;
The hills she moulded next, and sloped their steeps
Into the valleys down with gentle sweeps:
Then growth and verdure followed; spasms of fire
She needed not, to work out her desire.

MEPHISTOPHELES

Oh, that's your view! To you 'tis clear as light;
But those who saw all know 'twas different quite.
Mark! I was by, when with convulsive shock
The abyss burst up, with flames that roared and swirled,
When Moloch's hammer, smiting rock on rock,
Far in the air the splintered mountains hurled,
Strange massive boulders strew the country still;
The force that flung them there, who can explain?
As for philosophy, it never will:
There lies the rock, and there it must remain;
Thinking and theories are labour vain.
Your common folk, they only are cock-sure;
To try to shake their notions were mere waste,
Their wisdom long ago was quite mature:
A marvel 'tis, to Satan's credit placed.
On crutch of faith your pilgrim hobbles on
To Devil's Bridges, to the Devil's Stone.

FAUST

What nature is, seen from the point of view
Of devils, is worth consideration too.

MEPHISTOPHELES

A fig for Nature! What is she to me?
My honour's touched! Myself was there to see!
The people we, grand issues to achieve;
Convulsion, outrage, madness! See, believe!
But now no more with sayings dark to tease you,
Did nothing in our upper surface please you?
You saw, stretched out in boundless space before ye,
The kingdoms of the world, and all their glory.
Well, though you be so hard to satisfy,
Did nothing gladden either heart or eye?

FAUST

Oh yes! A grand idea lured me on.
Divine it!

MEPHISTOPHELES

That is quickly done.
I'd seek me out a city, which
Was in all urban horrors rich,
Close crooked lanes, high gable-peaks,
Cramped market-place, kale, turnips, leeks,

Shambles, where blue-fly swarms and feasts
On carcases of well-fed beasts:
There will you find at any time
Odours and bustle both sublime.
Vast squares I'd have, broad streets, that go
To make up an impressive show;
And lastly, where no gate confines,
Suburbs that spread in endless lines.
Of carriages I should have store,
To keep up an incessant roar,
And cheer me with the eternal flow
Of ant-swarms bustling to and fro.
And let me ride, or let me walk,
I still should be the pride, the talk
Of thousands, wheresoe'er I went.

FAUST

Such things can bring me no content.
One's pleased that men should multiply,
And in their way be fairly fed,
Be even trained and taught; but by and by
We find, that thus are only rebels bred.

MEPHISTOPHELES

Then, all for my delight, I'd rear a pile,
Where breezes freshliest blow, superb in style.
Hill, woodland, meadow, field, and glade,
Into a glorious garden should be made;
Smooth velvet lawns, enclosed in walls of green,
With shady groves, and winding walks between;
Tumbling cascades, from rock to rock that leap,
With water-jets of every varied sweep,
Majestic soaring some, with all around
Innumerable sprays, that hiss, and splash, and bound.
A dainty snug retreat I'd next prepare,
And lodge a bevy of fair women there,
Where through the illimitable hours I could
Enjoy the sweetest social solitude.
Women, I say; for, be it understood,
I never, never can my thoughts encumber
With the dear things but in the plural number.

FAUST

Vulgar and vile!   Sardanapalus!

MEPHISTOPHELES

　　　　　　　　　　　　　　Good!
Oh, if one might divine your purpose! High,
Beyond a doubt, it is, and noble too!
When you were sailing to the moon so nigh,
Was it a craze for her that wafted you?

FAUST

Not so! There still is scope for great
Achievements on this earthly sphere—
Things that shall make my memory dear.
Bold deeds alone my energy can sate.

MEPHISTOPHELES

So then, 'tis fame you would attain?
That you come fresh from heroines, is plain.

FAUST

To rule, to own, that is my thought.
The deed is all, the fame is nought.

MEPHISTOPHELES

Yet poets will turn up, to blaze
Your glory forth to after-days,
And set by folly fools a-craze.

FAUST

Where is the thing at which thou wilt not carp?
How shouldst thou know what man desires?
Thy odious nature, bitter, caustic, sharp,
How should it know what man requires?

MEPHISTOPHELES

Well, go your own way, since you must!
To me the full scope of your whims intrust!

FAUST

On the sea's wide expanse I turned to look;
It heaved, as from within, with sullen roar,
Then it drew backward, and its billows shook,
To storm the broad reach of the level shore.
And, as a tyrant, overbearing mood
Jars the free soul, that writhes a wrong to see,
Excites the feelings, stirs the passionate blood
Into a ferment, so that angered me.

I deemed it chance, the scene more closely eyed;
A little while, then backward rolled the tide,
And from the goal so proudly reached withdrew;
But, come the hour, the sport begins anew.

MEPHISTOPHELES (*ad spectatores*)

To me this pretty tale no news can tell;
Some hundred thousand years I've known it well.

FAUST (*continues with passionate warmth*)

Onward it sweeps by courses numberless,
Barren itself, to squander barrenness;
Now swelling, growing, rolling on, it drowns
In desolation leagues of wasted downs;
There riots, wave on wave, with wanton force,
Then ebbs—and nothing's been achieved, of course.
I might despair, to see the aimless way
Such lawless elements exert their sway.
Yet no despair shall my resolve benumb;
Here I might struggle, here might overcome!
Might? Shall! Howe'er the waves run high, and fleet,
Gently they lap around each hill they meet;
Rage how they may and proudly domineer,
Still puny heights their crests against them rear,
And puny chasms to suck them down are strong.
Straight plan on plan into my mind 'gan throng;
Mine, mine the joy, of joys most precious, be,
Back from the shore to bear the imperious sea,
The bounds to narrow of the watery track,
And far into itself to thrust it back!
My plans I shall develop bit by bit:
You know my wish; be bold, and further it!
[*Drums and warlike music are heard behind the spectators,
in the distance on the right.*

MEPHISTOPHELES

Oh, nothing easier! Hark, these drums afar!

FAUST

How! War again? All wise men shrink from war.

MEPHISTOPHELES

Or war or peace, 'tis wise to lose no chance
Of reaping gain from every circumstance.
Who'd let a favourable opening slip?
Here's one! Well, Faustus, get it in thy grip!

FAUST

Such riddling balderdash, I prithee, spare,
And what you drive at in a word declare!

MEPHISTOPHELES

As I was coming here, I learned that lately
The worthy Emperor has been worried greatly.
You know the man.   While we amused him, played
Into his hands the spurious wealth we made,
He held the whole world cheap; for he was young
When he succeeded to the throne, and so
To the false notion foolishly he clung,
That power and pleasure hand in hand might go,
And that 'twas fine, and the right thing to do,
To rule, and revel in enjoyment too.

FAUST

A great mistake.   He that is fit to rule
In ruling must a high contentment find;
Of lofty aims his bosom should be full,
Yet what they are, by none must be divined.
What's whispered in one loyal ear and wise,
When it is done, takes all men by surprise.
So shall he wear right worthily the crown,
So stand supreme.   Mere pleasure drags us down.

MEPHISTOPHELES

Not such is he! all times on pleasure bent!
Meanwhile the realm by anarchy was rent,
When high and low were each with each at feud,
When brother hunted brother, hacked and hewed,
Castle 'gainst castle warred, and town 'gainst town,
And guilds conspired to pull the nobles down.
Bishops against their flocks and chapters rose;
And men, if they but met by chance, were foes.
In churches murder, at each city gate
Thieves lay for merchants, travellers, in wait.
Thus all men grew pugnacious in their bent;
For life was constant warfare.   So things went.

FAUST

Went!   Limped along, fell down, got up, and then
Collapsed, and all aheap fell down again.

MEPHISTOPHELES

And yet this state of things none dared to blame,
For every man had some ambitious aim;
The very smallest his big project had,
But good men found things grow at last too mad.
Then rose the able in their might, and said:
'He that will give us peace shall be our head!
The Emperor cannot, will not!   Let us choose
One, will new soul into the realm infuse,
Quicken the world into a nobler life,
Make all men feel secure, end rapine, strife,
And peace and justice through the land diffuse!'

FAUST

A priestly twang in that!

MEPHISTOPHELES

        Priests too were there.
For portly paunch they wanted copious fare;
They had a deeper stake than all the rest.
Rebellion grew, they the rebellion blessed!
And the poor Emperor, whom we made so gay,
To battle moves, perhaps his last, to-day.

FAUST

It grieves me much—so good, so frank was he!

MEPHISTOPHELES

Pshaw!   While there's life, there's hope!   Come, let us see!
Let us but get him clear of this close valley!
He's safe for life, with one successful rally.
Which way the dice may tumble, who can tell?
Come luck, then vassals they will come as well!

      [*They climb up the central mountain-peak, and look
        down upon the army drawn up in the valley.   Drums
        and military music resound from below.*

Ha!   The position's chosen well, I see.
If we strike in, he's sure of victory.

FAUST

What now is in the wind?   Deceit!
Magic illusion!   Shows that cheat!

MEPHISTOPHELES

Warcraft, by which are battles won!
Think of the work you wish begun,
And to your grand idea cleave!
Save for the Emperor his throne and land;
Then, kneeling, from his hand in fief receive
A limitless expanse of ocean-strand.

FAUST

You've compassed many things, 'tis true:
Well, well, go on, and win a battle too!

MEPHISTOPHELES

No; you're to win it!   You must play
The general-in-chief to-day.

FAUST

An honour truly, to command,
Where I just nothing understand!

MEPHISTOPHELES

Leave to your Staff to see things straight,
And in the background calmly wait.
Long since I traced war's blunders to their source;
For triumph, on the elemental force
Of mountain and of man I rest:
Who into play can bring both these, is blest.

FAUST

Who are the armed men there below?
Have you stirred up the Hill-folk?

MEPHISTOPHELES

                          No!
But, like good Master Peter Squence,[1]
The whole squad in its quintessence.

---

[1] 'Peter Squenz' is the name given by Andreas Gryphius, in his seventeenth-century comedy based on the *Midsummer Night's Dream*, to Peter Quince.

Enter The Three Mighty Men (2 Sam. xxiii. 8)

MEPHISTOPHELES

Here my fine fellows come!   You see,
Of very different years they be—
Dress, armour different: you will not
Come badly off with such a lot.   [*Ad spectatores.*
There's not a child but loves to see
Men in cuirass and knightly gorget dight;
And, as these knaves quite allegoric be,
They will for that give all the more delight.

BULLY (*young, lightly armed, clad in motley*)

If one stare at me, eye to eye,
I dash my fist straight off into his chops;
And any coward, if he fly,
I clutch him by the hair until he stops.

HAVEQUICK (*manly, well armed, richly clad*)

Such pranks are idle and unfitting,
An utter waste of time and tide;
Seize, pillage, plunder, unremitting,
And think of nothing else beside!

HOLDFAST (*stricken in years, strongly armed, without other garment*)

No mighty boon in that, I say!
Wealth, even though great, soon slips away
In life's swift currents strong and deep.
To seize is well, but better 'tis to keep:
Leave the grey carlot free to act,
And he will keep your gear intact.
                    [*They descend the mountain together.*

ON THE SPUR OF THE MOUNTAIN

Drums and martial music heard from below. The EMPEROR'S
tent is pitched. EMPEROR, COMMANDER-IN-CHIEF, *Attendants*

COMMANDER-IN-CHIEF

I still am satisfied, 'twas best
To draw back to the valley here
Our forces, when so hotly pressed:
'Twill win the day for us, I'm clear.

EMPEROR

The event will show how that may be;
But this half flight, this yielding, troubles me.

COMMANDER-IN-CHIEF

Look at our right flank!   Ground, my liege, like this,
Not for the world would a true soldier miss;
The hills not steep, yet steeper than they show,
Odds in our favour, odds against the foe.
Whilst on the wave-like plain half hid we lie,
Their cavalry will never dare come nigh.

EMPEROR

Nought's left me but to praise; stout heart,
Stout arm, can here play well their part.

COMMANDER-IN-CHIEF

Here where the central plain spreads many a rood,
You see the phalanx in true fighting mood.
Their lances, by the early sun-rays kissed,
Shimmer and sparkle through the morning mist.
How dark waves to and fro the massive square!
There thousands hearts beat high, to do or dare.
How strong we are, by this you may divine;
To them I trust to break the enemy's line.

EMPEROR

Now for the first time this fair sight I see:
Worth twice its numbers such a host must be.

COMMANDER-IN-CHIEF

Nothing to say of our left flank have I;
The stubborn rocks stout heroes occupy.
Yon broken cliff, that gleams with arms, secures
The entrance to the pass, and so ensures,
That here the enemy, surprised, will break
Their force compact, and bloody shipwreck make.

EMPEROR

See, where they come, my traitor kin!   Oh, how
They called me cousin, uncle, brother!   Now
Still more and more presumptuous they grew,
Stripped me of power, of kingly reverence due,
Then, by their feuds, laid my whole kingdom waste,
And now in rebel league to crush me haste!
From side to side a while the people sway,
Then in the torrent's whirl are swept away.

COMMANDER-IN-CHIEF

A trusty spy, to gather news sent out,
Comes hurrying down the rocks; ill news, I doubt!

FIRST SPY

By what guile and daring may,
    And by many an artful track,
Here and there we forced our way,
    Yet small comfort bring we back.
Loyalty to thee was sworn
    By many in fine words; but all
Hung back, for they, they said, were worn
    By public peril, civic brawl.

EMPEROR

Oh, for themselves alone self-seekers care;
Duty, love, honour, gratitude, are nought.
When things are doing well, who takes to thought
How, when the next house burns, his own may fare?

COMMANDER-IN-CHIEF

Here comes another, slow, with heavy feet:
He quakes in every limb, and seems dead beat.

SECOND SPY

Glad were we, when we detected
    Tumult raging, wild and weird;

All at once, and unexpected,
  A new Emperor appeared.
Straight, submissive to his mandate,
  O'er the plains the people sweep;
His false flag, as he had planned it,
  They all follow—very sheep.

EMPEROR

A rival emperor as a boon I hail;
Emperor I never felt myself till now.
As a mere soldier did I don my mail;
For higher ends my casque now rings my brow.
At every fête, though brilliant it might be,
Complete throughout, yet danger lacked for me.
When, at your wish, to tilt at ring I went,
My heart beat high, I breathed the Tournament;
And had you not from war withheld me, fame
For deeds heroic would have crowned my name.
Mine was a soul, I felt, of dauntless mould,
When yonder sea of fire around me rolled;
It pressed upon me, threatening direful fate:
'Twas show, mere show, and yet the show was great.
Wild dreams I've had of victory and fame;
Now will I do what, left undone, was shame!
    [*Heralds are dispatched with a challenge to the rival
        Emperor. Enter* FAUST *in armour, his visor half
        closed.* THE THREE MIGHTY MEN *equipped and
        dressed as before.*

FAUST

Behold us here, unchid withal, we hope;
For foresight, even when things are safe, there's scope.
The Mountain-folk, thou knowest, think and brood,
Deciphering the signs, in thoughtful mood,
That all through nature and the rocks are strewed.
Spirits, that long have left the plains, cling still
With fondness to lone peak and misty hill.
Through labyrinthine chasms their work is sped,
'Mid gases' reek, by fumes metallic bred;
They separate, test, combine, and never rest,
Of something new for evermore in quest.
With the light hand of spiritual power
They build up forms translucent hour by hour;
Then in the crystal, dumb although it be,
The upper world and all it does they see.

EMPEROR

This I have heard, and I believe it true;
But what have we, friend, with all this to do?

FAUST

The sorcerer of Sabine Norcia thou
Hast to thy service bound—he serves thee now.
How dread the fate hung over him, and dire!
The brushwood crackled, up shot tongues of fire;
Piled were the sapless billets round him, which
Were intermixed with brimstone-rods, and pitch:
Save him nor man, nor God, nor devil could—
But thou didst burst these bonds of blazing wood!
This was at Rome.   That service ne'er forgot,
To guard thy welfare is his constant thought.
Still from that hour, of self unheeding, he
Questions the stars, the deeps, and all for thee.
He charged us, straight to make thy business ours,
And stand by thee.   Great are the mountains' powers—
Nature in them works so supremely free:
This stupid priests denounce as sorcery.

EMPEROR

On days of festal, when my guests I greet,
Who, brimmed with pleasant thoughts, for pleasure meet,
It gladdens me to see them throng and press,
And, with the crowd, the hall grow less and less;
But welcomer than all the man must be,
Who chivalrously comes to stand by me,
Here with the dawn, when perilous issues wait,
And o'er us darkly hang the scales of Fate.
But at this crisis grave, where now we stand,

Keep from thy ready sword thy stalwart hand,
Respect the hour, when mighty hosts draw near,
For or against me, to do battle here!
Self makes the man!   Who covets crown or throne
Must prove his claim by prowess of his own.
As for that phantom who against us stands,
Dubs himself Emperor, ruler of our lands,
The army's Duke, my nobles' rising sun,
Let him to death by mine own hand be done!

FAUST

Though it were glorious thus an end to make,
It were not well, my liege, thy life to stake.

With crest and plume is not the helmet dight?
It guards the head that nerves us for the fight.
Without the head what would the limbs avail?
If that grow torpid, these all faint and fail;
It that be hurt, all these are wounded too—
If healed, then vigour stirs in them anew:
Straight will the arm its stalwart right assert,
It lifts the shield to save the skull from hurt;
The sword as swiftly will its duty show,
Parry with vigour and return the blow;
The foot takes part in their success, and treads
Triumphant on the downstruck foemen's heads.

EMPEROR

Such is my anger; him I thus would treat,
So make his head a footstool for my feet.

HERALDS (*returning*)

Little honour, little profit,
　　Have we met with, where we went;
Rudely did they scorn and scoff it,
　　That brave challenge which you sent.
'Your Emperor!　Pshaw!　We mock and flout him!
　　Feeble echo in yon vale!
When we think or speak about him,
　　"Pshaw!" we say, "a bygone tale!"'

FAUST

Things have fallen out as they would wish them, who
Stand by your side unswervingly and true.
The foe draws near; thy troops on fire; do thou
Command the attack!　No better time than now.

EMPEROR

My claim to lead the host I here resign;
　　　　　　　　　[*To the* COMMANDER-IN-CHIEF.
And now that duty, good my lord, is thine.

COMMANDER-IN-CHIEF

Let the left wing set forward to the field!
The enemy's left, now coming up the slope,
Shall, ere they reach the top, be forced to yield;
With our young seasoned troops they cannot cope.

FAUST

Let this blithe hero here, I pray your Grace,
Within your ranks, and quickly, take his place;
And, with your troops incorporated so,
The sterling stuff that he is made of show.

[*Points to the right.*

BULLY (*advancing*)

Who looks me in the face, he runs the hazard
Of being well scored over cheek and mazzard;
Who turns his back to me—well, he may risk it,
But down he'll topple, cleft from chine to brisket.
And if your men will only then
With sword and mace strike home like me,
Your foes amain will strew the plain,
Bathed in their blood as in a sea.

[*Exit.*

COMMANDER-IN-CHIEF

Now let our central phalanx follow slow;
With force compact and wary meet the foe.
Already their right wing a check has met;
Their plans are by our tactics quite upset!

FAUST (*pointing to the middle one*)

Let him there also follow your commands!

HAVEQUICK (*advancing*)

With the army's pluck, heroic and fine,
Shall the thirst for plunder and pillage combine;
On this one object be all intent,
The rival Emperor's gorgeous tent!
Not long shall he flaunt it there in pride;
To the onslaught myself will the phalanx guide.

PILLAGE-FAST, SUTLER WOMAN (*fawning upon him*)

Although his wife I may not be,
He's the dearest of fancy men to me.
What a harvest awaits us there!   Your drab
Is a very devil to gripe and grab.
Where she plunders and rifles, no pity has she;
Once win, and to do what you like you're free.   [*Exeunt.*

COMMANDER-IN-CHIEF

As we foresaw, upon our left their right
Is hurled in force. Each man of ours will fight
To the last gasp to hold the foe in check,
That tries to storm the gorge's narrow neck.

FAUST (*beckons to the left*)

Pray you, sir, note yon fellow, too!   What harm,
If strength consents itself with strength to arm?

HOLDFAST (*advancing*)

For the left wing dismiss all care!
'Twill hold its own, when I am there.
The old one about him has all his wits;
What I once grasp, no lightning splits.   [*Exit.*

MEPHISTOPHELES (*descending from above*)

Look now, how there, behind our left,
From every jagged rocky cleft,
Armed men press onward, closely packed,
The pass still further to contract!
With casque, cuirass, sword, shield, and spear,
A bulwark at our backs they rear,
Waiting the signal to strike home.
                    [*Aside to the knowing ones.*
You must not ask me whence they come.
I've not been slow, since I went out,
I've cleared the armouries round about.
They stood on foot or horseback there,
As if the lords of earth they were;
Knights, kaisers, kings, they were of yore,
Now empty snail-shells, nothing more.
Many's the ghost himself with these has decked,
And to the life the Middle Ages played.
Whatever imps be now in them arrayed,
For this once they'll produce a rare effect.   [*Aloud.*
Hark!   What a temper they are in!
Mail clanks 'gainst mail with clattering din!
Torn banners, too, are fluttering there,
That longed again to breathe fresh air.
Here we have got an ancient people, who
Fain in this modern fray would mingle, too.
        [*Tremendous blare of trumpets from above; perceptible
            wavering in the hostile army.*

FAUST

Dark the horizon grows; meseems,
Breaks here and there in fitful gleams
A ruddy and portentous shine.
The spears, blood-boltered, flash and glare;
The rocks, the wood, the very air,
All heaven in sympathy combine.

MEPHISTOPHELES

The right flank stoutly holds its ground;
But, towering in their midst, I see
The giant Bully, dealing free
Those swashing strokes of his around.

EMPEROR

At first I saw one arm up; now
A dozen rage there.   Anyhow,
This can't be natural or right.

FAUST

Hast thou not heard of mists, that round
The coasts of Sicily abound?
There, hovering clear in broad daylight,
Uplifted high in middle air,
Mirrored in exhalations rare,
A wondrous vision meets the gaze—
Towns oscillating to and fro,
Gardens now high, now sinking low,
Picture on picture breaking through the haze.

EMPEROR

But yet, how strange!   See, each spear-head,
As if with lightning, flashes red!
While moves the host, on every lance
I see a flamelet flit and dance:
To me it looks too spectral quite.

FAUST

Forgive me, these things glimpses show
Of spirits gone hence long ago,
The famous Twins revealed once more,
By whom of old all seamen swore—
For our last stroke they nerve their might.

EMPEROR

To whom, then, do we owe it, say,
That nature, in this wondrous way,
For us should spells so rare unite!

MEPHISTOPHELES

To whom, but to that mighty master,
Who in his breast thy fate doth keep?
To see thee menaced with disaster,
Stirred feelings in him strong and deep.
So thou art saved, he gladly would
Meet death, to prove his gratitude.

EMPEROR

Round me that time with cheers and pomp they pressed.
Then I was something; this I wished to test,
So, without thinking, seized the chance, and there
Gave the white-bearded fellow some fresh air.
By this I robbed the clergy of a treat;
Thus was my fall in their good books complete.
Now, after all these years, am I to test
The outcome of a deed done half in jest?

FAUST

Rich interest follows generous deed.
Now turn your gaze on high!   He will
Some signal send, methinks.   Give heed!
It will anon be visible.

EMPEROR

An eagle hovers in the vaulted blue.
Him doth a griffin, fierce for fight, pursue.

FAUST

Now mark!   This augurs well, at least.
The griffin is a fabled beast;
What!   He to wrangle with the eagle,
A bird so real and so regal?

EMPEROR

See now, in circles wide they float,
Each coursing each—and now they clash
Together, and with gash on gash
Rend one another's breast and throat.

FAUST

Look, look! The sorry griffin, how,
All rent and scarred, he staggers, drops
His lion tail!   And see, he now
Is lost amid the pine-tree tops!

EMPEROR

May this portend what is to be!
Lost in amaze, I wait to see.

MEPHISTOPHELES (*towards the right*)

See, see! the enemy give back,
Pressed by our still renewed attack,
And, feebly keeping up the fight,
They 're falling back upon their right.
The left of their main body so
They into dire confusion throw.
Now on the right our phalanx brings
Its serried front, like lightning flings
Itself on the weak spot, and straight,
As ocean waves in stormy weather,
The forces, matched in bulk and weight,
In fray tumultuous clash together,
Nothing was ever better done;
For us the battle has been won.

EMPEROR (*on the left side, to* FAUST)

Look !   Yonder something seems amiss!
What , what can be the cause of this?
No stones upon the foe are hailed,
And they the lower cliff have scaled;
None keep the heights, a blow to strike,
Look there!   The foe, in serried mass,
Still pressing on and on, belike
Have gained possession of the pass;
Of ways unblest the issue plain!
These sleights of yours are all in vain.   [*Pause.*

MEPHISTOPHELES

My ravens here their flight are winging;
What can the message be they 're bringing?
The other side, I fear, prevails.

EMPEROR

What may these ill-starred birds presage?
Hither they bend their swarthy sails,
Straight from the rock-fight's fiery rage.

MEPHISTOPHELES (*to the Ravens*)

Sit down by me, at either ear!
Whom you protect need never fear,
For your advice is sound and sage.

FAUST (*to the* EMPEROR)

Hast never heard of pigeons, who
Back to their nest and fledglings flew
From regions strange to them and far?
That's the case here, though different.
The pigeon-post in peace is sent,
The raven-post's required for war.

MEPHISTOPHELES

They tell me of a grievous pinch.
Look how they're pressing, inch by inch,
Around our heroes' rocky wall!
The nearest heights are stormed, alas!
And, if we were to lose the pass,
Our case would be most critical.

EMPEROR

Betrayed!   I am betrayed at last!
'Tis you have round me drawn the net!
Horror! to feel it holds me fast!

MEPHISTOPHELES

Courage!   There's nothing lost as yet.
Patience unties the hardest knot;
Work's hottest, when the end's at hand.
I trusty messengers have got.
Command, that I may take command!

COMMANDER-IN-CHIEF (*who meanwhile has arrived*)

These men thou hast to counsel ta'en,
To me were, first and last, a pain.
The battle, now I cannot mend it,
'Twas they began, and they may end it.
My baton I to thee restore.

EMPEROR

Not so!   Retain it, till the Fates
Perchance may send us happier hours.
I shudder at this fellow's powers,
And his weird bird-confederates.

[*To* MEPHISTOPHELES.

Give you the baton?   Surely no.
You're not, methinks, the proper man.
Command!   Avert our overthrow!
And so betide, betide what can!
          [*Exit into the tent with the* Commander-in-Chief.

MEPHISTOPHELES

His baton!   Pooh!   What silly fuss!
Small profit would it bring to us.
There was a kind of cross upon it.

FAUST

What will you do?

MEPHISTOPHELES

          Do?   I have done it.
Hence, my black cousins, apt and fleet,
To the great mountain-lake!   The Undines greet,
And for the semblance of a flood entreat!
By arts, hard to divine, of female scheming,
They from the thing that is can part the seeming,
And, that it is the very thing, will swear.   [*Pause.*

FAUST

Our ravens have with flattery rare
Cajoled the water-nymphs from their lair.
See, trickling rills begin to gush!
From many a dry bare rocky brow
The springs in full swift volume rush.
Yon victory is no victory now.

MEPHISTOPHELES

Strange greeting that!   What follows next?
The boldest climber is perplexed.

FAUST

Brook downward bounds to brook in headlong course,
From the ravines they rush with twofold force;
And now in one bright arch the torrent sweeps.
Wide o'er the rocks it spreads, a shining flat,
Flashes and foams to this side and to that,
And ledge by ledge into the valley leaps.
What boots the bravest heart a tide to stay,
Must sweep before it everything away?
My very flesh to see such havoc creeps.

MEPHISTOPHELES

Nothing see I of all these water-lies;
Illusions these only for human eyes:
This wondrous hap to me is sheer delight.
Huddled in heaps, they turn in headlong flight,
Fancying, the fools, they will be drowned,
And puff and blow on solid ground,
Their arms, like swimmers, striking out.
Now all's confusion, utter rout!

> [*The Ravens have come back.*

To the great Master I'll speak well of you.
Now, would you prove yourselves true Masters too,
Hence to the smithy, belching fire,
Where the dwarf-folk, that never tire,
Strike sparks from metal and from stone;
Ask them for fire, while lightly chattering—
Fire brilliant, dazzling, sputtering, spattering,
Such as is but to fancy known.
Lightning, no doubt, far in the sky,
And stars, swift shooting from on high,
May any summer night be seen;
But lightning, on the brushwood gleaming,
And stars, that hiss on ground that's steaming,
Are not such common sights, I ween.
So, without fuss, you understand,
You first must beg, and then command.

> [*The Ravens fly away.   All happens as prescribed.*

Thick darkness settles on the foe!
Which way to turn, they do not know.
Meteors all round, and sudden light,
To dazzle and confound the sight!
Magnificent!　But now we want
Some sound to terrify and daunt.

FAUST

The empty arms, from ancient halls that came,
Find the fresh air breathe vigour through their frame.
They're rattling, banging, clattering up there—
A wonderful, discordant blare!

MEPHISTOPHELES

Quite right!　They're not to be kept back!
Now rings out knightly whack on whack,
As in the famous good old days.
Gauntlet, cuirass, and cuisses too,
As Guelphs and Ghibellines, renew
Full tilt their never-ending frays.

* N 335

Firm in transmitted rancour, they
A hate implacable display.
Now far and wide the tumult brays!
And so, at every devil's fête,
Nought works so well as party hate,
Down to the last convulsive throe.
Wild sounds, that scatter fear and panic,
Mingled with piercing yells Satanic,
Ring down into the vale below.

[*War tumult in the orchestra, passing at last into cheerful
military music.*

THE RIVAL EMPEROR'S TENT

Throne, Rich Surroundings. Havequick,
Pillage-fast

PILLAGE-FAST

We're first upon the field, you see.

HAVEQUICK

No raven flies so fast as we.

PILLAGE-FAST

Oh, look, what heaps of treasure there!
Where to begin?   To finish where?

HAVEQUICK

So crammed the place with plunder stands,
I know not where to lay my hands.

PILLAGE-FAST

That carpet suits me to a T;
My bed is often too hard for me.

HAVEQUICK

A Morgenstern of steel!   Just such
As I for years have longed for much!

PILLAGE-FAST

That scarlet cloak with golden seams,
One like it has often crossed my dreams!

HAVEQUICK (*taking the weapon*)

With this one makes short work.   A blow,
The fellow's dead, and on we go!
You've packed up such a lot, and yet
Not managed, the right sort to get.
Leave all that rubbish where it lay;
Take one of these small chests away!
The army's niggard pay they hold;
Its belly's stuffed with solid gold.

PILLAGE-FAST

'Tis mortal heavy!   More than I
Am fit to lift or carry.

HAVEQUICK

Try!
Quick, stoop!   Duck down, and let me pack
The box upon your sturdy back.

PILLAGE-FAST

Alack, alack!   I'm done for!   Whew!
It fairly breaks my back in two.
     [*The chest falls and breaks open.*

HAVEQUICK

There lies the red gold, all aheap;
Quick, quick, and up the shiners sweep!

PILLAGE-FAST (*crouches down*)

Into my lap with them!   With this
We shan't do very much amiss.

HAVEQUICK

There!   That's enough!   Off with you!   Pack!
        [*She rises.*
Your apron has a hole.   Alack!
Whether you stand or move, no matter,
The treasure recklessly you scatter.

HALBERDIERS (*of the true Emperor enter*)

This spot is sacred!   What are you about?
Rifling the Emperor's treasure-trove, I doubt?

HAVEQUICK

Limb, life we risked, and cheaply for his sake,
And of the booty now our share we take.
'Tis common usage, friend, the victor's due;
And as for us, why, we are soldiers too.

HALBERDIERS

That makes no part of our belief;
A soldier, quotha, and a thief!
The man who serves our Emperor, must
Be one whose honesty we trust.

HAVEQUICK

That honesty right well we know;
You name it 'Contribution,' though.
You're all on the same footing here;
The password of your trade is 'Give!'
                                        [*To* PILLAGE-FAST.
Start off with what you've sacked!   'Tis clear,
We're anything but welcome here.   [*Exeunt.*

FIRST HALBERDIER

The saucy knave!   Why broke you not
His pate across upon the spot?

SECOND HALBERDIER

Can't tell!   I felt unnerved.   They were
So phantom-like and weird a pair.

THIRD HALBERDIER

Something went wrong about my sight;
'Twas dazzled, I saw nothing right.

FOURTH HALBERDIER

What it all means, I fathom not.
All through the day it was so hot,
Oppressive, close, such sultry smother,
One kept his feet, down dropped another;
We groped and laid about us so,
A foeman fell at every blow;
Before our eyes there waved a mist,
Within our ears it buzzed and hissed:
So things went on, and here are we,
But know not, how things came to be.

Enter The Emperor *with four* Princes. The
Halberdiers *retire*

EMPEROR [1]

Well, leave him to his fate!   The day is ours.   In rout
The foe across the plains is scattered all about.
Here stands the empty throne, loot marks the traitor's place,
And, hung with tapestries, contracts the narrow space.
We with our own true guards in dignity the while,
Await the envoys here in high imperial style.
From all sides tidings come, glad tidings, hour by hour,
That peace is to a realm restored, that hails our power.
If, in the stand we made, some jugglery was wrought,
Yet, when all's said and done, 'twas we alone who fought.
Mere accidents in war will sometimes work to good—
Here meteors fall from heaven, there rains a shower of blood.
Sounds of a wondrous kind boom from the caverns near,
That make our hearts beat high, and fill the foe with fear.
A mark for lasting scorn, the vanquished prone is laid;
Praise to the victor's God exultingly is paid.
No need to give command, for all with one accord
From thousand throats do cry, 'We give Thee praise, O Lord!'
Yet—best and highest praise—I turn on mine own breast—
As rarely I have done—mine eyes in pious quest.
A young gay-hearted prince may waste the days are his;
The rolling years will teach how dear each moment is.
Therefore without delay, I link myself with you,
For home, and court, and realm, ye worthy Four and true.

[*To the first Prince.*

'Twas thou, Prince, who with skill didst well dispose our host,
Who in the crisis showed bold leadership the most;
Now what the time demands work thou, peace being restored,
Arch-Marshal henceforth be!   To thee I give the sword.

ARCH-MARSHAL

Thy faithful troops, till now required at home alone,
Will make thy frontiers safe, and safe with them thy throne,
Then be it ours, at feasts, when thronging guests are poured
Through thy ancestral hall, to dress thy festive board.
Thy shining sword I'll bear, and raise it by thy side,
Of sovereign Majesty the symbol, guard, and guide!

---

[1] For the scene of the Emperor rewarding his principal vassals for their
services in the war, which have been negative, the metre is changed, with
ironical intent, to alexandrines, six-footed rhyming couplets with a caesura
after the third foot.   This metre, imitated from the French classics, was the
one used in dignified or would-be dignified German drama from the seven-
teenth century until after 1770, but when Shakespearian blank verse had
become the vogue, the older metre began to produce a comic effect, suitable
for the mock-heroic parody in this scene.

EMPEROR (*to the second Prince*)

Thou, who dost valiant heart with courtesy unite—
Be thou Arch-Chamberlain!   The duties are not light.
Within our household be the head supreme of all;
Ill service do I get from servants prone to brawl.
By thy example taught, may they be more inclined
To be to me, the Court, and all, polite and kind!

ARCH-CHAMBERLAIN

The Master's lofty aims to further bringeth grace;
To bring help to the good, and not to harm the base,
To be straightforward, frank, and calm without deceit!
If thou, sir, knowst my heart, my joy is all complete.
Already on that feast to come my thoughts are bent,
The golden basin I to thee shall now present,
At meat and hold thy rings, that so thy hands may be,
Refreshed, as is my heart by happy smiles from thee.

EMPEROR

My mood is still too grave on festive thoughts to rest.
Yet be it so!   To start with cheerfulness is best.

[*To the third Prince.*

Arch-Steward I name thee!   In thy hands now I place
Fowl-yards, fish-ponds, and farms and conduct of the chase.
Give me each day my choice of viands and prepare
These dishes, as each month shall bring its own, with care.

ARCH-STEWARD

All meats will I forgo, and fast without regret,
Till some dish thou dost love before thee shall be set.
I and my kitchen-staff shall bring what's distant here,
And will accelerate the seasons of the year.
Yet not the luxuries wherewith thy table's graced,
But plain and solid fare is dearest to thy taste.

EMPEROR (*to the fourth Prince*)

Since revelry and feast perforce engage us now,
Young hero, fair as brave, my cupbearer be thou!
As Arch-Cupbearer, let this special care be thine,
To see our cellars stored with all the choicest wine.
But be thou temperate thyself, nor lose thy head,
By any tempting lures of social mirth misled.

ARCH-CUPBEARER

Even striplings, O my liege, if trust in them be shown,
Are found, ere one expects, to man's full vigour grown:
I too at that high feast shall duly take my place;
The Imperial sideboard I shall deck with royal grace,
With silver and with gold, magnificent to see;
But chief I'll set aside a beaker fair for thee—
A clear Venetian glass, where satisfaction waits,
Gives flavour to the wine, but ne'er inebriates.
Too great reliance some will place on such a prize;
But in due measure, Sire, a truer safeguard lies.

EMPEROR

What in this solemn hour I have on you conferred,
You've heard with confidence, relying on my word.
The Emperor's mighty word assures all gifts, of course,
Yet parchment's needed too, his mandates to enforce,
With signature and seal; the very man we need
I see approaching now.　He'll draw us up the deed.

Enter THE ARCHBISHOP—LORD HIGH CHANCELLOR

EMPEROR

When once an arch's curve is to the keystone braced,
Then is it for all time beyond all danger placed.
Thou seest four Princes here!　To these we have explained,
How in the days to come our Court shall be maintained.
But now, ye Five, on you and on your sapient power,
The weal of this whole realm is rested from this hour.
In landed wealth 'tis meet you shall all men outshine,
Therefore to you these lands I here at once assign,
The forfeit heritage of that revolted crew.
I give you fair domains—for staunch ye were and true—
And with them the full right, whene'er you see a chance,
By purchase, raid, exchange, their limits to enhance,
And power to exercise unchecked what rights to you,
As owners of the soil, by use and wont are due.
The judgments you pronounce are final.　No one may
Appeal to courts outside, when yours have had their say,
Tithe, toll, and impost dues, safe-conduct, duties, fees,
Are yours, and mining, salt, and coinage royalties.
That thus my gratitude effectively be shown,
I've raised you to a rank next only to my own.

ARCHBISHOP

Let me in name of all our deepest thanks express:
What makes us firm and strong, strengthens thy power no less.

EMPEROR

Even higher dignities I to you Five will give.
I live but for my realm, and so rejoice to live;
Yet thoughts of my long line withdraw my gaze from hours
Of stir and striving to the doom that ever lours.
I too, in God's good hour, must leave all I hold dear:
Then be it yours to choose one to succeed me here;
On holy altar raise him high, with crownèd brow,
And bring to peaceful close what was all storm but now.

LORD HIGH CHANCELLOR

Pride in our hearts, but bowed with humble mien we stand,
Thy vassals, princes all, the foremost in the land.
While yet the faithful blood runs in our veins we still,
One body, shall obey thy every wish and will.

EMPEROR

And now to end!   Let all that we to-day concede,
Be 'stablished for all time by manual-sign and deed.
You o'er your property shall hold dominion free,
On this condition, that it ne'er partitioned be:
Moreover, if you add to what you now receive,
You to your eldest sons the whole shall likewise leave.

LORD HIGH CHANCELLOR

On parchment I'll straightway record this statute, fraught
With weal for the realm and us, right happy in the thought.
Then, in the Chancery writ fair, the seal applied,
It shall be by thy hand solemnly ratified.

EMPEROR

I now dismiss you all, that you in private may
Reflect on the events of this momentous day.
          [*The Temporal Princes retire.   The* ARCHBISHOP *remains,
          and speaks in solemn tones.*

ARCHBISHOP

The Chancellor has retired, the Bishop stays behind,
To crave thine ear, impelled by grave misquiet of mind.
His father-heart is sad for thee, and in dismay.

EMPEROR

Dismay?   What troubles you on this so joyous day?

ARCHBISHOP

With bitter anguish, sir, at such a time I find
Thy hallowed head in league with Satan's self combined!
True, thou'rt secured upon thy throne—or so I hope—
But heedless, ah! of God, and our Holy Sire the Pope,
Who, when he hears of this, will straight pronounce his doom,
And with his lightnings will thy sinful realm consume.
He knows how at thy hest, the day that thou wert crowned,
Despite the solemn hour, the Sorcerer was unbound,
When from thy diadem the beam of grace was shed,
To mock all Christendom, first on that cursèd head.
But beat thy breast, and cede—'tis for thy spirit's health—
To Holy Church some slice of thy ill-gotten wealth:
The broad expanse of hills, where stood thy tent, and where
In thy defence were leagued foul Spirits of the Air,
Where to the Prince of Lies thou lentst thine ears of late—
That spot to pious use contritely dedicate,
With mountain and forest dense, as far as they extend,
And hilly slopes, green clad, that in broad meadows end;
Pellucid well stocked lakes, brooks numberless withal,
That, hurrying down like snakes, into the valleys brawl;
Then the broad vale itself, with meads, enclosures, plains:
Expressèd thus, penitence sure grace and pardon gains.

EMPEROR

This heavy sin of mine so weighs upon my breast,
I bid you take or leave whatever you think best.

ARCHBISHOP

First let the plot of earth by sin so desecrated
Be to the Lord Most High for ever consecrated,
In spirit I can see the walls rise ever higher;
The first beams of the sun illuminate the choir;
Now broadened to a cross, enriched by all the arts,
Longer and higher grows the nave, and glads all hearts;
Through stately portals throng the faithful, fired with zeal,
And far o'er hill and dale resounds the bells' first peal,
They clash and clang from towers that high aspire to heaven,
And penitents throng in, to whom new life is given.
On the high festive day—God send it to us soon!
Thy presence will adorn the Consecration.

EMPEROR

May this right noble work speak of my pious thought,
To praise God, and undo the sin that I have wrought.
Enough!   I already feel my spirit soaring higher.

ARCHBISHOP

This under hand and seal as Chancellor I require.

EMPEROR

A formal document, that gives the Church full right,
Lay thou before me; I will sign it with delight.

ARCHBISHOP (*has taken leave, but turns back
as he is going out*)

Then, as the work proceeds, 'tis meet thou dedicate
To it taxes, tribute, toll, and every due and rate,
For ever.   Much we need the fabric to maintain,
And staff to serve it well will cost vast sums, 'tis plain.
That progress may be swift on this bare cheerless spot,
Some of thy captured gold thou wilt to us allot.
We shall require, besides—I needs must thee remind—
Much far-off timber, lime, and stores of every kind.
Plain folk, urged by their priests, will do the carting, yes!
Who in her service works, him will the Church still bless.
                                                        [*Exit.*

EMPEROR

Oh, heavy is the sin that such dire penance craves!
They've brought me to a pass, these necromancing knaves!

ARCHBISHOP (*returning again, and making a deep
obeisance*)

Pardon, my liege, the realm's seashore to that vile man
Has been made over, but he will incur the Ban,
Unless there Holy Church in deep contrition thou
With tithes and taxes, rents and revenues endow.

EMPEROR (*losing his temper*)

There is no land there yet; just sea for far and wide.

ARCHBISHOP

His time will come who waits, with right upon his side.
We have thy royal word—no power may that gainsay.
                                                        [*Exit.*

EMPEROR (*alone*)

My kingdom, at this rate, will soon be signed away!

ACT V[1]

OPEN COUNTRY

WANDERER

THERE they are!   How well I mind them,
The dark lindens old and strong.
And I am again to find them
After years of travel long!
'Tis the old spot, unforsaken;
Still the sheltering cot is there,
As when billows tempest-shaken
Flung me on these sand-hills bare.
My kind hosts, I fain would greet them,
Brave good helpful souls, again:
But I scarce may hope to meet them;
They were aged even then.
Pious, ah, how pious were ye!
Shall I knock, or call?   What ho!
Hail, if kindly still as e'er, ye
Of good deeds the blessing know!

[1] The act opens many years after Faust has received his reward of 'the realm's seashore' from the Emperor.   The idyllic tone of the scenes with Philemon and Baucis, who might equally well have been called Darby and Joan, is in marked contrast with those in Faust's palace, where he is seen in all his power and glory, still discontented for the lack of that one portion of what was formerly the seashore occupied by the pious old couple.   His eviction of them raises the first of many questions which occur to the reader of this act, especially with regard to its moral implications.   'Man, while his struggle lasts, is prone to stray,' we have been told by the Lord, with regard to Faust, in the Prologue in Heaven, and in interpreting this key phrase we must remember the view of evil suggested in the same scene. 'Striving and erring are involved in one another and not to be disentangled' in this view, as Professor Barker Fairley reminds us.   Only the looker-on can keep his hands entirely clean; 'the man of action is always without conscience,' as one of Goethe's 'Maxims' says.   But this truth has not been so plainly brought home to us in most of the Second Part as in the First, unless (with Rickert) we look upon Euphorion as a kind of substitute hero of the end of the Helena act, displaying the excess we have learnt to expect in his father.   Again, what goal has Faust been striving to reach, and how far has he advanced in his long life?   Are we to take him as a model, or as a warning example?   Both views have been strongly argued, but on the whole it seems most likely that in *this* work (though certainly not in all his later works) Goethe is looking, as Viëtor says, 'for a standpoint above the plane of moral values' and suggesting that 'what makes Faust great is that in spite of all defeats he does not turn his back on life, but gives himself up to it wholeheartedly, whatever it may bring.'   Behind it all is the conviction that man and life and the universe are fundamentally good, and that is the sense of Faust's ultimate salvation.

BAUCIS (*very old*)

Hush, hush, stranger, hush!   No breaking
On my husband's spell of rest!
To give to his few hours of waking
Vigour, good long sleep is best.

WANDERER

Mother, thou still here, and he, too,
To receive the thanks I owe
For the young man's life, by ye two
Saved now many years ago?
Art thou Baucis, who so tended,
Nursed me back to life again?
                    [*The husband comes out of the cottage.*
Thou he (*turning to* PHILEMON), who with courage splendid
Snatched my treasure from the main?
Your fire, blazing fast and faster,
Your bell with its silver sound,
They from that so dire disaster
Me a safe deliverance found.
Let me on a little way there,
View the boundless ocean first;
Let me kneel, and let me pray there!
Seems my heart as it would burst!
                    [*He walks away upon the dunes.*

PHILEMON (*to* BAUCIS)

Quick, wife!   Spread the table under
The green shadow of our trees.
Let him go!   He'll start in wonder.
Not believing what he sees!
            [*Following the wanderer.   Standing beside him.*
Where the billows, wildly booming,
Savagely maltreated you,
Now 'tis like a garden, blooming
Fair as eye could wish to view.
Old in years as I was growing,
Help I could not, as of yore;
And, while my own strength was going,
Farther off, too, went the shore.
Great folks' serfs, with dauntless daring
Trenches dug and bulwarks spread,
Ocean's ancient rights impairing,
To be masters in its stead.

See, green fields on fields, and nigh them
Woodland, garden, mead, and town!
But now come, our viands, try them,
For the sun will soon be down.
Far out there, see, vessels beating
Up to port for night repair,
Bird-like to their nest retreating,
For there's now a harbour there.
Only on the sky-line yonder
May a streak of sea be seen;
All ways, far as eye can wander,
Lies thick-peopled land between.

IN THE LITTLE GARDEN

The three at table

BAUCIS (*to the stranger*)

Silent still?   And not a grain here
Yet has crossed your lips?

PHILEMON

                    Od's life!
Of our marvels more he'd fain hear:
You like talking; tell him, wife.

BAUCIS

Marvels! Ay!   If ever any;
Even yet they make me grew;
For in manner quite uncanny
The whole thing was carried through.

PHILEMON

Can the Emperor be to blame?   It
Was himself gave up the shore.
Did a herald not proclaim it,
Trumpeting, as he passed our door?
On our downs hard by their footing
First was planted.   There were seen
Bothies, tents.   But soon, upshooting,
Rose a palace 'midst the green.

BAUCIS

Vain all day their hacking, tearing,
Pick and shovel, stroke on stroke!
Where night-long great fires were flaring,
Stood a bank when morning broke.
Human victims surely bled there—
Through the dark their cries were borne;
Flashing fires to seaward sped there,
'Twas a great canal by morn.
He is godless, he has set his
Heart upon our cot, our wood.
A fine neighbour he, who'll get his
Will, and will not be withstood!

PHILEMON

Still he made a fairish tender—
A snug farm on his new land!

BAUCIS

Never your own knoll surrender!
Trust not what was sea and sand.

PHILEMON

To the chapel, on the dying
Rays of sunset there to gaze!
Let us ring, kneel, pray, relying
On the God of ancient days!

PALACE ¹

Spacious ornamental garden—wide, straight canal

FAUST (*in extreme old age, walking and meditating*)

LYNCEUS, THE WARDER (*through his speaking-trumpet*)

Sinks the sun, the ships are nearing
Port before the night shall fall,
And a stately bark is steering
Hither up the great canal.

¹ ' *War, commerce, piracy* . . .' It has been suggested that in his picture
of a bold seafaring community, not too particular in its methods of coloniza-
tion, Goethe was thinking of the English, for whom he frequently expressed
a not uncritical admiration in his later years, contrasting them with his
unpractical fellow countrymen. (See A. R. Hohlfeld, *Fifty years with
Goethe*, Madison, 1953.)

Her gay pennons brightly flutter;
On her stout masts swell the sails;
Blessings on thee seamen mutter;
Thee The Blest high fortune hails.

[*The chapel bell on the dunes rings.*

FAUST

Accursed bell! Its tinkle wounds me,
Like caitiff shot from hand unkind.
Unbounded is my realm before me,
Vexation stings me from behind.
It minds me by its hateful pealing,
My happiness is mixed with pine:
The clump of limes, the dusky shieling,
The crumbling chapel are not mine.
If there I wished an hour of leisure,
Shades not my own would blight the day,
They would be thorns to dash my pleasure.
Oh, would that I were far away!

WARDER (*as above*)

How blithely does the galley gay
Before the fresh breeze cleave its way!
How on it bears a towering hoard
Of sacks, chests, coffers, piled aboard!

[*A splendid galley, richly and showily laden with products
of foreign countries.*

MEPHISTOPHELES, THE THREE MIGHTY MEN

CHORUS

Back already, land we here!
All hail, master, patron dear!

[*They disembark; the goods are brought ashore.*

MEPHISTOPHELES

Well have we shown what we could do—
Content, if we are praised by you:
With but two ships we went away,
Now twenty have in port to-day.
By the rich cargo we have brought,
Behold, what great things we have wrought!
Free ocean sets the spirit free;
We make our own whate'er we see;
What's needed there's a hasty grip—
One grabs a fish, one grabs a ship.

Once we have three of these in store,
We never rest till we have four;
Then is the fifth in evil plight.
Who has the power, he has the right;
The WHAT's the question, not the HOW.
These seamen are as bold as ever:
War, commerce, piracy, are now
A Trinity, to be sundered never.

THE THREE MIGHTY MEN

No thank, or welcome! no welcome, or thank!
As if the things we have brought him stank!
Quite out of humour he looks, and grim;
This royal booty delights not him.

MEPHISTOPHELES

Expect no further reward; for you
Already have taken what was your due.

THE THREE MIGHTY MEN

You're only jesting? Fair is fair!
We all insist on an equal share.

MEPHISTOPHELES

First range in order, through hall and hall,
The things are richest, one and all.
The dazzling show when he comes to see,
And finds how precious and rare they be,
Be sure, he'll do the handsome thing,
And give the fleet high junketing.
To-morrow we'll have gay birds here,
You'll have your fun then, never fear!

[*The cargo is carried away.*

MEPHISTOPHELES (*to* FAUST)

With gloomy looks and brow austere
You of your high good fortune hear.
Success has on your wisdom smiled—
Ocean and shore are reconciled;
And from the shore the ocean sweeps
Your ships, and speeds them o'er its deeps.
Admit that from your palace here
Your arm clasps either hemisphere.
From this spot dated all the good—
'Twas here the first log-cabin stood:

A tiny trench was cut—no more—
Where plashes now the busy oar.
Your people's toil, your master-brain,
Have wrung this prize from land and main.
From here too—

FAUST

                    That accursèd here!
'Tis this which makes my heart so sick.
I needs must whisper in your ear,
It gnaws me, stings me to the quick;
The thought I can nor bear nor crush,
Yet must at the avowal blush—
The old folks must turn out up there.
I want that lime-grove for a site;
These few trees, not my own, they quite
The charm of all I own impair.
There, far and wide around to gaze,
From bough to bough I'd scaffolds raise,
Whence should be opened to the view
All that I've done, broad vistas through,
And at a glance might be surveyed
The master-work man's soul has made,
Winning, by well-concerted plan,
A wide and fertile home for man.
So we are kept upon the rack—
'Midst riches feeling what we lack.
The tinkling bell, the limes' perfume,
Haunt me like crypt's or church's gloom.
The will, with which no mortal copes,
Is broken on these sandy slopes!
How of the thought to be beguiled?
There goes the bell, and I am wild!

MEPHISTOPHELES

Of course, a great chagrin like this
Is gall and wormwood in your bliss.
Who but will own, this clink-clank must
Fill every fine ear with disgust;
And this curst ding-dong-bell, that shrouds
The cheerful evening sky with clouds,
Mingles with each event and mood
Down to the grave from babyhood,
Till life 'twixt ding and dong doth seem
The chaos of a faded dream.

FAUST

Marred at its height is our success,
By merely wilful stubbornness,
So that in angry, deep disgust,
One tires at last of being just.

MEPHISTOPHELES

Why fret?   Have you this many a year
Not worked at colonizing here?

FAUST

Go then—away the old folks clear!
The pretty little farm you know,
I picked out for them long ago.

MEPHISTOPHELES

We'll bear them off, and plant them there
Quite snug, or ever they're aware;
A pretty home, at any rate,
For usage rough will compensate.
                    [*Whistles shrilly; enter* THE THREE.

MEPHISTOPHELES

Come on! your lord's behests complete,
And he'll to-morrow feast the fleet.

THE THREE

He gave us scurvy welcome.   Least
He owes us is a rattling feast.

MEPHISTOPHELES (*ad spectatores*)

Here, too, befalls what long ago befell;
For we've a Naboth's vineyard here as well.

DEEP NIGHT

LYNCEUS (*sings on the watch-tower*) [1]

> For my keen vision noted,
> Set to watch day and night,
> To my tower devoted,
> The world's my delight.
> I scan the far forces,
> I mark what is near,
> Moon, stars in their courses,
> The woodlands, the deer.
> Thus a charm never-failing
> I see all around,
> And I am glad, hailing
> The joy I have found.
> O happy eyes, never
> Unblest; for whate'er
> Ye have looked on, wherever
> It met you, was fair.   [*Pause.*

> Not for my enjoyment merely,
> Am I stationed here so high;
> From the dark what horror drearly
> Breaks with menace on mine eye?
> Fire-flakes shooting up, I scan them
> Through the lindens' twofold night;
> Fiercelier, as the wind-gusts fan them,
> Rage the flames, and flash more bright.
> Ah, the cot's on fire, unheeded,
> Damp it was and moss-o'ergrown;
> Sorely swiftest help is needed,
> Help or succour there is none.
> Ah, the good old man and mother!
> Erst so careful they of fire,
> They will perish in the smother—
> Perish, oh disaster dire!
> All aglow within the lonely
> Dark hut!   Flames around it swell!
> Oh, if these good souls might only
> 'Scape from out yon blazing hell!

---

[1] The watchman into whose mouth Goethe puts the fine verses about the beauty of nature and the cruelty of man is given the same name (that of the steersman of the Argonauts, 'the lynx-eyed') as the watchman in the Helena act, but he is not thought of as the same person.

Tongues of flame shoot up and flicker
'Twixt the leaves and branches green,
Withered boughs, consuming quicker,
Blaze awhile, then fall between.
Eyes, shall you see this?   Ah me!
Must I so far-sighted be?
Crushed by falling branches, crashes
Down the chapel to the ground;
The steeple now with forkèd flashes,
Coiling serpent-like, is crowned.
Down to their roots the tree-trunks blighted
Glow red in the fiery blast!   *[Long pause.   Song.*
What erewhile the eye delighted
Hence hath with the ages passed.

FAUST (*on the balcony, facing the dunes*)

Aloft there what a cry of wailing!
Words and moans are now too late;
The warder grieves: though unavailing,
My grief for this rash act is great.
But though the linden-grove, ablaze there,
Lie all in ruin charred and black,
A stately tower I'll quickly raise there,
To look as far as eye can track.
There, too, I see the new home folding
Within its walls the aged pair,
Who, gratefully my care beholding,
Shall end their days in comfort there.

MEPHISTOPHELES *and* THE THREE *below*

We've come as fast as we could hie!
Your pardon!   Things have gone awry.
We knocked and kicked, and kicked and knocked,
And still the door they kept it locked.
We knocked and knocked, we shook it well,
And then the rotten fabric fell.
We shouted, threatened, loud and clear,
But could not make the people hear.
And, as folks do in such a mood,
Hear us they neither did nor would;
But we, remembering what you said,
Soon turned the old souls out of bed.
They made the business easy quite—
Down dead they fell, of simple fright.

A stranger whom they had aboard,
And who showed fight, was quickly floored.
In the short scrimmage—it fell out—
From cinders, that got strewn about,
The thatch caught fire.　'Tis blazing free,
A funeral-pyre for all the three.

FAUST

No ear to my commands you lent!
Not plunder, but exchange I meant.
This brutal outrage, mad and worse,
I curse it!　Hence! and 'mong you share my curse!

CHORUS

The ancient saw, we have it here:
To might give still a ready ear!
If bold, and reckless what befall,
Risk house and home, yourself—and all!

[Exeunt.

FAUST

The stars conceal their sheen and glow,
The fire begins to smoulder low;
A chilly breeze upon its wings
To me the smoke and smother brings.
Rash hest, too recklessly obeyed!
What there comes hovering like some spectral shade?

[Draws back.

MIDNIGHT [1]

Enter FOUR GREY WOMEN

FIRST

My name, it is WANT.

SECOND

It is DEBT they call me.

THIRD

My name is CARE!

FOURTH

Mine, NECESSITY.

THREE (*speaking together*)

The door it is bolted, we cannot go in;
A rich man dwells there, and we may not within.

WANT

I fade to a shade there.

DEBT

There I cease to be.

NECESSITY

There the eye is too dainty to look upon me.

---

[1] Of the four grey phantoms which appear out of the smoke of the burning cottage, only Care can attack the rich man Faust, and she speaks to him only after he has renounced the magic which since the compact has made him exempt from anxious thoughts about the future.   (Cf. note to p. 22.) The blinding of Faust has been variously interpreted.   Two things seem clear, that Faust is very old, and that when, losing his nerve at last or genuinely regretting the latest result of his wilfulness, he wishes to be a normal man again, the physical effects of age ironically rob him of precisely that sense without which the view-point he has just won on the old couple's land is useless to him.   He is exposed at last to the same lot, blindness, which (says Care) afflicts other men, through their irrational fears, all their lives.   But though he loses touch with material reality, his 'inner light' burns brighter than ever.   He is a stage nearer to being the pure 'entelechy' he becomes in the last scene of all, and only now has his vision of a possible state of contentment.   At this moment he dies, and the question of whether he has lost his wager with Mephistopheles or not is left open, except that his soul is 'saved,' as had been foretold in the 'Prologue in Heaven.'   There are many interesting points of contrast between this scene at midnight and the dawn scene at the beginning of the Second Part.

CARE

Ye sisters, ye neither can enter, nor dare;
But the keyhole's a portal sufficient for Care.

[CARE *disappears.*

WANT

Grey sisters, away!   Here no more may we bide.

DEBT

Where you go, there I go, and stick by your side.

NECESSITY

On your heels I will follow, Necessity saith.

THE THREE

The clouds they roll up, disappears star on star.
Behind there, behind!   From afar, from afar!
He is coming, our brother is coming—Death!

FAUST (*within the palace*)

I saw four come, and only three go hence.
Some words I heard, but could not catch the sense.
Necessity, said one, with muttered breath,
And then there came a rhyme ill-omened—DEATH:
A dull dead sound, of ghostly note, methought.
Not yet have I my way to freedom fought!
Could I sweep magic from my path, forgo
The spells of sorcery one and all, and so
Stand up before thee, Nature, just a man,
Then welcome, human lot, and mortal span!
Such was I once, ere I my studies fed
With the dark lore of arts inhibited—
Ere my chagrin in impious frenzy burst,
And mine own self and all the world I curst.
So now the very air do phantasms fill,
That how to 'scape them passes mortal skill.
Yea, if for us one day hath cheering gleams,
Night wilders us with spirit-haunted dreams.
The fresh green fields have made our pulses dance;
Then croaks a bird: what does it croak?—Mischance!
Beset by superstition night and morning:
Woe will betide, it augurs ill, gives warning.
And so we stand alone, scared, trembling, dumb.
I heard the door creak; in has no one come.

[*Shaken with apprehension.*

Is someone here?

CARE

So asked, I say, There is!

FAUST

Who, then, art thou?

CARE

Enough that here I be!

FAUST

Go, get thee hence!

CARE

My proper place is this.

FAUST (*at first incensed, then softening down*)

Take heed, Faust.   Use no spell of wizardry!

CARE

Though the ear may hear me not,
Fear is in the heart begot.
In for ever changing guise
Cruel power I exercise;
On the ocean, on the shore,
Sad companion evermore;
Always found, and sought for never,
Cursed, cajoled, and flattered ever!
Care hast thou, then, never known?

FAUST

I've galloped merely through the world, I own.
Each pleasure by the hair I'd seize,
Cast off whatever failed to please,
What 'scaped me let unheeded go.
First craving, then achieving, then
Longing for something new again;
And stoutly on through life went storming so,
Grandly at first, and foremost in the race,
But sagely now, and at a sober pace.
Of man and earth I know enough; what lies
Beyond is barricaded 'gainst our eyes.
Fool, who with blinking gaze out yonder peers,
And dreams of kindred souls in upper spheres!

Let him stand firm, and look around him here.
Not dumb this world to him that bears a brain:
Why through eternity should he career?
What things he knows will in his grasp remain.
So let him roam on through his earthly day;
Though spirits gibber, calmly hold his way;
And longing still, and still unsatisfied,
Accept his fate, let joy or grief betide.

CARE

Him I in my gripe have got
All the world availeth not.
Gloom upon him ever lies,
Suns set not for him, nor rise.
Sound in outward sense, and hale,
Darknesses within prevail.
Riches fineless may be his,
Yet he ne'er their master is.
Whim to him are good and ill;
He 'mid plenty hungers still.
Be it joy or be it sorrow,
Off he puts it till to-morrow,
All intent on what's to be,
Evermore unready he.

FAUST

Have done! This is for thee no place.
Nor me to listen to such trash befits.
Away! That litany so vile, so base,
Might rob the very sagest of his wits.

CARE

Shall he go? Or shall he come?
Doubt doth his resolve benumb;
On a beaten road, and straight,
He will pause and hesitate;
Lose himself more deeply, view
All things more and more askew.
Burden to himself and others,
Breath he breathes, yet breathing smothers,
Lifeless, though of living kind,
Not despairing, not resigned.
Such an all-adrift career—
Sad dejection, helpless fear,
Now exulting, now depressed,
Poor enjoyment, broken rest—
Chains him to the spot that bears him,
And in time for hell prepares him.

FAUST

O phantoms evil-starred!   'Tis thus you hurt
Man, whensoe'er ye hold him in your fangs;
Even days that might be happy ye pervert
Into a tangle of avoidless pangs.
'Tis hard, I know, from demons to get free;
The strong leash spirits weave few hands may sever;
Yet, mighty and insidious though it be,
Thy power, O Care, I will acknowledge never.

CARE

Then feel it now!   I leave behind
My curse on you, as swift away I wend.
Through their whole lives the race of man is blind;
You, Faust, be blind, now your life nears its end!
                                      [*She breathes upon him.*

FAUST (*blinded*)

Night seems to close in deeper—deepening still;
But all within is radiantly bright;
What I have thought I hasten to fulfil;
The master's bidding, that alone has might.
Up, vassals, from your lairs!   Give me to scan
The glad fulfilment of my daring plan.
Up! to your tools!   Ply shovel, pick, and spade!
Straight must the work be done, so long delayed.
Stern discipline, and toil intense,
Shall have the amplest recompense.
One mind to guide a thousand hands,
And perfected the work, my noblest, stands!

GREAT FORE-COURT OF THE PALACE

TORCHES

MEPHISTOPHELES (*as overseer, leading the way*)

This way, this way!   Come in, you
      Lemures, stumbling, hobbled—
Abortions, out of sinew,
      Bone, and tendon cobbled!

LEMURES (*in chorus*)

Here we are at your command!
  We've half heard why we came—it
Is all about a stretch of land,
  And we are to reclaim it.
Sharp-pointed stakes, long chains withal,
  To measure with, we've brought in.
On us why you were pleased to call—
  That we have clean forgotten.

MEPHISTOPHELES

The work here needs no artist-touches nice;
To measure from yourselves will quite suffice.
Let him that's tallest lie upon the ground,
And then you others lift the turf all round.
Prepare, as for our sires of old,
An oblong pit deep in the mold.
Out of the palace to the narrow home—
Such is the sorry end to which they all must come.

LEMURES (*digging with elvish gestures*)

In youth when I did live, did love,
  Methought 'twas very sweet;
Where mirth was free, and jollity,
  That place for me was meet.

But age with stealing steps
  Hath clawed me with his crutch.
A grave, its door I stumbled o'er;
  Why leave they open such?

FAUST (*comes out of the palace, groping by the door-posts*)

The clink of spades!   What rapture in the sound!
Hark! multitudes at work to do my bidding,
The soil of what disturbs it ridding,
Imposing on the waves a bound,
And drawing a strong curb the sea around!

MEPHISTOPHELES (*aside*)

Yet all your labour's spent for us alone.
With your fine dams and bulwarks vast,
You're but preparing a superb repast
For Neptune, the sea-fiend, to feast upon.
You're trumped and done for every way,
Into our hands the elements play,
Destruction onwards is striding fast.

FAUST

Inspector!

MEPHISTOPHELES

Here!

FAUST

Howe'er, where'er you may,
Get labourers, heaps on heaps.   Excite
By threats, cajoling, extra pay,
And extra cheer, to work with all their might.
Each day I'd have the tidings brought me, how
The trench is getting on, they're digging now.

MEPHISTOPHELES (*half aloud*)

Their talk to me, it is as if they gave,
Not tidings of a trench, but of—a grave.

FAUST

The marsh, that spreads hence to the mountain's base,
Empoisons all the land already gained;
But drain the noisome swamp off from the place,
My last, my highest aim were then attained.
Though not quite safe, still there would be broad lands,
Free for the tillage of a million hands!
Fields green and fertile; men and cattle both
Would to the virgin soil draw, nothing loath,
Hedging themselves betimes by dike and mound,
Which their bold busy hands will pile around.
Within, a very paradise; outside,
Howe'er may rage the angry baffled tide,
Striving to sap, to force an entrance, each
And all rush swiftly to close up the breach.
Yes!   This one thought absorbs me wholly—rife
With wisdom's final lesson, and most true;
He only merits freedom, merits life,
Who daily has to conquer them anew.
So, girt by danger, shall youth, manhood, age,
Pass kindly here their busy pilgrimage.
Such swarming multitudes I fain would see,
Free people standing on a soil as free;
Then to the passing moment might I say,
'Oh linger yet, thou art so fair!
So may the traces of my earthly day
Not with the ages fade away in air!'

In the foretaste of such high bliss, I seem
Even now to enjoy that moment all supreme.

[FAUST *sinks back; the* LEMURES *catch him and lay him upon the ground.*

MEPHISTOPHELES

Him does no pleasure sate, nor gain content!
From change to change his fancy ever went.
The last vile empty moment fain
Would he, poor creature, as it flies, retain.
He, who defied me with so high a hand,
Time masters him—there lies he on the sand.
The clock stands still——

CHORUS

          Stands still!   Hushed as midnight.
The index falls.

MEPHISTOPHELES

It falls; 'tis finished quite!

CHORUS

'Tis past!

MEPHISTOPHELES

          Pshaw!   Past?   A stupid phrase!   Why past?
Past and pure nothingness are one at last!
What boots this evermore creating, when
Things all sweep into nothingness again?
'There!   Now 'tis past!'   From this what can we glean?
'Tis all the same as though it ne'er had been;
Yet round and round it goes, as though it were.
Eternal Void I, for my part, prefer.

BURIAL

LEMUR (*solo*)

Who has with shovel and with spade
    Built up the house so vilely?

CHORUS OF LEMURES

For thee, sad guest, in hempen vest,
    'Tis finished much too highly.

LEMUR (*solo*)

Who has so badly furnished it?
Chairs, tables, where are any?

CHORUS OF LEMURES

'Tis snug and strong, not let for long,
The claimants are so many.

MEPHISTOPHELES

The body's down, and if the spirit would
Only come out, I very quickly should
Show it my blood-writ bond; but nowadays
Men have, alas, so very many ways
Of getting souls out of the devil's clutch!
The old way out of date has grown,
The new we do not fancy much—
Else had I managed all alone.
To help from others I must now resort.
We're altogether in a sorry plight.
Long well-established usage, ancient right,
Who can rely on them, or who, in short,
Trust anything to be what once it was?
Once with the latest breath out came the soul:
Like cat on mouse emerging from its hole,
Snap! and I had it fast within my claws!
Now it hangs back, and is averse to quit
The loathsome corpse, that foully harbours it;
The elements, that hate each other, send
It ignominiously packing in the end.
For days and hours, perplex me how I will,
'When?' 'How?' and 'Where?' is the cursed question still.
Old Death has lost his power so swift and stout,
The 'Whether' even hangs in tedious doubt.
Ofttimes on rigid limbs I've gloated, then
Found 'twas all sham: they moved, got up again.
                              [*Fantastic gestures of conjuration.*
Hither away!   Faster than e'er you flew,
Lords of the straight, lords of the crookèd horn,
Chips of the old block, devils bred and born,
And bring the jaws of hell along with you!
Hell has jaws manifold, that gape to suit your
Different shades of dignity and rank;
But people, too, in this their final prank,
Will not be so particular in future.
                              [*The ghastly jaws of Hell open on the left.*

The corner teeth gape wide; from the abyss
The raging stream of fire leaps forward, and I see,
Through whirling smoke and flames, that roar and hiss,
The City of Fire, where flames eternal be.
Up to the very teeth the blazing eddies play:
The damned swim up in hope to 'scape their doom;
But the Hyena crunches them, and they,
Howling in pain, their fiery path resume.
Much more is left to spy in corners there;
In compass small such agony supreme!
Nought could serve better sinful folk to scare;
But they regard it all as lies, and fraud, and dream.

[*To the stout devils, with short straight horns.*

You of the fiery cheeks, you all aglow,
Full fed on brimstone, fat and broad of beam!
Short, clumsy, stiff-necked, watch you here below
If anything like phosphorus shall gleam.
That is the soul, Psyche with wings; these steal,
'Tis then a loathsome worm, and nothing more,
The moment I have stamped it with my seal,
Off with it to where hell's fires whirl and roar!
The nether regions be your care,
Ye paunches!   Duty bids you so.
If the soul has its favourite lodging there,
With certainty one cannot know.
Within the navel it delights to dwell;
'Twill give you thence the slip.   So watch that well!

[*To the lean devils, with long crooked horns.*

You giants, capering round with limbs disjointed,
Strike out into the air; no pause, but snatch,
Your arms outstretched, your talons sharply pointed,
That you the flighty, fluttering thing may catch!
It finds, no doubt, its ancient home a bore,
And the first wish of genius is to soar.

[*Glory from above on the right.   Heavenly host.*

CHORUS OF ANGELS

Kin to the blest above,
Envoys of heavenly love,
Onwards still follow,
Bearing in trust
Pardon to sinners,
Life to the dust!
With slow-beating wings,
As along ye are sped,
On all living things
Benign influence shed!

MEPHISTOPHELES

I hear discordant sounds, a hideous noise,
Come with the unwelcome radiance from above;
A mawkish chant it is of girls and boys,
Such as your canting tricksters dearly love.
You know how we, by curses agonized,
Plotted destruction to the human race:
The most disgraceful things that we devised
Seem to their pious souls not out of place.
They come, a sneaking, hypocritic set—
So have they snatched from us full many a prize:
With our own arms they fight us; for what yet
Are they, but devils clothed in masking guise?
Lose here, and you're eternally disgraced.
To the grave!   Cling to its margin!   Haste ye, haste!

CHORUS OF ANGELS (*scattering roses*)

Roses that dazzle so,
Balm-breathing, living,
Fluttering to and fro,
Inly life giving,
Floating on leafy wing,
Blossoms half opening,
Hasten to blow!
Scatter around you Spring,
Verdure and glow,
Paradise bring
To the sleeper below!

MEPHISTOPHELES

Why do you duck and shrink?   Is that hell's wont?
Stand fast, and let them scatter as they may!
Each to his place!   Fools, show a steady front!
They think, forsooth, with such flower-rubbish they
Can fiery fiends as with snowflakes o'erlay!
Before your breath 'twill shrivel, melt away.
Blow then, ye blowers!   Gently, gently there!
The whole troop blench before your scorching air.
Not quite so strong!   Shut mouth and nostrils to.
You've blown a deal too fiercely.   Pest, that you
To hit the due proportion never learn!
You more than shrivel—you scorch, you wither, burn.
They flutter down with poisonous, piercing flame;
Stand close, and meet them fearlessly!   Oh, shame!
What!   Quailing still?   All courage gone and spent!
A strange, bewitching glow the devils scent.

CHORUS OF ANGELS

Flowers, blest and beautiful,
Flames, gladsome, bright,
On hearts that are dutiful
Shed pure delight,
Love every way.
Words with pure truth that ring,
Clear as heavens opening,
To hosts immortal bring
Everywhere day.

MEPHISTOPHELES

Curse on these idiots, ill-bestead!
The Satans turn heels over head!
Round, round like wheels they spin, the paunchy brutes,
And plunge tail-foremost into hell again.
I hope you'll find your well-earned hot bath suits;
But I will here, here at my post remain.
                [Striking aside the roses that hover around him.
Off, Jack o' Lanterns! Pugh! For all your flash,
Grasped, and what are you but mere loathsome squash?
What! flickering still? Begone with you! They cling
About my neck—like pitch and brimstone sting.

CHORUS OF ANGELS

What with your nature wars,
You must abjure it;
What on your spirit jars,
Do not endure it:
If it will force its way,
Front it we must and may;
Only the loving love
Heavenward can sway.

MEPHISTOPHELES

I burn all over, head, heart, liver, bone!
A hyperdiabolic element! They are
More piercing than the fires of hell by far!
Ha! now I see why ye make such wild moan,
Ye hapless lovers! who, though sweethearts spurn,
To look at them your necks can't choose but turn.
Why to that side is even my head bowed?
I, that to deadly strife with them am vowed!
* o 335

Time was, to see them set me on the rack.
What strange thing's this has pierced me through and
     through?
These dear young things are charming to the view;
Why can I curse them not?   What holds me back?
And if I let them o'er me mastery get,
Who then henceforward may be called the fool?
The pretty rascals, I detest them, yet
They strike me as by much too beautiful;
Fair children, pray inform me, are you not
Of the great race of Lucifer begot?
You are so pretty, fain I'd kiss you; you,
Methinks, appear at the right moment, too.
It is so nice, so natural, as though
I'd met with you a thousand times before.
You set one's concupiscence all aglow;
Each time I look, you charm me more and more.
Come nearer!   Oh, vouchsafe me but one glance!

CHORUS OF ANGELS

Behold us!   Why recoil as we advance?
We still advance; if stay thou canst, then stay!
          [*The angels drawing round, occupy the whole space.*

MEPHISTOPHELES (*who is thrust into the proscenium*)

You rail at us as spirits damned, and you
Are of sheer wizardry the masters true;
For you lead man and womankind astray.
How cursèd this adventure is!
Love's element, can it be this?
A raging fire fills all my frame;
Scarce on my neck I feel the scorching flame.
You hover to and fro; come down, and sway
Your gracious limbs in somewhat worldlier way.
It suits you well, I grant, that earnest style,
Yet fain I'd see you but one moment smile;
That were for me beyond all utterance sweet:
A smile, I mean, like that when lovers meet.
A slight turn of the mouth—the thing is done.
You there, tall shapely lad, I like the best:
Only that priest-like air is not my taste,
Give me one loving glance, one, only one!
A scantier robe, too, were more seemly, kind;
These sweeping folds too decent are by far.
They turn about!   To view them from behind—
They're quite too toothsome, the young rogues, they are!

CHORUS OF ANGELS

Ye loving flames, quicken
More clearly and calm,
To souls remorse-stricken
Let truth bring a balm!
So themselves from the thrall
Of the ill they may wrest,
Thenceforth in the All-in-all
Merge and be blest!

MEPHISTOPHELES (*pulling himself together*)

How is 't with me?   Like Job, from head to heels,
All boils, a horror to one's self; but yet
Triumphant, when one probes himself, and feels
Reliance on himself and on his race.
The noble devil-parts all keep their place;
'Tis but skin-deep this lickerish fuss and fret;
Those plaguy flames already are burnt out,
And now I curse you all, right round about!

CHORUS OF ANGELS

The man o'er whom
You, holy flames, brood,
Is purged from death's gloom,
Lives blest with the good.
In unison blending,
Sing, upwards ascending;
The air, it is purified,
Spirit, breathe free!

[*They ascend, bearing away with them the immortal
part of* FAUST.

MEPHISTOPHELES (*looking around*)

But how is this?   Where have they gone?
Ye milksop chits, you have outwitted me!
Away to heaven they've with their booty flown;
That's why they nibbled at this grave, I see!
Great and unique the prize they have withdrawn
Out of my very fingers.   The high soul,
That by its own free act I held in pawn,
They've filched away, clean out of my control.
And now, to whom shall I complain?   Who, who
Will vindicate for me my well-earned right?
In your old days you've been bamboozled; you
Have well deserved your present direful plight.

I've bungled quite discreditably—great
Outlay have lost, and shamefully withal;
Let vulgar lust, a silly amorous heat,
The devil's tough well-seasoned self enthral.
If after all that he has seen and known,
He lets such childish stuff his wits benumb,
Not small the folly is, I needs must own,
To which such weakness could at last succumb.

MOUNTAIN DEFILES, FOREST, ROCK, WILDERNESS [1]

HOLY ANCHORITES
(Dispersed along the slopes, stationed among the clefts)

CHORUS AND ECHO

Forests are waving here,
Rocks beetle vast and sheer,
Roots to the ground are braced,
Stem thick with stem enlaced;
Brooks leap and sparkle clear,
Sheltering caves darkle near;
Harmlessly gliding round,
Dumb lions roam,
Honour the hallowed ground,
Love's blessèd home.

[1] There is no real contradiction between the implications of Faust's words to Care, about the folly of other-worldly longings, and the Christian symbolism of the last two scenes, and there is no question of a death-bed conversion of Goethe himself. 'Old men will always be mystics,' he said in his *Maxims and Reflections*, as their hold on life relaxes, but in all essentials he remained a liberal humanist, whose religion was not a separate field of experience from his science, philosophy, and poetry. (Cf. the last recorded *Conversation with Eckermann*, of 11th March 1832). At the close of his drama, as at the beginning, or in the scene introducing Mephistopheles, he made use of any elements in the Christian tradition which served his poetic purpose, with a kind of playful irony which should warn us not to take anything at its face value in isolation, but only as one element in a meaningful whole. The idea of divine grace seems to be brought in almost as an afterthought, and it is probably a reflection of the untroubled conscience which Kierkegaard and those who followed him found so distressing, like the words in the *Nature Fragment* fifty years earlier: 'She has brought me here; she will lead me out again. I trust myself to her.' Others, like Carlyle, found Goethe, and German literature, in a positive sense, religious, proclaiming a living religion which had 'its dwelling and birth-place in the soul of man.'

PATER ECSTATICUS (*hovering up and down*)

Joy evermore burning,
Love's fiery yearning,
Heart-anguish glowing,
God's bliss o'erflowing.
Arrows, pierce through me,
Lances, subdue me,
Clubs, crush, confound me,
Lightnings, flash round me!
Kill every trace in me
Of what is base in me!
Shine, star, evermore,
Eternal love's core!

PATER PROFUNDUS (*lower region*)

As the rock chasm here at my feet
Rests all its weight on yon deep chasm beneath;
As countless sparkling rills together meet,
Ere in the torrent's fall they foam and seethe;
As the tree-stem shoots evermore above,
High and more high by its own inward strain—
Such and so worketh the Almighty Love,
That mouldeth all things, and doth all sustain.
Around me here is a tumultuous roaring,
As though the wood and precipices shook;
And yet 'tis only the delightsome pouring,
Down the steep cleft, of the abounding brook,
Will fertilize anon the valley near.
The lightning, which spread wreck and death before,
Does it not serve to purge the atmosphere,
That vapour in its breast and poison bore?
Envoys of love are these; and they proclaim
What, evermore creating, girds us round.
Oh, may't in me, too, light a holy flame,
When my chilled soul, in chains of anguish bound,
Perplexed with thronging doubts, and ill at ease,
Is tossing to and fro, and sunk in gloom!
O God, my torturing thoughts appease,
My hungering heart illume!

PATER SERAPHICUS (*middle region*)

Through the pine-trees' waving hair,
Lo, a dawn-cloud onward rolls!
Tell me, my heart, what dwells in there?
Is it a host of infant souls?

CHORUS OF BLESSED BOYS

Tell us whither we are going—
Father, tell us, who are we?
Happy are we; bliss o'erflowing
To us all it is, To Be.

PATER SERAPHICUS

Boys, at dead of midnight born,
Soul and sense but half awake,
Straightway from your parents torn,
Rank with angel hosts to take!
Come, draw near; obey your feeling:
One is here, whose love is true.
Happy ye! no trace revealing
Of earth's rugged ways in you.
Drop into my eyes, an organ
    Fit for man and earthly sphere;
Use them as your own, to gaze on
    All that lies around us here!
                    [*He takes them into himself.*
These are trees; these, rocky ridges;
    This a river, that its steep
Down-rush to the chasm abridges
    By one mighty arching leap.

BLESSED BOYS (*from within*)

'Tis all grand, but sad it makes us—
    'Tis too sombre, too immense;
With uneasy dread it shakes us—
    Father, father, take us hence!

PATER SERAPHICUS

Mount to higher spheres supernal,
Ever, all unconscious, grow;
By God's influence eternal,
Through His presence, strengthened so!
For, sublimed there, reigns the healing
Power, that feeds the spirit's mood;
Everlasting love's revealing,
Quickening pure beatitude.

CHORUS OF BLESSED BOYS (*circling round the
                    topmost peak*)

        Hands intertwine in
        A circling ring,
        Feelings divine in
        Gladsomeness sing!

God teaches you; hear Him,
Trust in His grace:
You, who revere Him,
Shall look on His face!

ANGELS (*hovering in the higher sphere, bearing the
immortal part of* FAUST)

Rescued from the Evil One
Is our brother's soul here;
Who hath nobly wrestled, run,
Him can we enrol here.
And if 'twas love divine's behest,
That sin should not defeat him,
Then will the spirits of the blest
With cordial welcome greet him.

THE YOUNGER ANGELS

Roses that from hands were sent,
Loving—holy—penitent,
Helped us to inflict defeat,
And our lofty task complete,
Rescuing this precious soul
From the Evil One's control.
As we strewed them on their head,
Demons shrank and devils fled.
Not the wonted pangs of hell,
But love's anguish on them fell.
Even the Arch-Fiend with pain
Quivered, pierced through every vein.
Shout aloud through all the sky!
We have triumphed!   Victory!

THE MORE ADVANCED ANGELS

Alas! still with earthly taint
Is he encumbered,
Not yet with the pure, a saint,
May he be numbered.
When spirit-force strong
Hath the earthly attracted,
And this with itself has
Inwoven and compacted,
No angels can part what
Is twofold, yet one,
By love Everlasting
This alone may be done.

THE YOUNGER ANGELS

Round yonder peak on high,
Mist-like and trailing,
Spirits of good I spy
Hitherward sailing.
Now clears the cloud away;
I see a bright array
Circling and soaring,
Boys, blessèd boys they be,
Set from earth's burden free,
Rapt and adoring;
Drinking in quickened life
From all the beauty rife,
Fresh to their gaze unfurled,
Here in the upper world.
Let him, where they begin
Perfected bliss to win,
Be mated with them!

THE BLESSED BOYS

Him we are fain to
Receive as a chrysalis;
Thus we attain to
The pledge of angelic bliss.
Flossy veils round him press.
Gently undo them!
Growing in saintliness,
He will burst through them.

DOCTOR MARIANUS (*in the highest, purest cell*)

Here the outlook is free,
Spirit raised high.
Women are passing me
Climbing the sky,
And in their midst, serene,
Star-crowned, resplendent,
Lo! there is Heaven's queen,
In glory transcendent!   [*Enraptured.*
Ruler of sky and earth below,
    In Thy azure vaulted
Unto me vouchsafe to show
    Thy mystery exalted!
Bless all that in man's heart hath fired
    Emotions gentler, dearer,
And, with a saintly love inspired,
    To Thee stills draws it nearer!

If Thy behests inspire our will,
    What then may daunt or curb it?
But if Thou biddest us be still,
    Our calm, what may disturb it?
Virgin pure from spot or taint,
    Mother, holy, tender,
Queen, elect of us, and saint,
    Throned with God in splendour!

    Light cloudlets free
       Around her are bent;
    Women they be,
       That have sinned and repent—
    Sinned in their weakness
       Of nature too tender,
    Now in all meekness
       Kneeling to render
    Lowly contrition,
       Imploring remission
    Of sins from her grace.

To thee, whom passion could not touch,
    Still, still it hath been granted,
That those who fall, through loving much,
    May come with trust undaunted.
'Tis hard from ruin to defend
    Them, so their weakness blindeth;
And who by his own strength may rend
    The fetters passion bindeth!
How on smooth slippery slope the feet
    Slide swift to their undoing!
Whom fool not words and glances sweet,
    And flattery's subtle wooing?

MATER GLORIOSA *comes floating forward*

CHORUS OF REPENTANT WOMEN

    Upward thou'rt soaring
       To regions eternal;
    Hear our imploring,
       Thou, peerless, supernal,
    Thou rich to o'erflowing
       In pardoning grace!

MAGNA PECCATRIX (St Luke vii. 36–50)

By the love, that bent in weeping
    O'er thy Son, divinely born,
His feet with balmy tear-drops steeping,
    Spite of Pharisaic scorn;
By the box, that dropped profusely
    Ointment precious, odour fine;
By the tresses clustering loosely,
    That did wipe the limbs divine!

MULIER SAMARITANA (St John iv. 4–42)

By the spring, whereto in dim
    Far ages Abraham's flocks were led;
By the pitcher's cooling rim,
    That touched His lips, the Saviour dread;
By the clear, full source that now
    Wells out there in stream abundant,
Through the universe to flow,
    Ever sparkling and redundant!

MARIA AEGYPTIACA

By that hallowed spot and dear,
    Where was laid the Lord Immortal;
By the arm in warning clear
    Raised, that thrust me from its portal;
By the forty years I passed,
    In deserts lone, of true repentance;
By what on the sand at last
    I traced, a blessèd farewell sentence!

THE THREE

Thou, who from the greatly sinning
    Never dost avert Thy face,
Still for their repentance winning
    An eternal resting-place,
To her, who only once forgot
    Herself, vouchsafe Thy blessing—
To her, who fell, yet weeted not,
    Wherein she was transgressing!

UNA PENITENTIUM (*formerly called* GRETCHEN)

Incline, incline,
Thou peerless one, bright
With effulgence of light,
Unto my bliss thy glance benign!
My early love, my lover,
All trial, struggle over,
Returns to me—is mine!

THE BLESSED BOYS (*circling round and drawing near*)

Already us far above
Towers he in might;
Richly our fost'ring love
Will he requite.
From life were we brought, ere
Its lessons could reach us;
But he hath been taught there,
And he will teach us.

UNA PENITENTIUM

In rapt amazement he is lost,
While round the choir celestial shineth;
He grows so like the heavenly host,
That his fresh life he scarce divineth.
Lo, every bond of earth hath he
Off with its whilom vesture flung,
And, in celestial panoply
Arrayed, comes stately forth and young!
Vouchsafe, I may his teacher be—
Still dazzles him the unwonted light.

MATER GLORIOSA

Come! Mount to higher spheres! and he
Will follow, holding thee in sight.

DOCTOR MARIANUS (*prostrate on his face in prayer*)

Touched hearts, that true repentance know,
Gaze on those pitying eyes,
And, ever grateful, ever grow
More meet for Paradise!
May every better thought serene
Be to thy service given!
Oh, bless us, Virgin, Mother, Queen,
Omnipotent in heaven!

CHORUS MYSTICUS

All in earth's fleeting state
As symbol showeth;
Here, the inadequate
To fullness groweth;
Here is wrought the ineffable,
Through heavenly love;
The Ever-Womanly
Draws us above.[1]

> [1] 'Him who dare name?
>   Or who proclaim,
>   Him I believe,'

Faust had said to Margaret (p. 129), and similarly in the poem *Prooemion* of 1816, Goethe spoke of God as 'so often named, but still unknown in His essence,' and continued:

> Strain eye and ear till sight and sound be dim,
> Thou'lt find but faint similitudes of Him;
> Yea, and thy spirit in her flight of flame
> Still tries to gauge the symbol and the name.
>   (Translation by J. A. Symonds.)

It is in that sense that earthly experience, in which we see the Divine in a glass darkly, instead of face to face, is 'merely a symbol.' The Chorus Mysticus suggests a fourfold contrast. In the first two lines it is what has already been explained. In the third and fourth it is between the final inadequacy of earthly existence and the longed-for perfection, the fullness of life beyond life. In the fifth line it is between the familiar thoughts and feelings which we can express in words, and the as yet unknown life of pure spirit which no words can describe. The last lines give new expression to the mystical analogy between earthly and heavenly love. Again the former foreshadows and is continuous with the latter, so that Goethe can think of the essence of womanhood as identical with the urge to the highest spirituality. 'What brings Dante and Goethe together in spite of all their difference is their common belief in the redeeming power of love. Gretchen, like Beatrice, helps the celestial embassy; Gretchen, like Beatrice, leads Faust at last through the spheres.' (Lowes Dickinson.)

EVERYMAN'S LIBRARY

A Selected List

In each of the thirteen classifications in this list (except BIO-GRAPHY) the volumes are arranged alphabetically under the authors' names, but Anthologies, etc., are listed under titles. Where authors appear in more than one section, a cross-reference is given. The number at the end of each item is the number of the volume in the series.

EVERYMAN'S LIBRARY

BIOGRAPHY

Baxter (Richard), Autobiography of 868

Blake (William), Life of. By Alexander Gilchrist. Illustrated 971
(See also POETRY AND DRAMA)

Brontë (Charlotte), Life of. By Mrs. Gaskell 318
(See also FICTION)

Burney (Fanny), Diary (1779–1840) 960

Burns (Robert), Life of. By J. G. Lockhart 156
(See also POETRY AND DRAMA)

Byron's Letters 931
(See also POETRY AND DRAMA)

Carlyle's Reminiscences 875
(See also ESSAYS and HISTORY)

Cellini's Autobiography 51

Cowper (Wm.), Selected Letters of 774
(See also POETRY AND DRAMA)

Dickens (Charles), Life of. By John Forster. 2 vols. 781–2
(See also FICTION)

Evelyn's Diary. 2 vols. 220–1

Fox (George), Journal of 754

Franklin's Autobiography 316

Gibbon's Autobiography 511
(See also HISTORY)

Goethe, Life of. By G. H. Lewes 269

Hudson (W. H.), Far Away and Long Ago (autobiography of his youth) 956

Johnson (Dr. Samuel), Life of. By James Boswell. 2 vols. 1–2

Johnson's Lives of the Poets. 2 vols. (See also TRAVEL) 770–1

Keats (John), Life and Letters of. By Lord Houghton 801
(See also POETRY AND DRAMA)

Lamb (Charles), Letters of. 2 vols. 342–3
(See also ESSAYS and FOR YOUNG PEOPLE)

Mahomet, Life of. By Washington Irving 513

Napoleon, Life of. By J. G. Lockhart 3

Nelson, Life of. By Southey 52

Newcastle (First Duke of), Life of, and other writings. By the Duchess of Newcastle 722

Outram (Sir J.), The Bayard of India. By Capt. L. J. Trotter 396

Pepys's Diary. New enlarged edition. 3 vols. 53–5

Plutarch's Lives of Noble Greeks and Romans. Dryden's Translation. 3 vols. 407–9

Rousseau, Confessions of. 2 vols. 859–60
(See also ESSAYS and PHILOSOPHY)

Swift's Journal to Stella. Ed. J. K. Moorhead 757
(See also ESSAYS and FICTION)

Vasari's Lives of the Painters. 4 vols. 784–7

Walpole (H.), Selected Letters of 775

Wellington, Life of. By G. R. Gleig 341

Woolman's (John) Journal and Other Papers 402

CLASSICAL

Aeschylus' Lyrical Dramas 62

Aristophanes' Comedies. 2 vols. 344, 516

Aristotle's Poetics, etc., and Demetrius on Style, etc. 901
„ Politics 605
(See also PHILOSOPHY)

Caesar's War Commentaries 702

Cicero's Essays and Select Letters 345

Demosthenes' Crown and other orations 546

Epictetus, Moral Discourses, etc. Elizabeth Carter's Translation 404

Euripides' Plays in 2 vols. 63, 271

Herodotus. 2 vols. 405–6

Homer's Iliad 453
„ Odyssey 454

Horace. Complete Poetical Works 515

Lucretius: On the Nature of Things 750

Marcus Aurelius' Meditations 9

Ovid: Selected Works 955

Plato's Dialogues. 2 vols. 456–7
„ Republic 64

Sophocles' Dramas 114

Thucydides' Peloponnesian War 455

Virgil's Aeneid 161
„ Eclogues and Georgics 222

ESSAYS AND BELLES-LETTRES

Anthology of English Prose 675

Arnold's (Matthew) Essays 115
(See also POETRY)

Bacon's Essays 10
(See also PHILOSOPHY)

Bagehot's Literary Studies. 2 vols. 520–1

Burke's Reflections 460
(See also ORATORY)

Canton's The Invisible Playmate 566
(See also FOR YOUNG PEOPLE)

Carlyle's Essays. 2 vols.   703–4
,,   Past and Present   608
,,   Sartor Resartus and Heroes and Hero Worship   278
(*See also* BIOGRAPHY *and* HISTORY)
Castiglione's The Courtier   807
Century of Essays, A. An Anthology of English Essayists   653
Chesterfield's (Lord) Letters to his Son   823
Coleridge's Biographia Literaria   11
,,   Essays and Lectures on Shakespeare, etc.   162
(*See also* POETRY)
De Quincey's(Thomas)Opium Eater 223
Dryden's Dramatic Essays   568
Eckermann's Conversations with Goethe   851
Emerson's Essays. 1st and 2nd Series 12
,,   Representative Men   279
Gilfillan's Literary Portraits   348
Hamilton's The Federalist   519
Hazlitt's Lectures on the English Comic Writers   411
,,   The Round Table and Shakespeare's Characters   65
,,   Spirit of the Age and Lectures on English Poets   459
,,   Table Talk   321
Holmes's Autocrat of the Breakfast Table   66
Hunt's (Leigh) Selected Essays   829
Johnson (Dr. Samuel), The Rambler   994
Lamb's Essays of Elia   14
(*See also* BIOGRAPHY *and* FOR YOUNG PEOPLE)
Landor's Imaginary Conversations and Poems: A selection   890
Lynd's (Robert) Essays on Life and Literature   990
Macaulay's Essays. 2 vols.   225–6
(*See also* HISTORY)

Machiavelli's The Prince   280
Milton's Areopagitica, etc.   795
(*See also* POETRY)
Mitford's Our Village   927
Montaigne's Essays. Florio's translation. 3 vols.   440–2
Newman's University Education, etc.723
(*See also* PHILOSOPHY)
Prelude to Poetry, The. Ed. by Ernest Rhys   789
Quiller-Couch's (Sir Arthur) Cambridge Lectures   974
(*See also* FICTION)
Rousseau's Emile, or Education   518
(*See also* BIOGRAPHY *and* PHILOSOPHY)
Ruskin's Sesame and Lilies, The King of the Golden River, etc.   219
,,   Stones of Venice. 3 vols.   213–15
Spectator, The. By Addison, Steele, and others. 4 vols.   164–7
Spencer's (Herbert) Essays on Education   504
Steele's Tatler   993
Sterne's Sentimental Journey and Journal and Letters to Eliza   796
(*See also* FICTION)
Stevenson's Virginibus Puerisque and Familiar Studies of Men and Books 765
(*See also* FICTION, POETRY, *and* TRAVEL)
Swift's Tale of a Tub, The Battle of the Books, etc.   347
(*See also* BIOGRAPHY *and* FICTION)
Table Talk. Ed. by J. C. Thornton 906
Thackeray's (W. M.) The English Humorists and The Four Georges.   610
(*See also* FICTION)
Thoreau's Walden   281
Trench's On the Study of Words and English Past and Present   788
Tytler's Principles of Translation   168
Walton's Complete Angler   70

FICTION

Ainsworth's Old St. Paul's   522
,,   Rookwood   870
,,   The Tower of London 400
,,   Windsor Castle   709
American Short Stories of the 19th Century   840
Austen's (Jane) Emma   24
,,   ,,   Mansfield Park   23
,,   ,,   Northanger Abbey   25
,,   ,,   Pride and Prejudice 22
,,   ,,   Sense and Sensibility 21
Balzac's (Honoré de) Wild Ass's Skin 26
,,   ,,   Eugénie Grandet 169

Balzac's (Honoré de) Old Goriot   170
,,   ,,   The Cat and Racket, and Other Stories 349
,,   ,,   Ursule Mirouët 733
Barbusse's Under Fire   798
Blackmore's (R. D.) Lorna Doone   304
Borrow's Lavengro   119
,,   Romany Rye   120
(*See also* TRAVEL)
Brontë's (Anne) Tenant of Wildfell Hall   685
,,   (Charlotte) Jane Eyre   287
,,   ,,   Shirley   288

Everyman's Library—Fiction—Continued

Brontë's (Charlotte) Villette 351
    ,,   ,, The Professor 417
    (See also BIOGRAPHY)
    ,, (Emily) Wuthering Heights 243
Burney's (Fanny) Evelina 352
Butler's (Samuel) Erewhon and Erewhon Revisited 881
    ,,   ,, The Way of All Flesh 895
Collins's (Wilkie) The Moonstone 979
    ,,   ,, The Woman in White 464
Converse's (Florence) Long Will 328
    (See also FOR YOUNG PEOPLE)
Dana's Two Years before the Mast 588
Defoe's Captain Singleton 74
    ,, Journal of the Plague Year 289
    ,, Moll Flanders 837
    (See also TRAVEL and FOR YOUNG PEOPLE)
CHARLES DICKENS'S WORKS:
    Barnaby Rudge 76
    Bleak House 236
    Christmas Books 239
    David Copperfield 242
    Dombey and Son 240
    Great Expectations 234
    Hard Times 292
    Little Dorrit 293
    Martin Chuzzlewit 241
    Nicholas Nickleby 238
    Old Curiosity Shop 173
    Oliver Twist 233
    Our Mutual Friend 294
    Pickwick Papers 235
    Tale of Two Cities 102
    (See also BIOGRAPHY)
Disraeli's Coningsby 535
Dostoevsky's (Fyodor) The Brothers Karamazov. 2 vols. 802-3
    ,,   ,, Crime and Punishment 501
    ,,   ,, The Idiot 682
    ,,   ,, Letters from the Underworld and Other Tales 654
    ,,   ,, Poor Folk and the Gambler 711
    ,,   ,, The Possessed. 2 vols. 861-2
Du Maurier's (George) Trilby 863
Dumas's Black Tulip 174
    ,, The Count of Monte Cristo. 2 vols. 393-4
    ,, Marguerite de Valois 326
    ,, The Three Musketeers 81
    ,, Twenty Years After 175
Edgeworth's Castle Rackrent and The Absentee 410
Eliot's (George) Adam Bede 27
    ,,   ,, Middlemarch. 2 vols. 854-5
    ,,   ,, Mill on the Floss 325

Eliot's (George) Romola 231
    ,,   ,, Silas Marner 121
English Short Stories. Anthology. 743
Fenimore Cooper's The Last of the Mohicans 79
    ,,   ,, The Prairie 172
Fielding's Amelia. 2 vols. 852-3
    ,, Jonathan Wild and The Journal of a Voyage to Lisbon 877
    ,, Joseph Andrews 467
    ,, Tom Jones. 2 vols. 355-6
Flaubert's Madame Bovary 808
    ,, Salammbô 869
    ,, Sentimental Education 969
France's (Anatole) At the Sign of the Reine Pédauque and The Revolt of the Angels 967
French Short Stories of the 19th and 20th Centuries 896
Gaskell's (Mrs.) Cranford 83
Gogol's (Nicol) Dead Souls 726
    ,,   ,, Taras Bulba and Other Tales 740
Goldsmith's Vicar of Wakefield 295
    (See also POETRY)
Goncharov's Oblomov 878
Gorki's Through Russia 741
Grossmith's (George and Weedon) Diary of a Nobody. Illustrated 963
Hawthorne's The House of the Seven Gables 176
    ,, The Scarlet Letter 122
    (See also FOR YOUNG PEOPLE)
Hugo's (Victor) Les Misérables. 2 vols. 363-4
    ,,   ,, Notre Dame 422
    ,,   ,, Toilers of the Sea 509
Jefferies' (Richard) After London and Amaryllis at the Fair 951
    (See also FOR YOUNG PEOPLE)
Kingsley's (Charles) Hereward the Wake 296
    ,,   ,, Westward Ho! 20
    (See also POETRY and FOR YOUNG PEOPLE)
Loti's (Pierre) Iceland Fisherman 920
Lover's Handy Andy 178
Lytton's Last Days of Pompeii 80
Marryat's Mr. Midshipman Easy 82
    (See also FOR YOUNG PEOPLE)
Maupassant's Short Stories 907
Melville's (Herman) Moby Dick 179
    ,,   ,, Typee 180
Mérimée's Carmen, with Prévost's Manon Lescaut 834
Mickiewicz's (Adam) Pan Tadeusz 842
Mulock's John Halifax, Gentleman 123
Pater's Marius the Epicurean 903
Poe's Tales of Mystery and Imagination 336
    (See also POETRY)

Prévost's Manon Lescaut, with Méri-mée's Carmen 834

Quiller-Couch's (Sir Arthur) Hetty Wesley 864
(*See also* ESSAYS)

Radcliffe's (Ann) Mysteries of Udolpho. 2 vols. 865–6

Reade's (C.) The Cloister and the Hearth 29

Richardson's (Samuel) Clarissa. 4 vols. 882–5

,, ,, Pamela. 2 vols. 683–4

Russian Authors, Short Stories from 758

SIR WALTER SCOTT'S WORKS:
Bride of Lammermoor 129
Guy Mannering 133
Heart of Midlothian, The 134
Ivanhoe. Intro. Ernest Rhys 16
Kenilworth 135
Old Mortality 137
Quentin Durward 140
Redgauntlet 141
Rob Roy 142
Talisman, The 144

Shelley's (Mary) Frankenstein 616

Shorter Novels, Vol. I. Elizabethan 824

Shorter Novels, Vol. II. Jacobean and Restoration 841

Shorter Novels, Vol. III. 18th Century 856

Sienkiewicz (Henryk), Tales from 871
,, ,, Quo Vadis? 970

Smollett's Humphry Clinker 975
,, Roderick Random 790

Somerville and Ross: Experiences of an Irish R.M. 978

Sterne's Tristram Shandy 617
(*See also* ESSAYS)

Stevenson's Dr. Jekyll and Mr. Hyde, The Merry Men and Other Tales 767

Stevenson's The Master of Ballantrae and The Black Arrow 764

,, Treasure Island and Kid-napped 763
(*See also* ESSAYS, POETRY, *and* TRAVEL)

Surtees's Jorrocks's Jaunts and Jollities 817

Swift's Gulliver's Travels. Unabridged Edition, with contemporary maps 60
(*See also* ESSAYS *and* BIOGRAPHY)

Thackeray's Esmond 73
,, Newcomes. 2 vols. 465–6
,, Pendennis. 2 vols. 425–6
,, Vanity Fair 298
,, Virginians. 2 vols. 507–8
(*See also* ESSAYS)

Tolstoy's Anna Karenina. 2 vols. 612–13
,, Master and Man, etc. 469
,, War and Peace. 3 vols. 525–7

Trollope's (Anthony) Barchester Towers 30
,, ,, Dr. Thorne 360
,, ,, Framley Parsonage 181
,, ,, The Last Chronicles of Barset. 2 vols. 391–2
,, ,, Phineas Finn. 2 vols. 832–3
,, ,, The Small House at Allington 361
,, ,, The Warden 182

Turgenev's Fathers and Sons 742
,, Liza, or A Nest of Nobles 677
,, Smoke 988
,, Virgin Soil 528

Twain's (Mark) Tom Sawyer and Huckleberry Finn 976

Voltaire's Candide, etc. 936

Zola's (Émile) Germinal 897

HISTORY

Bede's Ecclesiastical History, etc. 479

Carlyle's French Revolution. 2 vols. 31–2
(*See also* BIOGRAPHY *and* ESSAYS)

Chesterton's (Cecil) History of the United States 965

Creasy's Fifteen Decisive Battles of the World 300

Gibbon's Decline and Fall of the Roman Empire. Ed. by Oliphant Smeaton, M.A. 6 vols. 434–6, 474–6
(*See also* BIOGRAPHY)

Green's Short History of the English People. 2 vols. 727–8

Holinshed's Chronicle as used in Shakespeare's Plays 800

Lutzow's Bohemia: An Historical Sketch. Revised edition 432

Macaulay's History of England. 4 vols. 34–7
(*See also* ESSAYS)

Maine's Ancient Law 417

Motley's Dutch Republic. 3 vols. 86–8

Paston Letters, The. 2 vols. 752–3

Prescott's Conquest of Mexico. 2 vols. 397–8

,, Conquest of Peru 301

Stanley's Lectures on the Eastern Church 251

Thierry's Norman Conquest. 2 vols. 198–9

Villehardouin and De Joinville's Chronicles of the Crusades 333

Voltaire's Age of Louis XIV 780

Everyman's Library

ORATORY

Anthology of British Historical Speeches and Orations 714

Burke's American Speeches and Letters 340
(*See also* ESSAYS)

Fox (Charles James): Speeches (French Revolutionary War Period) 759

Lincoln's Speeches, etc. 206

PHILOSOPHY AND THEOLOGY

A Kempis' Imitation of Christ 484

Aquinas, Thomas: Selected Writings. Ed. by Rev. Fr. D'Arcy 953

Aristotle's Ethics 547
(*See also* CLASSICAL)

Bacon's The Advancement of Learning 719
(*See also* ESSAYS)

Berkeley's (Bishop) Principles of Human Knowledge, New Theory of Vision 483

Browne's Religio Medici, etc. 92

Bunyan's Grace Abounding and Mr. Badman 815
(*See also* ROMANCE)

Burton's (Robert) Anatomy of Melancholy. 3 vols. 886–8

Chinese Philosophy in Classical Times. Trans. and ed. by E. R. Hughes 973

Descartes' (René), A Discourse on Method 570

Hindu Scriptures 944

Hobbes's Leviathan 691

Hume's Treatise of Human Nature. 2 vols. 548–9

James (William): Selected Papers on Philosophy 739

Kant's Critique of Pure Reason 909

King Edward VI. First and Second Prayer Books 448

Koran, The. Rodwell's Translation 380

Law's Serious Call to a Devout and Holy Life 91

Leibniz's Philosophical Writings 905

Locke's Two Treatises 751

Malthus on the Principles of Population. 2 vols. 692–3

Mill's (John Stuart) Utilitarianism, Liberty, Representative Government 482

More's (Sir Thomas) Utopia 461

New Testament 93

Newman's (Cardinal) Apologia pro Vita Sua 636
(*See also* ESSAYS)

Nietzsche's Thus Spake Zarathustra 892

Paine's (Tom) Rights of Man 718

Pascal's Pensées 874

Ramayana and the Mahabharata, The 403

Renan's Life of Jesus 805

Robinson, Philosophy of Atonement 637

Rousseau's (J. J.) The Social Contract, etc. 660
(*See also* ESSAYS *and* BIOGRAPHY)

St. Augustine's Confessions 200

„   The City of God. 2 vols. 982–3

St. Francis: The Little Flowers, and The Life of St. Francis 485

Spinoza's Ethics, etc. 481

Swedenborg's (Emanuel) The True Christian Religion 893

POETRY AND DRAMA

Anglo-Saxon Poetry. 794

Arnold's (Matthew) Poems 334
(*See also* ESSAYS)

Ballads, A Book of British 572

Beaumont and Fletcher, The Selected Plays of 506

Blake's Poems and Prophecies 792
(*See also* BIOGRAPHY)

Browning's Poems. Vol. I, 1833–44 41

„   Poems. Vol. II, 1844–64 42

„   Poems and Plays, Vol. IV, 1871–90 964

„   The Ring and the Book 502

Burns's Poems and Songs 94
(*See also* BIOGRAPHY)

Byron's Poetical Works. 3 vols. 486–8
(*See also* BIOGRAPHY)

Calderon: Six Plays, translated by Edward FitzGerald 819

Chaucer's Canterbury Tales 307

„   Troilus and Criseyde 992

Coleridge, Golden Book of 43
(*See also* ESSAYS)

Cowper (William), Poems of 872
(*See also* BIOGRAPHY)

Dante's Divine Comedy 308

Donne's Poems 867

Dryden's Poems 910

Eighteenth-Century Plays 818

English Galaxy of Shorter Poems 959

Everyman and other Interludes 381

FitzGerald's Omar Khayyám, etc. 819

Golden Treasury of Longer Poems 746
Goldsmith's Poems and Plays 415
  (*See also* FICTION)
Gray's Poems and Letters 628
Heine: Prose and Poetry 911
Ibsen's Brand 716
  „   A Doll's House, The Wild Duck,
    and The Lady from the Sea 494
  „   Ghosts, The Warriors at Helge-
    land, and An Enemy of the People 552
Ibsen's Peer Gynt 747
  „   The Pretenders, Pillars of
    Society, and Rosmersholm 659
International Modern Plays 989
Jonson's (Ben) Plays. 2 vols. 489–90
Keats's Poems 101
  (*See also* BIOGRAPHY)
Kingsley's (Charles) Poems 793
  (*See also* FICTION *and* FOR YOUNG PEOPLE)
La Fontaine's Fables 991
Langland's (William) Piers Plowman 571
Lessing's Laocoön, etc. 843
Longfellow's Poems 382
Marlowe's Plays and Poems 383
Milton's Poems 384
  (*See also* ESSAYS)
Minor Elizabethan Drama. 2 vols. 491–2
Minor Poets of the 18th Century 844
Minor Poets of the 17th Century 873

Molière's Comedies. 2 vols. 830–1
New Golden Treasury, The 695
Palgrave's Golden Treasury 96
Poe's (Edgar Allan) Poems and Essays 791
  (*See also* FICTION)
Pope (Alexander): Collected Poems 760
Restoration Plays 604
Rossetti's Poems and Translations 627
Shakespeare's Comedies 153
  „   Historical Plays, Poems,
    and Sonnets 154
  „   Tragedies 155
Shelley's Poetical Works. 2 vols. 257–8
Sheridan's Plays 95
Silver Poets of the 16th Century 985
Spenser's Faerie Queene. 2 vols. 443–4
  „   Shepherd's Calendar, etc. 879
Stevenson's Poems 768
  (*See also* ESSAYS, FICTION, *and* TRAVEL)
Swinburne's Poems and Prose 961
Tchekhov. Plays and Stories 941
Tennyson's Poems, 1829–92. 2 vols.
  44, 626
Webster and Ford. Plays 899
Whitman's (Walt) Leaves of Grass 573
Wilde (Oscar): Plays, Prose Writings,
  and Poems 858
Wordsworth's Longer Poems 311

REFERENCE

Biographical Dictionary of English
  Literature 449
Everyman's English Dictionary. Ed.
  by D. C. Browning, M.A. 776

Literary and Historical Atlas. America.
  Many coloured and line Maps; full
  Index and Gazetteer 553

The following volumes in this section are now in the special edition of
Everyman's Reference Library:

Atlas of Ancient & Classical Geography
Dictionary of Dates
Dictionary of Quotations and Proverbs
Dictionary of Non-Classical Mythology
Dictionary of Shakespeare Quotations

Smaller Classical Dictionary. (Revised
  from Sir William Smith)
Thesaurus of English Words and
  Phrases. (Revised from Peter Roget)

ROMANCE

Aucassin and Nicolette, with other
  Medieval Romances 497
Boccaccio's Decameron. (Unabridged.)
  2 vols. 845–6
Bunyan's Pilgrim's Progress 204
  (*See also* PHILOSOPHY)
Burnt Njal, The Story of 558
Cervantes' Don Quixote. 2 vols. 385–6
Chrétien de Troyes: Eric and Enid, etc.
  698

Heimskringla: Sagas of the Norse Kings
  847
Kalevala. 2 vols. 259–60
Mabinogion, The 97
Malory's Le Morte d'Arthur. 2 vols. 45–6
Marie de France, Lays of 557
Nibelungs, The Fall of the 312
Rabelais' The Heroic Deeds of Gar-
  gantua and Pantagruel. 2 vols. 826–7

SCIENCE

Boyle's The Sceptical Chymist 559
Darwin's The Origin of Species 811
(*See also* TRAVEL)
Euclid: the Elements of 891
Faraday's (Michael) Experimental Researches in Electricity 576
Harvey's Circulation of the Blood 262
Howard's State of the Prisons 835
Locke's Essay on Human Understanding 984
Marx's (Karl) Capital. 2 vols. 848–9

Owen's A New View of Society, etc. 799
Pearson's (Karl) The Grammar of Science 939
Ricardo's Principles of Political Economy and Taxation 590
Smith's (Adam) The Wealth of Nations. 2 vols. 412–13
White's Selborne. New edition 48
Wollstonecraft (Mary), The Rights of Woman, with John Stuart Mill's The Subjection of Women 825

TRAVEL AND TOPOGRAPHY

A Book of the 'Bounty' 950
Borrow's (George) The Bible in Spain 151
(*See also* FICTION)
Boswell's Tour in the Hebrides with Dr. Johnson 387
(*See also* BIOGRAPHY)
Cobbett's Rural Rides. 2 vols. 638–9
Cook's Voyages of Discovery 99
Crèvecœur's (H. St. John) Letters from an American Farmer 640
Darwin's Voyage of the Beagle 104
(*See also* SCIENCE)

Defoe's Tour through England and Wales. 2 vols. 820–1
(*See also* FICTION *and* FOR YOUNG PEOPLE)
Kinglake's Eothen 337
Polo's (Marco) Travels 306
Portuguese Voyages, 1498–1663 986
Stevenson's An Inland Voyage, Travels with a Donkey, and Silverado Squatters 766
(*See also* ESSAYS, FICTION, *and* POETRY)
Wakefield's Letter from Sydney, etc. 828
Waterton's Wanderings in South America 772

FOR YOUNG PEOPLE

Aesop's and Other Fables 657
Alcott's Little Men 512
,, Little Women & Good Wives 248
Andersen's Fairy Tales. Illustrated by the Brothers Robinson 4
Browne's (Frances) Granny's Wonderful Chair 112
Bulfinch's The Age of Fable 472
Canton's A Child's Book of Saints. Illustrated by T. H. Robinson 61
(*See also* ESSAYS)
Carroll's Alice in Wonderland, Through the Looking-Glass, etc. Illustrated by the Author 836
Collodi's Pinocchio: the Story of a Puppet 538
Converse's (Florence) The House of Prayer 923
(*See also* FICTION)
Defoe's Robinson Crusoe. Parts I and II 59
(*See also* FICTION)
Fairy Tales from the Arabian Nights. Illustrated 249
Grimms' Fairy Tales. Illustrated by R. Anning Bell 56
Hawthorne's Wonder Book and Tanglewood Tales 5
(*See also* FICTION)

Howard's Rattlin the Reefer 857
Hughes's Tom Brown's Schooldays. Illustrated by T. Robinson 58
Jefferies's (Richard) Bevis, the Story of a Boy 850
(*See also* FICTION)
Kingsley's Heroes 113
,, Water Babies and Glaucus 277
(*See also* POETRY *and* FICTION)
Lamb's Tales from Shakespeare. Illustrated by A. Rackham 8
(*See also* BIOGRAPHY *and* ESSAYS)
Lear: A Book of Nonsense 806
Marryat's Children of the New Forest 247
,, Masterman Ready 160
(*See also* FICTION)
Mother Goose's Nursery Rhymes. Illustrated 473
Sewell's (Anna) Black Beauty. Illustrated by Lucy Kemp-Welch 748
Spyri's (Johanna) Heidi. Illustrations by Lizzie Lawson 431
Stowe's Uncle Tom's Cabin 371
Verne's (Jules) Twenty Thousand Leagues Under the Sea 319
Wyss's Swiss Family Robinson. Illustrated by Charles Folkard 430